teach yourself...
WordPerfect 6.1
for Windows

by Jan Weingarten

MIS:
PRESS

A Subsidiary of
Henry Holt and Co., Inc.

First Edition—1995

Library of Congress Cataloging-in-Publication Data

Weingarten, Jan
    Teach yourself-- WordPerfect 6.1 for Windows / Jan Weingarten
        p. cm
    Includes index.
    ISBN 55828-425-7
    1. WordPerfect for Windows (Computer file) 2. Word processing.
 I. Title.
 252.5.W655W452 1995
 652.5'536--dc20   94-45640
                                                             CIP

Printed in the United States of America.

10 9 8 7 6 5 4 3 2

MIS:Press books are available at special discounts for bulk purchases for sales promotions, premiums, fund-raising, or educational use. Special editions or book excerpts can also be created to specification.

For details contact: Special Sales Director
                        MIS:Press
                        a subsidiary of Henry Holt and Company, Inc.
                        115 West 18th Street
                        New York, New York 10011

Editor in Chief: Paul Farrell   **Managing Editor:** Cary Sullivan

Development Editor: Judy Brief   **Technical Editor:** Kristy Clason

Copy Editor: Gwynne Jackson   **Production Editor:** Anthony Washington

Associate Production Editor: Maya Riddick

Dedication

For Cyrille, my favorite WordPerfect expert

Acknowledgments

Writing is in many ways a team sport, and without the support and dedication of the following team members, this book would not have happened:

Preeminent template designer supreme, Ted Clifford. He created the templates on disk for the original edition of this book. For this edition, he carefully redesigned them to work with WordPerfect 6.1.

My crack team of assistants: Kayla Mohammadi, Joshoa List, Matt Griscom, DeLois Gibson, and Vernell Hollingsworth. They revised, captured screens, did document clean-up, and kept me from going totally over the edge.

My brother, John Weingarten, who stepped in at the 11th hour to revise a few chapters.

My editor at MIS:Press, Judy Brief. Judy should be well on her way to sainthood after this project. She held up remarkably well through all the tight deadlines and last-minute changes (except for that one time I made her sick).

The rest of the MIS:Press team: Shari Chappell, Copy Edit Manager supreme; Gwynne Jackson, Copy Editor extraordinaire; Brian Oxman, copy edit and revision god; Anthony Washington, Production Editor and layout guru; and Maya Riddick, Associate Production Editor and layout goddess.

My agent at Waterside Productions, Matt Wagner. Thanks, Matt. You keep getting me into gigs and out of trouble.

Table of Contents

SECTION II:
BEYOND THE BASICS

**SECTION IV:
FILE MANAGEMENT
AND PRINTING**

**SECTION VI:
AUTOMATION TOOLS**

SECTION VII:
ORGANIZATIONAL AND
REFERENCING TOOLS

Introduction

If you already own WordPerfect 6.1 for Windows, give yourself a pat on the back—you made a wise decision. WordPerfect's user-friendly approach and impressive collection of features have secured its position as the most popular word processing software on the market. With this new release, WordPerfect has truly become a power-packed dynamo without peer.

With WordPerfect's vast potential, it's easy to become overwhelmed and intimidated. Where do you start? Which features do you really need?

Teach Yourself WordPerfect 6.1 for Windows is the answer. You don't need to have any experience with computers or word processing—this book takes you by the hand and makes sense out of the maze of features. I won't throw a lot of jargon at you—I'll use real English and examples you can relate to to introduce you to the necessary computer terminology. Stick with me and you'll be speaking computerese and producing impressive-looking documents in no time.

WHERE SHOULD YOU START?

Even if you're a new user, Chapter 1, *Jumpstart,* will have you creating an actual document right away. I'll walk you through starting Windows and WordPerfect. Then you'll create, save, spellcheck, and print your first document.

If you've never used a mouse or are new to Windows, you might want to take a look at Chapter 2, *Getting Started with WordPerfect for Windows*, before you do the *Jumpstart* chapter. I'll give you mouse and keyboard techniques, talk in more detail about starting and exiting Windows and WordPerfect, and explain the WordPerfect screen.

If you're an old hand with mice and Windows (or even a medium hand), you can probably skip right to Chapter 3, *Power Tools*. Even if you've used an earlier version of WordPerfect for Windows, look through this chapter—WordPerfect has made several additions to its arsenal of power tools.

Chapter 4, *Using Help*, is probably the most important chapter in the whole book. WordPerfect's online Help system gives you the tools you need to figure out how to do just about anything. Even if you only skim through the rest of the book, make sure you're comfortable navigating through Help.

HOW THIS BOOK IS ORGANIZED

Section I: Getting Started takes you through the basics. After the *Jumpstart* chapter, Chapters 2 through 8 give you essential tools for creating and working with WordPerfect documents. You'll start Windows and WordPerfect and learn to recognize the different parts of the WordPerfect screen. You'll learn how to navigate your way around the document screen, move and copy text from one place to another, and recover when you make a mistake (like accidentally pressing the wrong key). *Basic Formatting* and *Basic Layout* give you essential skills for creating and formatting WordPerfect documents. You'll learn how to center, bold, and underline text; set tabs; change margins and line spacing; and work with other elements of line, page, and paragraph formatting.

Section II: Beyond the Basics covers more advanced formatting techniques, including headers and footers, page numbering, hyphenation, and working with different paper sizes. You'll use WordPerfect's powerful find and replace feature to locate text or codes anywhere in a document. And you'll learn how to use WordPerfect's proofreading tools—Speller, Thesaurus, and Grammatik—to catch errors and find just the right words.

In *Section III: Dressing It Up—Fonts and Graphic Elements,* you'll learn how to spice up your documents by adding graphics images, lines, and borders. And you'll use different fonts (type styles) to add impact. This section also covers WordPerfect's TextArt feature, which allows you to perform all sorts of contortions with your text—you can stretch or twist lines of text into several different shapes and styles.

In *Section IV: File Management and Printing,* you'll learn how to use WordPerfect's file management tools to find files in different directories, create new directories, and move or copy files. You'll also learn how to make the most of WordPerfect's printing capabilities—printing a whole document or selected parts of it, cancelling print jobs, and more.

In *Section V: Tables and Columns,* you'll work with the tables feature to easily arrange text and numbers in columns and rows. You'll learn to adjust table formatting, and I'll introduce you to WordPerfect's spreadsheet features, which enable you to use tables for complex calculations. Then I'll show you how to work with newspaper-style columns and mailing labels.

Section VI: Automation Tools covers WordPerfect's powerful collection of tools that can save you time by automating the process of document creation. Macros, styles, and templates can all be used to keep you from having to enter the same text and codes over and over. In addition to saving you time, these features will help you achieve consistency in your formatting. And you'll see how the merge feature makes short work of creating form letters.

Section VII: Organizational and Referencing Tools teaches you how to organize material and work efficiently with long documents. This section covers outlines, cross referencing, tables of contents, indexing, footnotes, and working with several documents at once.

LOOK OUT FOR THESE

Throughout the book, I'll point out additional information, tips, and shortcuts, and I'll also tell you what to watch out for. Look for the following:

KEYBOARD

This icon indicates a keyboard alternative to an action that can be performed with the mouse. In some cases, the keyboard alternative is actually a shortcut—when that's the case, I'll point it out.

NOTE

When you see this, it means there's some information that you should pay particular attention to. It might be a tip or some additional information that will help you make sense of what's being discussed.

ROADMAP

I've used this icon primarily in the Jumpstart chapter. Because this chapter takes you through a lot of features very quickly, the roadmaps point you to the chapter in this book where you can learn about specific features in more detail.

SHORTCUT

I use this icon to let you know when there's an easier way to do something.

WARNING

Pay attention when you see this. I'll tell you what to watch out for when you're working with certain features.

WHAT ABOUT THE DISK?

The disk that's included with this book contains 20 templates that can help you do all sorts of cool things, from creating a three-fold brochure to balancing your checkbook. Appendix C tells you what the templates do and how to use them.

WordPerfect 6.1 for Windows

SECTION I

GETTING STARTED

CHAPTER 1

Jumpstart

(My Boss Is Breathing Down My Neck and I Don't Have Time to Read the Whole Book Right Now)

Let's talk about:

- ❖ Starting WordPerfect
- ❖ Entering text
- ❖ Saving a document
- ❖ Spell checking a document
- ❖ Making minor editing changes
- ❖ Printing a document
- ❖ Exiting WordPerfect
- ❖ Exiting Windows

JUMP RIGHT IN, THE WATER'S FINE

This chapter is for all you Type-A personalities who can't be bothered with a lot of details—*just give it to me straight*. And that's exactly what you'll get here. No frills, no tricks, just the basics. By the end of the chapter you'll be able to create, save, spell check, and print a simple document. You'll also know how to get into and out of WordPerfect and Windows.

Obviously, there's much more to mastering WordPerfect for Windows (or they wouldn't have paid me to write this book), but it all builds on the basics of typing, saving, and printing. If you can do that, you can start to produce real documents right away.

I'm not going to get into any shortcuts in this chapter. You'll have to stick with me a little longer to get those. (Yes, you're right—that *was* a blatant attempt to get you to keep reading.) I'm also not going to give you a lot of explanations and tell you *why* things are the way they are. What you will get are bare-bones techniques to get you started until you learn all about neat stuff like Power Bars, Toolbars, and QuickMenus, all of which streamline the process of choosing commands.

ROADMAP

As we create the sample document, I'll point out *Roadmaps* along the way, directing you to areas of this book where you can get more information.

Ready? Let's do it.

Starting WordPerfect

I'm assuming that you've started Windows and that Program Manager, with all of its pretty little icons, is on your screen (see Figure 1.1).

Click here

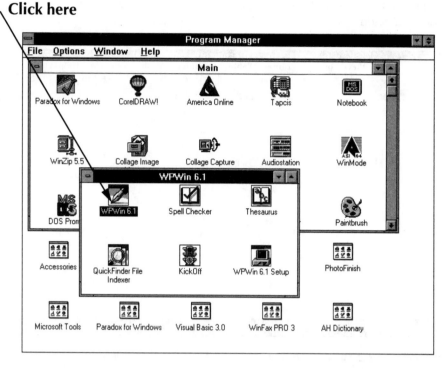

Figure 1.1 *The Program Manager screen with the WPWin 6.1 group window open.*

ROADMAP

If you need help opening Windows, refer to the "Starting Windows" section in Chapter 2.

Do It

Double-click on the WPWin 6.1 icon to start WordPerfect for Windows:

1. Move the mouse pointer to the WPWin 6.1 icon inside the WPWin 6.1 group window.

2. Double-click the left mouse button.

Depending on how fast your computer is, this might take a little time, but pretty soon you should see the WordPerfect screen (see Figure 1.2).

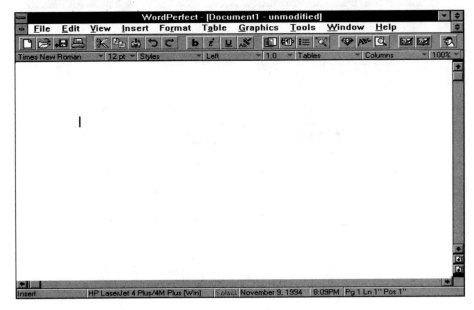

Figure 1.2 *When you first start WordPerfect, this is what you should see.*

If the WPWin 6.1 icon isn't visible on your screen, you might have to open the WPWin 6.1 group window. Chapter 2, "Getting Started with WordPerfect," covers starting WordPerfect in more detail.

ROADMAP

Just Type

That's all you have to do now. There's a whole bunch of stuff on the screen, but you don't really have to deal with it to create a simple document. You can just start typing.

Do It

Let's enter some text:

1. Type today's date and press **Enter** twice.

2. Type the following name and address, pressing **Enter** after each line:
   ```
   Ms. Florence Fellows
   682 Fallible Point
   Federal Way, WA 98107
   ```

3. Press **Enter** once more to add an extra line between the address and the salutation.

4. Type: **Dear Ms. Fellows,** and press **Enter** twice.

5. Type the following text, mistakes and all (and if you make a few more of your own, no problem—you can fix them later). Don't press **Enter** at the end of each line. The only time you need to press **Enter** is at the end of a paragraph.

   ```
   I enjoyed are conversashun yesterday and am am
   pleased that you will represent our new line of
   waterproof sundresses. I know that these will be hot
   items in the damp NOrthwest. Now women will be able
   to venture out in their summer best, confidunt that
   they will not be caught unawares by our changeable
   weather.
   I will call you as soon as I have more information
   abot the shipping schedule.
   Sincerely,
   Sarah Sewell
   Marketing Manager
   ```

Your letter should look like Figure 1.3.

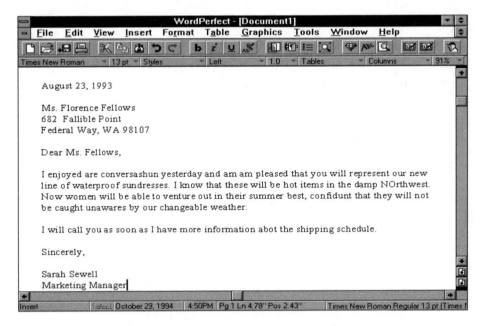

Figure 1.3 *Hey, you just typed a whole letter!*

Saving Your Masterpiece

Saving should always be the first thing you do after creating a document. Until you save your document to disk, it only exists in the computer's temporary memory. If the power goes out or you turn off your computer without saving, all of your work could be lost. In fact, if your document is much longer than the one we just created, you should save it while you're in the middle of creating it, and then save it frequently while you're working. This is something I'll keep bugging you about throughout the book—saving documents often is one of the best habits you can get into (unless you *really* like to type the same stuff over and over).

Do It

To save your file:

1. Click on the word **File** on the menu line (just below where it says WordPerfect at the very top of your screen). Or press **Alt+F**. That opens the File menu (see Figure 1.4).

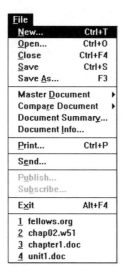

Figure 1.4   *This is the File menu.*

KEYBOARD

To press **Alt+F**, hold down the **Alt** key while you press the letter **F**, then release both keys. For any menu selection, the letter that's underlined is the one you press, either on its own or in combination with the **Alt** key.

2.   Click on **Save As**… (or press the letter **A**). Any time a menu item has an ellipsis (…) after it, you'll see a *dialog box* when you choose that item. The dialog box is WordPerfect's way of saying it needs more information—in this case, it needs to know what name you want to give your file (see Figure 1.5).

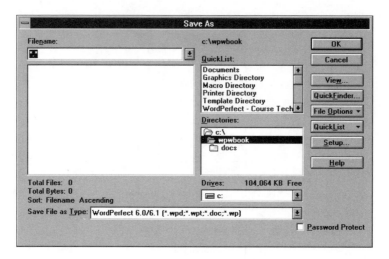

Figure 1.5 *Choosing* **Save As** *opens the Save As dialog box.*

3. When the Save As dialog box opens, it looks like there are a lot of choices to make, but all you have to do is type a name for the document—the insertion point is already in the right place for you to start typing. Type **FELLOWS.LTR**.

4. Click **OK**, or press **Enter**. Notice that the OK button has a darker border around it than the other buttons. That indicates that it's the default button: its action will be executed if you press **Enter**. So, pressing **Enter** in this case is just like clicking on **OK**.

After you choose **OK,** the Save As dialog box disappears and you're back at the main WordPerfect screen.

Once you've used Save As to save a document for the first time, you can choose **Save** from the File menu at any time to save the document. WordPerfect won't ask you any questions—it'll just do it. It's very fast, and it's a good idea to do this on a regular basis—any time you've made major changes to your document or added a lot of text.

ROADMAP

Go to Chapter 5, "Editing 101," to learn more about saving documents.

Spell It Right

Once you've entered your text and saved the document, the next step is to make sure everything's spelled right. Wait—don't pull out your dictionary and start looking up every word. WordPerfect has a built-in feature that automatically checks your document. You might be wondering why we didn't spell check the document before saving it. That would've saved some time, right? Well, yeah, but there's a method here.

Any time you run a spell check or send a document to the printer (or do other complex things like running a merge) there's a possibility that something could go wrong. Your computer could freeze up. If that happens before you save, you could lose all your work. I don't want to scare you; it's not going to happen often, but I'd rather be safe than sorry. (How's that for a tired but true cliche?)

Do It

Let's run a spell check:

1. With FELLOWS.LTR on the screen, click on the **Tools** menu (or press **Alt+T**).

2. Click on **Spell Check** (see Figure 1.6). At this point you don't have to worry about all of the Spell Checker options. The Spell Checker automatically checks the whole document unless you specify something else.

Figure 1.6 *Choose **Spell Check** from the Tools menu (or press the letter **S**).*

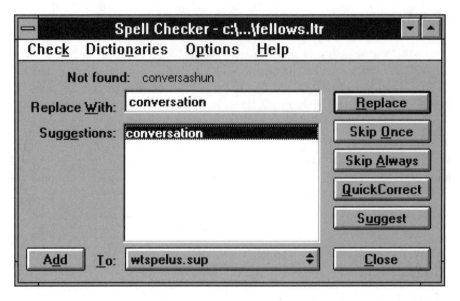

Figure 1.7 *The Spell Checker dialog box is displayed. The spell checker highlights the first word it finds that's not in its dictionary (in this case, conversashun) and waits for your action.*

ROADMAP

Go to Chapter 11, "Proofreading Tools," to learn about the different tasks you can perform with the Spell Checker.

3. When the Spell Checker stops on a word, there are several choices you can make. Most of them are covered in Chapter 11—you just need to deal with a couple for now:

❖ If the Spell Checker stops on a word that's spelled correctly but isn't in WordPerfect's dictionary (a good example of this would be someone's name), you can choose **Skip Once** to skip over the word without making any changes (with Skip Once, the Spell Checker stops the next time it sees the same word). Choose **Skip Always** to skip over the word every time the Spell Checker sees it during the current spell check session.

❖ If the word really is misspelled, choose one of the words from the Suggestions box. If you see the correct spelling there, double-click on that word. You can also use your **Up Arrow** and **Down Arrow** keys to highlight the correct word and then press **Enter**.

ROADMAP

If the word you want isn't in the Suggestions list, you can edit the spelling manually. You'll know more about this after reading Chapter 11, "Proofreading Tools."

4. Go through the letter, skipping or replacing words as necessary.

5. Click on the **Yes** button (or press **Enter**) to close the Spell Checker (see Figure 1.8).

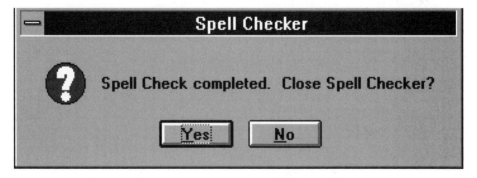

Figure 1.8 *You'll see this dialog box when the spell check is completed.*

6. Click on **File**, then **Save**, to save the document.

All of the changes you make during the spell check are stored in the computer's temporary memory (RAM) until you save the document again. You should always save your work right after spell checking.

Fixing Mistakes

What, you're not perfect? You mean there are still some problems with your letter even after running the spell check? Well, join the club. Fortunately, WordPerfect gives you multiple ways to clean up your work. For now, I'll give you a basic tool that will let you change a word or letter here and there.

The word *are* in the first sentence should really be *our*. Why didn't that get caught during the spell check? Okay, I'll give you the brief version of minilecture #3248 (which will be repeated at length in Chapter 11): *A spell checker does not take the place of proofreading your work.* *Are* is a real word, and it's spelled correctly, even though it's not the word you meant to use. 'Nuff said for now.

Do It

Let's fix it:

1. Move the mouse pointer (which is now a thin vertical line that looks like the capital letter "I") so that it's anywhere in the word *are*, and click the left mouse button. The insertion point (the flashing vertical line) is displayed at the point where you click the mouse.

2. Get rid of the word *are* by pressing **Delete** or **Backspace** a total of three times. The key you press depends on where the insertion point is:

    ❖   If the insertion point is just after the letter you want to delete, press **Backspace**.

    ❖   If the insertion point is just in front of the letter you want to delete, press **Delete**.

3. Type **our**. Until you learn more techniques for deleting and changing text, you can always delete one character at a time with Backspace or Delete, then type in whatever you want to replace it with.

4. Don't forget to save again.

ROADMAP

You've probably already noticed that the mouse pointer changes shape depending on what's happening. Chapter 2, "Getting Started with WordPerfect," explains the different shapes and when they're displayed.

The Last Step—Printing

Finally, we can print the letter and get that boss off your back! Again, no details here—just the basics so that you have the tools you need to print a document until you get a chance to delve into printing in more depth.

Do It

To print your file:

1. With your letter on your screen, click on **File** (or press **Alt+F**).
2. Click on **Print** (or press **P**).

NOTE

Notice the black dot next to **Full Document** in Figure 1.9. That means that WordPerfect will print the whole document unless you make another selection. For now, you don't have to worry about all of the choices in the dialog box.

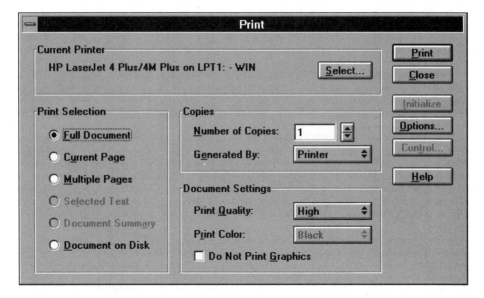

Figure 1.9 *Here's the Print dialog box.*

3. Click **Print** to start printing (or press **P**).

ROADMAP

If Windows and WordPerfect have been set up properly on your computer, you shouldn't have to worry about selecting a printer. But if you can't get the letter to print, don't worry. It's probably just a matter of changing a couple of settings. Take a look at Chapter 16, "Printing," to find out more.

Exiting WordPerfect

Let's pretend that letter was the only thing you needed to do today (we can dream, can't we?), so it's time to get out of WordPerfect and turn off the computer. So, without further ado....

Do It

Exit WordPerfect:

1. Click on **File** (or press **Alt+F**).
2. Choose **Exit** from the File menu (or press the letter **X**).

If you haven't made any changes to your document since the last time you saved it, choosing Exit from the File menu takes you right out of WordPerfect and back to the Program Manager window.

If any changes have been made, you'll see the dialog box shown in Figure 1.10. If you want to save the changes, choose **Yes**. Otherwise, choose **No**. After choosing Yes or No, WordPerfect closes and you'll be back at the Program Manager window.

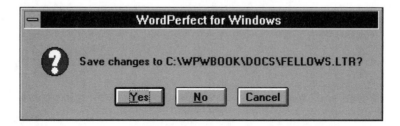

Figure 1.10 *If any changes have been made to your document, this dialog box is displayed when you try to exit WordPerfect.*

Exiting Windows

If you're really done for the day, you probably want to turn off your computer and go home (I know I do). There's only one more thing to do before you can hit that power switch: exit Windows. Here's where you start to see the beauty of Windows. Because all Windows programs and Windows itself comply with certain standards, you can use the same technique to exit Windows that you just used to exit WordPerfect.

Do It

Let's exit Windows:

1. Click on **File** (or press **Alt+F**).
2. Choose **Exit Windows** from the File menu (or press the letter **X**).
3. A dialog box is displayed to make sure you really want to exit Windows. Click **OK** to exit Windows (or press **Enter**).

After you choose **OK**, Program Manager disappears and you are returned to a DOS prompt that should look something like this:

```
C:\WINDOWS>_
```

It might look a little different on your computer. For example, your prompt could just say **C:**, or it might have a string of names instead of or in addition to **WINDOWS**. The important thing is that the screen should be empty except for the prompt line.

Once you're at a DOS prompt, you can safely turn off your computer.

Never turn off your computer without exiting all the way out of Windows.

THE END . . . AND THE BEGINNING

Give yourself a pat on the back. You got in and out of both Windows and WordPerfect, you created a document, saved it, checked the spelling, made an editing change, and printed. Whew! There's a lot more to learn, but you've got the basic ingredients. Everything else will build on the basic elements you learned in this chapter.

In the next chapter, "Getting Started with WordPerfect," you'll learn the techniques for using the mouse and keyboard. Then you'll learn how to recognize and work with different elements of the WordPerfect screen: dialog boxes, scroll bars, pull-down menus, and much more.

Getting Started with WordPerfect

(It's Elementary, Dear Watson)

Let's talk about:

- ❖ Why Windows?
- ❖ Using a mouse
- ❖ Using the keyboard
- ❖ Starting Windows
- ❖ Starting WordPerfect
- ❖ Understanding the WordPerfect screen
- ❖ WYSIWYG

WINDOWS WARMUP

Wait! Don't turn the page yet. I can hear you thinking, "I didn't buy this book to learn about Windows. I'll just skip right over to the WordPerfect stuff." Well, hold on a minute. I'm only going to talk about "Windows stuff" that you actually need to know in order to use WordPerfect. In fact, I'll use WordPerfect as an example, so you can use this chapter to start getting familiar with the WordPerfect screen. So, stick with me for a little while (unless you're an old hand with Windows and really don't need this introduction, in which case you have my permission to skip ahead).

Why Windows?

Okay, everyone's talking about Windows, and your best friend finally convinced you that you absolutely had to buy Windows and WordPerfect for Windows. So you did. But was it the right thing to do? The answer is an unequivocal *yes*. Why, you may ask? In a word: standardization.

What that means is that once you learn techniques for working with any Windows program (in this case, WordPerfect for Windows), you have the basic tools for working in any other Windows program. For example, you use the same method to save files and exit the program no matter which program you're using.

Windows' standardization extends to printing. Instead of having to set up a printer every time you install a new program, when you install a Windows application, it *knows* what printer you have by looking at your Windows setup. If you get a new printer, all you have to do is install and set it up in Windows, and all of your Windows programs can automatically use it.

There are many more advantages to Windows, which you'll discover as you delve further into it. For now, just be aware that a lot of what you learn in this book will apply to the next Windows program you decide to master.

If You're New to Windows

I'm going to assume that Windows is already installed on your computer (if you're smart, you got that friend who talked you into buying it to install it for you). If it's not, refer to the booklet, *Getting Started with Microsoft Windows*, that came with your Windows software.

Windows 3.1 comes with a brief on-screen tutorial that I highly recommend, especially if you've never used a mouse. The tutorial lets you practice different mouse techniques and familiarizes you with some of the Windows elements.

To run the tutorial, choose **Windows Tutorial** from Program Manager's Help menu and follow the on-screen instructions. If that last sentence sounded like Greek, don't worry for now. Just keep reading—I'll tell you how to access menus (and where to find them!).

Using a Mouse

Before we go any further, I have one question. Do you have a mouse? No? You mean you went out and got Windows *and* WordPerfect for Windows, and you *still* don't have a mouse?? Well, go get one. A mouse is very important (if not crucial) to Windows and Windows applications. You can use Windows and WordPerfect without a mouse, but you won't be able to take advantage of a lot of nifty shortcuts, and some things will be downright cumbersome to accomplish.

Got your mouse now? Good. Let's go. Just rest your hand lightly on that little critter with your index finger over the left button and your middle finger over the right button. The left button is the one you'll use most of the time. A lot of Windows programs don't even use the right mouse button, but WordPerfect for Windows uses it to get to some shortcut features. If your mouse has three buttons, ignore the middle one—you won't use it at all in WordPerfect for Windows.

NOTE

Lefties unite! For all you lefties out there, don't fret. Microsoft thought of you when they designed Windows. You can swap the left and right mouse buttons to make it easier to operate the mouse. "Customizing the Mouse and Other Pointing Devices" in your Windows manual tells you how to make this change. If you've swapped the mouse buttons, you'll have to mentally reverse any instructions I give for using the mouse. When I write "click the left mouse button," you'll click the right one.

Click, Click, Click . . . What a Drag

Click and drag. There, you just learned most of the mouse lingo you need to know. What's the rest? Pointing. That's all there is to it. You point, you click, or you drag. There are some fancy combinations, like double-clicking, quadruple-clicking, and dragging and dropping, but they're just extensions of the basic techniques.

❖ **Point.** This means that you move the mouse pointer (the little arrow that moves around on your screen when you move the mouse) to a particular spot. If I write "point to the **Save** button," move the mouse until the arrow is on the Save button.

❖ **Click.** If I write "click on the **File** menu," point to the File menu, press down on the mouse button (in this case it would be the left button), and then let go. It's called clicking because with most mice you'll hear a little click when you let go of the button.

❖ **Double-click.** Double-clicking is something you'll be doing a lot. All it means is that you point at the item in question and click the left mouse button (press and let go) twice in fairly rapid succession. This action might seem awkward at first, but with a little practice you'll be double-clicking with the best of them.

❖ **Drag.** This is a technique in which you point at the item and hold down the left mouse button while you move the mouse to a new location. When the object you're dragging is where you want it, release the mouse button.

The mouse pointer is a tricky little devil—it actually changes its shape depending on what you're doing. The two shapes you'll see most of the time are an arrow (or some variation of an arrow) and an I-beam (sort of like a capital letter I). A regular arrow means that you can make a selection from a menu or dialog box; the arrow changes to a double-arrow to let you know you can change the size of a window or dialog box. The I-beam indicates you're in an area where text can be entered. Throughout this book, I'll use the term *mouse pointer* when I tell you to do something with the mouse, and I'll explain what's happening to the shape when it's important.

Using the Keyboard

There isn't much I need to tell you about the keyboard. When you're entering text, you can type the same way you would on a typewriter. But I do want to point out a few added attractions.

Special Keys

Your computer keyboard contains special keys that WordPerfect uses for different purposes at different times. How's that for a vague statement? All it means is that WordPerfect takes advantage of all of the extra keys to give you shortcut methods for accomplishing tasks.

NOTE

I emphasize mouse use in this book, since in most cases the mouse is the easiest way to do things. But I'll give you keyboard alternatives for most procedures and let you know when the keyboard method is actually a shortcut. Sometimes using the keyboard can save you time. As you become more familiar with WordPerfect, experiment with the mouse and the keyboard in various situations. The whole idea is to use whichever method feels most comfortable and efficient to you.

I'll point out specific keyboard alternatives as we go along. For now, here are the basics:

❖ **Function keys.** These are the strange-looking keys numbered **F1** through **F12** (your keyboard might only go up to **F10**). Depending on what kind of keyboard you have, these keys are either at the top of your keyboard or in a block to the left of the main typing area. As the name implies, function keys are assigned specific functions. For example, you can press **F7** to indent a paragraph of text in WordPerfect.

❖ **Ctrl, Alt, and Shift.** These keys are used in combination with other keys to extend a key's power or to change what the key does. For example, pressing **F7** by itself indents a paragraph, but **Shift+F7** is used to center a line of text. If I write "press **Shift+F7**," hold down the **Shift** key while you press the **F7** key, and then release both keys at the same time. Don't worry if using these combination keystrokes seems awkward at first; it takes practice, and you'll get plenty of that throughout this book.

❖ **Esc.** This is the cancel key. If you open a menu or dialog box by mistake, just press **Esc** to back out of it.

❖ **Other special keys.** As we work through WordPerfect's features, I'll point out other keys that can be used as mouse alternatives (and, in some cases, shortcuts). The **Home**, **End**, **PageUp**, and **PageDown** keys make it easy to move around in a document or dialog box. You'll use the **Delete** key to delete text and other objects and the **Insert** key to change your typing mode.

NOTE

WordPerfect comes with a template (a plastic strip that sits on your keyboard) that tells you how all of the function keys are used. The template also lists several Control-key shortcuts; for example, **Ctrl+T** is a shortcut for starting a new document.

Starting Windows

If you haven't started Windows yet, go ahead. We're going to start practicing, so loosen up that clicking finger. Depending on how your computer is set up, Windows might start automatically when you turn on your computer. If it doesn't, you'll probably see something like this:

```
C:\>_
```

This is called a *DOS prompt*. (I won't get into why it's called a DOS prompt. For the purposes of this book, you just need to know that it is.) Yours might look a little different, but all you need to do is type **WIN** and press **Enter** to start Windows.

If your computer is set up differently (for example, someone might have set you up so that a menu appears on your screen when you start your computer), check with the nice person who installed Windows and set up your system for instructions on starting Windows.

Have you started Windows? Just checking. Figure 2.1 shows an opening Windows screen.

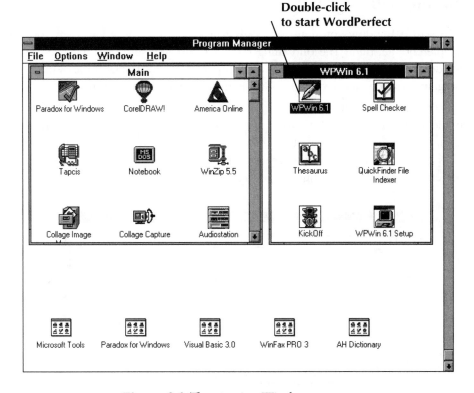

Figure 2.1 *The opening Windows screen.*

Your screen might not look quite like this. One of the neat (and initially confusing) things about Windows is that you can change just about everything, including the arrangement of the screen. But even if your screen has a different number of windows (the boxes with little pictures in them) or they're arranged differently, you still have access to the same features and you use them the same way.

The screen that you see when you start Windows is called Program Manager. You can think of Program Manager as the brains behind Windows. Whenever Windows is running, so is Program Manager. The important thing to know is that the Program Manager screen is your starting point for getting where you want to go in Windows.

Starting WordPerfect

You start a Windows program by double-clicking on its program icon. Sounds simple enough, right? The only thing you have to make sure of is that the group window containing the icon you want is open. Figure 2.1 shows the WPWin6.1 program group window with the WordPerfect for Windows icon inside it.

To start WordPerfect for Windows, you need to be able to see the WPWin 6.1 icon. If the WPWin 6.1 program group is minimized (that means it's been shrunk down to a little box at the bottom of your screen), you have to double-click on the icon to open the group window. Figure 2.2 shows the Windows screen with the WPWin program group reduced to an icon.

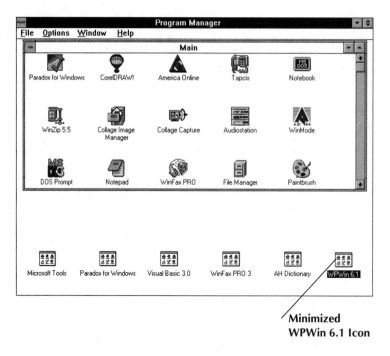

Figure 2.2 *The WPWin 6.1 group minimized.*

Do It

It's time to start WordPerfect for Windows. Just point at the WPWin 6.1 icon (that pretty little picture of a fountain pen you see in Figure 2.1) and double-click. With any luck, you should see the opening WordPerfect screen, and it should look like Figure 2.3.

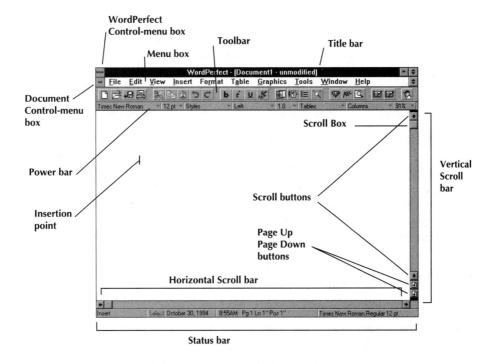

Figure 2.3 *The opening WordPerfect screen.*

ANATOMY OF THE WORDPERFECT SCREEN

Get used to looking at this screen; it's the starting point for everything you'll do in WordPerfect. Let's get acquainted with it by going over the elements shown in Figure 2.3.

Control Menu Boxes

The little boxes in the upper-left corner of the screen are called *Control menu boxes*. The one on top is for WordPerfect, and the one underneath is for your current document. Double-clicking on WordPerfect's Control menu box lets you exit WordPerfect, and double-clicking on the document's Control menu box allows you to close the current document.

Every Windows program has a Control menu box. Double-clicking on it is a great shortcut for exiting out of any Windows application.

NOTE

The Title Bar

The *title bar* is the highlighted strip at the top of the document window. After you save a document, its name is displayed in the title bar. Keep an eye on the title bar. As you move your mouse pointer around the screen or select menu items, you'll see Help Prompts that explain what will happen when you click on a button or give you hints about how to use a feature.

The Insertion Point

The insertion point is the blinking vertical line near the top of your screen. It is where text will appear when you start typing. Go ahead, try it. Just type a word or two and notice that the insertion point moves to reflect the new text location. Always make sure your insertion point is where you want it to be before you type.

Scroll Bars

Because your computer screen is smaller than a standard piece of paper, parts of your text are usually hidden, even if your document is only one page long. And in a longer document, of course, you can only see a small part of it at a time. You'll learn different techniques for moving around in documents in Chapter 5, "Editing 101." For now, I just want you to be familiar with the scroll bars. The vertical and horizontal scroll bars make it easy to view different parts of your document. I'll use the vertical scroll bar for the following examples. The horizontal scroll bar does the same thing, except it moves you left and right instead of up and down.

NOTE

In order to use the scroll bars, you must have text on the screen.

❖ Click on the black up or down arrow at the top and bottom, respectively, of the vertical scroll bar to move up or down a line at a time. Hold the arrow down to move continuously.

❖ The *scroll box* reflects your location in the document. For example, when the scroll box is at the top of the scroll bar, you're at the beginning of the document. If the scroll box is in the middle, you're somewhere in the middle of the document. To scroll to an approximate position in your document, just drag the scroll box up or down.

❖ The teeny little up and down arrows at the bottom of the vertical scroll bar (the ones that look like they're on top of a little piece of paper) are for moving you up or down a page at a time. Position your mouse pointer over the up arrow at the bottom of the scroll bar and look at the title bar. You should see a Help Prompt that says *Previous Page—View the Previous Page.* Now you know what will happen if you click on the button.

WARNING

The scroll bars change your view of the document, but they don't have anything to do with where text appears when you type. For example, if you're typing text at the beginning of a document and you use the vertical scroll bar to move to the bottom of the document and start typing, the text still appears at the top of the document. You have to move your insertion point before you can type in a new location. After you use the scroll bar to bring a different part of the document into view, position your mouse pointer in the document window and click the left mouse button where you want to enter text. That repositions your insertion point.

The Menu Bar

The *menu bar* is right under the title bar. You open a menu by clicking on its name.

To open a menu with the keyboard, press the **Alt** key to activate the menu bar. Use the **Left Arrow** or **Right Arrow** key to highlight your menu choice. Then press **Enter**. You can also open a menu by holding down the **Alt** key while you press the underlined letter for the item you want.

In Figure 2.4, I clicked on **Format** to pull down (or open) the Format menu.

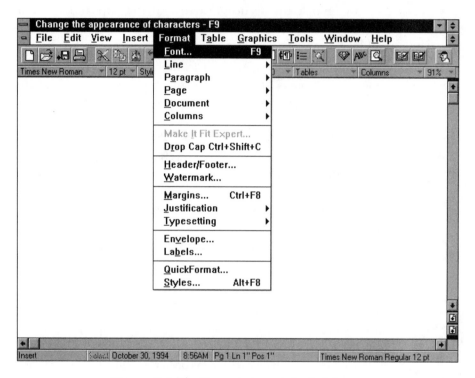

Figure 2.4 *The Format menu is pulled down.*

Once you've opened a menu, you can choose an item by either clicking on it or typing the underlined letter for the item. You can also use the **Up Arrow** and **Down Arrow** keys to highlight the item you want, and then press **Enter**.

For now, don't worry about what the features actually *do*. In this chapter we're concentrating on *how* the menus and dialog boxes work. We'll get to all of the specific features later.

NOTE

You will notice that some of the menu items have three little dots after them, and some of them have right-pointing triangles. Why? The symbols tell you what will happen if you choose that item:

❖ An ellipsis (...) signifies that choosing the item opens a dialog box. The dialog box gives you options or asks for more information before it executes the command. I'll talk about dialog boxes in a separate section in this chapter.

❖ A right-pointing triangle lets you know that choosing the item opens a *cascading menu*, which gives you another set of commands to choose from. In Figure 2.5, I clicked on **Line** from the Format menu. This gave me a cascading menu with choices that are all related to working with lines of text. Notice that there are ellipses after some of the items on the cascading menu. A dialog box is displayed when you choose an item followed by an ellipsis, whether it is on the main menu or a cascading one.

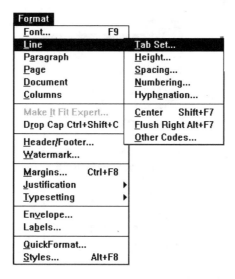

Figure 2.5 *The cascading Line menu.*

❖ If a menu item is displayed without an ellipsis or triangle, choosing the item causes an action to happen. For example, choosing **Center** from the cascading Line menu shown in Figure 2.5 centers a line of text without any further input from you.

❖ Have you noticed the key combinations listed next to some of the menu items? Those are keystroke alternatives or shortcuts that you can use instead of choosing the item from a menu. For example, I could press **Shift+F7** to center a line of text instead of choosing **Center** from the cascading Line menu.

In addition to ellipses, triangles, and shortcut keys, there are two more items you might see on menus:

❖ **Check marks.** When you see a check mark next to an item, as shown in Figure 2.6, the menu item is a *toggle*—you choose the same item to turn the feature on and off. A check mark next to it means that it's turned on, or activated. For example, in Figure 2.6, the Power Bar and Status Bar are turned on. To turn off the Power Bar and remove the check mark, I would click on its name in the menu.

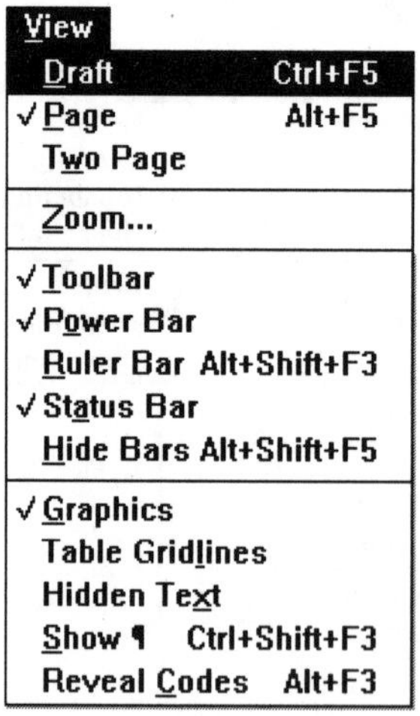

```
View
   Draft              Ctrl+F5
 √ Page               Alt+F5
   Two Page
   Zoom...
 √ Toolbar
 √ Power Bar
   Ruler Bar Alt+Shift+F3
 √ Status Bar
   Hide Bars Alt+Shift+F5
 √ Graphics
   Table Gridlines
   Hidden Text
   Show ¶    Ctrl+Shift+F3
   Reveal Codes   Alt+F3
```

Figure 2.6 *The View menu with check marks next to activated items.*

❖ **Dimmed items.** If a menu item is dimmed, the command is not currently available. For example, in the cascading Endnote menu shown in Figure 2.7, Edit is dimmed. In this case, there is nothing to edit because I haven't created any endnotes yet.

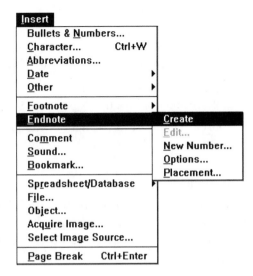

Figure 2.7 *The cascading Endnote menu.*

Closing a Menu

You can close a menu by clicking anywhere outside the menu. (You can also close a menu by clicking on the menu's name, but the entire screen is a much bigger target.)

To close a menu with the keyboard, press **Esc** twice. Pressing **Esc** the first time closes the menu, but the menu bar is still active. You have to press **Esc** again to move your insertion point back into the document area.

The Status Bar

The *Status Bar* (at the bottom of the document window) gives you information about what's going on in your document. You can also double-click on some of the Status Bar items to make things happen.

❖ The information on the far left is called the *General Status field*. (That's where it says *Insert* in Figure 2.3.) As you work with different features, this area displays specific information. For example, when your insertion point is in a table, the General Status field tells you where you are in the table. When you're just entering regular text, the General Status field tells you whether you're in Insert or Typeover mode, and you can switch between the two by double-clicking on the word **Insert** or **Typeover**. (Chapter 5 explains the Insert and Typeover modes.)

❖ The Printer field displays information about the currently selected printer. Double-clicking on this field opens the Select Printer dialog box.

❖ The Select On/Off field (just to the right of the Printer field) is activated when text or codes are selected. Double-click on this field to turn Select mode on or off.

❖ The Date and Time fields display the current date and time.

❖ The Combined Position field at the right end of the Status Bar tells you where your insertion point is located. *Pg* is the page number, *Ln* is the distance from the top of the page, and *Pos* is the distance from the left edge of the page.

NOTE

The items just described appear on the Status Bar when you first install WordPerfect, but the Status Bar can be customized to show or hide whatever pieces of information you want. For example, you can have the Status Bar display the current font or tell you whether Caps Lock is on. Appendix B contains instructions for customizing the Status Bar.

Dialog Boxes

Choosing a menu command that's followed by an ellipsis opens a dialog box. Dialog boxes are the meat and potatoes of WordPerfect: except for some very basic commands, almost everything you do in WordPerfect happens through a dialog box. As you'll see throughout this book, dialog boxes come in many guises and can contain all sorts of different options. In this section, I'll use a few representative dialog boxes to show you some of the common elements that you will encounter. Figure 2.8 shows the Font dialog box. I opened it by choosing **Font** from the Format menu (you can also open the Font dialog box by pressing **F9**).

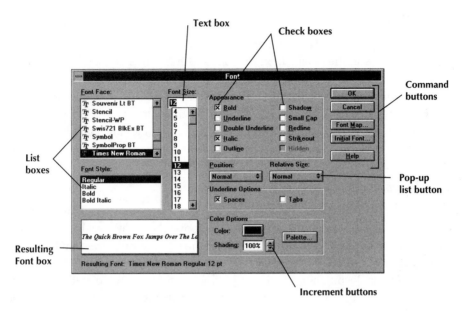

Figure 2.8 *The Font dialog box.*

Command Buttons

Look at the buttons on the right side of the dialog box. These are called *command buttons*; you press them to make something happen. If there's an ellipsis after the name in the command button, choosing it opens another dialog box with more options.

Most dialog boxes have OK, Cancel, and Help command buttons. Choose **OK** to execute your commands after you've entered all the required information or made whatever choices you want to make in the dialog box. Choose **Cancel** to close the dialog box without executing any commands. Choose **Help** to open a Help window for the feature you're using (you'll learn all about using Help in Chapter 4). The other command buttons are specific to the dialog box you're using.

Command buttons can be anywhere in the dialog box. Notice the Palette command button in the Color Options area of the Font dialog box.

Check Boxes

All of the options in the Appearance area have check boxes next to them. Notice that there are Xs in the boxes next to Bold and Italic. I've chosen those options by clicking on them or pressing the **Alt** key and the underlined letter. Check boxes are toggles—you select a check box item by clicking on it, and clicking on the same item again unselects it. You can select as many check boxes as you want. For example, I could choose to apply Bold, Underline, and Italic to the same section of text.

Text Boxes

A *text box* is an area where you can type specific information in a dialog box. In the Font dialog box, there's a text box just above the Font Size list. (Font size has to do with the size of your text.) The text inside the box (the number 12) is highlighted, or *selected*. To change the number, just start typing. When text is selected in your document or in a text box, it's automatically deleted as soon as something else is typed. You'll see text boxes in dialog boxes where you need to enter specific information, such as a number or the name of a file.

List Boxes

A *list box* is just a box that has a bunch of choices. In the Font dialog box, there are list boxes for Font Face, Font Size, and Font Style. You choose an item from a list box by clicking on it or by using your **Up Arrow** and **Down Arrow** keys to highlight the item. (Font Size is an example of a situation where you can either type your choice in the text box or select an item from the list box.) If all of the choices don't fit in the list box, there are scroll bars that let you move through the list. (I'll explain scroll bars a little later in this chapter.)

Pop-Up Lists

Notice that there are up and down arrows in the Position box. That means you'll get a *pop-up list* when you choose that option. Pop-up lists are a little funny. If you click (press the mouse button and let go) on the button, the list pops up and pops right back down. To use a pop-up list, you have to hold down the mouse button while you drag the highlight bar to the choice you want.

Increment Buttons

The up and down arrows next to the Shading text box are examples of *increment buttons.* These buttons are displayed next to text boxes where you're supposed to type in a number. They look very much like the pop-up list arrows—the only difference is that there's a line between the up and down arrows for increment buttons and no line between the arrows for pop-up lists. Increment buttons are an alternative to typing a number in the text box. You can click on the up arrow to increase the number or or the down arrow to decrease the number. If the number is already as high as it can go for that option, you'll hear a little click and the number won't change. For example, you can't go any higher than 100% for Shading, so if you try to click on the up arrow, nothing will happen.

Let's look at another dialog box for a few more examples. Figure 2.9 shows the Open File dialog box.

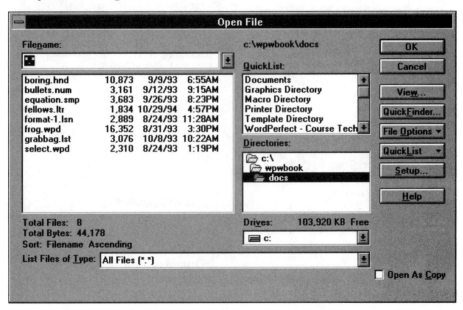

Drop-down list button

Figure 2.9 *The Open File dialog box.*

Use this dialog box to open a document that's already been created. Notice there's a text box where you can type the name of a file. There are also Filename and Directory list boxes and, of course, the **OK**, **Cancel**, and **Help** command buttons. In addition, there's something new.

Drop-Down Lists

The down arrows next to the Drives and List Files of Type boxes indicate *drop-down lists*. When you click on the arrow, you get a list of choices. Unlike a pop-up list, the drop-down list stays on the screen when you press and release the mouse button. Figure 2.10 shows the Drives drop-down list.

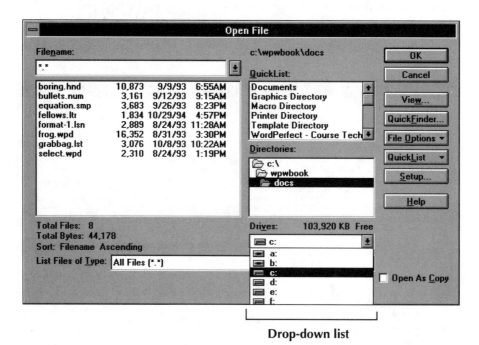

Figure 2.10 *The Drives drop-down list.*

Just click on the selection you want.

Radio Buttons

There's one more dialog box button we haven't talked about. Take a look at Figure 2.11. This is the Zoom dialog box, which I opened by choosing **Zoom** from the View menu.

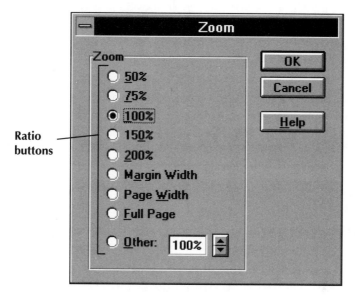

Ratio buttons

Figure 2.11 *The Zoom dialog box.*

Hey, we haven't seen those little round buttons before. They're like check boxes, only different.

The buttons next to the choices in the Zoom dialog box are called *radio buttons*. You can only choose one radio button at a time. Think of it like the buttons on your car radio—you can only tune in one station at a time. When you click on a choice to select a radio button, the previous choice is automatically deselected. Even though you can only select one radio button in each group, a dialog box can contain more than one group of radio buttons. When there is more than one group of radio buttons, you can select one radio button from each group.

Now you've seen a few examples of dialog boxes. Each has a different purpose, but you use the same techniques to work with them. By the time you finish this book, you'll be a dialog box expert.

Moving Dialog Boxes

Dialog boxes can sometimes pop up where you don't want them to. They might end up hiding text that you need to see. No problem. Did you notice that dialog boxes all have title bars, just like the WordPerfect window? You can move a dialog box anywhere on your screen by positioning your mouse pointer over the title bar and dragging the box. As you drag, a dotted outline of the box is displayed and moves with you. When the outline is where you want the box to be, release the mouse button.

NOTE

You can work with several documents at one time, and you can change the size of the document window to see more than one document on-screen. See Chapter 26, "Working with Multiple Documents," for information on moving, sizing, and minimizing documents. That chapter also has information on switching between documents and other programs.

WYSIWHAT???

Windows (and most Windows programs, including WordPerfect) use what's called a WYSIWYG display. *WYSIWYG* stands for *what you see is what you get*, and it means that what you see on the screen is a close approximation of what you'll see on the printed page. For example, if you change the size of your type or add a graphics image or footnote, you'll see all of those elements on your screen. In a non-WYSIWYG environment, a graphics image might appear as an empty box, and your text always appears the same size, which makes it hard to tell how the document will look when it's printed.

WordPerfect has two full WYSIWYG displays: Page and Two Page. The only difference between them is that Page displays one page at a time on your screen, and Two Page displays two pages side by side. Figure 2.12 shows a document in Page view, and Figure 2.13 shows the same document in Two Page view.

There's also a Draft view mode, which is a partial WYSIWYG display. In Draft view, you can still see different type styles and sizes, but headers, footers, and some other formatting features don't display on your screen. At times, using Draft view can speed things up. Because Draft view doesn't display as many different screen elements, you can move through a document faster.

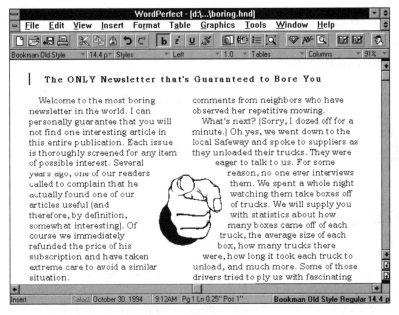

Figure 2.12 *Page view.*

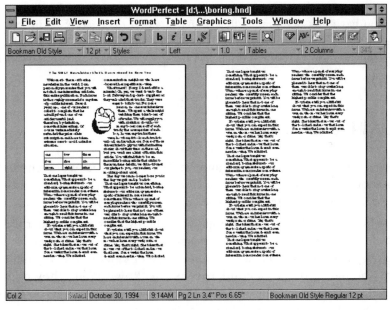

Figure 2.13 *Two Page view.*

Changing the View Mode

Open the View menu by clicking on **View** or by pressing **Alt+V**. Then choose **Draft**, **Page**, or **Two Page**.

NOTE

Page view is the default, which means that it is what you get automatically unless you choose another view mode. I've used Page view for all of the figures in this book. If you're using Draft view, sometimes your screen won't match what you see in the book.

EXITING WORDPERFECT

Close WordPerfect by double-clicking on the Control menu box. Make sure you click on the top Control menu box—the one on the title bar. The Control menu box on the menu bar is for the document window—double-clicking on it just closes the document on your screen, but it does not close WordPerfect.

You can also exit WordPerfect by pressing **Alt+F4** or choosing **Exit** from the File menu.

If you have any documents that aren't saved, a dialog box is displayed that asks if you want to save them. Choose **Yes** to save or **No** to close the documents without saving them. You'll be returned to the main Windows screen.

FROM HERE . . .

Let's see, we've opened Windows and opened and closed WordPerfect. We've talked about menus, scroll bars, and dialog boxes. Are we done yet? Is it lunch time? Nope. There are a few more bases to cover before you get a break.

Did you notice that I skipped right over the two rows just under the menu bar? Well, that's not because they're insignificant; it's because they're important enough to get their own chapter (with a couple of other features). The top row is the Toolbar and the second row is the Power Bar; they're part of WordPerfect's arsenal of power tools. The next chapter zeros in on these and other tools that will speed up and simplify your work.

CHAPTER 3

Power Tools

(There Must be an Easier Way to Do This)

Let's talk about:

- ❖ The Power Bar
- ❖ Toolbars
- ❖ QuickMenus
- ❖ The Ruler Bar

I don't know about you, but I'm really lazy. If there's an easy way to do something, I'm all for it. And even then, I'll usually try to find an even easier way. Well, those friendly WordPerfect programmers busted their you-know-whats so that we wouldn't have to. This chapter introduces you to a bunch of cool tools that put most of WordPerfect's features just a mouse click away.

One reason I want you to know how to use these tools before we go much further is that, whenever possible, the shortcut tools will be the method we'll use to get things done. One caveat here: all of the tools discussed in this chapter require a mouse. If you don't have one, it doesn't mean you can't use WordPerfect for Windows (and throughout the book, I'll give you alternative methods for doing things without a mouse), but it does mean that you won't be able to take advantage of a lot of great shortcuts.

ROADMAP

This chapter focuses on using the shortcut tools *out of the box*. But most of them can be customized in various ways (such as moving them to different parts of the screen, changing the way they look, or displaying different items). You'll find information on customization in Appendix B.

THE POWER BAR

The Power Bar is a group of buttons arranged horizontally along the top of your screen (see Figure 3.1). When you install WordPerfect, the Power Bar is displayed by default, but you can hide it if you choose. It's so handy that I can't think of a good reason to turn it off (unless you don't have a mouse), but let's turn it off and back on just to get a good sense of where it is on the screen.

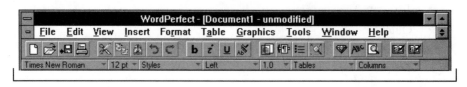

Power bar

Figure 3.1 *The Power Bar gives you quick access to a whole bunch of commonly used features.*

Do It

To hide or display the Power Bar:

1. Click on **View** (or press **Alt+V**) to open the View menu.

NOTE

Any time you see a check mark next to a menu item (as in Figure 3.2), you can click on the item (or type the underlined letter) to deactivate the feature. Clicking on it when there's no check mark activates the feature. It's just like flicking a switch: the same action turns it on and off.

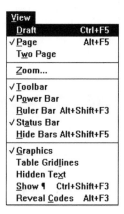

Figure 3.2 *Notice that there's a check mark next to the Power Bar option on the View menu.*

2. Choose **Power Bar** (or press **O**) to turn off the Power Bar. Pay attention to your screen—notice that the Power Bar disappears.

3. Repeat steps 1 and 2 to turn the Power Bar back on, and watch your screen as the Power Bar reappears.

What do the Buttons Do?

Good question. Even though the buttons display text instead of pictures, it's not entirely clear what each one does. Well, WordPerfect thought of us here, too. If you move the mouse pointer to any of the buttons (don't click—just point), and hold it there for a moment, you'll see a box that tells you what the button does. If you want a more detailed explanation, look at the title bar. The description under the mouse pointer is called a *QuickTip*, and the title bar message is called a *Help Prompt*.

Do It

Move your mouse pointer over any of the buttons on the Power Bar—you don't have to click on anything; just move the mouse. Check out the QuickTip just below the mouse pointer and the Help Prompt on the title bar. Play around with this a bit and get a sense of the different options you can access from the Power Bar. In Figure 3.3 my mouse pointer's on the button that says *Left*. The QuickTip tells me that this button's for justification. If that doesn't help me enough, I take a look at the title bar, where it says *Align text in document*.

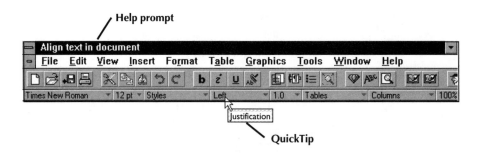

Figure 3.3 *Mouse pointer on the Justification button.*

How do I Use the Buttons?

Okay, now you know how to figure out what the buttons do, but how do you use them? Click. That's it. Just click once on any of the buttons to get to the feature described.

Depending on the feature, clicking on a Power Bar button might give you a list of choices, or it might simply implement the feature. That all depends on whether there are further choices that need to be made. Don't worry about what the individual buttons actually accomplish for now. The goal here is just to be able to use them. As we get into different features throughout the book, we'll make extensive use of the Power Bar and you'll find out what the specific buttons do.

Do It

Let's use the Justification button as an example.

1. Move your mouse pointer to the Justification button. (Remember, you can glance at the QuickTip or Help Prompt to make sure you're on the right button.)

2. Click the left mouse button. That's all there is to it. The Justification drop-down list is displayed, as you can see in Figure 3.4.

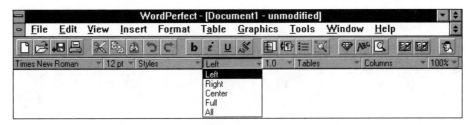

Figure 3.4. *The Justification drop-down list.*

3. Since we're just using this as an example, click anywhere outside the drop-down list to close it.

That's pretty much it for the Power Bar. You know how to figure out what the buttons do and you know how to use them. From now on, you'll use them a lot.

TOOLBARS

Toolbars are like the Power Bar, only different. Does that explain it enough for you? No? Okay, I'll tell you a little more. Like the Power Bar, Toolbars have buttons that you click on to make something happen. The most obvious difference is that, by default, the Toolbar displays pictures instead of text. Another difference is that you can have as many different Toolbars as you want, and you can move the current Toolbar to different locations on the screen. Check out Appendix B if you want to create your own Toolbars or move them around.

Do It

You use exactly the same method to display the Toolbar that you used for the Power Bar.

1. To activate the Toolbar, choose **Toolbar** from the View menu (or press **Alt+V, T**).

2. If the Toolbar is already displayed (see Figure 3.5), choosing **Toolbar** makes it disappear.

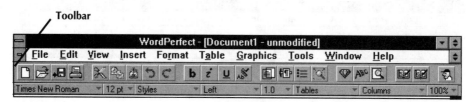

Figure 3.5 *By default, the Toolbar is displayed between the Menu Bar and the Power Bar.*

What do the Buttons Do?

Those pictures are pretty cryptic, aren't they? But no problem—QuickTips and Help Prompts are there to assist you, just as they are for the Power Bar.

Why are some of the buttons grayed-out (or dimmed)? Think back to Chapter 2. Any time an item is dimmed in a menu or dialog box, it means that item is not currently available. Usually something else needs to happen before the feature can be used. For example, the Cut and Copy buttons are dimmed because you have to have text selected before you can perform either of these actions.

Do It

Let's use the Print button as an example:

1. Move your mouse pointer to the Print button 🖶 (use the QuickTip and Help Prompt to make sure you're in the right place).

2. Click the left mouse button. That's all there is to it. The Print dialog box is displayed, as you can see in Figure 3.6.

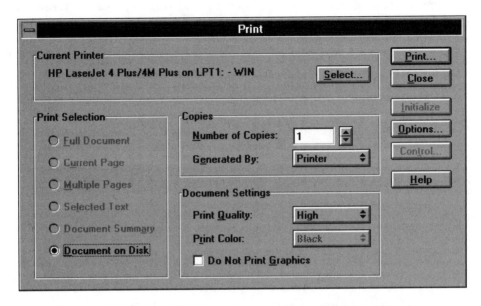

Figure 3.6 *The Print button takes you right to the Print dialog box.*

3. Since we're just using this as an example, click on the **Close** button (or press **C**) to close the Print dialog box.

Do you remember how you accessed the Print dialog box in Chapter 1? You opened the File menu and then chose **Print**. With the Toolbar, one click and you're there.

Choosing Different Toolbars

WordPerfect comes with 13 predefined Toolbars. If you're working with a particular feature, you can choose a special Toolbar to streamline your efforts. For example, if you're doing a lot of document formatting, there's a Format Toolbar that makes it easier to get to options that would otherwise be buried under several menus and dialog boxes.

The default 6.1 WordPerfect Toolbar is displayed unless you make another choice. It includes options that WordPerfect decided would apply to most general situations. Throughout the book, we'll make use of different Toolbars as appropriate.

How do you choose a different Toolbar? You could choose **Preferences** from the Edit menu and then double-click on the Toolbar icon. This brings up the Toolbar Preferences dialog box with a list of available Toolbars. At this point, you can double-click on the Toolbar you want. After that, you still have to close the Preferences dialog box.

I bet you're thinking that sounds like a lot of effort for something that's supposed to save time. If it's that much work to change Toolbars, why bother? You're right. And, of course, WordPerfect has most graciously provided you with a much easier way to switch Toolbars. It's time to introduce you to QuickMenus. That's the next power tool I'll be discussing in this chapter, but it's such an obvious choice here that we'll use it without getting into any major explanations.

Do It

Let's use a QuickMenu:

1. Move your mouse pointer so that it's anywhere on the Toolbar.

2. Click the right mouse button. A list of available Toolbars is displayed (see Figure 3.7).

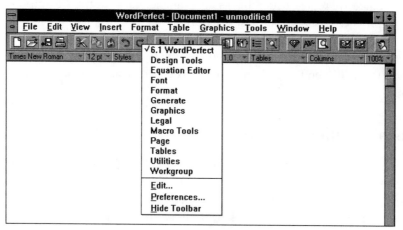

Figure 3.7 *The current Toolbar (in this case, the 6.1 WordPerfect Toolbar) has a check mark next to it.*

3. Click on the Toolbar you want. The current Toolbar is automatically replaced by the one you select.

QUICKMENUS

WordPerfect's menu system is designed to make it easy to get to the features you need, but it can be confusing and intimidating when you sometimes have to wade through layers of menus to get to the right one.

QuickMenus to the rescue! You saw an example in the last section, when we used a QuickMenu to change Toolbars. When you clicked the right mouse button anywhere on the Toolbar, you got a menu that gave you options specifically related to Toolbars. That's the whole idea behind QuickMenus: to narrow down the possible choices. With a QuickMenu, you get only those menu items that relate to the specific feature or document area in you're working.

Where are the QuickMenus?

QuickMenus are all over the place. Unlike the Power Bar and Toolbars, you don't turn on a QuickMenu by selecting it from a pull-down menu. The neat thing about QuickMenus is that you don't even have to know what you want or what features are available in a particular area—just click the right mouse button, and if a QuickMenu pops up, it tells you which features are appropriate for that section of the document.

For example, what if you want to create a header (text that will print at the top of every page), but you don't know how to get to the Header feature through the pull-down menus? Easy! <u>Move the mouse pointer up near the top of the page and click the right mouse button</u>. This QuickMenu has only two items: Header/Footer and Watermark. That really narrows your choices, doesn't it? Just click on **Header/Footer**, and you're on your way. What's a watermark? Hey, don't even think about it now—we'll get there (but for the terminally curious, it's in Chapter 14, "Borders, Lines, and Watermarks").

Figures 3.8 through 3.15 show you most of the QuickMenus that are accessible from the main document screen and tell you where your cursor needs to be to access them. A lot of the items on the QuickMenus are probably unfamiliar to you. That's okay. Don't worry about *what* the items are—we'll get to that as we cover the individual features. For now, as with the Power Bar and Toolbars, the idea is simply to become familiar with the concept of QuickMenus.

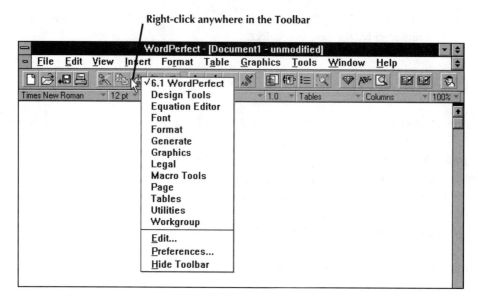

Figure 3.8 *The Toolbar QuickMenu lets you quickly switch between Toolbars and includes options for editing and customizing.*

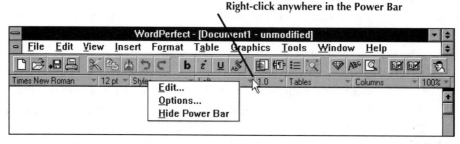

Figure 3.9 *From this QuickMenu, you can get right to the Power Bar Options dialog box, where you can change the settings for the Power Bar.*

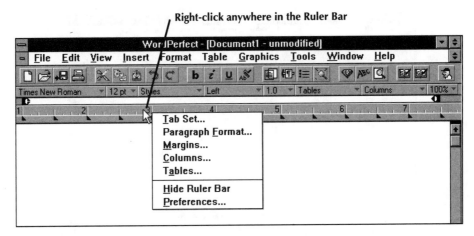

Figure 3.10 *This is the Ruler Bar's QuickMenu, which can whisk you away to some commonly used formatting and layout features. (The Ruler Bar is covered in the next section of this chapter.)*

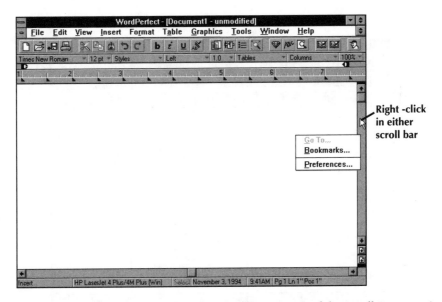

Figure 3.11 *By clicking the right mouse button on one of the Scroll Bars, you're within easy reach of any location in your document.*

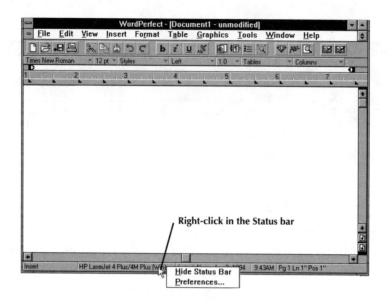

Figure 3.12 *Right-click on the Status Bar to hide or customize it.*

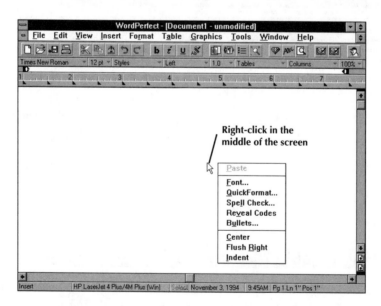

Figure 3.13 *Click the right mouse button just about anywhere in the document window for instant access to often-used features.*

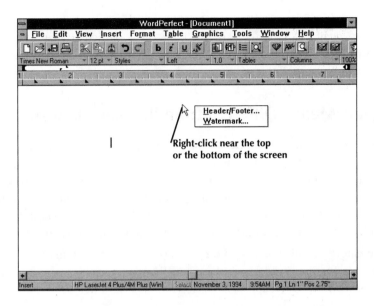

Figure 3.14 *Right-click near the top or bottom of a page to create a header or footer.*

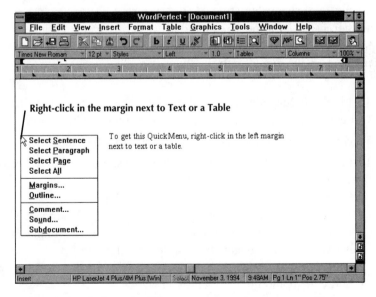

Figure 3.15 *Right-click in the left margin next to text or a table to access this QuickMenu.*

WordPerfect has hidden a few more QuickMenus throughout the program. Some of them are available when you're working on a particular feature or have a graphic image on your screen. We'll talk about and use most of them as we work our way through the features.

Are QuickMenus Different from Regular Menus?

Nope. When you choose **Header/Footer** from a QuickMenu, it's the same as choosing it from a pull-down menu or dialog box. QuickMenu items are no different from regular pull-down menu items. If an item is followed by an ellipsis (...), choosing that item activates a dialog box. If there's a check mark next to an item, that item is turned on or selected. If there's nothing next to an item, clicking on it causes an action to happen without any further input.

To create the QuickMenus, WordPerfect just grouped items from the pull-down menus for easier access and copied them to QuickMenus. So it doesn't matter how you get to a feature—the end result is the same.

Using QuickMenus

The best way to practice using QuickMenus is to start clicking your right mouse button in different areas of the screen and see what happens. I'll give you a few basic instructions, and then I'd like you to take a few minutes to explore QuickMenus before we move on to the Ruler Bar.

❖   To trigger a QuickMenu, click the right mouse button. The QuickMenu you get depends on where your mouse pointer is when you click.

❖   To choose a QuickMenu item, click on it with either mouse button.

❖   To turn off a QuickMenu, click the left mouse button anywhere outside the menu.

If you don't get the QuickMenu you intended, just try clicking in a slightly different location. For example, if you're trying to get the main document window QuickMenu and you get the one for headers and footers instead, it probably means that you clicked a little too high on the screen. Click again, a little lower, and you should get the menu you want.

THE RULER BAR

With the Power Bar, Toolbars, and QuickMenus, virtually all of WordPerfect's features are a mouse click away. Can it get any easier than that? Sure it can. How about changing margin and tab settings without having to select a feature at all? Take a look at Figure 3.16

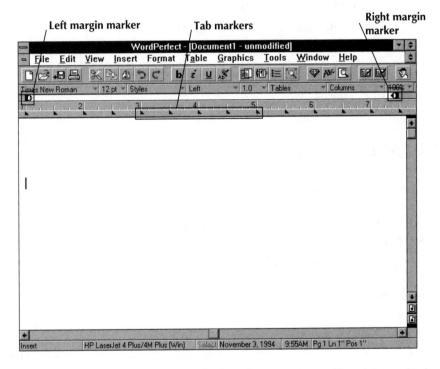

Figure 3.16 *When the Ruler Bar is displayed, you can see all margin and tab settings.*

The Ruler Bar is displayed just below the Power Bar; it gives you visible margin and tab markings. The markings aren't just window dressing: you can change a tab or margin setting just by dragging the appropriate marker to a new location on the ruler.

The Ruler Bar also has its own QuickMenu that contains several formatting and layout options (see Figure 3.10).

For now, I'll just show you how to activate the Ruler Bar. In Chapter 8, "Formatting: The Sequel," you'll learn how to make it do your bidding.

Do It

To activate or deactivate the Ruler Bar:

1.   Click on **View** (or press **Alt+V**) to open the View menu.
2.   Choose **Ruler Bar** (or press **Alt+Shift+F3**).

If there's a check mark next to this item, the Ruler Bar is already on. Just like the Power Bar and Toolbar options, the Ruler Bar is a toggle; choosing it turns it on if it's off or off if it's on.

FROM HERE . . .

The power tools you learned about in this chapter are heavily used throughout the book. From now on, when I tell you about a feature, I'll emphasize the easiest method, and that'll usually mean making use of the Power Bar, Toolbars, QuickMenus, or Ruler Bar.

At this point, make sure that the Power Bar, the WordPerfect 6.1 Toolbar, and the Ruler Bar are all displayed. This would be a good time to go back through this chapter and make sure you feel comfortable displaying all four power tools.

The next chapter, "Getting Help," will make you even more self-sufficient (uh-oh, I better stop with this self-sufficiency stuff or I'll be out of a job). I'll give you resources that will help you figure out any WordPerfect problem on the spot.

After that, we'll really start digging into WordPerfect's goodies. We'll learn how to perform all of your word-processing tasks in the easiest way possible.

CHAPTER 4

Getting Help

(We All Need a Little Help From Our Friends)

Let's talk about:

- ❖ Using the WordPerfect Help system
- ❖ Running the tutorial
- ❖ Searching for help on a specific topic
- ❖ Using coaches
- ❖ Using Help to get information about your system

I know you're chomping at the bit—you want to *use* WordPerfect, not take detours to learn about useless stuff like the Help system. Well, it's far from useless. In fact, if this is the only chapter you read, you'll have all of the resources you need to navigate your way through WordPerfect's features. WordPerfect's on-line help is a great way to get immediate information that can lead you through whatever feature you're working on.

With WordPerfect's Help system, you have several different ways to get the information you want. You can search for help on a specific topic, use the glossary to look up a definition, or let one of the coaches actually walk you through a procedure. There's even a tutorial that contains on-screen lessons to guide you through the basics of creating and formatting documents.

USING HELP

Let's jump right in.

1. Open the Help menu by clicking on **Help** or pressing **Alt+H**. Figure 4.1 shows the Help menu. You can choose Help options from this menu. We'll get into most of them in a bit.

Figure 4.1 *The Help menu.*

2. Choose **Contents**, which opens the WordPerfect Help Contents window, shown in Figure 4.2.

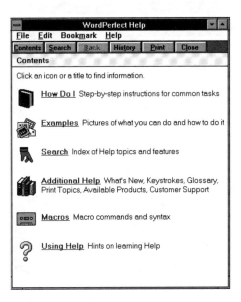

Figure 4.2 *The WordPerfect Help Contents window.*

F1 is a quick keyboard shortcut for opening the Help Contents window.

3. Move your mouse pointer around the window. Notice that the pointer turns into a hand when you move over one of the green underlined items. The hand tells you that you can click on the item to get more information.

4. To find out what kinds of information you can get, click on **Using Help** (the last green item on the list). This takes you to the Using Help window, shown in Figure 4.3.

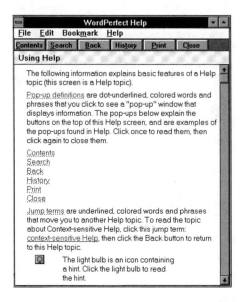

Figure 4.3 *The Using Help window.*

This is a great place to start with Help. The Using Help window contains and explains most of the elements you'll run into as you use Help. Play around with it for a bit. Click on a couple of the words that are underlined with dashes to get pop-up definitions of the word. Click to display the definition, then click again to make it disappear.

The words with solid underlines take you to another help window for that topic. Click on context-sensitive help to jump to a help screen that gives you information about context-sensitive help and tells you how to use it.

As you work with Help, you'll see light bulbs like the one in the Using Help window. Click on the light bulb for a hint about the Help topic you're in.

Before you move on, take some time to explore the Using Help window. All of the definitions, hints, and additional help windows give you valuable information about the Help system.

If you want even more detailed information about using Help, press **F1** (or choose **How to Use Help** from the Help window's Help menu). You'll get the Contents for How to Use Help window, shown in Figure 4.4. Click on any of the underlined items to jump to the help topic you want.

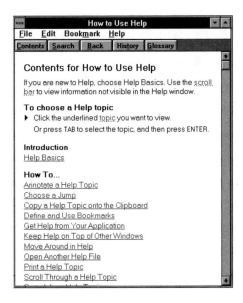

Figure 4.4 *The Contents for How to Use Help window.*

Closing Help

Just click on the **Close** button (located beneath the menu bar) to exit Help. You can also close the Help window by double-clicking on its Control menu box or by choosing **Exit** from Help's File menu. Close the Help window before you move to the next section.

HOW DO I DO THIS?

WordPerfect's Help system is ready and waiting to answer those "How do I do this?" questions. In fact, if you pull down the main Help menu (from WordPerfect, not from inside Help), you'll see an option called *How Do I.*

1. Choose **How Do I** from the Help menu to open the window shown in Figure 4.5. You can also choose **How Do I** from the Contents list inside Help. Press **F1** to open the Help Contents window and choose **How Do I** to get to the window shown in Figure 4.5.

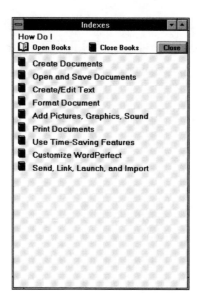

Figure 4.5 *The How Do I window.*

The topics in the How Do I window all finish the question "How do I?" The items are grouped into major categories like *Create Documents* and *Add Pictures, Graphics, Sound* to make it easier to find what you want. For example, you may be saying to yourself, "How do I change margins?"

2.   Click on **Format Document**. I guessed that margins would be in the Formatting section. In a bit, I'll show you how to search for a particular topic if you're not sure where to find it.

3.   The book icon next to Format Document opens and there's a list of formatting topics from which to choose.

4.   Choose **Change Tabs, Margins, Line Spacing**.

5.   Now you're down to the detailed topic listings. They're displayed in green underlined text. Choose **Set Margins**. Clicking on a green underlined *How Do I* topic opens the Help window for that topic, as you can see in Figure 4.6.

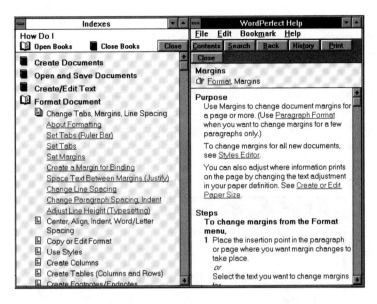

Figure 4.6 *The Margins Help and How Do I windows side by side.*

The How Do I window remains on the screen; you can choose as many different How Do I topics as you want. Each time you click on a different topic in the How Do I window, the Help window for that topic replaces the one that's currently displayed.

To close How Do I:

1. Click on the **Close** command button in the How Do I window. Notice that the Help window stays open.

2. Close the Help window by clicking on its **Close** command button (or pressing **Alt+F4** or **Esc**).

SEARCHING FOR HELP ON A SPECIFIC FEATURE

The Help system contains an alphabetical index of all WordPerfect features. But if Help just presented you with a list, you'd have to do an awful lot of scrolling to find what you want, since there are about a kazillion features. So Help helps you out by giving you a way to search through the index and get the specific help you need. Suppose you want to find out how to add the date to a document.

1. From the WordPerfect window, choose **Search for Help on** from the Help menu. Or, from a Help window, click on the **Search** command button. Either way, the dialog box shown in Figure 4.7 is displayed. Notice the instructions at the top of the dialog box. Your insertion point is inside the text box, all ready for you to start typing.

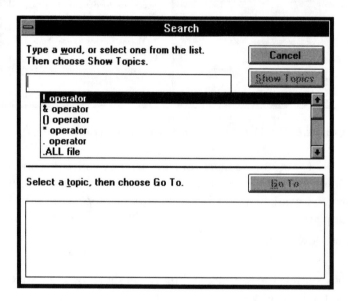

Figure 4.7 *The Search dialog box.*

2. Type the word you want to search for. For this example, type **date**. As you type, notice that the selection bar moves through the list to highlight the word you type.

3. Click on **Show Topics** or press **Enter**. The bottom list box displays a list of Help topics that are related to the word you selected, as shown in Figure 4.8.

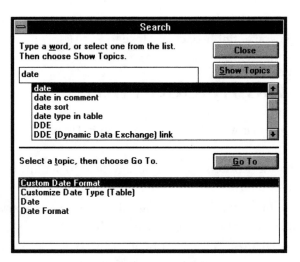

Figure 4.8 *When you choose Show Topics, a list of related topics is displayed in the bottom list box.*

4.   Double-click on the topic you want to get help on. (For this example, choose **Date**.) Or highlight the topic and choose **Go To** (or press **Enter**). The Help window for the topic you choose opens, as shown in Figure 4.9.

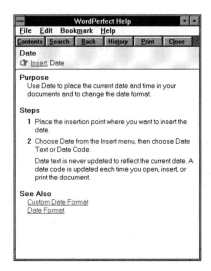

Figure 4.9 *The Date Help window.*

If you want to do another search, just click on **Search** and repeat steps 2 through 4. When you're finished, click **Close** to exit Help.

NAVIGATING THROUGH HELP

Here are a few tips that will help you get around in Help:

❖ Click on the **Contents** button at any time to return to the main Help Contents window.

❖ You can move backward through the Help topics you've used in the current Help session by clicking on the **Back** button.

❖ Click on **History** to get a list of all of the Help topics you've looked at during the current session. The list can hold up to 40 items; they're listed in reverse order, so the topics you used most recently are at the top of the list. Just double-click on a topic to reopen its Help window.

❖ You can get a printout of a Help topic by clicking **Print** or choosing **Print Topic** from Help's File menu.

❖ To print several Help topics at once, choose **Print Topics** from Help's File menu. This option allows you to select multiple Help topics and send them to the printer.

❖ If you want the Help window to remain visible while you work on your document, choose **Always on Top** from Help's Help menu. Just click in your document window to work on the document, and click in the Help window if you want to look up another topic. Choose **Close** when you're finished using Help.

CONTEXT-SENSITIVE HELP

Sometimes you want specific help on the feature you're trying to use, and it would be really nice if you could just tell WordPerfect, "I want help on what I'm doing right now—you figure it out for me." Well, you can. In fact, there are a couple of ways to get context-sensitive help. *Context-sensitive* just means that WordPerfect figures out what you're trying to do based on the context (which dialog box you're in, which button you're pointing to, or which menu item is highlighted).

❖ Press **F1** when a menu item is highlighted to get specific help about the highlighted item.

❖ When you're in a dialog box, press **F1** or click on **Help** to get a Help window for that dialog box feature.

Help: What Is?

There's also a great feature called *Help: What Is?* that lets you use Help to ask the question "What will happen if I press this key (or take this action)?" **Shift+F1** gives you help that is specific to the feature you are using. Let's try it.

1. Press **Shift+F1** to activate Help: What Is? A bubble with a question mark in it will attach itself to your mouse pointer.

2. Point at a menu item, a button, or a particular area of the window and click the left mouse button. For this example, click anywhere on the Ruler Bar. The Help window for the Ruler Bar is displayed, as shown in Figure 4.10.

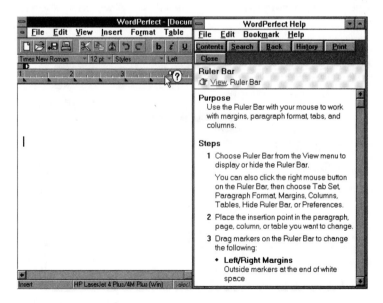

Figure 4.10 *Context-sensitive help for the Ruler Bar.*

3. If you want, jump to a related topic by clicking on any of the underlined items.

4. When you're done, close the Help window.

You can also use Help: What Is? to find out what a particular keystroke will do. For example, if you press **Shift+F1** and then press the **Tab** key, you'll get the Tab Key Help window.

USING THE GLOSSARY

The glossary contains definitions of most of the words you'll encounter as you work with WordPerfect. To use the glossary:

1. Open the Help Contents window by choosing **Contents** from WordPerfect's Help menu or pressing **F1**.

2. Click on **Additional Help**, then click on **Glossary** in the Additional Help window.

3. Click on **Glossary** to display the Glossary window, shown in Figure 4.11.

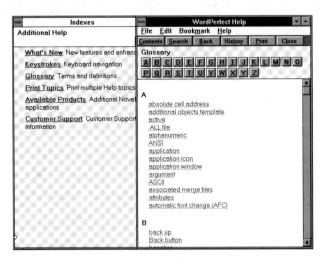

Figure 4.11 *Help's glossary window.*

4. Click on any of the letter buttons to get a list of available glossary items for that letter of the alphabet. For this example, click on **D**.

5. Click on the item for which you want to see a definition. For now, click on **dialog box** to display a pop-up box that tells you what a dialog box is, as shown in Figure 4.12.

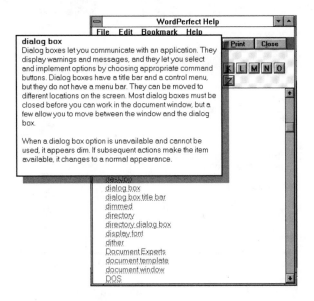

Figure 4.12 *The glossary with a definition box open.*

6. When you're done reading the definition, click anywhere on the screen to close the definition box, and choose **Close** to close the Help window.

GETTING SOME COACHING

WordPerfect includes several coaches that actually walk you through some common procedures. Unlike a Help window, a coach is right there at your side throughout the procedure, and it even shows you what to do next (if you ask nicely). Let's say you want to create a footnote, but you've never done it before, so a little assistance is in order.

1. Choose **Coaches** from WordPerfect's Help menu. The Coach dialog box, shown in Figure 4.13, is displayed. The list box contains a list of the available coaches. When a particular coach is highlighted, a short description is displayed in the Description box.

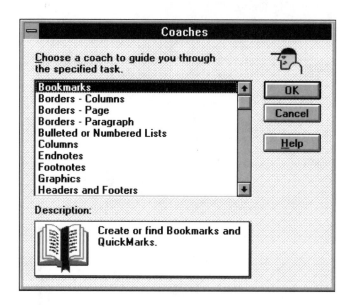

Figure 4.13 *The Coach dialog box.*

2. Click on the coach you want to use and choose **OK**. For this example, choose **Footnotes**. Your personal coach is displayed in the form of a dialog box, as shown in Figure 4.14. It describes the feature you are about to use and tells you about some of the available WordPerfect options for the feature.

3. Choose **Continue**.

4. Choose **Quit Coach** from any of the coach dialog boxes if you want to end the coaching session. If you are in the middle of a coaching session, just choose **Yes** when asked if you want to quit. The coach disappears, but anything that you added to your document while you were using the coach remains on screen.

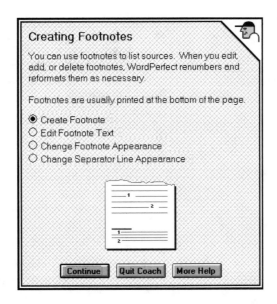

Figure 4.14 *The opening coach dialog box for Creating Footnotes.*

The coach tells you what to do to complete the procedure. Just follow along. Where appropriate, a coach displays a **Show Me** button. If you choose **Show Me**, the coach actually pulls down a menu or opens a dialog box for you and tells you where you need to click next. In Figure 4.15, when I clicked on **Show Me** the coach pulled down the Insert menu, opened the cascading Footnote menu, and moved the mouse pointer to **Create**. All I have to do now is click on **Create**.

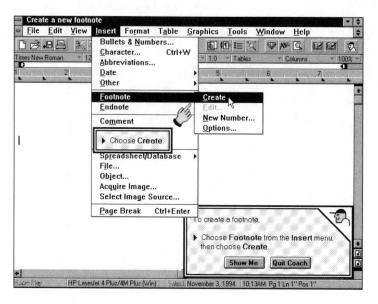

Figure 4.15 *The coach is showing me what to do next.*

Coaches are a great way of learning how to do different things in WordPerfect. You're actually doing the work in a real document, but the coach is guiding you every step of the way.

RUNNING THE TUTORIAL

WordPerfect's on-line tutorial contains four lessons that take you through the basics of creating and formatting documents. The tutorial is a useful tool for familiarizing yourself with basic word-processing concepts and learning how WordPerfect does things.

You can use the tutorial in a couple of different ways. You could run through all four lessons to get a quick overview of the basics before you continue with this book. Or you could complete different lessons at different points to review and reinforce what you've learned. For example, you might want to complete the first lesson, "Starting Out," at this point and wait until you've finished Chapter 7, "Basic Formatting," before running the second and third lessons, "Editing Text" and "Formatting Text."

I'll give you instructions to get you started with the tutorial. Once you start it, all you have to do is follow the on-screen instructions—WordPerfect tells you what to do next.

1. Choose **Tutorial** from the Help menu. The opening dialog box for the tutorial is displayed, as shown in Figure 4.16.

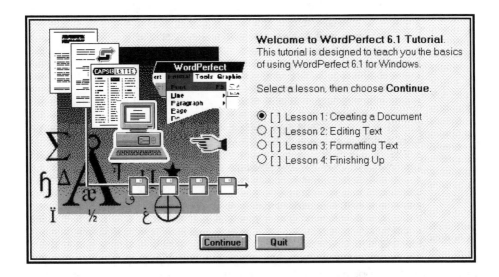

Figure 4.16 *The opening Tutorial dialog box.*

Even though the dialog boxes for coaches and the tutorial look a little different, they work just like any dialog box. Click on a radio button to make a selection or on a command button to make something happen.

NOTE

2. Click on the lesson you want and choose **Continue**. In Figure 4.17, I clicked on **Lesson 1** and chose **Continue** to move to the opening dialog box for Lesson 1. The opening dialog box for each lesson tells you approximately how long it will take to complete the lesson, gives you a brief description of the lesson's contents, and gives you an opportunity to proceed or go back to the main menu.

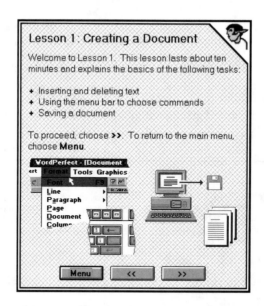

Figure 4.17 *The opening dialog box for Lesson 1.*

3.   To proceed with the lesson, click on the **>>** button.

Every tutorial dialog box has **Menu**, **<<**, and **>>** command buttons. You can return to the main menu at any time by clicking on **Menu** in each of the two dialog boxes that appear. From there, you can exit the tutorial by choosing **Quit**. The **>>** button advances you to the next lesson step, and the **<<** button takes you backward a step at a time. If something isn't clear and you want to review a few steps, just press **<<** until you return to the point you want.

USING EXAMPLE DOCUMENTS TO GET HELP

Take a look at Figure 4.18. Choose **Examples** from the Help Contents window to use this help feature that gives you samples of different document styles. You can find out how to work with a particular feature by clicking the arrow that points to the appropriate part of the document. You don't have to know the name of the feature—just find something you'd like to be able to do, and click.

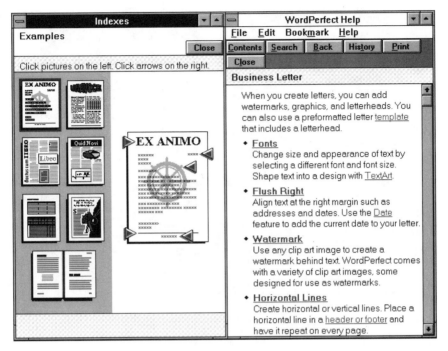

Figure 4.18 *The Examples window.*

USING THE UPGRADE EXPERT

If you are upgrading from a previous version of WordPerfect or from another word processor, this Help option is a must-see. Choose **Upgrade Expert** from the Help menu to get the dialog box shown in Figure 4.19.

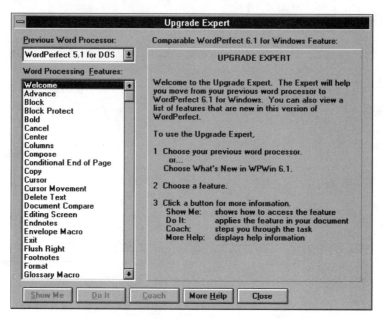

Figure 4.19 *The Upgrade Expert.*

GETTING SYSTEM AND WORDPERFECT VERSION INFORMATION

It is often helpful to know how WordPerfect and Windows are using your system's resources. In addition, if you call WordPerfect's telephone support line, they'll want to know the date on your WordPerfect program and your license number. All of this information is available in one place.

Choose **About WordPerfect** from the Help menu to display the dialog box shown in Figure 4.20.

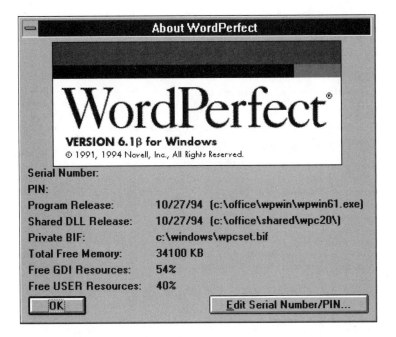

Figure 4.20 *The About WordPerfect dialog box.*

If you entered your license number when you installed WordPerfect, the license number is displayed here. If not, choose **Edit Serial Number/PIN** to open a dialog box that lets you type your license number in a text box. The *PIN* (personal identification number) is used when you call WordPerfect's telephone support.

The Program Release, Total Free Memory, and Free Resources information can help WordPerfect Support (or someone else who is helping you troubleshoot a problem) figure out what's going on.

FROM HERE . . .

As you work through this book and begin creating your own documents, don't forget about Help. If you want to review something I've talked about or get a different perspective on it, try Help. I won't cover every single detail about every single feature, so you can use Help when you're ready to delve a little deeper. I definitely suggest that you give the coaches a try too—it's nice to have a helping hand when you're learning a new feature. And if you haven't already, why don't you run Lesson 1 of the tutorial before reading the next chapter? It will reinforce a lot of the material I've covered, and you'll be all set to move on.

In the next chapter, "Editing 101," you'll learn more about the basics of opening, creating, and saving documents. We'll make some changes to the document you created in the Chapter 1, and you'll learn techniques for efficiently moving around in a document. I'll even show you how to recover when you do something you didn't mean to do.

CHAPTER 5

Editing 101

(Throw Out Those Red Pencils and Erasers)

Let's talk about:

- ❖ Opening a document
- ❖ Moving around in a document
- ❖ Adding text
- ❖ Deleting text
- ❖ Undeleting and undoing (the Oops! features)
- ❖ Closing a document without saving
- ❖ Saving a document

Pop quiz time. What's the first thing that happens after you finish creating a document? Give up? Come on, think about it—as soon as you're done and the document's no longer on your screen, you remember something that needs to be added. (Or am I the only one that happens to?)

In the old typewriter days, this meant either starting over or scrawling a note in the margin before you mailed the letter. Even a minor error could cause you to have to retype a lengthy document. Well, as far as I'm concerned, one of the greatest things about computers is that I *never* have to retype. I can bring that document back to the screen, get rid of what I don't want, add what I do, and move the rest of it around in any order I desire.

In this chapter, you'll bring a document you already created back to the screen and learn how to make simple changes. Then, in Chapter 6, "Moving and Copying Text," you'll learn how to take chunks of text and move them around.

OPENING AN EXISTING DOCUMENT

When you're staring at an empty WordPerfect document screen, you have two choices: You can start creating a new document (that's what we did in Chapter 1), or you can open a document that's already been created.

KEYBOARD

If you click on the **New Blank Document** button 📄 on the Toolbar (or press **Ctrl+N**), you get a blank document screen like the one you used in Chapter 1. But if you choose **New** from the File menu (or press **Ctrl+T**), you get the New Document dialog box shown in Figure 5.1. This allows you to choose a template to give your document a basic layout.

ROADMAP

As you can see, you can choose from several categories, including business, fax, legal, letter, and memo. Document templates can save you a lot of effort—check out Chapter 23 for the complete scoop.

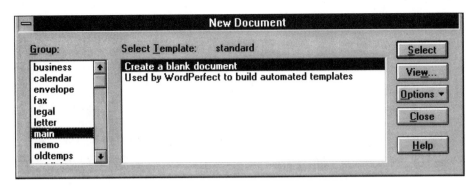

Figure 5.1 *The New Document dialog box.*

Do It

Let's open the document you created in Chapter 1.

1. Click on the **Open** button 🖼 on the Toolbar. The Open File dialog box, shown in Figure 5.3, is displayed. You can also choose **Open** from the File menu or press **Ctrl+O**.

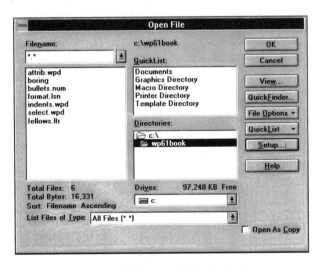

Figure 5.2 *The Open File dialog box.*

2. Double-click on the file you want to open (in this case, **FELLOWS.LTR**). If necessary, use the vertical scroll bar until the file you want to open is visible.

KEYBOARD

Press the **Tab** key to move into the Filename list box. Use the **Up Arrow** and **Down Arrow** keys to select the file you want. Then press **Enter** to open the file. If you can't see all of the files, you can use the **Down Arrow** to move through the list. If you know the name of the file, just type it in the Filename text box and then press **Enter**.

ROADMAP

FELLOWS.LTR should be back on your screen at this point. If you had a problem opening it, refer to Chapter 15, "Managing Files," for help. Take a look at the sections on understanding and changing directories. It's possible that you inadvertently saved FELLOWS.LTR in a different directory We're not going to get into all that directory stuff now—just hang in there and it'll all become clear.

SHORTCUT

If you've worked on a document recently, there's an even easier way to open it. WordPerfect keeps track of the last four documents you've opened, and they're listed on the bottom of the File menu. To open one of the documents, just click on its name. Or, if you're using the keyboard, press the number next to the name.

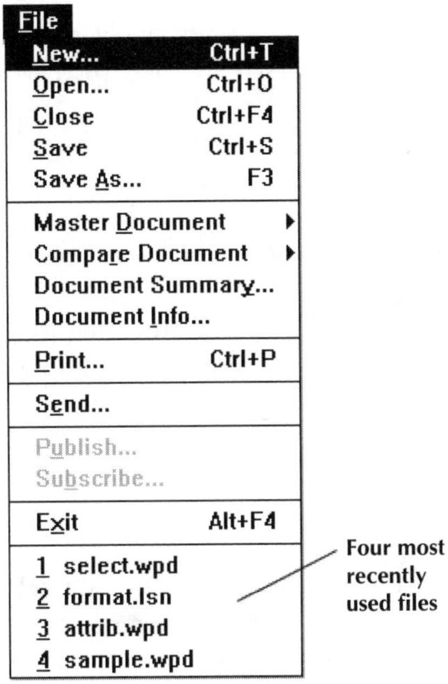

```
┌─────────────────────────────┐
│ File                        │
│  New...            Ctrl+T    │
│  Open...           Ctrl+O    │
│  Close             Ctrl+F4   │
│  Save              Ctrl+S    │
│  Save As...          F3      │
│                             │
│  Master Document        ▶   │
│  Compare Document       ▶   │
│  Document Summary...        │
│  Document Info...           │
│                             │
│  Print...          Ctrl+P    │
│                             │
│  Send...                    │
│                             │
│  Publish...                 │
│  Subscribe...               │
│                             │
│  Exit              Alt+F4    │
│                             │
│  1  select.wpd              │
│  2  format.lsn              │
│  3  attrib.wpd              │
│  4  sample.wpd              │
└─────────────────────────────┘
```

Four most
recently
used files

Figure 5.3 *The File menu with the four most recently opened documents listed at the bottom.*

MOVING AROUND A DOCUMENT

Okay, the document's on your screen. Now what? How do you move your insertion point to the part of the document you want to change? As usual, there are several answers. You can always just click the left mouse button anywhere on the screen to move your insertion point to a new location. But what if your document is several pages long and you want to get to a particular page or the end of the document? I'll give you a whole list of shortcut methods for moving to different parts of a document.

A lot of the movement shortcuts use keyboard combinations, and this is one situation where I'm going to encourage you to use the keyboard. When you're typing and editing, your hands are on the keyboard, and a keyboard shortcut can be a lot quicker than reaching for the mouse.

NOTE

You can't move your insertion point past the area that has text and formatting codes. To WordPerfect, the blank area beyond where you've entered text or codes doesn't exist until you type something or add some formatting. If you try to move beyond the current document area, the insertion point will just move to the last text or code in the document. For example, if you click the mouse button anywhere below the signature lines in FELLOWS.LTR, the insertion point moves to the end of *Marketing Manager,* because that's the end of the document.

Before I give you the movement lists, let's add a little to your letter to give you more to work with. In the process, I'll show you a couple of keyboard shortcuts that, in my humble opinion, beat the heck out of the mouse alternatives.

Do It

1. With FELLOWS.LTR on the screen, press **Ctrl+End** to move your insertion point to the end of the document. How's that for a slick shortcut? **Ctrl+End** always takes you to the very end in an instant, even if the document is 100 pages long. The mouse alternative in this case would involve pointing to the vertical scroll box and dragging it all the way to the bottom of the scroll bar.

2. Now we'll add a couple of pages so that you'll have a longer document to play with. Press **Ctrl+Enter** to insert a hard page break. Notice that the Status Bar changes to show that you're on page 2.

3. Type **Page Two** on the second page so we'll have a frame of reference.

4. Add one more page break (by pressing **Ctrl+Enter**), and type **Page Three** on the third page.

5. Press **Ctrl+Home** to move your insertion point back to the top of the document.

Table 5.1 contains a list of keyboard shortcuts that will get you where you want to go. Don't even try to memorize these, just refer to them and use them as you work with WordPerfect. The ones you find yourself using frequently will quickly find their way into your memory bank. In Table 5.1, a plus sign (+) between the keys means that you hold down the first key while you press the second and then release both keys. A comma means that you press and release the first key before you press the second.

Table 5.1 Moving the insertion point with the keyboard.

To get here	Press these keys
One character to the right	**Right Arrow**
One character to the left	**Left Arrow**
Next word	**Ctrl+Right Arrow**
Previous word	**Ctrl+Left Arrow**
Beginning of the current line	**Home**
Beginning of the current line (before any formatting codes)	**Home, Home**
End of the current line	**End**
Up one line	**Up Arrow**
Down one line	**Down Arrow**
Next Paragraph	**Ctrl+Down Arrow**
Previous paragraph	**Ctrl+Up Arrow**
Top of the current screen	**Page Up**
Bottom of the current screen	**Page Down**
First line of the previous page	**Alt+Page Up**
First line of the next page	**Alt+Page Down**
Beginning of the document (after most formatting codes)	**Ctrl+Home**
Beginning of the document (in front of any formatting codes)	**Ctrl+Home, Ctrl+Home**

Do It

Take a few minutes to move through your letter using these keystroke combinations. Try moving word by word (you can hold down the **Ctrl** key and keep pressing the **Left Arrow** or **Right Arrow** key to move several words at a time). Then move up and down through the paragraphs, move between the pages, and move to the beginning and end of lines. In other words, just play around for a bit. Notice that the Pg, Ln, and Pos entries change as you move the insertion point.

Are you done playing? It's time to use the mouse. As I said before, the keystroke combinations are quick, but you have to know which one to use in a particular situation. The main advantage to using the mouse is that you don't have to remember all those keystrokes—you just click or drag, either in the document window or on the scroll bars.

I'm not going to give you the mouse information in a table, because it takes a little more explaining.

❖ Click the left mouse button to move the insertion point to any location visible on the screen. If you're used to using the mouse a lot anyway, this can be easier than dealing with all those keystroke combinations.

❖ If you can't see the area you want to move to, use the scroll bars to bring the text into view, and then click inside the document window to move the insertion point.

NOTE

Remember that the scroll bars just change your *view* of the screen—they don't move the insertion point. Check this out by dragging the vertical scroll box to the bottom of the scroll bar. Notice that the page and position information on the Status Bar don't change until you click the left mouse button in the document window.

ADDING TEXT

Now that you can move around your document, adding text where you want is simple. Just move your insertion point to the location where you want the new text and start typing.

Insert and Typeover Modes

When you first start WordPerfect, you are in *Insert* mode. This means that when you type, the characters are inserted to the left of your insertion point, and the text that follows is pushed to the right to make room for the added text. Most of the time, Insert mode works fine—your existing text automatically reformats as you add new text.

Sometimes, though, you don't want to push the existing text out of the way; you want to replace it. That's where *Typeover* mode comes in handy. Typeover does exactly what it sounds like—in Typeover mode, you are typing over your existing text, and the existing text does not move to make way for new text.

So why use Typeover? There's a good example in your letter. In Chapter 1, you replaced the word *are* with *our*. Because we were using only basic techniques, you deleted *are* and then typed in the word *our*. Since both words have the same number of letters, it would have been quicker to just turn Typeover on and type the correct word right over the wrong one.

Let's add some text to your letter, using both Insert and Typeover modes. We'll start by adding a sentence in Insert mode, and then switch to Typeover mode to make a correction.

Do It

1. Move your insertion point just in front of the word *Now*, as shown in Figure 5.4. As you type new text, it will be inserted in front of the insertion point, and the rest of the text will move over to make room.

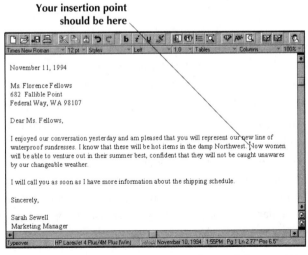

Figure 5.4 *The insertion point is in front of the word* Now.

2. Type **Because of our new fashion breakthrough**, and press the **Spacebar** once. Turn Typeover mode on by pressing the **Insert** key (or double-clicking on **Insert** on the Status Bar).

NOTE

The Insert key is a toggle: If Typeover is on, pressing **Insert** turns it off; if Typeover is off, pressing **Insert** turns it on.

3. Your insertion point should still be in front of the letter *N* in the word *Now*. Because *Now* is no longer the beginning of the sentence, the first letter shouldn't be capitalized. Since we're just replacing one letter with another, this is a perfect use for Typeover.

4. Type a lowercase **n**. Notice that it replaces the capital *N*, and the rest of the text stays put.

5. Save the letter by clicking on the **Save** button ▣ on the Toolbar (or press **Ctrl+S**).

DELETING TEXT

In Chapter 1, you learned how to delete one character at a time using the **Delete** and **Backspace** keys. Backspace deletes the character to the left of the insertion point. Delete gets rid of the character to the right of the insertion point. Well, that's okay, but it could get pretty tedious if you have a lot to delete.

Fortunately, WordPerfect is no slouch in this area, either. There are several methods for deleting text—you'll probably end up using different ones depending on your needs.

You can delete text using the keyboard or the mouse. As with moving your insertion point, using keystrokes can often be easier and faster than switching to the mouse. The main advantage of the mouse methods is that you don't have to remember a particular keystroke combination. For now, we'll try a little of both. (I'll even throw in some QuickMenu action.)

Do It

1. Place your insertion point anywhere in the word *now*.

2. Press **Ctrl+Backspace** to delete the entire word.

KEYBOARD

Ctrl+Backspace always deletes the word where the insertion point is located. You can delete several words by holding down the **Ctrl** key while you press the **Backspace** key as many times as you want. Doing this deletes words from the insertion point forward. For example, if you held down the **Ctrl** key after you deleted the word *now*, and pressed the **Backspace** key four more times, you would delete the words *women will be able*.

3. Move the insertion point anywhere in the sentence that begins *I will call you*, move your mouse pointer into the left margin area, and click the right mouse button. (You can tell you're in the margin when the mouse pointer changes from an *I* to an arrow.)

4. The QuickMenu shown in Figure 5.5 should be displayed. If it isn't, move your mouse pointer a little and try again. Choose **Select Sentence**. Notice that the entire sentence is selected: it has a dark box around it, and the letters appear in reverse color, as shown in Figure 5.6.

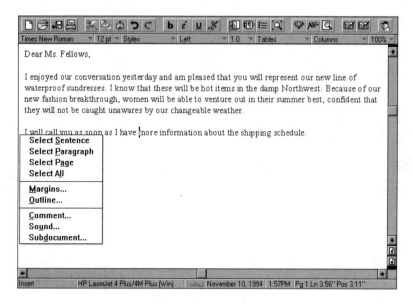

Figure 5.5 *This is the QuickMenu you get when you click in the left margin next to text.*

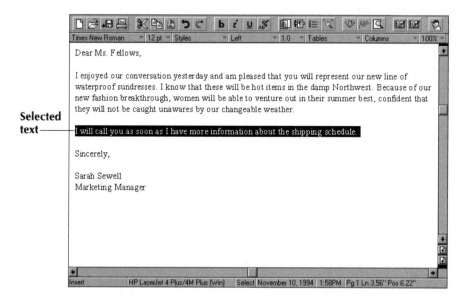

Figure 5.6 *The entire sentence beginning with* I will call you *is selected.*

5. Press the **Delete** key.

Chapter 6, "Moving and Copying Text," gets into a lot more detail on different methods for selecting text. The main thing to note here is that, once text has been selected, you can always delete it by pressing **Delete**.

ROADMAP

Deleting Text with Keyboard Shortcuts

As you saw, pressing **Ctrl+Backspace** deleted a word in a flash—you didn't have to select it first or lift your fingers off the keyboard to reach for the mouse. There are two more keyboard shortcuts that will come in handy:

❖ **Ctrl+Delete** deletes from the insertion point position to the end of the current line.

❖ **Ctrl+Shift+Delete** deletes everything from the insertion point position to the end of the current page.

Use caution with these keystrokes because you are not prompted for confirmation. WordPerfect just goes ahead and performs the deletion.

WARNING

Deleting Text with the Mouse

Once you have selected text, you can click the right mouse button anywhere on the document editing screen and choose **Delete** from the QuickMenu. You can select text using any of the methods that are covered in the next chapter. You can also delete selected text by pressing the **Delete** or **Backspace** keys.

UNDELETE AND UNDO (OR OOPS! I DIDN'T MEAN TO DO THAT)

So, you selected a bunch of text, and just as your finger hit the **Delete** key, you said to yourself, "I didn't want to delete that sentence!" Happens all the time. That's why those lovely WordPerfect folks gave you two Oops features. Both of them are designed to help you recover from those inevitable slips of the finger. Whenever you say Oops!, think Undelete or Undo.

Why do I need two features, and what's the difference between them, you ask? Read on.

There are four main differences between Undelete and Undo:

1. Here's the biggie: Undo doesn't *necessarily* undelete text, it just reverses your last editing change. For example, if you delete a sentence and then type a new word, choosing **Undo** *deletes the new word* rather than undeleting the sentence, since entering the new word was your last editing change.

2. Undelete keeps track of the last three things you deleted. Undo can track up to 300 editing changes.

3. Undelete restores text or formatting codes wherever your insertion point is located when you give the Undelete command. Undo restores text or formatting codes to their original location.

NOTE

Undelete can be used as a quick-and-dirty way to move text. You can delete something, move your insertion point to a new location, and use Undelete to restore the text.

4. Undelete displays the deleted text and asks if you want to restore it. Undo reverses the last action without asking you for confirmation.

Knowing these differences allows you to make the best use of the two features. You can actually use Undo as a deletion shortcut. For example, if you've just typed a sentence and change your mind, choose **Undo** and the sentence is gone.

Undelete

WordPerfect keeps track of your last three deletions by storing them in a temporary location called a *delete buffer.*

Do It

To use Undelete:

1. Choose **Undelete** from the Edit menu (or press **Ctrl+Shift+Z**). As you can see in Figure 5.7, when you choose **Undelete**, your last deletion is displayed on the screen, and the Undelete dialog box is displayed. You can choose to restore the text that's displayed, or you can cycle through the text in the delete buffer by choosing **Next** or **Previous**.

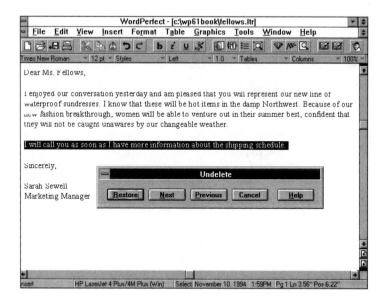

Figure 5.7 *The Undelete dialog box.*

2. When the text you want to restore is displayed, choose **Restore**.

NOTE

If you don't see selected text on-screen when you choose **Undelete**, it might be behind the Undelete dialog box. Just move the dialog box out of the way by pointing at the box's Title Bar and dragging it to a new location.

Undo and Redo

Because Undo reverses your most recent editing actions, it can be used to delete or restore text or formatting codes—it all depends what you did last. And if you want to undo the Undo, there's a Redo feature.

Do It

1. Type a few words so that you can see what happens when you choose **Undo**.

2. Click the **Undo** button ⬛ on the Toolbar. You can also choose **Undo** from the Edit menu or press **Ctrl+Z**. Notice that the text you just typed is gone. If you type several words without stopping, that's all considered one editing action. But as soon as you press any other editing keys or choose another feature, it becomes another action. For example, if you type **more information**, both words are considered one action. But if you press the **Backspace** key after typing the last *n* in information, choosing Undo only restores the *n*.

3. Now what if you want those pearls of wisdom you typed back on screen? Simple. Just Choose **Redo** from the Edit menu (or press **Ctrl+Shift+R**).

Undo and Redo History

How can WordPerfect (and you) possibly keep track of the last 300 things you've done? With a little help from the Undo/Redo History menu. It lists all the recent actions you've taken and allows you to undo or redo as many levels as you want.

Do It

1. Type a couple of lines of text.

2. Delete several words or phrases, add some additional text (a few words will do), and then make a couple more deletions.

3. Choose **Undo/Redo History** from the Edit menu to open the dialog box shown in Figure 5.8. Your list won't look exactly like mine, but it should have several actions listed.

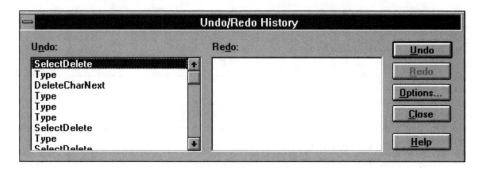

Figure 5.8 *The Undo/Redo History dialog box.*

4. Select one of the actions in the Undo list (any action but the first one) and choose **Undo**. Notice that all of the actions above the one you selected are also highlighted. That's because WordPerfect can't undo or redo something you did several steps ago without also undoing or redoing the actions that brought you to that point. Also notice that the items you undo are moved into the Redo list. If you change your mind about all or part of the redo, select the item or items you want and choose **Redo**.

Undo and Redo Options

I told you that WordPerfect can keep track of up to 300 actions, but by default it only saves the last 10 actions. That's because storing a whole bunch of actions can use up a lot of memory. But if you have plenty of memory and want to track lots of stuff, here's the scoop.

Do It

1. Choose **Options** from the Undo/Redo History dialog box. This opens the dialog box shown in Figure 5.9.

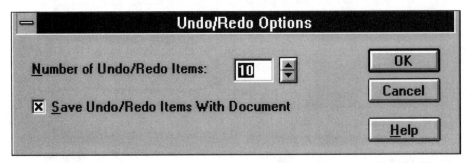

Figure 5.9 *The Undo/Redo Options dialog box.*

2. To change the number of actions WordPerfect tracks, enter a number in the **Number of Undo/Redo Items** text box (or click on the incrementing up and down arrows until the number you want is displayed).

3. By default, WordPerfect saves the Undo/Redo History with each document. This means you can undo or redo stuff even in later editing sessions. It's a handy feature, but the history can cause "file bloat"— because WordPerfect saves the history information each time you save the document, your documents can end up taking up a lot of disk space. If you find that this is a problem deselect **Save Undo/Redo Items with Document**.

CLOSING A DOCUMENT WITHOUT SAVING

In the Delete, Undelete, and Undo sections, you probably messed around with your document quite a bit. Sometimes a document gets so messed up that you just wish you could start over. Well, you can. Remember that everything you type only exists in the computer's temporary memory until you save it. That means you can close the document without saving at any time, and any changes you've made will be lost. That can sometimes be a good thing. The next time you open the document, it'll be just the way it was before you made all those changes. Let's try this with FELLOWS.LTR.

Do It

1. Choose **Close** from the File menu (or press **Ctrl+F4**).

Figure 5.10 *This dialog box is displayed if any changes have been made since the last time the document was saved.*

2. If a dialog box displays, choose **No** to close the document without saving the changes.
3. Open FELLOWS.LTR again. (If you need a little help, refer to the section on opening a document earlier in this chapter.)

SAVING

We talked briefly about saving in Chapter 1. Now it's time to jump in a little further. As I've mentioned (and will probably mention many more times), frequent saving is very, very important. In fact, now that you know how to close a document without saving, you have a pair of tools that can really free you to experiment with WordPerfect without fear. As long as you save your document before you do anything drastic or try a feature you're not sure of, you can always close the document without saving and go back to the original version if things don't turn out.

Naming Documents

For FELLOWS.LTR, I told you what to name the file, but I didn't give you any information to help you name your own files. There are a few rules you need to follow, and a few that are optional.

Rules

WordPerfect didn't make these rules up. They apply to any file that you create on a computer that uses DOS or Windows.

❖ A filename can have up to eight characters (in FELLOWS.LTR, FELLOWS is the name).

❖ A filename can have an optional extension of up to three characters (in FELLOWS.LTR, the extension is LTR). Anything after the period is called the *extension*. Note the word *optional*. A filename doesn't *have* to have an extension.

❖ A filename can't have any spaces in it. For example, you can't name a file MY NOTE, even though that's less than eight characters. The space makes it an invalid filename. (To find out how you can get around this, see the next rule.)

❖ A filename *can* contain hyphens (-), underline characters (_), and many other symbols. In addition to hyphens and underline characters, the following are all acceptable: ! @ # $ % ^ & ( ) { } ~. So, to get back to rule 3, if you want a file called MY NOTE, just stick a hyphen or underline character in between the words—MY_NOTE is a perfectly acceptable filename, and the underline character separates the words so the name still makes sense to you.

❖ You can use numbers in a filename. You might want to use numbers to identify filenames by date. For example, you could identify a series of meetings by using MTG as the extension and the date as the filename, such as 05-12.MTG, 10-16.MTG, and 11-14.MTG.

❖ Avoid using the following extensions: COM, EXE, BIN, SYS, and BAT.

These are extensions that DOS and other programs use for special files, such as the ones that start programs.

❖ You can type a filename in either uppercase or lowercase letters or even mix up the cases, it doesn't make any difference. In this book, I'm showing all filenames in uppercase just so they'll stand out.

NOTE

Don't worry too much about which symbols you can and can't use. If you try to use a symbol that WordPerfect won't accept as part of a valid filename, the dialog box in Figure 5.11 (or a similar one) is displayed. Just choose **OK** (or press **Enter**) to close the dialog box and try another name.

WARNING

Note that WordPerfect does not prevent you from using inappropriate extensions.

Figure 5.11 *This dialog box or a similar one is displayed if you try to save a file with an invalid name.*

In Figure 5.11, I tried to use quotation marks as part of the filename, and they are not acceptable.

Suggestions

As long as you follow the rules, anything goes as far as naming files. It's a good idea to develop a file-naming system that works for you. When you look at a list of files, it should be easy to find the one you want. The following suggestions might help:

❖ Be consistent with your filenames. For example, don't name one meeting file 11-12.MTG and the next one MEETING.DEC.

❖ Use extensions that describe the type of document. For example, you could use LTR for letters, MEM for memos, and RPT for reports.

WordPerfect uses a default extension of WPD, which stands for WordPerfect document. This extension is used for your documents unless you specify something else. I find that having the same extension for all of my WordPerfect documents is too limiting, but if you use a lot of different programs, there is some value to being able to identify a WordPerfect document by its extension. You'll have to make your own decision on this as you go along.

Saving an Existing Document

Earlier in this chapter, I had you save FELLOWS.LTR by clicking on the **Save** button 🖫 on the Toolbar. In Chapter 3, I told you that the Power Bar and Toolbars were usually the quickest way to access features, and clicking on the **Save** icon is definitely quick. When you're typing along, however, it can be easier to press a couple of keys than to reach for the mouse.

Ctrl+S is the keystroke shortcut for Save, and it can become almost automatic to press **Ctrl+S** every so often without missing a beat. Whichever method you prefer, get in the habit of saving often.

Saving a Document with a Different Name

Sometimes you might want to use a document for a different purpose. Let's say you really like FELLOWS.LTR, and you want to use it as a sort of blueprint for another letter. There are methods for copying part of the text to another document, but it can be easier just to give the document a different name and then make the changes you want.

Do It

1. Choose **Save As** from the File menu (or press **F3**). The Save As dialog box is displayed with the current filename selected, as shown in Figure 5.12.

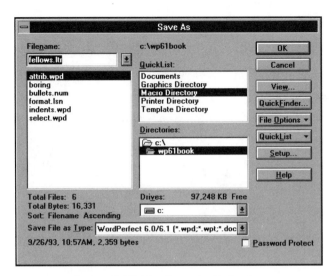

Figure 5.12 *The Save As dialog box.*

2. As soon as you start typing, the old filename disappears. Type in the new name (use **NEW.LTR** or a name of your choosing) and choose **OK** (or press **Enter**).

You now have a new document that contains the text from FELLOWS.LTR. You can change the new document in any way you like without affecting FELLOWS.LTR.

Open as Copy

The Save As procedure I just told you about works great, but in WordPerfect 6.1 there's an even better way to accomplish the same thing. Take a look at Figure 5.13. See the checkbox in the lower right corner? If you check it, WordPerfect opens the document in *read-only* mode. That means you can edit the document, but WordPerfect won't let you save it with its original name. This is a great way of keeping yourself from inadvertently saving over a file you didn't mean to change. If you choose **Save** with a file that's been opened as a copy, you get the Save As dialog box and are forced to give the document a different name.

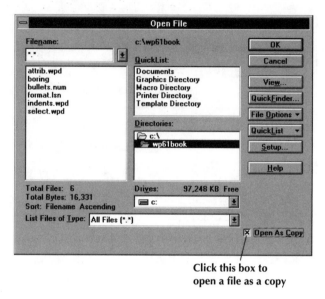

Click this box to
open a file as a copy

Figure 5.13 *The Open File dialog box with **Open as Copy** checked.*

FROM HERE . . .

We're about to move into deeper waters (but not too deep). In the next chapter, you'll learn how to move and copy blocks of text to different locations, and in Chapter 7, "Basic Formatting," we'll start adding some pizazz to the page with tabs, indents, bold, and underline.

Before you move on, you should be comfortable with what we covered in this chapter. You should be able to open a document, move through it using the mouse and the keyboard, and add and delete text. You should also be able to recover (remember the Oops! features—Undelete and Undo) when you delete text by mistake or want to reverse an editing action. And you can close a document without saving if you've made changes that you can't recover from with Undelete and Undo. Finally, you learned more about saving: you understand filenames, you know how to save a document while you're working on it, and you know how to save a document with a different name.

CHAPTER 6

Moving and Copying Text

Let's talk about:

- ❖ Selecting text
- ❖ Understanding the Clipboard
- ❖ Cutting, copying, and pasting
- ❖ Using drag and drop

So, you can add new text and you can delete text you don't want. But in this chapter you'll start to see the real power of WordPerfect. *Selecting* (or highlighting) text is the springboard for innumerable nifty tricks. We'll talk about all the cool things you can do with selected text, and you'll move and copy blocks of text all over the place.

BEFORE YOU START

Open **FELLOWS1.LTR** to give yourself something to play with in this chapter. As I show you how to use various selection and move and copy techniques, try them out on this document. Go ahead—mess it up. If you practice every time I give you a set of steps or a new way to do something, you'll be an old pro in no time. Then, at the end of the chapter, you can close the document without saving it so your original FELLOWS1.LTR will still be intact.

ROADMAP

See the "Open as Copy" section later in this chapter for another alternative.

SELECTING TEXT

Pay attention here. Once you learn about selecting text, you'll use this newfound skill throughout the book. After you select a block of text, you can apply almost any WordPerfect feature to that block. For example, you can change the font (type style) for a particular section of text, or you can choose to spell check only a selected block of text (this can come in handy when you've added text to a document and don't want to spell check what you've already done).

As you progress through WordPerfect's features, you'll rely heavily on selecting. And, since selecting text is a major component of moving and copying, I figure this is as good a place as any to show you the basics.

NOTE

So far we've just worked with text, so that's what we're talking about in this chapter. But anything that can be put into a WordPerfect document can be selected, moved, or copied. That includes formatting codes, graphic images, tables, and columns. The selection techniques in this section work for any WordPerfect object.

As with deleting text and moving around in a document, selecting can be done with both the keyboard and the mouse, and one method might be better than the other at various times. I'll show you both methods, and where appropriate, give you my preferences. (Actually, I'll probably give you my preferences whether or not it's appropriate.)

Selecting Text with the Mouse

The basic method for selecting text with the mouse is really easy, but it's not necessarily the most efficient. You just hold down the left mouse button and drag it across the text you want to select. When you've selected what you want, release the mouse button. This method works, and its main advantage is that you don't have to remember any special techniques, but it's not very precise. You have to pay close attention as you move the mouse, and it's easy to select too much or too little. I'm not saying you shouldn't use this technique—just that the other methods are usually quicker and even easier.

When you do drag to select text, WordPerfect automatically selects word by word rather than character by character. Here's what happens. Say you position your mouse pointer in the middle of the word *spring* and begin to drag. At first, only the portion of the word following your insertion point is selected. But as soon as you drag past the end of the word, WordPerfect selects the entire word. And if you then drag onto another word, that whole word will be selected. The selection highlight appears to jump from word to word as you drag.

If you want to be able to select character by character, hold down the **Alt** key as you drag. Table 6.1 shows mouse shortcuts for selecting text.

Table 6.1 Mouse shortcuts for selecting text.

To Select	Do this
A word	With the insertion point anywhere in the word, double-click the left mouse button.
A sentence	With the insertion point anywhere in the sentence, triple-click the left mouse button.
A paragraph	With the insertion point anywhere in the paragraph, quadruple-click. Clicking four times in a row can be a little tricky and take some practice. If you don't get it right away, don't worry. You might want to try the **Shift+Click** method instead (it's coming up in the next section).

The Best Shortcut of All

That heading's not too opinionated, is it? Anyway, in my (maybe not so humble) opinion, if you don't remember any other methods for selecting text, remember this one. It can be used for any chunk of text, and it doesn't involve any fancy moves like quadruple-clicking while standing on your head. Here it is.

Do It

1. Place your insertion point where you want the selection to begin.

2. Move your mouse pointer to where you want the selection to end (but don't click yet). You can use any of the movement shortcuts you learned in the last chapter—it doesn't matter *how* you move to the end—just get there.

3. Hold down the **Shift** key while you click the left mouse button.

4. If you didn't select quite enough, just move the mouse pointer down to where you want it and **Shift+Click** again. It's easy to extend the selection.

NOTE

This doesn't work for decreasing the size of the selection. If you've selected too much text, hold down the **Shift** key while you press the **Left Arrow** or **Up Arrow** key until the selected area is the size you want. You can also increase or decrease the size of a selection by holding down the **Shift** key while you drag the mouse pointer to the right or left.

That's it. I probably use this method more than any other. I don't have to worry about whether I want to select a sentence, a paragraph, or some other chunk of text. Having categorically stated that this is *absolutely the best way* to select text, I must admit that there are a couple of situations where another method actually works better.

The Second-Best Shortcut of All: The QuickMenu

Shift+clicking works great for most text chunks, with two exceptions that I can think of: selecting a page and selecting the whole document. If you know that you want to select the whole page, there's no need to go through the process of moving the mouse pointer just so you can **Shift+Click** at the end of the page, especially when there's a special shortcut: a QuickMenu.

Do It

1. Click the right mouse button in the left margin next to text.

```
Select Sentence
Select Paragraph
Select Page
Select All

Margins...
Outline...

Comment...
Sound...
Subdocument...
```

Figure 6.1 *This QuickMenu lets you select a sentence, a paragraph, the current page, or the entire document. (It also has a few other options that we'll get to in later chapters.)*

2. Choose **Select Page** to select the current page or choose **Select All** to select the entire document. You can also choose **Select Sentence** or **Select Paragraph**, and sometimes you might prefer this method to Shift+clicking.

You can also access these options by choosing **Select** from the Edit menu (and if you don't have a mouse, that's the only way you can get to them). Remember, QuickMenus don't give you any options that aren't available on the regular pull-down menus. The QuickMenus just make the options easier to get to.

Selecting Text with the Keyboard

If you don't have a mouse, you've still got many nifty options for selecting text. In fact, you mousers might want to take heed of some of these shortcuts.

The key (and I mean that literally) to selecting with the keyboard is **Shift**. Use the **Shift** key in conjunction with other keyboard combinations to select various portions of text. Table 6.2 lists several keystroke combinations you can use to select text.

KEYBOARD

You can use **F8** instead of the **Shift** key. **F8** turns Select mode on, then you can use any of the keystrokes in Table 6.2 (without holding down the **Shift** key). To turn Select mode off, press **F8** again.

Table 6.2 Keyboard shortcuts for selecting text.

To Select	Use These Keys
One character to the right	**Shift+Right Arrow**
One character to the left	**Shift+Left Arrow**
One word to the right	**Shift+Ctrl+Right Arrow**
One word to the left	**Shift+Ctrl+Left Arrow**
From the insertion point down one line	**Shift+Down Arrow**
From the insertion point up one line	**Shift+Up Arrow**
From the insertion point to the end of the current line	**Shift+End**
From the insertion point back to the beginning of the current line	**Shift+Home**
From the insertion point to the end of the current paragraph	**Shift+Ctrl+Down Arrow**
From the insertion point to the beginning of the current paragraph	**Shift+Ctrl+Up Arrow**
From the insertion point to the end of the document	**Shift+Ctrl+End**
From the insertion point to the beginning of the document	**Shift+Ctrl+Home**

A few of these keystroke combinations definitely have their uses. Did you notice that most of the instructions started with *From the insertion point?* That's how these methods differ from the choices on the QuickMenu (or pull-down menu). If you choose **Select Paragraph** from the QuickMenu, the entire paragraph is selected, regardless of the location of your insertion point. If you want to select only a portion of the paragraph, place your insertion point where you want to begin and use the keystroke shortcut (in this case, **Shift+Ctrl+Down Arrow**).

Deselecting Text

No matter how large an area of text you've selected, you can deselect it by clicking anywhere outside the selected area. If you don't have a mouse, you can press one of the arrow keys or **Ctrl+Z** (the shortcut for **Undo**).

What Can You Do with Selected Text?

Here are a few of the operations you can perform on a block of text. You can:

- ❖ Save it
- ❖ Spell check it
- ❖ Delete it
- ❖ Move or copy it
- ❖ Change its formatting
- ❖ Print it
- ❖ Change the text from uppercase to lowercase (or vice versa)

To do any of these, just select the text you want the change to apply to, and then implement the feature. As you've already seen, to delete text, select it and then press the **Delete** key. It's just as easy to use selected text with other features; you'll see for yourself as we get to the different features. Now, let's do some selecting, moving, and copying.

MOVING AND COPYING TEXT

WordPerfect makes it easy to shuffle text around to your heart's content. You can take a block of text and put it wherever you want, even in another document. WordPerfect calls the process of copying and moving text *cutting and pasting.*

These terms come from the old days of manual page layout and pasteup, when you literally had to cut out a piece of text using an X-acto knife. Then you took that piece and used rubber cement or wax to paste it in a new location. And you had to use rulers and stuff to make sure you pasted it in straight. Fun, huh? And not real practical, except in a commercial environment.

ROADMAP

For more about copying text between documents, see Chapter 26, "Working with Multiple Documents."

But now, through the magic of modern technology, cutting and pasting is yours to command with just a few mouse clicks or keystrokes.

Before we get into the mechanics of cutting, copying, and pasting, you need to know what happens to the text when you cut or copy it.

The Clipboard

Windows has a special area that stores the last thing you cut or copied. When you cut or copy something from WordPerfect for Windows, it goes into the Windows Clipboard. Because the Clipboard is shared by all Windows programs, anything in the Clipboard can be pasted into any other Windows program.

The Clipboard can only hold one thing at a time. Whenever you cut or copy something, it replaces whatever was in the Clipboard. When you choose the **Paste** command, whatever is in the Clipboard is moved back into your document.

Even though the Clipboard only holds one thing, you can add to it by using the **Append** command on the Edit menu. If you choose **Append** with text selected, a copy of that text is added to the end of whatever's currently in the Clipboard. This can be useful if you want to compile different sections of a document and put them in a new location.

Cutting Versus Copying

Once you select a block of text, you can choose to either cut or copy it to the Clipboard. When you cut text, it is removed from the document and placed in the Clipboard. When you copy text, the original text stays where it is and a copy of it is placed in the Clipboard. That's the only difference.

Drag and Drop

Drag and drop is a Windows technique that makes moving and copying super simple. With this technique, pasting isn't a separate step—it's part of the same process.

Do It

To move text with drag and drop:

1. Select the text.
2. Hold down the left mouse button while you drag the text to a new location. Notice that a box with a dotted shadow attaches itself to the mouse pointer.
3. Release the mouse button, and the text is pasted at the location of the insertion point.

To copy text with drag and drop:

1. Select the text.
2. Hold down the **Ctrl** key while you drag the text to its new location. Notice that a box with a solid shadow attaches itself to the mouse pointer.
3. Release the mouse button, and a copy of the text is pasted in at the location of the insertion point, but the original text remains where it was.

Move and Copy Methods

Dragging and dropping is usually the easiest way to move or copy text. There are a few situations, however, when other methods might work better. The most obvious, of course, is if you don't have a mouse—You can't use drag and drop with the keyboard. In addition, if you're working in a long document and you want to move or copy some text to a location several pages away or if you are selecting a really large block of text, it can be a pain to drag the selection over that distance. Instead, try the techniques that follow. I'm not going to tell you which of the following three methods is best—it's really a matter of preference.

If you have a mouse, the QuickMenu and Toolbar are both good choices. With the QuickMenu, you have to activate the menu and then make a selection. With the Toolbar, you just click on an icon. On the other hand, you have to move the mouse farther to get to the Toolbar. I suggest you try both and see what works best for you. The third method, using the keyboard, is the obvious choice if you don't have a mouse. And, if you're a speedy typist and like to keep your hands on the keyboard, the keyboard shortcuts can save you time even if you do have a mouse.

Do It

Use the QuickMenu to cut and paste:

1. Select the text.
2. Click the right mouse button anywhere in the document window (except near the very top or bottom of the page) to display the QuickMenu.

Figure 6.2 *This QuickMenu is displayed when you click the right mouse button in the document window when text is selected.*

3. Choose **Cut** if you want to move the text to the Clipboard, or choose **Copy** to leave the text where it is and place a copy in the Clipboard.

4. Move the insertion point to the location where you want the text to be inserted.

5. Activate the QuickMenu by clicking the right mouse button in the document window.

6. Choose **Paste**.

Use the Toolbar to cut and paste:

1. Select the text.

2. Click on the **Cut** button ✂ to move the text to the Clipboard.

3. Instead of step 2, you could click on the **Copy** button 📋 to leave the text where it is and place a copy in the Clipboard.

4. Move the insertion point to the location where you want the text to be inserted.

5. Click on the **Paste** 📋 button.

Use the keyboard to cut and paste:

1. Select the text.

2. Press **Ctrl+X** or **Shift+Delete** to move the text to the Clipboard, or press **Ctrl+C** or **Ctrl+Insert** to leave the text where it is and place a copy in the Clipboard.

3. Move the insertion point to where you want the text to be inserted.

4. Press **Ctrl+V** or **Shift+Insert** to paste the text into your document.

Ctrl+X, **Ctrl+C**, and **Ctrl+V** are all keyboard shortcuts for items than can also be accessed through the pull-down menu. (Any time you don't remember the shortcuts, you can choose **Cut**, **Copy**, or **Paste** from the Edit menu.)

FROM HERE . . .

In the next chapter, we'll add some formatting codes to your text. Before you move on, make sure you feel comfortable selecting text. Think of selecting as your base camp—you'll always come back to it and branch out from there. The cutting, copying, and pasting techniques you learned in this chapter will also stand you in good stead. All of the elements that you add to your document can be dragged, dropped, cut, copied, and pasted.

CHAPTER 7

Basic Formatting

(As We Boldly Go Where No Word Processor Has Gone Before)

Let's talk about:

- ❖ Understanding codes
- ❖ Tabs and indents
- ❖ Center and flush right
- ❖ Bold and underline
- ❖ Adding the date
- ❖ Changing text to uppercase or lowercase

WHY DO I NEED TO KNOW ABOUT CODES?

So far, everything you've done has been obvious—you type text and you can see it on the screen. You press the **Enter** key and the insertion point moves down to the next line. Simple and straightforward, right? But as you start to add other elements to your documents, it's important to know what's going on behind the scenes.

Whenever you do anything to your document besides typing text, WordPerfect inserts a code that can only be seen in a place called the *Reveal Codes window*. I can feel your eyes starting to glaze over ("Oh no, she's going techie on me"), but try to stay with me for just a bit. These codes are the framework for everything that happens in WordPerfect. If something doesn't look the way you think it should, the problem can usually be solved by taking a look at the codes. There's probably either a missing code, a code that shouldn't be there, or a code that's in the wrong place.

One reason I'm introducing you to Reveal Codes near the beginning of the book is so you can start getting used to it right away. A lot of beginners get intimidated by the whole idea of codes, but if you take it slowly and work with them as you learn new features, they'll be second nature in no time.

While you're learning WordPerfect, try to get in the habit of turning Reveal Codes on every time you add a new feature. Just turn Reveal Codes on to see what the code looks like, then turn it off. If you do that often enough, the Reveal Codes screen won't look like hieroglyphics when you really need to use it.

Using Reveal Codes

Codes are very polite creatures: they never show themselves unless invited. There are three main ways to turn on Reveal Codes:

1. Choose **Reveal Codes** from the View menu (shown in Figure 7.1), or

2. Press **Alt+F3**, or

3. Position your mouse pointer on the little black bar at the top or bottom of the vertical scroll bar (just above the up arrow or below all of the arrows at the bottom) until the pointer turns into a double-headed arrow. As you drag the bar, a thick black line is displayed across the document window. The Reveal Codes window takes up the space left below the black line when you release the mouse button.

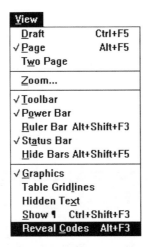

Figure 7.1 *You can turn on Reveal Codes from the View menu.*

Notice that the shortcut keystroke (**Alt+F3**) is listed next to Reveal Codes, and that Reveal Codes is a toggle (you use the same action to turn it off that you use to turn it on).

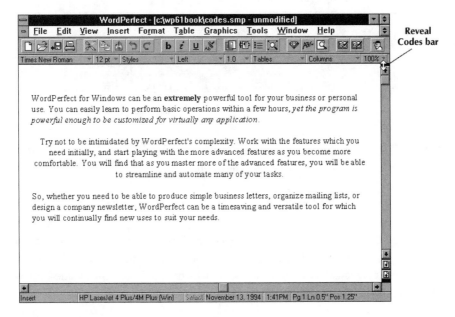

Figure 7.2 *The vertical scroll bar with the pointer on a Reveal Codes bar.*

Whichever method you use to turn on Reveal Codes, you end up with your screen split into two parts, as shown in Figure 7.3. It will be less confusing if you remember that what you're seeing in Reveal Codes is exactly what's in the document window—if you look at where the insertion point is in the document window and then look at the insertion point in Reveal Codes, you'll see that they're in the same location. Reveal Codes is sort of like an x-ray of your document. The document window shows your document all prettied up with skin and hair and makeup, and Reveal Codes strips all of that away (yuck).

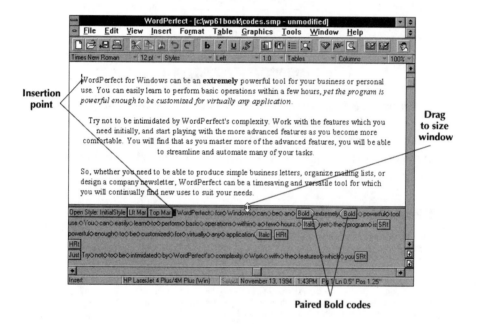

Figure 7.3 *A document with some formatting codes displayed in the Reveal Codes window.*

There are a few things in Figure 7.3 that I'd like to point out to you:

1. The sizing bar at the top of the Reveal Codes window can be used to change the size of the window at any time. Just move the mouse pointer over the bar until the pointer turns into a double-headed arrow, and drag the bar up or down.

2. The insertion point looks a little different in the Reveal Codes window, but it works exactly the same as in the document window. You can press the **Backspace** key to delete the text or code to the left of the insertion point, or press **Delete** to delete whatever's to the right of the insertion point.

3. Notice that there are two codes for Bold: The first one turns Bold on, and the second one turns it off. Anytime you have one code that turns a feature on and another that turns the same feature off, these are called *paired codes.* Any text that's between the two codes is affected by the code.

4. The diamonds between words indicate spaces.

ROADMAP

Don't worry about the InitialStyle code a the beginning of the document. This will be explained in Chapter 22, "Working with Styles."

You don't have to work with Reveal Codes on all the time, nor do I recommend it. It would drive you nuts to have all of that on the screen the whole time you're typing! Use Reveal Codes as a troubleshooting tool, or when you're doing complex formatting and need to know where your codes are. Turn Reveal Codes on when you need it, and then get rid of it.

Hiding Reveal Codes

You can turn Reveal Codes off the same way you turned it on, with an added QuickMenu shortcut:

1. Choose **Reveal Codes** from the View menu, or

2. Press **Alt+F3**, or

3. Drag the sizing bar (at the top of the Reveal Codes window) down until Reveal Codes disappears, then let go of the mouse button, or

4. Use the QuickMenu. Press the right mouse button when you're inside the Reveal Codes window, and choose **Hide Reveal Codes**.

That's enough about codes for now. I'll point some of them out to you as we go along and remind you to turn Reveal Codes on from time to time. But wait: before we leave this subject, there's just one more little thing you should know about.

Auto Code Placement

For the most part, when you insert a code, whatever it does takes effect from wherever your insertion point is located when you activate the feature. That means that if you turn Bold on, everything from the insertion point onward is boldfaced (until you turn Bold off). But it doesn't always work this way. WordPerfect does this really helpful thing that can, however, confuse you if you don't know it's happening.

Some codes (like top and bottom margins or headers and footers) should only appear at the beginning of a page. Others, like line spacing or tab settings, should only appear at the beginning of paragraphs. If you change your top margin with your insertion point in the middle of a page, WordPerfect will very nicely move the code to the top of the current page. This is called *Auto Code Placement*, and it can really keep you from getting into trouble with codes. Just be aware that a code won't *necessarily* end up where you think you put it. I'll let you know which features use Auto Code Placement as we get to them, and I'll tell you where the code will end up in each instance.

Creating a Sample Document

So we've got something to play around with for this chapter, I'd like you to type the following text just as you see it. We'll make it look pretty later. (This document was actually written by one of my students who "saw the light" about Reveal Codes.)

```
The Revealing Facts about Reveal Codes
by Margaret Nevins
    I am a computer novice. My level of understanding these
strange creatures called computers is very minimal. The
other day I needed to edit some old reports that were
created in another program. Jan decided it was a good time
to teach me how to convert them to the new format. The
first thing she said was "turn your Reveal Codes on." (I
never used Reveal Codes...too confusing!)
```

Let me tell you something—I discovered a very helpful new language. I am here to tell you Reveal Codes is fun—it is sooooo easy and helpful!

Looking at the codes was the only way I could really tell what was going on. Because the document I was working on was over 30 pages long, I was forced into using Reveal Codes for a long time. Lo and behold—I began to like it. "To know me is to love me" or something like that.

Save this document as FORMAT.LSN, and leave it on your screen. We'll use it throughout this chapter. (The LSN extension stands for *lesson*, so you'll be able to tell what this document is for when you see it in a file list.)

Tabs and Indents

When you press the **Tab** key, WordPerfect moves the insertion point to the next tab stop and indents the text for the current line. Pressing the Indent key (**F7**) also moves the insertion point to the next tab stop, but an indent affects the entire paragraph. When you press **F7**, all of your text is indented until you press the **Enter** key. Figure 7.4 shows examples of tabbed and indented text.

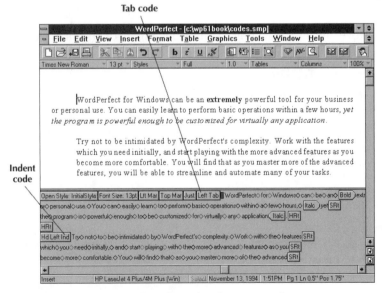

Figure 7.4 *Tab and indent examples.*

In Figure 7.4, I pressed the **Tab** key to indent the first line of the first paragraph. I indented the second paragraph using the Indent feature. Notice the Tab and Indent codes in the Reveal Codes window.

When you install WordPerfect, tab stops are automatically set every half inch, so you can use the Tabs and Indents right out of the box. In the next chapter, you'll learn how to change tab settings and set tab stops wherever you want them.

Do It

The text you just typed is all in a block at the left margin. Let's add some tabs and indents to make it look better.

1. Turn Reveal Codes on and notice what happens as you add tabs and indents.

NOTE

Take a look at the Status Bar when you insert tabs or indents. The Pos indicator changes to reflect the current tab position.

2. Move the insertion point to the beginning of the first paragraph (just before the sentence *I am a computer novice.*).

3. Press the **Tab** key.

4. Move the insertion point to the beginning of the second paragraph (just before the sentence beginning with *Let me tell you something*). We'll indent the entire paragraph to set it off from the rest of the text.

5. Press **F7** and notice that the whole paragraph moves over.

KEYBOARD

F7 is the quickest ways to indent a paragraph, but you have a couple of other options. Indent is on the QuickMenu that you get if you click the right mouse button anywhere in the document window. You can also choose **Paragraph** from the Format menu and **Indent** from the cascading Paragraph menu.

6. Move the insertion point to the beginning of the last paragraph and press the **Tab** key. Your document should now look like Figure 7.5.

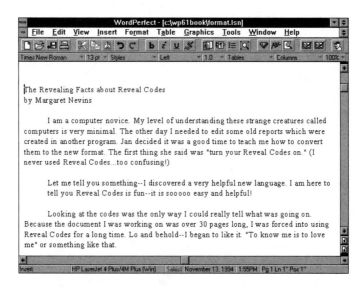

Figure 7.5 *The first line of the first and last paragraphs is indented, and the whole middle paragraph is indented to make it stand out.*

WARNING

Don't use the Spacebar to indent text! With most type styles (or fonts, as you'll learn in Chapter 12), each character takes up a different amount of space, so there's no such thing as a standard character width. When you press the Spacebar to line up text, it might look okay on the screen, but ends up being a zig-zag mess when you print. A good rule: Use the Spacebar only to add spaces between words. Always use tabs or indents to indent text.

Different Kinds of Indents

You just used a left indent, where the whole paragraph moves over to the next tab stop. Figure 7.6 shows the other types of indents and how you create them.

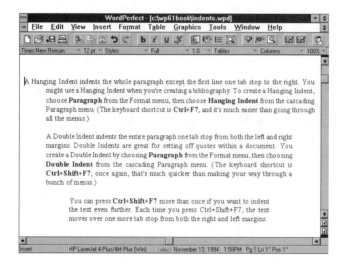

Figure 7.6 *In addition to left indents, which indent the entire paragraph from the left margin, you can also create hanging indents and double indents. The sample text here gives you instructions for creating these indents.*

Tabs and indents can be inserted at any time. It doesn't make any difference whether you add them before you type your text or apply them to text that's already there (as we did in this case).

Center and Flush Right

WordPerfect makes it easy to center text between the left and right margins. You can also center text over a particular tab stop. And it's a snap to make text line up with the right margin.

Like most WordPerfect formatting codes, you can center text or align it with the right margin either before or after you type.

If you want several lines of text to be centered or flush right, it's more efficient to use the Justification feature, which we'll get to in the next chapter.

ROADMAP

Centering Text between the Margins

The keyboard's the easiest way to go here. Just press **Shift+F7** and start typing. Or, if there's already text on the line, place your insertion point at the beginning of the text before you press **Shift+F7**.

Do It

1. Move your insertion point to the beginning of the first line of FORMAT.LSN (*The Revealing Facts about Reveal Codes*).

2. Press **Shift+F7** and watch the text move to the center of the page.

3. Move your insertion point to the end of the document (**Ctrl+End**) and press the **Enter** key twice.

4. Press **Shift+F7** and type:

Wow, this is easy! I just centered this line of text without even breathing hard.

5. Take a look at Reveal Codes and notice the codes in front of the line of centered text.

That was easy, wasn't it? And did you notice that you got exactly the same result whether you inserted the Center code before or after the text was typed?

Centering Text on a Specific Position

If you move your insertion point to any point other than the left margin before you press the Center key (**Shift+F7**), the text will be centered over that position. You can center text over more than one position on a line.

NOTE

If you want to center more than one entry on a line, make sure there's enough space between the entries. If there isn't, the text could overlap.

Do It

1. Move your insertion point to the end of the document and press the **Enter** key twice.
2. Press the **Tab** key three times.
3. Press **Shift+F7**.
4. Type: **This text is centered over a tab stop.**
5. Take a look at Reveal Codes and notice how this code differs from the code for centering text between the margins.

Flush Right

The ability to line text up at the right margin is really useful. I remember (in the all-but-forgotten typewriter days) trying to count how many characters I had to type and then backspacing that many times from the right margin. If I counted wrong, or if the text got changed, too bad. Well, I don't have to do that kind of finagling anymore. I just choose the Flush Right feature, and WordPerfect does the rest. (I told you I was lazy!)

Do It

1. Move your insertion point to the beginning of the byline (*by Margaret Nevins*).
2. Press **Alt+F7** and watch that text zip on over to the right margin.
3. Move your insertion point to the bottom of the document and press the **Enter** key twice.
4. Press **Alt+F7** and type: **The End**. Notice that the text actually works its way *in* from the right margin as you type. (I always like to watch that trick.)

With both center and flush right, if your text wraps to the next line, the second line won't be centered or flush right. As mentioned earlier, center and flush right are best for single lines of text. You can, however, select multiple lines of text and press **Shift+F7** (center) or **Alt+F7** (flush right).

Changing Text Appearance

There are any number of ways you can change the appearance of your text. For now, we'll focus on bold, underline, and italic, since they're all fairly common, and they're all just a click away on the Toolbar. In fact, move your mouse pointer over the Toolbar right now and see if you can pick out the **Bold**, **Underline**, and **Italic** buttons.

You can turn on any of these text attributes before you type, or you can apply them to selected text. We'll try it both ways.

NOTE

The techniques you use are the same for any text attribute. So when I talk about paired italic codes, for example, I'm not just talking about italic. You would do exactly the same thing to turn off a bold or underline code.

Do It

1. Select the word *Revealing* on the first line of your document. (Try double-clicking on the word to select it.)

2. Click on the **Bold** button 🅱 on the Toolbar (or press **Ctrl+B**).

3. Select the word *very* in the second sentence.

4. Click on the **Underline** button 🆄 on the Toolbar (or press **Ctrl+U**).

5. Move your insertion point to the end of the second text paragraph (after *soooo easy and helpful*) and press the **Spacebar** once. Make sure Reveal Codes is on before you do the next step—I want you to see what happens when you choose an appearance code without any text selected.

6. Click on the **Italic** button 🅸 on the Toolbar (or press **Ctrl+I**). Notice that WordPerfect inserted *two* italic codes, and your insertion point's between them. Anything you type between the two codes will be in italic.

7. Type: **I'm hooked.** Because your insertion point is still between the two italic codes, you have to do something to get out of there, or whatever you type next will also be italic.

8. Click on the **Italic** button again (or press **Ctrl+I**). Notice that the insertion point moves past the ending italic code. The next thing you type will be in normal text.

NOTE

All paired codes are toggles: You know what that means—you perform the same action to turn them on and to turn them off.

Applying More than One Attribute

What if you want to bold, underline, *and* italicize the same word or phrase? You could select the text and then click on the **Bold**, **Underline**, and **Italic** buttons in succession, but there's an easier way. The Font dialog box lets you change all of the appearance items you want in one fell swoop. Not only that, the dialog box gives you access to even more appearance options.

WARNING

Be careful when applying attributes and changing type sizes and styles. Your document can easily end up with a ransom note appearance. Use your own judgment, but don't overdo it with too many different options. For a good example of going too far, take a look at what we've done to FORMAT.LSN (especially after the next section). Normally you wouldn't use bold, italic, and underline in the combinations and to the extent we have on this page.

Do It

1. Select the phrase *Reveal Codes is fun* in the middle paragraph.

2. Choose **Font** from the Format menu (or press **F9**).

   Here's a neat trick you can use as an alternative to get to a lot of dialog boxes. Just double-click on any Power Bar button that's associated with a particular feature to open the dialog box for that feature. For example, double-clicking on the following buttons will take you to the Font dialog box: **Font Face** or **Font Size**.

   In Figure 7.7, you can see the Font dialog box. There's a whole lot of stuff you can do in here, but we'll save most of it for Chapter 12, "A Look at Fonts." For now, we'll concentrate on the check boxes in the

Appearance section. Notice that our old standbys are there: bold, italic, and underline. You've also got double underline and a few others we won't deal with right now. The main thing to note is that everything's in one place. You can check as many of the boxes as you want and then choose **OK**—it's a one-step process.

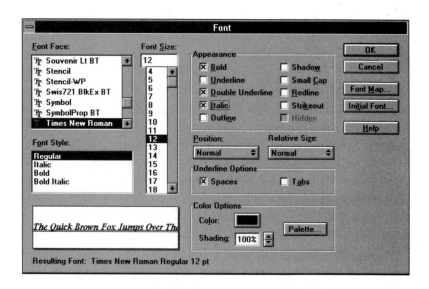

Figure 7.7 *The Font dialog box.*

3. Click in the check boxes next to **Bold**, **Double Underline**, and **Italic**.

   Keyboard alternative: You can select check boxes with the keyboard by holding down the **Alt** key while you press the underlined letter for the option you want. In this case, you would press **Alt+B** for Bold, **Alt+D** for Double Underline, and **Alt+I** for Italic.

4. Choose **OK** to accept your changes and close the Font dialog box.

NOTE

If you check a box by mistake, just click again on the same box to uncheck it.

Adding the Date

In Chapter 1, I had you type the date at the top of the letter, but that's an awful lot of work, isn't it? Not only that, but you actually have to *know* what today's date is. Ready for a shortcut?

Do It

1. Move your insertion point to the top of the document (**Ctrl+Home**).

2. Press **Ctrl+D**.

    Menu alternative: Choose **Date** from the Insert menu and **Date Text** from the cascading Date menu.

3. Press the **Enter** key twice to insert a couple of lines between the date and the title.

Yup, that's all there is to it.

What Just Happened Here?

It looks like magic, but there's a simple explanation. Your computer keeps track of the date, and WordPerfect can use that information to insert the current date in your document at any time.

The feature you just used is called *Date Text*. It inserts the current date as text. Once you've used this feature, the date is just like regular text. If you retrieve the document tomorrow it will still have today's date. That's okay, but what if you want the document to have the current date, even if you print it two weeks from now?

NOTE

If your computer date is incorrect, the date used for the date text feature will also be incorrect.

The Date Code Feature

When you use the Date Code feature, the date is inserted as a code (remember to look at Reveal Codes when we do this), and WordPerfect uses that code to update the document every time it's opened or printed. With Date Code, your document can always have the current date—you'll never have to remember to change the date before the document goes out (or remember after the document has already gone out, which is more my style).

Do It

1. Move your insertion point to the date text you just inserted. Take a look at it in Reveal Codes, noting that it's just regular text.

2. Delete the date text.

3. Press **Ctrl+Shift+D** (or choose **Date** from the Insert menu and **Date Code** from the cascading Date menu).

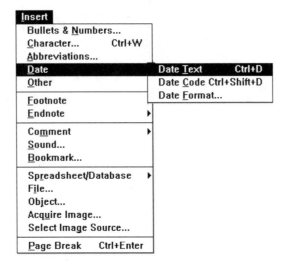

Figure 7.8 *The cascading Date menu.*

Changing the Date Format

You can change the way the date is displayed when you choose **Date Text** or **Date Code**. You can even include the time of day. By default, the date appears with the month spelled out, followed by the day of the month and then all four digits of the year (like this: *August 23, 1993*), just like it appeared in FORMAT.LSN. I guess WordPerfect figured that was the most commonly used format. But sometimes you might want the date to look different. Here's how:

Do It

1. Choose **Date** from the Insert menu.

2. Choose **Date Format** from the cascading Date menu.

3. Choose the format you want from the Document Date/Time Format dialog box. You can either double-click on the selection you want or highlight it and choose **OK** (or press the **Enter** key).

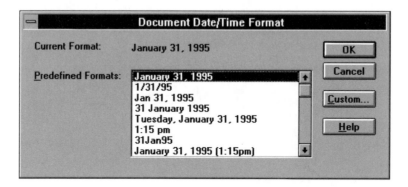

Figure 7.9 *The Document Date/Time Format dialog box.*

Changing the date format won't change the format of any dates that you've already inserted using the Date Text feature, but it could change the format of Date Codes, depending on where your insertion point is when you change the format. The Date Format code is inserted wherever your insertion point is when you access the Date/Time Format dialog box, and any Date Codes that follow the date format code are affected by the format change. Also, any date text that you add after the format change takes on the new format. Keep in mind, though, that the format change is only for the current document.

ROADMAP

If you want to permanently change the date format, see Appendix B, "Customizing WordPerfect."

Changing Text to Uppercase or Lowercase

Have you ever turned **Caps Lock** on by mistake and typed several lines of text before you realized it? No? You mean I'm the only one again? Oh, well. Anyway, whether you need to change text that's all in caps to lowercase, or decide to change a title to uppercase text, WordPerfect can handle that chore with ease. Let's try it.

Do It

1. Select the title line (*The Revealing Facts about Reveal Codes*). Let's convert all of the text to uppercase.

2. Choose **Convert Case** from the Edit menu.

3. Choose **Uppercase** from the cascading Convert Case menu, as shown in Figure 7.10.

   Keyboard alternative: You can select text and then press **Ctrl+K** to cycle between uppercase and lowercase. Just stop when the text is the way you want it.

4. Now what if you want to change the title back so the first letter of each word is capitalized? Just select the title again and choose **Initial Caps** from the Convert Case menu.

   WordPerfect does the job for you—it knows which words should and shouldn't be capitalized. Note: You can't use the **Ctrl+K** shortcut to switch to intial caps.

NOTE

The Convert Case feature only works when you have a block of text selected. If you try to access the Convert Case menu without text selected, all of the options are dimmed.

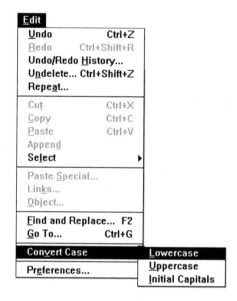

Figure 7.10 The Cascading Convert Case menu.

Wrapping It Up

We've messed around quite a bit with this poor old document. I hope you've managed to learn a few things (and had some fun) along the way. At this point, the document on your screen should look something like Figure 7.11. If it doesn't, or if there's anything we covered in this chapter that's a little fuzzy, take the time to review it now.

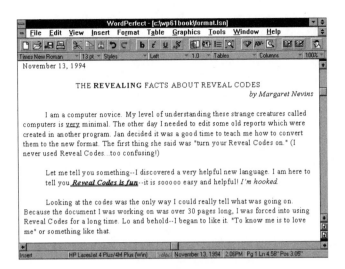

Figure 7.11 *FORMAT1.LSN after a lot of formatting changes.*

Do It

Save the document as FORMAT1.LSN. And take a break—you've earned it.

FROM HERE...

Let's see, what did we cover here? Codes, tabs, indents, center, flush right, bold, underline, italic, dates, converting case.... Whew, it's *definitely* time for a break—that was quite an accomplishment.

You should have a pretty good understanding of Reveal Codes. As you work with new features, remember to take a look at the codes (even if I forget to remind you). You know how to use tabs and indents, and you'll learn how to change the tab settings in the next chapter. And you have several tools for changing the appearance of your text. And you never have to actually *type* the date again! Finally, you've got a way to recover when you hit that **Caps Lock** key by mistake. Actually, you've got two ways to recover (don't forget **Undo**).

WordPerfect 6.1 for Windows

CHAPTER 8

Formatting: The Sequel

(It Gets Even Better)

Let's talk about:

- ❖ Changing the view
- ❖ Setting margins
- ❖ Setting tabs
- ❖ Changing line spacing
- ❖ Changing justification settings

When you install WordPerfect for Windows, it uses the following default settings:

- ❖ One-inch margins top and bottom
- ❖ One-inch margins left and right
- ❖ Tab stops every one-half inch
- ❖ Single line-spacing
- ❖ Left justification (ragged-right margins)

This is another case where those WordPerfect folks show how helpful they can be. Without these default settings, we couldn't have created the documents we have as easily as we have. We would have had to set margins, tabs, and line spacing before we could create even a simple document. So the defaults make it possible to get up and running quickly, and they're fine for *generic* documents, but it's time to branch out a little. Who wants to be generic?

In this chapter, you'll learn how to change the margins, the tab settings, the spacing between the lines, and how the text is lined up on the page. As I've mentioned before, all of WordPerfect's defaults are just a place to start—any of them can be changed to suit your needs.

Pregame Check

Is FORMAT1.LSN still on your screen, or did you take a break after the last chapter? It's okay, you can admit it—you *deserved* that break. But it's time to go back to work, and you need a document to work with.

Do It

1. Close FORMAT1.LSN if it's on screen. We need to go back to the plain vanilla version you created at the beginning of the last chapter so you'll be able to see the full effects of the changes we're going to make.

2. Open FORMAT.LSN. It should look like Figure 8.1—no tabs, no indents, no nuthin'. If you already saved it with some tabs or indents, you can practice your deletion techniques by getting rid of them now. (Don't worry about any bold, italic, or underline codes—they won't get in the way here.)

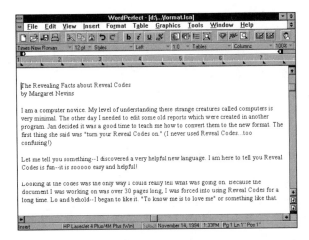

Figure 8.1 *Your document should look pretty much like this.*

3. Turn **Reveal Codes** on and notice that there are two HRt codes between each paragraph. Those are the codes that were inserted when you pressed the **Enter** key.

4. Delete one of the HRt codes after each paragraph so that it looks like there are no spaces between the paragraphs. The document should now look like Figure 8.2.

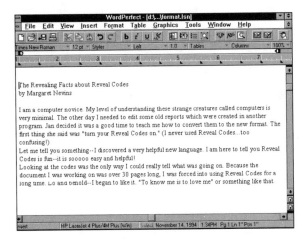

Figure 8.2 *FORMAT.LSN with only one hard return between each paragraph.*

And one more thing. We'll be making a lot of the changes in this chapter through the magic of the Ruler Bar.

5. If the Ruler Bar isn't visible, turn it on by choosing **Ruler Bar** from the View menu (or pressing **Alt+Shift+F3**).

All set? Let's go.

Changing the View—Zooming In and Out

This topic might seem like a slight departure from the subject at hand, but trust me, it's not. A standard sheet of paper is 8.5" wide and 11" tall. Most computer monitors are wider than they are tall (sort of like a piece of paper turned over on its side), so you usually don't see your document the way it's actually going to look on paper.

By default, WordPerfect displays your text at its actual size for easy readability. If the display area of your monitor is 7" high (that's pretty standard), you can only see about two thirds of a page at a time. That's okay when you're entering text and changing simple attributes. But when you start making more complex changes, sometimes you want to be able to zoom out and see what the whole page looks like, or zoom in to enlarge a particular part of the document. It can be really handy to see the entire page when you're changing margins and other settings that affect the appearance of the page.

Do It

1. Choose **Zoom** from the View menu to open the Zoom dialog box shown in Figure 8.3.

2. Click one of the radio buttons to select a zoom option, then choose **OK**.

3. Try the different zoom options to see what they look like.

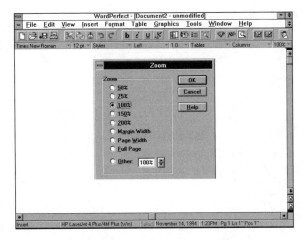

Figure 8.3 *The Zoom dialog box.*

As you do this, notice that the numbers and markings on the Ruler Bar stretch and shrink as necessary. Figures 8.4 through 8.7 show the same document at different Zoom settings.

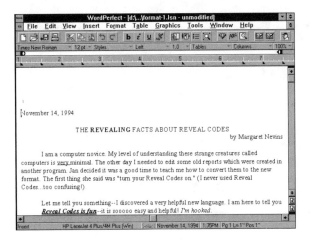

Figure 8.4 *100% Zoom.*

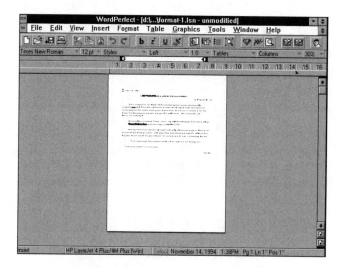

Figure 8.5 *Full Page view.*

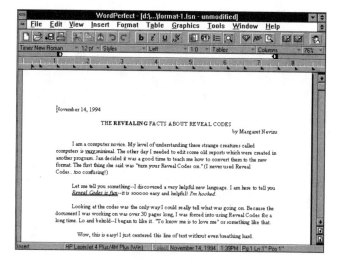

Figure 8.6 *Page Width view.*

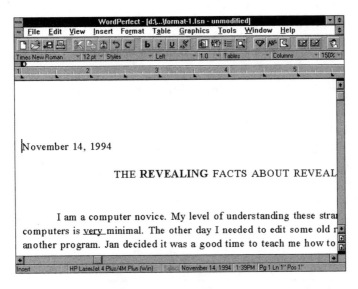

Figure 8.7 *150% Zoom.*

Remember, 100% is the default. If you want your document to look like it did at the beginning, just choose 100%.

From time to time I'll ask you to change your Zoom option when we're working on a particular feature. Now you'll know what I mean and how to do it.

Changing the Zoom setting doesn't affect the way the document will print; it only changes the way the document looks on your screen.

Changing Margins

It's a snap to change left and right margin settings in WordPerfect for Windows—just drag one of the margin markers on the Ruler Bar to the location you want. If you want to enter precise measurements for your left and right margins, or if you want to change the top and bottom margins, use the Margins dialog box. I'll show you both ways.

Changing Left and Right Margins with the Ruler

Make sure your insertion point is at the very top of FORMAT.LSN (right in front of the date), and take a look at the Status Bar. The Pos indicator should say 1". That means the text will print 1" in from the left edge of the page. I want you to take note of this position, because it's about to change right before your eyes.

There's one kind of tricky thing about the Ruler Bar. Do you see what look like inward-pointing triangles just above the 1" and 7.5" marks? Each triangle looks like it's one piece, but the one at the left margin is actually three separate markers: for the left margin, first line indents, and left margin adjustments. The marker at the right margin is two pieces: for the right margin and right margin adjustments. In Figures 8.8 and 8.9, I'll show you what I mean.

Figure 8.8 *The Ruler Bar with all three markers at the left margin.*

Because all of the markers start out at the left margin, it's hard to tell them apart, but in Figure 8.9 I've moved the first line indent and paragraph margin markers so you can see what's going on.

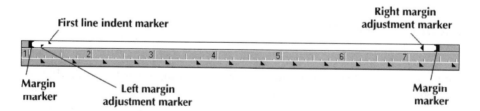

Figure 8.9 *Now you can see that there are actually three separate markers at the left margin and two at the right margin.*

It's important to be aware of this so that you don't grab the wrong marker by mistake. Right now, we're just moving the margins. We'll deal with first line indents and paragraph adjustments in a little bit. And as we go through the steps, I'll give you some tips that'll help you make sure you have the correct marker.

Do It

1. Make sure your Zoom setting is at 100%. This will give you the best view of what's happening with the Ruler for now.

2. Move your mouse pointer to the left margin marker on the Ruler Bar.

3. Hold down the left mouse button and look at the right corner of the Status Bar. Also notice the dashed vertical line that appears—this serves as a visual guide while you move the margin.

NOTE

You can always tell whether you have the correct marker by checking the Status Bar. The right corner displays the appropriate position information as soon as you press the left mouse button on any of the Ruler Bar markers.

4. Drag the margin marker toward the right until the Status Bar tells you that the left margin is at 1.25". (It doesn't have to be *exactly* 1.25—just get it close.) Figure 8.10 shows the margin marker as it's being moved.

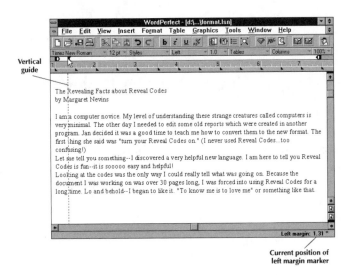

Figure 8.10 *As you move the margin marker, the vertical guide makes it easy to see where you are, and the Status Bar gives you a precise measurement.*

5. When the margin marker is where you want it, release the mouse button and watch the text move over.

I had you look at the Status Bar because I wanted you to know what was happening, but you don't always have to watch it while you're changing margins or tabs. If a precise measurement is important, the Status Bar information is great—otherwise, there's nothing wrong with "eyeballing" it. Just move the markers until they look right to you. And if you don't like where they end up, just move them again. The Ruler makes it easy to play with the settings until you get them right.

NOTE

Remember Auto Code Placement? That's the feature I told you about in the last chapter that moves codes to appropriate locations. Margin settings are one of the codes affected by Auto Code Placement. A left or right margin change can only take effect at the beginning of a paragraph. If your insertion point is in the middle of a paragraph when you change left or right margin settings, the margin code moves to the beginning of that paragraph, and the margin change is in effect from that location onward until you specify another setting.

Changing Margins with the Margins Dialog Box

You can use the Margins dialog box to enter exact settings for your left and right margins (and it's the *only* way to change top and bottom margins—there's no handy ruler for that). Getting to the Margins dialog box from the Ruler is easy—just double-click on one of the margin markers or click the right mouse button on the Ruler (anywhere above the tab markers), and choose **Margins** from the QuickMenu.

NOTE

Since the margin markers, first line indent markers, and paragraph adjustment markers are virtually on top of each other, it can take a bit of mouse dexterity to double-click on the correct marker. Using the QuickMenu is much easier, since you have most of the Ruler as your target.

Do It

1. Move your insertion point to the second paragraph (anywhere in the phrase *I discovered a whole new language*). I want you to see where the different margin codes end up when the insertion point's in the middle of the document.

2. Change your zoom setting to **Full Page** so you can see what's happening to the page as we make the changes. Notice that there's a special Zoom button 🔲 on the Toolbar. Its sole function is to change your zoom setting to Full Page. Click on it to change to Full Page view, then click on it again when you're ready to return to your previous zoom setting.

3. Click the right mouse button anywhere on the Ruler Bar above the tab marker line to open the QuickMenu.

NOTE

If you click on the line that has the tab markers, you get a different QuickMenu. If that happens, just click again a little higher on the Ruler.

4. Choose **Margins**. The Margins dialog box is displayed, as shown in Figure 8.11. You can also access the Margins dialog box by pressing **Ctrl+F8** or by choosing **Margins** from the Format menu.

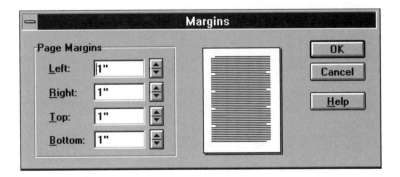

Figure 8.11 *The Margins dialog box.*

5. Tab to the appropriate box and type a number. For this document, change the margins as follows:

    ❖ Left: 2

    ❖ Right: 3

    ❖ Top: 2

    ❖ Bottom: .5

    Keyboard alternative: You can move to different text boxes in a dialog box by pressing the **Alt** key with the underlined letter for that box. For example, press **Alt+R** to move to the Right margin box. You can also press the **Tab** key to cycle between the options.

    Notice the little picture of a page next to the margin setting text boxes. As you enter numbers, the picture changes to show you how the page will look with the new settings. You can experiment with different numbers and get a good idea of how they will affect your document before you leave the Margins dialog box.

6. When you've completed your settings, choose **OK**. (OK is the default, so you can just press **Enter** when you're ready.)

7. Turn Reveal Codes on and find the margin codes. The left and right margin settings you just inserted should be at the beginning of the paragraph that starts with *Let me tell you something*. The top and bottom margin codes should be at the top of the document. Auto Code Placement moves top and bottom margin codes to the top of the current page.

Figure 8.12 shows FORMAT.LSN with the margin changes, and in Figure 8.13, I've expanded the Reveal Codes window so you can see all the codes for the document.

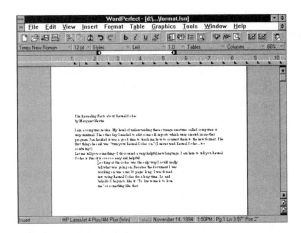

Figure 8.12 *FORMAT.LSN with margin changes.*

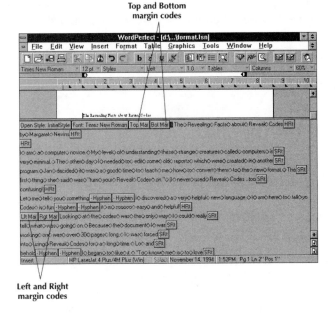

Figure 8.13 *The expanded Reveal Codes window for FORMAT.LSN.*

You can use margin changes for different effects. If you have a really short letter, wider left and right margins and a larger top margin can make the text look a little less lonely on the page. And if you need to squeeze an extra line or two onto a page, lopping a little off the top or bottom margin can often be your salvation. But WordPerfect 6.1 comes with a cool new feature that can automatically take care of a lot of this kind of stuff. Read on.

Make It Fit

The Make It Fit Expert is like a magic wand that allows you to shrink or expand a document to fit a certain number of pages. Without this Expert, you would have to tweak margin settings, font size and line spacing until the documents fits in the desired space. Suppose you change your left margin, then take a look at your document and realize that didn't quite do the trick. Then you have to decide whether to make another margin adjustment, or perhaps change the line spacing or font size. This maneuvering could go on for quite awhile.

With the Make It Fit Expert, you just tell WordPerfect how many pages you want the document to be. Then you specify which options it's okay to change. For example, you could say that it's okay to change the line spacing but not the left margin.

Do It

1. Click on the **Make It Fit button** 🔲 on the Toolbar (or choose **Make It Fit Expert** from the Format menu). This opens the Make It Fit Expert dialog box, shown in Figure 8.14.

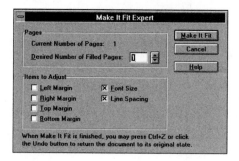

Figure 8.14 *The Make It Fit Expert.*

2. The Pages section tells you the current number of pages in the document. If you want to expand the document, enter a larger number in the **Desired Number of Filled Pages** text box; if you want to shrink the document, enter a smaller number.

3. In the Items to Adjust section, check the boxes for the features you want to allow WordPerfect to mess with. If you don't check a particular feature, WordPerfect doesn't consider that feature in its calculations. For example, if you leave Top Margin unchecked, WordPerfect will leave the top margin alone when it changes the document.

4. Choose **Make It Fit** to close the dialog box and see the results.

Paragraph Adjustments

Here's where you see why I had you get rid of the tabs and scrunch up FORMAT.LSN with no spaces between the paragraphs. WordPerfect's paragraph formatting features can take care of these tasks automatically.

Changing First Line Indents with the Ruler

In the last chapter, you pressed the **Tab** key at the beginning of each paragraph to indent the first line. With the First Line Indent feature, you can indent all of your paragraphs at once. And it's just as easy as it was to change margins—you just move a marker on the Ruler Bar.

Do It

1. Change back to 100% zoom.

NOTE

Full Page view is great for seeing the layout of the page, but it's just about impossible to read the text at that setting. I usually zip back and forth between 100% and Full Page several times while I'm working on a document—with the Toolbar, it's really easy. I use 100% for typing and editing and zoom out to Full Page to change settings that affect the look of the page (or just to take a peek at how the page is shaping up).

2. Move your insertion point to the beginning of the first text paragraph (in front of the sentence *I am a computer novice*).

3. Move your mouse pointer to what you now know is more than just the left margin marker on the Ruler Bar.

4. Hold down the left mouse button on the top half of the inward-pointing triangle and look at the right-hand corner of the Status Bar. It should say *First Line Indent*, followed by a measurement.

5. Drag the First Line Indent marker toward the right until the Status Bar tells you that the First Line Indent is at 1.5". (Again, don't worry about exact positioning.)

6. Release the mouse button.

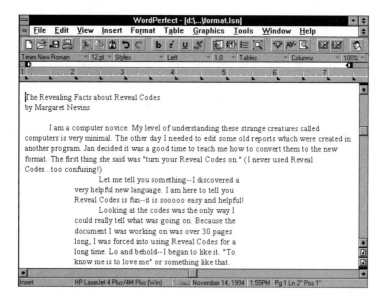

Figure 8.15 *The first line of each paragraph is indented.*

Notice that this trick worked even for the second and third paragraphs, which have different margins. Look at the First Line Indent code in Reveal Codes (the code is at the beginning of the paragraph). It's telling you that the first line of each paragraph will be indented that amount *from the left margin*, no matter where the margin is set.

Changing the Spacing between Paragraphs

It's time to add some space between the paragraphs. To do that, you need to open the Paragraph Format dialog box.

Do It

1. Make sure your insertion point is somewhere in the byline paragraph (*by Margaret Nevins*), because we want these settings to affect everything from there on down.

2. Click the right mouse button anywhere on the Ruler Bar above the tab marker line to open the QuickMenu.

3. Choose **Paragraph Format**. The Paragraph Format dialog box is displayed, as shown in Figure 8.16. You can also access the Paragraph Format dialog box by choosing **Paragraph** from the Format menu and then choosing **Format** from the cascading Paragraph menu.

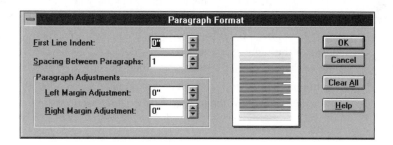

Figure 8.16 *The Paragraph Format dialog box.*

NOTE

While we're in here, take a look at the First Line Indent option. You can make precise changes to the First Line Indent setting by entering a number in the text box. Depending on your needs, this can be a good alternative to using the Ruler Bar.

4. Use the mouse or press the **Tab** key to place your insertion point in the Spacing Between Paragraphs text box.

5. Enter a number. In this case, enter the number **2**. But what does the number *mean?* It's a multiple of your line spacing. If your text is single-spaced, entering **2** in this text box is like changing your line spacing to double between paragraphs.

6. When you're done changing settings, choose **OK** (or press **Enter**).

NOTE

Did you see the **Clear All** button in the Paragraph Format dialog box? If you change a bunch of settings and decide they're all wrong, just click on this button and you're back to the defaults, which are 0 for everything except Spacing Between Paragraphs (the default for that is 1). What this button is really good for though, is if you move one or more of the indent markers on the Ruler by mistake and you can't figure out how to get it back where it was. Especially if you've done a few more things since moving the markers and it's too late to use Undo.

NOTE

Yes, two notes in a row. Is this your lucky day or what? Here it is: in most circumstances, don't bother with the Paragraph Adjustment (Left and Right Margin Adjustment) options in the Paragraph dialog box. They work pretty much like the regular margins, and it's confusing to have two different codes that do essentially the same thing. If you want to change your margins for a particular paragraph or section of text, just select the text you want and use any of the techniques for changing margin settings.

NOTE

Hey, I'm on a roll here, why not go for three in a row? Want to know the big advantage of using the First Line Indent and Spacing Between Paragraph features over pressing the **Tab** key at the beginning of each paragraph and the **Enter** key twice at the end of each paragraph? They allow you to change your mind without paying a penalty. If you decide that you want the first line moved over just a little farther or a little more space between the paragraphs, you just change one setting and it's done. (P.S. You can enter any measurement you want for the Spacing Between Paragraphs. It doesn't have to be a whole number. You can use any increment that's acceptable for line spacing, from 0.1 to 160.)

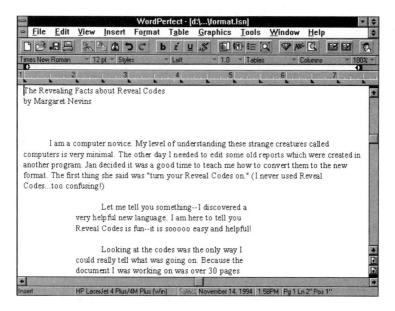

Figure 8.17 *Hey, this is starting to look pretty good!*

Setting Tabs

In Chapter 7, you used tabs and indents to move the insertion point over to the next tab stop. You didn't have to change any settings since WordPerfect comes with tab stops every one-half inch. These settings are okay if you're just using tabs to indent the first line of paragraphs, but you may need to create custom tab settings for lists, charts, or any documents with unusual formats. You'll see that creating custom tab settings with the Ruler is just as easy as changing your margins.

WARNING

With tabs, as with most other formatting codes, the new setting takes effect from the point it is placed in the document (because of Auto Code Placement, that's at the beginning of the paragraph for tabs). This means that a new tab setting will affect any tabs or indents that come after the tab set code in the document. The new setting won't affect any tabs or indents that are in front of the code.

Four Types of Tab Stops

WordPerfect has four different types of tabs, and the tab markers on the Ruler change so you can see what kind of tabs you have. Figure 8.18 shows examples of each tab type and points out the different tab markers.

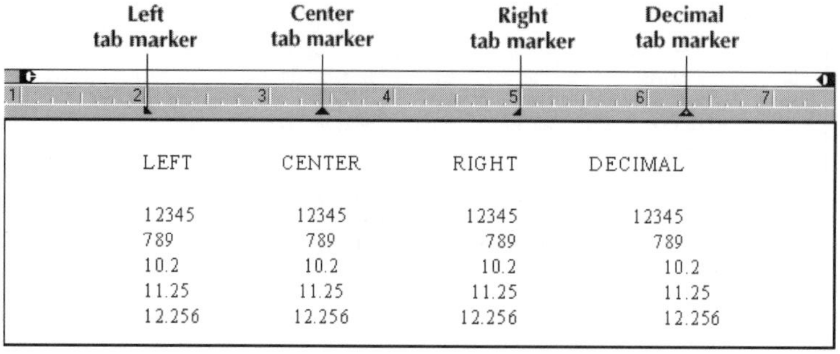

Figure 8.18 *Examples of different tab types.*

- ❖ Left tabs are the default. With a left tab, the left edge of the text lines up at the tab stop, and the text moves over to the right as you type.
- ❖ With right tabs, the right edge of the text lines up at the tab stop, and the text moves to the left as you type.
- ❖ With center tabs, the text is centered over the tab stop.
- ❖ With decimal tabs, the text lines up on a decimal point (or any other alignment character that you choose). The text in front of the alignment character acts like it's right-aligned (moving to the left as you type). The text after the alignment character is left-aligned (it moves to the right as you type).

Changing Tabs with the Ruler

You can add, move, or delete tab stops by dragging tab markers or clicking on the Ruler. For this section, try to recreate the document in Figure 8.18. Start by typing all of the text and numbers, pressing the **Tab** key only once between each column. The columns won't be lined up properly at first (in fact, they'll look really weird), but as you delete and move tabs, the text will move around and line up.

Do It

1. To move a tab stop, just drag a tab marker to a new location on the Ruler. When you hold down the left mouse button on a tab marker, notice that you have a vertical guide to help you with placement, just like you do for margins and first line indents. The Status Bar also gives you information while you're dragging a tab marker.

2. To delete a tab stop, just drag the tab marker down and off the Ruler, then release the mouse button.

3. To add a tab stop, position the mouse pointer on the Ruler where you want the new tab stop and click the left mouse button in the area just below the measurement markings. Because left tabs are the default, when you add a tab stop it's automatically a left tab unless you specify another type.

If you want the new tab stop to be something other than a left tab, right-click on the Ruler Bar anywhere in the row that displays the tab markers and choose the tab type you want from the QuickMenu. (There's also a choice on this menu that clears all of your tab settings so you can start from scratch.) All of the tabs you add will be the new type until you make another selection.

NOTE

You can move or delete more than one tab stop at a time by selecting a group of tab markers. Just hold down the **Shift** key while you drag across the tab markers, then release the **Shift** key. (Careful with this one—if your mouse pointer is a little too low, you'll end up moving a tab stop instead of selecting. The best way to ensure that you will select instead of move is to position your mouse pointer slightly in front of the first tab you want to select before you start dragging.) Once you have a group of tab stops selected, you can delete them by dragging the selection off the Ruler, or move them by dragging the selection to a new location.

Using the Tab Set Dialog Box

Most of your tab setting changes can be made with the Ruler, but the Tab Set dialog box contains some options that aren't available on the Ruler. (And, if you don't have a mouse, the dialog box is the only way to fly.) Let's open the dialog box, and then I'll tell you about it.

Do It

❖ Double-click on any tab marker,

❖ Or choose **Line** from the Format menu, then choose **Tab Set** from the cascading Line menu,

❖ Or choose **Tab Set** from the Ruler Bar's QuickMenu.

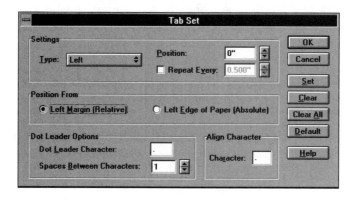

Figure 8.19 *The Tab Set dialog box*

❖ The Settings area is where you can choose a tab type, enter a specific position for a tab stop, or specify the spacing for evenly spaced tabs. If you want to set more than one tab stop while you're in the Tab Set dialog box, be sure to choose **Set** rather than **OK** after you enter a number in the **Position** text box. As soon as you choose **OK**, the dialog box is closed.

❖ Tabs can be positioned from the left margin or from the left edge of the page. By default, tabs are *relative* (positioned from the left margin). Relative tabs "float" in relation to the left margin. When the left margin is changed, the tabs change with it.

Because of relative positioning, the number you enter in the Position text box won't match the number on the Ruler (the Ruler measures from the left edge of the page). For example, if your left margin is set at 1" and you set a relative tab at 2" (by typing **2** in the Position text box), the tab marker on the Ruler will end up at the 3" mark. The tab stop is 2" from the *margin*, but 3" from the *left edge of the page*. This can be a little confusing unless you realize what's happening.

❖ Dot Leader Options lets you change the character that's used for dot leaders and the amount of space between the characters. *Dot leader*—hey, there's a new term for you. A dot leader is a series of dots that *lead* your eye from the insertion point position to the next tab stop. Figure 8.20 shows a document that's a typical example of how dot leaders might be used.

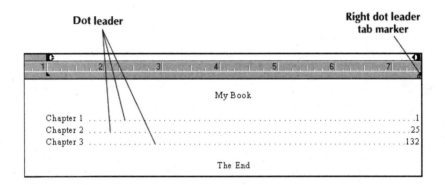

Figure 8.20 *Dot leaders are often used for tables of contents. There's a right-aligned dot leader tab at the right margin (notice the tab marker).*

❖ Align Character lets you change the alignment character that's used when you choose Decimal Tabs. Your text will align on whatever character you enter in this text box.

ROADMAP

Press **Ctrl+W** with your insertion point in either the **Dot Leader Character** or **Align Character** boxes, and you can choose from about a kazillion different characters. Just make sure you delete the current contents of the text box first. You could have a row of musical notes as your dot leader or a happy face for your alignment character. These special characters can be inserted anywhere in a document—you'll learn more about this in Chapter 12, "A Look at Fonts."

❖ Choose **Set** after you enter a number in the **Position** box.

❖ You can delete an individual tab setting by entering its position in the **Position** text box and then choosing **Clear**. Deleting a tab stop is *so* much easier on the Ruler—don't even bother using this button unless you don't have a mouse.

❖ The **Clear All** button deletes all of the current tab settings. It's usually a good idea to do this so you can start with a clean slate before you create custom tab settings.

❖ The **Default** button sets the tabs back to the original setting of one tab every 0.5". This can be really handy if you've used custom tab settings for a particular section and want to get back to the default settings for the rest of the document. Just move your insertion point to where you want the default tab settings to begin, open the Tab Set dialog box, choose **Default**, and choose **OK**.

NOTE

One last tab note. It's easy to set your own evenly spaced tabs like the ones WordPerfect uses for a default. Choose **Clear All** to get rid of all the current tab settings. Specify where you want the tabs to start by entering a number in the Position text box. Then specify how much space you want between each tab stop by choosing **Repeat Every** and entering a number in that text box. Then choose **OK**. Presto chango—evenly spaced custom tabs. For example, if you enter **1** in the Position text box and **1.25** in the **Repeat Every** box, you'll end up with tab stops every 1.25" starting 1" from the left margin.

Changing Line Spacing

By default, documents that you create in WordPerfect are single-spaced, and that's what we've worked with so far. But what if you need to give your boss a double-spaced draft so she can mark it all up with her red pencil? By now you probably have the idea that this'll be a piece of cake, and you're right.

NOTE

Line Spacing is another one of those codes that gets moved to the beginning of the paragraph by Auto Code Placement.

Do It

1. Move your insertion point to the top of the document.
2. Click on the **Line Spacing** button on the Power Bar.
3. Click on one of the menu choices, then release the mouse button.

The line spacing choices on the Power Bar are pretty limited. Choose **Other** from the Power Bar's Line Spacing menu to open the dialog box shown in Figure 8.21. You can also choose **Line** from the Format menu and **Spacing** from the cascading Line menu.

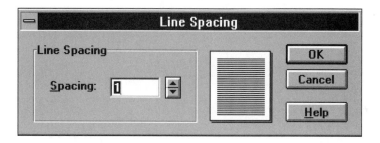

Figure 8.21 *The Line Spacing dialog box.*

The Line Spacing dialog box allows you to set your line spacing at any increment from .01 all the way up to 160. (If any of you can think of a reason you would ever set your line spacing to 160, please let me know.)

Justification

No, this isn't where I make you justify your existence—*justification* refers to how your text is aligned on the page. Figure 8.22 shows examples of paragraphs with left, full, center, and right justification. Figure 8.23 shows what happens if you choose **All** from the Justification menu.

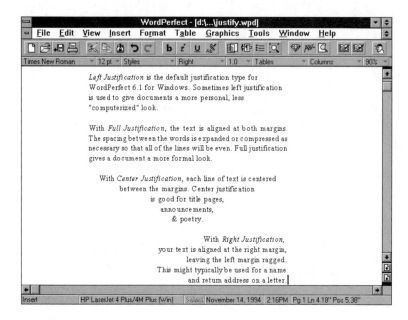

Figure 8.22 *Each paragraph has a different justification setting.*

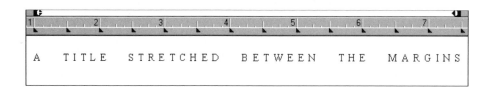

Figure 8.23 *When you choose **Justification**, **All**, the space between each letter is adjusted so that they are evenly spaced between the left and right margin.*

Do It

1. Place your insertion point anywhere in the paragraph where you want the justification change to take effect. (Remember, Auto Code Placement moves the code to the beginning of the paragraph.)

2. Click on the **Justification** button on the Power Bar.

3. Click on one of the choices on the pop-up menu and release the mouse button.

For this feature, the keyboard options are useful shortcuts even if you have a mouse:

❖ **Ctrl+L** for left justification

❖ **Ctrl+R** for right justification

❖ **Ctrl+E** for center justification

❖ **Ctrl+J** for full justification

There isn't a keyboard shortcut for **Justification**, **All**. Choose **Justification** from the Format menu, then choose **All** from the cascading Justification menu.

FROM HERE ...

In the next chapter, you'll learn to enhance your documents even further. Before you move on, take some time to practice what you learned in this chapter. Write a letter to your mom (or do some real work if you must)—show her that you know how to set margins and tabs wherever you want them, that you can change the spacing between lines and paragraphs, and align the text four different ways.

And one more thing—did you remember to look in Reveal Codes to see what the justification and tab setting codes look like? Yeah, I know: nag, nag, nag. Well, it's for your own good. You'll thank me for it later. (Whoa, where did that come from? It must be all that talk about writing letters to Mom.)

WordPerfect 6.1 for Windows

SECTION II

BEYOND
THE BASICS

CHAPTER 9

Advanced Formatting

(Finishing Touches)

Let's talk about:

- ❖ Creating headers and footers
- ❖ Adding page numbers
- ❖ Using hyphenation
- ❖ Keeping text together
- ❖ Working with advance codes
- ❖ Delaying or suppressing codes
- ❖ Changing the paper size

Congratulations! As a graduate of Section I, you can create and edit WordPerfect documents and make basic formatting and layout changes. But there's more to life than the basics. In this chapter, I'll show you tricks and features that will allow you to enhance and streamline the process of putting a document together.

Before You Start

For this chapter, you need to have a document that's longer than one page. If you already have a two- to five-page document that you want to use for practice, go ahead and open it. (Make sure you save it with a different name so your original doesn't get messed up.) Otherwise....

Do It

1. Open **FORMAT1.LSN**.
2. Move your insertion point to the end of the document and add a page break (**Ctrl+Enter**).
3. Type some text on the second page. (You can just type **This is page two** if you want—it doesn't have to be anything fancy.)
4. Add a couple more pages by repeating steps 2 and 3.
5. Save the document as **LONGDOC.WPD** and leave it on your screen.

Headers and Footers

Headers and footers make it easy to repeat the same text on every page (or selected pages) of your document. What's the difference between headers and footers? C'mon, take a wild stab at it. That's right—headers appear at the top of a page and footers at the bottom. That's the *only* difference. Other than that, everything that I say about headers can be applied to footers (and vice versa).

Why use headers and footers? Have you ever typed a title and page number at the bottom of every page of a document? You have? Then I bet you can guess what's coming next. You end up adding a couple of lines of text to the first page, and the text that used to be at the bottom of each page is now somewhere in the middle. So you have to adjust the position of each and every title and page number. Imagine this process repeated *ad infinitum* every time a small change is made to the document (maybe you don't have to imagine—maybe you've been there).

Headers and footers let you completely bypass this time-wasting nightmare. If you use these features, you only enter the information once, and the text stays where it's supposed to be no matter how many changes you make to your document. In addition, if you want to change something about the header or footer itself, you only do it once.

What Can You Put in a Header or Footer?

Almost anything you can put in a document—text, numbers, graphic images, lines, borders—can go in headers and footers. If you can do it in a document, you can probably do it in a header or footer. You can use all the techniques you've already learned to move the insertion point and make formatting changes. Any features that aren't available in headers or footers are dimmed on the pull-down menus.

Creating a Header or Footer

We'll add a header so that the title, date, and page number appear on every page of LONGDOC.WPD.

Do It

1. Make sure your insertion point is somewhere on the first page.
2. Choose **Header/Footer** from the Format menu. The Headers/Footers dialog box is displayed, as shown in Figure 9.1.

NOTE

You can also access the Header/Footer dialog box by clicking the right mouse button near the top or bottom of a page to open the Header/Footer and Watermark QuickMenu, and then choosing **Header/Footer.**

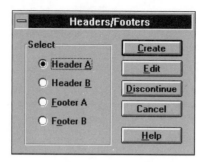

Figure 9.1 *The Headers/Footers dialog box.*

3. Choose **Header A**, **Header B**, **Footer A**, or **Footer B** (in this case, accept the default, which is Header A).

4. Choose **Create** (or press **Enter**). Your text jumps down on the page to make room for the header, and the Feature Bar shown in Figure 9.2 is displayed. Notice that it says *Header A* after the document name in the Title Bar.

    A Feature Bar is used just like the Power Bar and Toolbars. You just click on one of the buttons for quick access to a particular option. If you don't have a mouse, you can access any Feature Bar button by holding down **Alt+Shift** while you press the underlined letter for that option. For example, to choose **Pages**, you would press **Alt+Shift+A**.

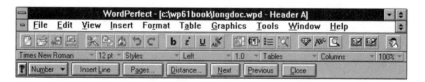

Figure 9.2 *The Header or Footer Feature Bar is displayed below the Ruler Bar.*

5. Type the text for your header or footer, using any formatting options you want. For this example:

    ❖ Type **Revealing Facts** at the left margin.

    ❖ Without pressing the Spacebar, press **Shift+F7** to center the date code.

    ❖ Press **Ctrl+Shift+D** to insert a date code.

    ❖ Press **Alt+F7** so that the page number is aligned flush right.

❖ Click on the **Number** button and choose **Page Number** to insert a code that prints the correct page number on each page.

6. Click on the **Pages** button to tell WordPerfect whether you want the header or footer to appear on every page, odd pages, or even pages.

7. Click on the **Distance** button to adjust the amount of space between the header or footer and the document text.

8. Choose **Close** from the feature Bar when you're done to turn off the Header/Footer Feature Bar and return to your document text.

9. Press **Alt+PageDown** to move your insertion point to the beginning of the second page. Notice that your header is right there with the correct page number, as shown in Figure 9.3.

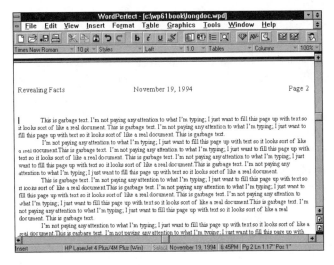

Figure 9.3 *Page 2 of LONGDOC.WPD with header.*

NOTE

If you're only going to use one header or footer, use A. Header/Footer B is for documents that use multiple headers or footers. For example, each even-numbered page of this book shows the page number followed by the title of the book at the left margin, while the odd-numbered pages have the chapter number and title followed by the page number at the right margin. This could be accomplished by using Header A for odd pages and Header B for even pages.

Discontinuing a Header or Footer

To turn off a header or footer in the middle of a document, just move your insertion point to the page where you want the header or footer to stop. From the Headers/Footer dialog box, select the desired header or footer and choose **Discontinue**.

NOTE

If you don't want headers or footers to appear on particular pages, use the Delay or Suppress feature (both of which are discussed later in this chapter) instead of Discontinue.

Editing a Header or Footer

It's easy to edit a header or footer. Just click anywhere in the header or footer text, and change whatever you want. If the Feature Bar is not active, just click the right mouse button when your insertion point is in the header or footer area and choose **Feature Bar** from the QuickMenu. A few notes about editing headers and footers:

❖ This won't work with the keyboard—you can't just move your insertion point into a header or footer. To edit a header or footer with the keyboard, you have to open the Headers/Footers dialog box, select the desired header or footer, and choose **Edit**.

❖ If you're working in a document and some features don't work the way you think they should, or some menu items don't seem to be available, you might have accidentally clicked in a header or footer area without realizing it. Take a look at the Title Bar—if the word *Header* or *Footer* appears after the document name, you need to leave that area before you can access the regular document features. Just click anywhere in the document text and you'll be back in the normal editing area.

❖ When you choose **Edit** from the Headers/Footers dialog box, the header or footer that's just above the insertion point location is the one that's selected. So if you have more than one header or footer in your document, move your insertion point just past the appropriate header or footer code before you edit.

Page Numbering

You just saw how simple it is to add a page number code to a header or footer. But if you don't want to include a lot of text and formatting along with the page number, you can use the page numbering feature instead—it's no muss, no fuss. Just access the Page Numbering dialog box, pick a location, add a little text if you want, and you're done. There are more options you can play with, but it can be as simple as that.

By default, page numbering is turned off. If you print a document, it won't have any page numbers. Even though you see page numbers on the Status Bar, you have to tell WordPerfect when you want the numbers to appear on the printed page.

Do It

1. Make sure your insertion point is on the page where you want the page numbering to start. (For this example, it should be on the first page.)

2. Choose **Page** from the Format menu, then choose **Numbering** from the cascading Page menu. The Page Numbering dialog box is displayed, as shown in Figure 9.4.

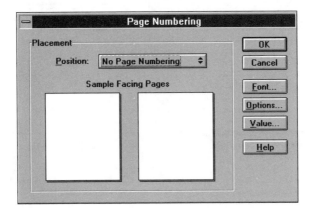

Figure 9.4 *The Page Numbering dialog box.*

3. Choose the placement of the page numbers from the Position pop-up list. For this lesson, choose **Alternating Bottom**.

NOTE

Before you leave this dialog box, play around with the choices on the pop-up list and notice what happens in the Sample Facing Pages area. As you make different selections, it gives you a preview of the placement of page numbers.

4. If you just want the page number without any accompanying text or formatting, choose **OK** (or press **Enter**) to close the dialog box and insert the page numbering code in your document. (Don't forget to take a look at the code.) Figure 9.5 shows what LONGDOC.WPD looks like with a header and page numbers.

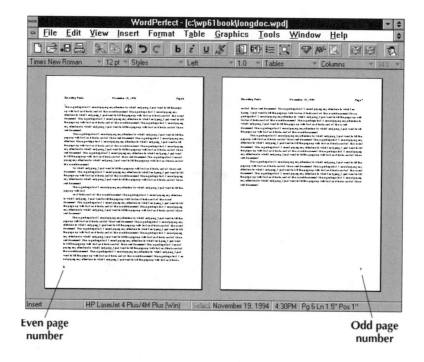

Even page number

Odd page number

Figure 9.5 *When you choose alternating page numbers, even page numbers are at the left margin, and odd page numbers are at the right margin.*

Did you see how easy it was to set the page number position? To create alternating page numbers with a header or footer, you would have to use two separate headers or footers (one on odd pages and one on even pages), and then within the header or footer you would have to use flush right to get the page number at the right margin on the odd pages. But if all you want is the page number, there's no contest between the two features—the alternating page number feature is the way to go.

Page Numbering Enhancements

We just inserted the most basic kind of page numbering—just the number at a specified position. You can get a lot fancier with page numbering, and this section offers some examples to give you a taste of the power of the page numbering feature. There are three buttons in the Page Numbering dialog box that let you embellish your page numbers.

In this section I'm using page numbers for all the examples. Secondary, chapter, and volume numbers work exactly the same way. The only difference is that chapter and volume numbers don't increase automatically; you have to change the value every time you want to update the number. A suggestion: don't mess with secondary, chapter, and volume numbers until you feel pretty comfortable with using all of the options on regular page numbers.

Font

If you don't specify anything else, your page numbers will print in the same type size and style as your document text. You can change style or size for your page numbers by choosing **Font**. Just change any of the settings you want in the Page Numbering Font dialog box and choose **OK**. (The Page Number Font dialog box is identical to the Font dialog box, which is covered in detail in Chapter 12, "A Look at Fonts.")

Options

Choosing the **Options** button takes you to the Page Numbering Options dialog box, shown in Figure 9.6. This is where you add text to the page number or change the numbering type.

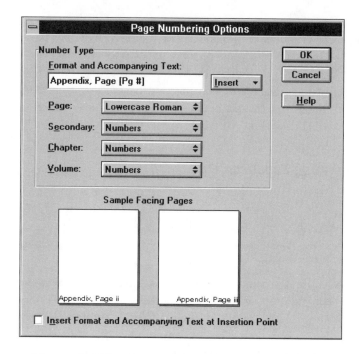

Figure 9.6 *The Page Numbering Options dialog box.*

To include text with the page number, enter it in the **Format & Accompanying Text** box. I've entered some sample text in Figure 9.6. The text in brackets is the code that inserts the page number. When you print, the actual page number is printed in place of this code. Don't delete this code, or the page number won't print. (If you delete the code by mistake, you can add it again by choosing **Page** from the Insert pop-up list.)

Your page numbers can print as regular numbers (the default), uppercase or lowercase letters, or uppercase or lowercase Roman numerals. Make your choice from the pop-up lists for **Page**, **Secondary**, **Chapter**, or **Volume**. In Figure 9.6, I changed the numbers for **Page** to **Lowercase Roman** (which might be appropriate for an introduction or appendix).

Value—Changing the Starting Page Number

The Value button takes you to the Numbering Value dialog box, shown in Figure 9.7.

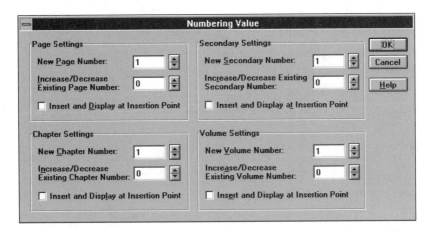

Figure 9.7 *The Numbering Value dialog box.*

This dialog box might look a little intimidating, but all you have to focus on for now is the **New Page Number** option in the Page Settings area. Unless you change this setting, WordPerfect assumes you want to begin your document with page one and number all of the pages consecutively (a fairly reasonable assumption). But sometimes you might want a document to begin with a different page number or change the numbering in the middle of a document (for example, you might want to skip a couple of page numbers if you're going to manually insert some data from another source after the document is printed). Just type the new starting page number in the **New Page Number** text box. The new number takes effect at the top of the current page.

There's one other option you should know about in this dialog box. Choose **Insert and Display at Insertion Point** to insert the page number at any location in your document.

Hyphenation

As you type, WordPerfect wraps your text to the next line when you get to the right margin. If the word you're typing is too long to fit on the line, the whole word moves down. If the word is really long, you might want to hyphenate it to make your lines look better. When you're using full justification, wrapping a long word to the next line can leave a lot of unsightly gaps between the remaining words on the line.

You can just type a hyphen in the middle of the word. That'll take care of the problem for the time being. But what if you change your margins or add some text in front of the word? That hyphen's still sitting there in the middle of the word, even though the word's now in the middle of a line.

But you know I'm going to give you an easier way. Just turn the Hyphenation feature on and WordPerfect does the rest.

Do It

To turn hyphenation on:

1. Move your insertion point to the paragraph where you want to start hyphenating.

2. Choose **Line** from the Format menu, then choose **Hyphenation** from the cascading Line menu.

3. Click on the **Hyphenation On** check box in the Line Hyphenation dialog box, shown in Figure 9.8, and choose **OK** (or press **Enter**).

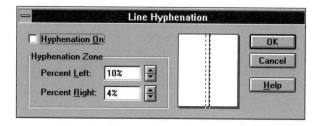

Figure 9.8 *The Line Hyphenation dialog box.*

Hyphenation Prompts

After you turn hyphenation on, you might be stopped by a Position Hyphen dialog box, shown in Figure 9.9, as you move through your document. This just means that WordPerfect has found a word that it thinks should be hyphenated and wants some input from you.

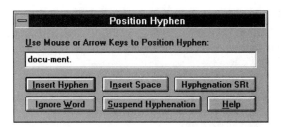

Figure 9.9 *The Position Hyphen dialog box.*

1. Choose **Insert Hyphen** to accept the way WordPerfect has hyphenated the word. If you want to move the hyphen, use the **Left Arrow** or **Right Arrow** key, and then choose **Insert Hyphen** when the hyphen is positioned where you want it.

NOTE

Pay close attention to the Position Hyphen text box before you accept WordPerfect's choice of position. Even though WordPerfect checks its own internal dictionary before placing a hyphen, I've found that it comes up with some pretty strange choices. I've seen it try to hyphenate one syllable words, or hyphenate a word right in the middle of a syllable. Don't assume that WordPerfect's choice is correct.

2. Choose **Insert Space** if you want to break the word with a space instead of a hyphen.

3. Choose **Hyphenation SRt** if you want to break the word without using a hyphen. (This is handy if you've connected words with slashes, like writer/consultant.) This option allows a line break after the slash without inserting a hyphen or a space.

4. Choose **Ignore Word** if you don't want the word to be broken at all. With this option, the entire word wraps to the next line.

5. Choose **Suspend Hyphenation** if the hyphenation prompts start bugging you (this can happen if you're making a lot of formatting changes or spellchecking). This option just turns off hyphenation during the current procedure—it automatically goes back on when you're finished.

NOTE

Don't turn hyphenation on until you've typed your text. If you have hyphenation on while you're typing, the position prompts can get really annoying.

Different Kinds of Hyphens

There are three kinds of hyphens you can manually insert while you're typing:

❖ **Regular hyphen**. That's what you get when you press the **Hyphen** key. The hyphen is part of your text, so it won't move or change when the text reformats. It allows words to be broken at the end of a line, but the hyphen is still visible if the text happens to be in the middle of a line.

❖ **Hyphen character**. Insert a hyphen character by pressing **Ctrl+ –**. (This is sometimes called a *hard hyphen.*) Use a hyphen character if you don't want the words on either side of the hyphen to break between lines. For example, if you separate a date with hyphens (12-01-22), use a hyphen character instead of a regular hyphen to make sure the date doesn't get split in the middle.

❖ **Soft hyphen**. To insert a soft hyphen, press **Ctrl+Shift+ –**. A soft hyphen lets you tell WordPerfect to hyphenate a particular word if necessary, even if the hyphenation feature is turned off. The word is hyphenated if it falls at the end of a line, but the hyphen is invisible if the word is in the middle of a line.

All of these hyphens can also be inserted through the Other Codes dialog box. It's much easier to use the keyboard shortcuts, but if you don't remember them, just choose **Line** from the Format menu, then choose **Other Codes** from the cascading Line menu. The Other Codes dialog box is displayed, as shown in Figure 9.10. Choose the code you want from the Hyphenation Codes area and choose **OK**.

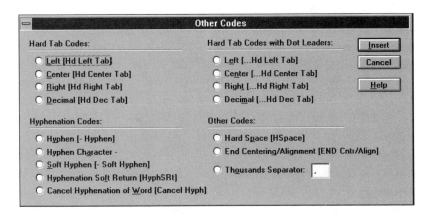

Figure 9.10 *The Other Codes dialog box.*

There are two other hyphenation options you can select in this dialog box:

- ❖ **Hyphenation soft return.** This is like telling WordPerfect to insert a soft hyphen, only there's no hyphen. If the words are at the end of a line, they'll be split at the location of this code. If they're in the middle of a line, nothing happens.

- ❖ **Cancel hyphenation of word**. Insert this code if you don't want a particular word to be hyphenated under any circumstances.

Keeping Text Together

As you're typing along, WordPerfect moves the text to the next page as soon as you get to the bottom margin. It doesn't care whether it's breaking a two-line paragraph or ripping a heading from its accompanying text—it just does it. But there are four different features that put you in control of how text gets split between pages. The first, hard page breaks, are inserted with a keystroke or by choosing **Page Break** from the Insert menu. You get to the other three through the Keep Text Together dialog box, shown in Figure 9.11. To access this dialog box, choose **Page** from the Format menu, then choose **Keep Text Together** from the cascading Page menu.

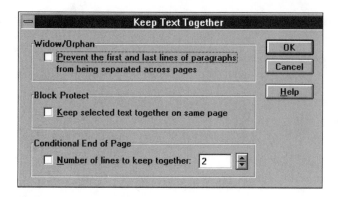

Figure 9.11 *The Keep Text Together dialog box.*

Hard Page Breaks

You've already done this. Any time you want to force WordPerfect to start a new page, just press **Ctrl+Enter** or choose **Page Break** from the Insert menu. After you've read the rest of this section, however, you might not use this as often.

Hard page breaks aren't as flexible as some of the other options. If you insert a hard page break and then make changes that affect the pagination, you have to go back and delete the hard page break and insert it in a new location.

Widows and Orphans

Widows are single lines of text that get stranded all by themselves at the top of a page, while their *orphans* are left alone at the bottom of a page. Let's take pity on those poor widows and orphans by turning on WordPerfect's widow/orphan protection. (Bet you didn't know WordPerfect was such a civic-minded program.)

❖ Just check **Widow/Orphan** in the Keep Text Together dialog box and choose **OK**.

ROADMAP

It's a good idea to turn on widow/orphan protection as a default, so that it's automatically taken care of for all your documents. You can do this by adding a widow/orphan code to your initial codes style. See Chapter 22, "Working with Styles," to learn how to do it.

Block Protect

This feature is great when you have a chart, list, or quotation that you don't want split between pages. Here's what you do:

1. Select the text you want protected.

2. Choose **Keep Selected Text Together on the Same Page** from the Keep Text Together dialog box and choose **OK**.

WordPerfect inserts paired block protection codes at the beginning and end of the selected text. Any text you type between the codes will be part of the protected block.

You can't protect a block that's longer than one page.

NOTE

Conditional End of Page

If your document has headings, you usually want to make sure that there's at least a line or two of text on the same page as the heading. It looks pretty stupid to have a heading all by itself at the bottom of a page.

Conditional End of Page is the feature of choice for this situation—you can tell WordPerfect to keep a specific number of lines together with the heading. If that number of lines won't fit on the page, the whole group is moved to the next page.

1. Make sure your insertion point is at the beginning of the first line you want to keep together.

2. Check **Number of Lines to Keep Together** in the Keep Text Together dialog box, then type a number in the text box and choose **OK**. (Don't forget to count blank lines when you're figuring out how many lines you want to keep together. If your text is double-spaced, each line counts as two.)

Advance

Advance codes are another way of getting control over where your text ends up on the page. You can move text or codes to a specific position without adding a lot of unnecessary hard returns or tabs.

Why use advance codes? What if the logo on your letterhead paper takes up the top two inches of the page? The first page of each letter has to start at least 2" down, but you want the rest of the pages to start 1" from the top. You don't want to change your top margin for the first page and then change it back (you could, but that's an extra step). Just insert an advance code that tells WordPerfect to move the insertion point down 2" from the top of the page, and you're all set.

Do It

To insert an advance code:

1. Choose **Typesetting** from the Format menu, then choose **Advance** from the cascading Typesetting menu. The Advance dialog box is displayed, as shown in Figure 9.12.

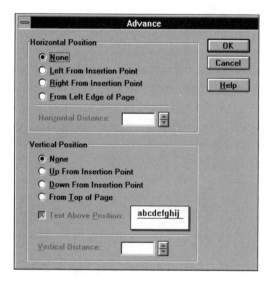

***Figure 9.12** The Advance dialog box.*

2. Select the advance option you want.

3. Enter the distance you want to move the text in the appropriate text box.

❖ **From Left Edge of Page** and **From Top of Page** are both *absolute settings*. Text remains in the position you choose, regardless of what happens with the rest of the text on the page. For example, if you advance the first line of text on your letterhead down 2" from the top of the page, the text following that advance code is *always* 2" from the top of the page, even if you add text or hard returns above the code.

❖ **Left from Insertion Point**, **Right from Insertion Point**, **Up from Insertion Point**, and **Down from Insertion Point** are all *relative settings*. Their position on the page depends on the position of the insertion point. If your insertion point is at Ln 5" and you enter an advance code that moves the insertion point down one inch, the insertion point past the advance code will initially be at Ln 6". But if you add text that moves the insertion point down to Ln 5.5", the advance code moves the insertion point relative to the new location. If you look at the Status Bar past the advance code, it shows Ln 6.5".

❖ If you choose **From Top of Page**, you can tell WordPerfect whether you want the text to print above or below the position by checking or unchecking the **Text Above Position** check box.

From Top of Page can only be used for the current page. You can't advance text to an absolute position on a different page.

The Advance feature can be handy for filling out preprinted forms. You can measure where you need to fill in information and use **From Top of Page** and **From Left Edge of Page** codes to position each response exactly where you want it.

Delaying and Suppressing Codes

Why would you want to delay or suppress a code? If you don't want the code, don't put it in in the first place. Is that what you're thinking? Well, believe me, there are reasons. Take a look at LONGDOC.WPD for a prime example. We added a header to the document, but there's already a title and page number on the first page.

Often you don't want headers or footers on the first page. You could move your insertion point to the beginning of the second page before you create the header or footer, but that could create problems if you add text and the top of page two isn't the top of page two anymore.

It's much better to group your page formatting codes in one location and use Suppress and Delay to control where they appear. Here's the difference between them and when should you use them:

❖ Use **Suppress** to keep a header, footer, watermark, or page number from appearing on a particular page. Suppress works only for the page where your insertion point is located when you access the feature. You have to insert a suppress code on each page where you don't want the header, footer, or watermark.

ROADMAP

I know we haven't talked about watermarks yet. That comes in Chapter 14.

❖ Use **Delay** to move formatting codes a specified number of pages. Using LONGDOC.WPD as an example, **Suppress** works great if you want the header to start on the second page. But if for some reason you don't want the header to start until page 4, **Delay** would make more sense. Just tell WordPerfect to delay the header code for three pages.

❖ A major difference between the two features is that you add a suppress code after you've already created the page number, header, footer, or watermark. When you use Delay, activate the delay feature before you create the formatting feature.

Adding a Suppress Code

1. Make sure your insertion point is on the page where you want to suppress the page numbering, header, footer, or watermark.

2. Choose **Page** from the Format menu, then choose **Suppress** from the cascading Page menu. Figure 9.13 shows the Suppress dialog box.

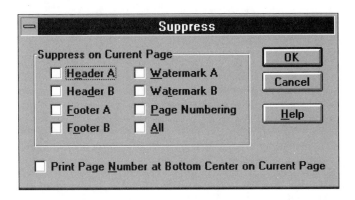

Figure 9.13 *The Suppress dialog box.*

3. Check the boxes for all of the items you want to suppress, or check **All** to suppress all of them, and choose **OK**.

The **Print Page Number at Bottom Center on Current Page** option can be useful if your page number is included in a header or footer that you want suppressed, but you still want the page number to print on that page. Or you might have used the page numbering feature to put the page numbers at the top of the page, but you have one page with a chart where you want the page number to move to the bottom. (This option is dimmed when Page Numbering or All is checked.)

Creating a Delay Code

1. Place your insertion point on the page where you want the delay codes to appear (not the page where the feature itself will appear). For example, if you're delaying codes from the beginning of the document to the third page, your insertion point should be on page one.

2. Choose **Page** from the Format menu, then choose **Delay Codes** from the cascading Page menu.

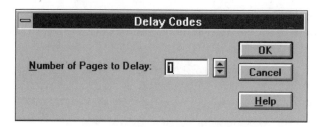

Figure 9.14 *The Delay Codes dialog box.*

3. Enter a number in the text box and choose **OK**. This number isn't a page number—it's the number of pages between the current page and where you want the delayed feature to appear. For example, if you're on page 1 and you want a feature delayed until page 3, enter **2** in the **Number of Pages to Delay** text box. The Define Delayed Codes window, shown in Figure 9.15, is displayed.

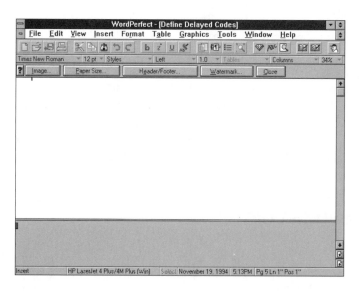

Figure 9.15 *Add codes in the Define Delayed Codes window.*

Notice that the Title Bar tells you where you are, and a Reveal Codes window opens up so you can see what you're adding. There's also a special Feature Bar for delay codes that gives you quick access to some commonly delayed codes.

4. Add the codes or create the feature you want to delay. Enter codes in this area just like you would in the document window. For example, if you want to delay a header code, create the header using exactly the same techniques I showed you earlier in this chapter. The only difference is that you're creating it in the Delay Codes window. (Features that aren't available in the Delay Codes window are dimmed on the menus and Power Bar and Toolbar.)

5. When you're done, choose **Close** from the Feature Bar.

Changing Paper Size

Everything we've done so far has been formatted for a standard 8.5" x 11" sheet of paper, with the text printed across the width of the page (called *portrait orientation*). That's WordPerfect's default, and it's probably what you'll use most of the time. But not always. What about envelopes and labels? And what if you want the text to print across the long side of the page (called *landscape orientation*)?

It's easier than you might think. WordPerfect comes equipped with definitions for a bunch of different paper sizes, including envelopes and labels. You just pick the one you want and away you go. (You can also create your own custom paper size definitions when you get really brave.)

Do It

1. Make sure your insertion point is on the page where you want the paper size change to take place.

2. Choose **Page** from the Format menu, then choose **Paper Size** from the cascading Page menu. The Paper Size dialog box is displayed, as shown in Figure 9.16.

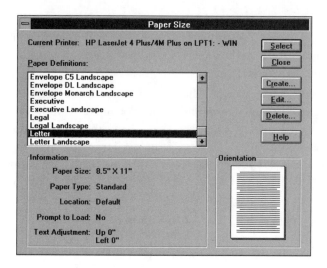

Figure 9.16 *The Paper Size dialog box.*

The choices in this dialog box depend on what printer you have, so your list might look a little different. Before going one to the next step, I want you to pay attention to a couple of things. The Information area gives you details about the highlighted selection, and the Orientation area has a little picture, so you don't have to rely on just the name.

3. Highlight the size you want in the **Paper Definition** list, then choose **Select**.

Don't use the **Paper Size** feature for envelopes. There's a much easier way—WordPerfect has its own envelope feature, which you'll learn about in Chapter 16.

ROADMAP

FROM HERE ...

At this point you can create and edit complex documents. You can add headers, footers, and page numbers (and you know how to keep them from printing on certain pages). You have three different techniques for keeping text together on a page, and you can use advance codes to move text or codes to specific locations on a page. And last but not least, you can even change the size of the paper your document is printed on.

If you'd like a little practice with this, go back and play with LONGDOC.WPD. If you didn't already, suppress the header on page 1. Then advance the first paragraph down 1" and add a footer that's delayed until page 4. Before you leave this chapter, you should feel comfortable with formatting, because we're moving past it for a while. In the next chapter, you'll use features that'll help you find your way around longer documents.

CHAPTER 10

Finding Your Way

(Help! I'm Lost)

Let's talk about:

- ❖ Finding text and codes
- ❖ Replacing text and codes
- ❖ Replacing word forms
- ❖ Getting to a specific page or location with Go To
- ❖ Using Bookmarks to mark your place

You've written your masterpiece. It's beautifully formatted. It has headers and footers, and there isn't a widow or orphan in sight. Now what? In my experience, a bunch of major editing changes. You need to add a sentence in that paragraph where you quoted Sally Swensen, but you can't remember what page that was on. You just found out that every place where you used the word *hippopotamus*, it was really supposed to be *antelope*. And your boss just said "Oh, by the way, all of those italic headings need to be changed to bold." In the middle of all this, you get a frantic phone call. You have to leave for a while, but you want to be able to pick up where you left off when you come back.

We've been through enough by now that you probably realize this is all going to be a breeze. Yup. Just do a quick search for *Swensen*, replace *hippopotamus* with *antelope*, and replace italic with bold. And when you have to leave, stick an electronic bookmark in the document so you can get right back to the same place.

Prep Work

Before you perform all these wonderful feats, type the following short paragraphs (I won't make you type a lot—we'll just pretend this is a long document) so we've got something to work with in this chapter:

```
    As some of you may know from our last newsletter,
our photographic safari in search of the wild
hippopotamus is selling out fast. I never realized
there were so many hippopotamus enthusiasts in our
small town! I am thrilled with the response and look
forward with great anticipation to this trip.
    So hurry up if you want to be part of this
hippopotamus happening. In the words of Sally
Swensen, who led our last excursion, "The
opportunity to see a hippopotamus up close is not
to be taken lightly."
```

Make sure the last sentence (the one in quotes) is in italics. We're ready to go.

Find

With the Find and Replace feature, you can quickly move to any text or code in your document. The Find and Replace Text dialog box has an assortment of options that allow you to zero in on just what you want (and replace it with something else if you choose). Let's start by doing a simple text search and branch out from there.

Do It

To search for text:

1. Make sure your insertion point is located where you want the search to begin. (Actually, you'll discover some options in a bit that let you get around this, but for now, place your insertion point at the beginning of the sample text.)

2. Choose **Find and Replace** from the Edit menu (or press **F2**).

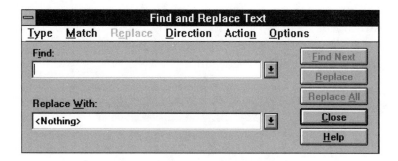

Figure 10.1 *The Find and Replace Text dialog box.*

3. Enter the text you want to search for in the Find text box. In this case, type **swensen**.

NOTE

It doesn't matter whether you enter the text in uppercase or lowercase. Find isn't case sensitive by default—it finds anything that matches the characters in the text box. If you want an exact match, choose **Case** from the Match menu.

4. Choose **Find Next**.

The text that's found is selected. If you click anywhere in the document and start typing at this point, the selected text is replaced by whatever you type. If you don't want to type over the text, just click again to unselect it.

The Find and Replace Text dialog box remains on the screen so that you can do a series of searches if you want. As soon as you click anywhere in the document window, the dialog box becomes inactive, but it doesn't go away. When you're done using the dialog box, just click on its **Close** button.

Finding More than One Occurrence of a Search String

What you're searching for, whether it's text or codes (or a combination of both) is called the *search string.*

In the example above, Find took you right to *Sally Swensen.* But maybe you're not sure that's the only place you mentioned her. You want to find out if her name appears anywhere else in the document. With the Find and Replace Text dialog box still on screen, just choose **Find Next** again, and the search continues. You can keep clicking on Find Next until WordPerfect has found all occurrences of the word or phrase. When there aren't any more to find, you'll see the dialog box displayed in Figure 10.2.

Figure 10.2 *This dialog box appears when there are no more occurrences of a search string to be found.*

NOTE

This dialog box means that WordPerfect sees no more occurrences of the word or phrase *in the direction you are searching* (in this case, from the insertion point forward). If you start your search from the very beginning of your document, you can be confident that **Find** will uncover all of the occurrences if you just keep choosing **Find Next**.

But what if you didn't start right at the beginning? You could put the insertion point right at the beginning of your document and start over. There's a better way, though—in the Find and Replace Text dialog box, see what happens when you click on the **Direction** menu: you can choose **Forward** (the default) or **Backward**. If you select Backward, the Find Next button changes into a **Find Prev** button; clicking this button with the mouse (or pressing **Alt+F**) finds the next occurrence by searching backward from the insertion point.

KEYBOARD

Shift+F2 is a great shortcut for searching for the next occurrence. You can let WordPerfect find the first place the word or phrase appears and then close the Find and Replace dialog box. Then just keep pressing **Shift+F2** until you've found all occurrences. **Alt+F2** does the same thing in reverse—each time you press **Alt+F2**, WordPerfect searches backward to the next occurrence.

Searching for Codes

Any code that can be included in a WordPerfect document can be included in a search string. You can search for codes by themselves or in combination with text. For example, if you know you turned on italics right before you used quotation marks, you could search for the **Italc On** (italics on) code followed by a quotation mark to find the right spot.

Do It

1. Choose **Find and Replace** from the Edit menu (or press **F2**).

2. Choose **Codes** from the Match menu. The Codes dialog box is displayed, as in Figure 10.3.

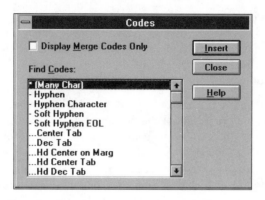

Figure 10.3 The Codes dialog box.

3. Add a code from the Find Codes list to your search string by highlighting the code and then choosing **Insert** (you can also double-click on a code). The code is displayed in the text box at the location of your insertion point, and the Codes dialog box stays on screen. This makes it easy to insert more than one code in a search string. When you're through adding codes, choose **Close** from the Codes dialog box.

4. When your search string is complete, choose **Find Next** or **Find Previous** to begin the search.

Turn Reveal Codes on before you search for a code, so you'll be able to see where the insertion point ends up in relation to the code.

You can combine multiple codes with text in a search string. The search string in Figure 10.4 shows a number followed by a tab, a Bold On code, and some text.

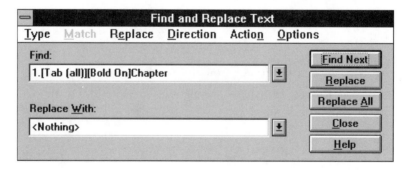

Figure 10.4 A sample search string that combines text and codes.

Using Wildcards

WordPerfect has two special codes that can be used as wildcards. Wildcards can help if you don't know the spelling of a word. For example, you could use wildcards to replace the letters you're not sure of in *hippopotamus.*

❖ **[?(One Char)]** takes the place of one character.

❖ **[*(Many Char)]** can take the place of any number of characters, including zero.

Let's say you don't know whether there's one *p* or two, that you have no idea what happens between the first *o* and the *m,* and that you're not sure whether that last vowel is an *a* or a *u.* Figure 10.5 shows how you'd set up your search string.

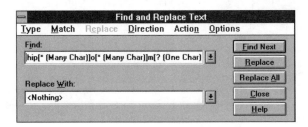

Figure 10.5 *This search string finds anything that starts with* hip, *has multiple (or no) letters between the* p *and the* o *and between the* o *and the* m, *and exactly one letter between the* m *and the final* s.

❖ You insert wildcards in a search string by choosing them from the Codes dialog box.

SHORTCUT

Here's a shortcut for selecting codes from the Codes list. If you know how the code looks (and this can be a little tricky; WordPerfect uses some strange and often inconsistent abbreviations—for example, the code for a left tab is *Left Tab,* and the code for a left margin is *Lft Mar*), make sure the Find Codes list is active (by clicking in it or tabbing to it) and just start typing. As soon as you type the first letter, a text box appears above the list and the selection bar moves to the first code that begins with that letter. Keep typing just long enough to get the selection bar to move to the code you want—you don't have to type the whole thing.

NOTE

The *(Many Char)* code is at the top of the list in the Codes dialog box, but the *?(One Char)* code isn't. WordPerfect put this one a ways down the list, after the codes for tabs and hyphens. To use the shortcut to find it, click in the Codes dialog box (but be sure Display Merge Codes Only is not selected) and type **?**. *?(One Char)* should then be selected in the list.

Refining the Search

You can set up some pretty fancy search strings. Now it's time to look at the other options on the Find menus that can help you fine-tune your search. The options on the Match menu let you narrow your search criteria.

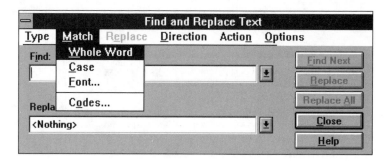

Figure 10.6 *The Match menu.*

❖ Choose **Whole Word** if you want to make sure that the search finds whole words only. If this box isn't checked, a search for *cot* also finds *apricot, cottage,* and *ascot*—in other words, any word that has the letters *cot* in it. When **Whole Word** is checked, the words *Whole Word* appear below the Find text box.

❖ Choose **Case** if you want to search for an exact match of the word or phrase in your search string. If Case isn't checked, a search for *COT* finds *cot, Cot,* and *COT.* With the option checked, only *COT* is found. When **Case** is checked, the words *Case Sensitive* appear below the Find text box.

❖ Choose **Font** to narrow your search to text in a specific type size or style. This option takes you to a Match Font dialog box, where you make your selections.

❖ You've already seen what happens when you choose **Codes**. This is how you access the Codes dialog box to insert codes in your search string.

The options on the Action menu tell WordPerfect what to do when it finds the search string in the following cases (see Figure 10.7):

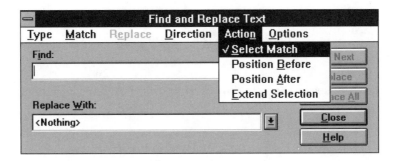

Figure 10.7 *The Action menu.*

❖ **Select Match** is the default. As you saw earlier, WordPerfect selects the search string when it finds it.

❖ Choose **Position Before** if you want the insertion point to end up at the beginning of the search string,

❖ Choose **Position After** if you want the insertion point to end up at the end of the search string.

❖ **Extend Selection** is a fancy way of selecting a block of text. Place your insertion point where you want the selection to begin, press **F2** to open the Find and Replace Text dialog box, type the ending word in the Find text box, and choose **Find Next**. The area from the insertion point to the word you search for is selected. This won't work, though, if the *Wrap* option is selected (I'll get to that in just a bit).

Use the Options menu to tell WordPerfect where to start the search and how much of the document it should include in the search (see Figure 10.8). By default, a search begins at the location of your insertion point and continues to the end or beginning of the document, depending on whether you choose **Find Next** or **Find Previous**.

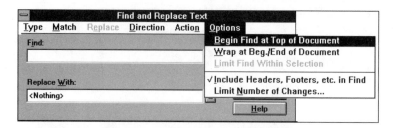

Figure 10.8 The Options menu.

❖ Choose **Begin Find at Top of Document** if you want the search to begin at the top of the document, regardless of where your insertion point is located.

❖ Choose **Wrap at Beg./End of Document** if you want to search the entire document starting from the insertion point location. If you choose **Find Next** with this option checked, Find searches from the insertion point to the end of the document, then wraps back to the beginning and searches to the insertion point location again. If you choose **Find Previous**, Find searches backward to the beginning of the document, then moves to the end and searches back to the insertion point.

❖ You can search a block of selected text by choosing **Limit Find Within Selection**. Make sure the text is selected before you access the Find and Replace Text dialog box; otherwise this option is dimmed. This can really speed things up if you know that what you want to search for is in a particular area of your document.

❖ **Include Headers, Footers, etc**. is checked by default. This means that Find searches through headers, footers, footnotes, endnotes, tables of contents, and most other areas of your document. If you know that what you want to find is in the regular document text, you can speed up your search by unchecking this option.

NOTE

When you open the Find and Replace Text dialog box, the last thing you searched for will be in the Find text box. Since the text or code is selected, as soon as you start typing or choose a code the whole selection disappears—you don't have to delete it first. Also keep in mind that the Find and Replace Text dialog box can end up covering what you want to find. You can just move the box out of the way by dragging its title bar.

You can do two *types* of searches. So far we've been talking about text searches. As you've seen, a text search can include codes, but the codes that you choose from the Codes dialog box are generic. For example, if you insert a **Lft Mar** (left margin) code in a search string, the search will stop every time it finds a left margin code. It doesn't pay any attention to the specific margin setting.

What if you have 89,000 left margin codes in your document and you want to find the one where you changed the left margin to 1.38"? You don't want to stop at every single margin code along the way. A specific codes search is the answer. Let's try it and you'll see what I mean.

Do It

To search for specific codes:

1. Choose **Type** from the pull-down menu on the Find dialog box, as shown in Figure 10.9.

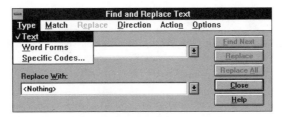

Figure 10.9 *The Type menu.*

2. Choose **Specific Codes**. The Specific Codes dialog box, shown in Figure 10.10, is displayed. You can search for and replace specific settings for any of the codes in this dialog box.

Figure 10.10 *The Specific Codes dialog box.*

3. Select the code you want and choose **OK** or press **Enter.** For this example, I'm choosing **Lft Mar**. (You can also double-click on the code.) The Find and Replace Left Margin dialog box, shown in Figure 10.11, is displayed. The Find and ReplaceText dialog box is replaced by a dialog box that's specific to the code you've selected.

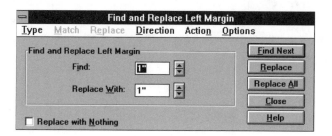

Figure 10.11 *The Find Left Margin dialog box.*

4. Type a setting in the Find box. Using this example, you would type **1.38**.

You can also click on the up or down arrow to the right of the Find text box, or use the **Up** and **Down Arrows** on your keyboard.

NOTE

5. If you want to replace the old margin setting with a new one, just type a setting in the Replace With text box. Or, you can select the **Replace with Nothing** check box if you want to delete the code.

6. Choose **Find Next** or **Find Previous** to start the search.

After you enter a setting for the code, a specific codes search is just like a text search. You can change any of the options on the Action and Options menus (the Match menu is dimmed because none of its options apply to specific codes searches) before you start the search.

You can only search for one specific code at a time. You can't combine specific codes with text or with other codes.

NOTE

Replace

Now you know how to use the Find and Replace Text dialog box to find text. But what about that *Replace* in the title? No problem. If you already know what you want to replace a set of text or codes with, just type a replacement string in the Replace With text box and let WordPerfect do the work for you.

Let's make all of the changes I talked about in the first paragraph of this chapter. No, you don't have to hastily shuffle the pages and reread the beginning of the chapter—I'll walk you through it. First we'll replace *hippopotamus* with *antelope* (and you don't even have to remember how to spell *hippopotamus*).

Do It

To find and replace text:

1. Choose **Find and Replace** from the Edit menu (or press **F2)**.

2. Enter the text or codes you want to search for in the Find text box. For this example, use **hippopotamus**, and include wildcards for the parts you're not sure of.

3. Enter the replacement text or codes in the Replace With text box. Type **antelope** (see Figure 10.12).

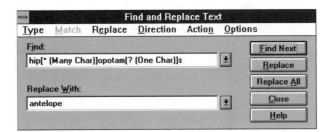

Figure 10.12 *The find and replace strings for our example.*

Don't press **Enter** until you've completed your find and replace strings and made any changes you want on the menus. Notice that Find Next is the default button—as soon as you press **Enter**, WordPerfect tries to initiate a search whether you're ready or not. Click or press **Tab** to move among the text boxes.

SHORTCUT

It's time-consuming to enter all those codes and text. What if you have to suspend this search and run a search for something else (e.g. *rhinoceros*)? To return to your original task, do you have to retype and rearrange everything? Of course not. WordPerfect's right on top of this one. The Find and Replace With text boxes have little down arrows next to them. If you click on one of these arrows, you'll get a *history list* that contains search strings you've already used. To reuse one of the strings, just select it from the list (use the scroll bar to move through the list if the item you want isn't visible).

4. Choose any options you want from the Match and Options menus.

NOTE

Limit Number of Changes lets you narrow the area that's affected. If you're working in a really long document and know that the search string occurs a lot, you can choose this option and enter a number in the box that is displayed to specify the number of times you want to find and replace the search string.

5. Choose **Forward** or **Backward** from the Direction menu.

6. Choose **Find Next**, **Replace**, or **Replace All**.

❖ Choose **Find Next** to locate the first occurrence of the search string.

❖ When you choose **Replace** the first time, it simply finds the first occurrence of the search string. After that, choosing **Replace** searches for and replaces the next occurrence.

❖ Choose **Replace All** to move through your document and replace every occurrence of the search string without stopping.

WARNING

When you're replacing one word with another, be sure you check **Whole Word** (on the Match menu) or you could end up with some weird results. If you don't do this, every time WordPerfect finds the search string it'll replace it, even if the search string falls in the middle of another word. For example, you could enter *bed* as a replacement for *cot* and end up with *apribed*, *bedtage*, and *asbed*. Not a pretty sight.

Refining the Replace Text

When you put your insertion point in the Replace With text box, the Replace menu becomes active (unless Word Forms is selected). This is very similar to the Match menu, with a couple of differences.

❖ There is no Whole Word selection under Match, since the entire Replace With text box is used anyway.

❖ If **Case** is not selected, the first letter of the replacement is capitalized in the document if and only if the first letter of the search string or word was capitalized in the document.

❖ If **Case** is selected, capitalization always appears in the document the same way it does in the Replace With text box.

❖ If **Font** is not selected, the replacement will appear in the document in the same font as the string it replaced.

❖ If **Font** is selected, a dialog box opens up, and you can select the font that the replacement string will use every time it appears in your document.

That's the replace process in a nutshell. You can enter codes in Replace With strings exactly the way you do in Find strings. Specific codes searches also work the same.

NOTE

You can use Replace to get rid of repeated text or codes. If you don't put anything in the Replace With text box and then choose **Replace** or **Replace All**, WordPerfect finds whatever's in the search string and replaces it with nothing. In other words, it's gone. This is really nifty if you have to delete a particular word or code throughout your document. For example, if you want to delete all the bold codes, just insert a **Bold On** code in the Find text box, leave the Replace With text box blank, and choose **Replace All**.

I didn't forget the other search we have to do. Before you move on to explore a Find and Replace goodie, new with WordPerfect 6.1, practice by replacing the italic codes in your sample text with bold. Okay, now you may continue.

Finding and Replacing Word Forms

Check out the Find and Replace Text dialog box once again. Select **Word Forms** from the Type menu. Notice that both the Find and the Replace With text boxes now have little notes underneath them.

What are word forms, anyway? WordPerfect programmers know that many words appear with different endings. For example, the words *walk*, *walks*, *walked*, and *walking* may all appear somewhere in your document. These are just different forms of the word *walk*.

Suppose you're almost finished writing a lengthy article on the Key West Golf Club, and you realize that using the verb *stroll* instead of *walk* would be more flattering to the golfers. The Word Forms option allows you to find and replace all forms of a word with the equivalent forms of another word.

In your golfing document, you could open the Find and Replace Text dialog box, select Word Forms, type **walk** in the Find text box and **stroll** in the Replace With text box. Selecting the **Replace All** button will replace all forms of *walk* with the appropriate forms of *stroll*—and WordPerfect considers capitalization, too (if **Case** is not selected under the Replace menu)! The golfers will be very pleased.

Go To

Want to get quickly to page 162? Don't want to press **Alt+PageDown** 161 times? Use Go To. In addition to moving you at breakneck speed to a specific page, this handy-dandy feature can whisk you to a Bookmark or table (I know, you don't know about Bookmarks or tables yet, but when you do, you'll know how to find them).

There's another neat trick that Go To can perform: It can reselect a block of text. Say you selected some text and made it bold. After you unselect the text and move your insertion point down a ways in the document, you realize you also wanted the text in italics. You don't have to find your way back to the text and reselect it—just choose **Reselect Last Selection** from the Go To dialog box.

Do It

To go to a specific page:

1.   Choose **Go To** from the Edit menu, or click the right mouse button on one of the scroll bars and choose **Go To** from the QuickMenu (or press **Ctrl+G**).

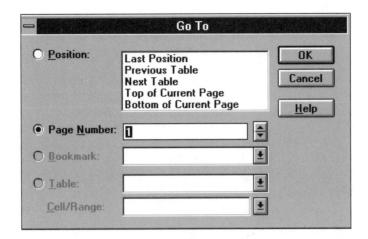

Figure 10.13 *The Go To dialog box.*

2. Select the option you want and choose **OK**.

❖ If you choose **Page Number**, enter the page number you want to move to in the text box.

❖ If you choose **Position**, highlight the position you want to move to. You get different choices in the Position list if you have text selected or if you're in a column or table when you choose Go To.

❖ Choose **Last Position** to move back to your last insertion point location in the document.

❖ If you have bookmarks in your document, you can choose the one you want from the drop-down list.

❖ If your document contains tables, their names appear in a drop-down list.

NOTE

The **Last Position** option can be a lifesaver when you accidentally move to another location in your document. Suppose you meant to press **Ctrl+Right Arrow** to move to the next word, but you pressed **Ctrl+End** by mistake. Now you're at the end of your document and you don't even remember where you were before. Just choose **Last Position** from the Go To dialog box and you're back where you started. If you've typed anything in the meantime, you're out of luck. Once you've entered text or codes anywhere, that's considered your last position.

KEYBOARD

There's a keyboard shortcut that'll get you to your last position even faster. Just press **Ctrl+G**, **Alt+P**, **Enter**. You don't even have to wait for the Go To dialog box to be displayed. This works because **Last Position** is always the first item in the Position list.

Bookmarks

Remember that frantic phone call you got at the beginning of the chapter? Well, now you're back and want to pick up where you left off. Forward-thinking person that you are, you stuck a bookmark in your document before you left, so you can quickly move to the right location. How did you stick a bookmark on a computer screen? Simple, through the magic of modern technology (and those ever-helpful and under-sung WordPerfect programmers).

There are two kinds of bookmarks you can create:

❖ **QuickMark**. This is, as the name implies, a generic quickie. You don't give it a name (actually, *QuickMark* is its name), and you can only have one QuickMark at a time in a document. QuickMarks are ideal for those times when you need to temporarily mark a spot before you leave your document (like the frantic phone call scenario).

❖ **Named Bookmark**. You can have as many of these as you want. When you create the bookmark, you assign it a unique name, and then you can locate the bookmark by its name at any time. Named bookmarks are great for marking areas in a document that need more work or information. For example, you could have a bookmark called *check date* that reminds you that you still need to check the date for an event.

Do It

To create a QuickMark:

1. Place your insertion point where you want the QuickMark.

2. Choose **Bookmark** from the Insert menu, or click the right mouse button on one of the scroll bars and choose **Bookmarks** from the QuickMenu.

3. Choose **Set QuickMark**.

KEYBOARD

Instead of steps 2 and 3, you can press **Ctrl+Shift+Q** to create a QuickMark.

To find a QuickMark:

1. Move your insertion point anywhere *other* than where the QuickMark is located so you can see what happens.
2. Choose **Bookmark** from the Insert menu, or click the right mouse button on one of the scroll bars and choose **Bookmarks** from the QuickMenu.
3. Choose **Find QuickMark**.

KEYBOARD

Instead of steps 1 and 2, you can press **Ctrl+Q** to find the QuickMark.

Turn Reveal Codes on and notice that your insertion point is to the right of the Bookmark code. Move your insertion point to the left of the code—the code expands to show the name of the Bookmark (in this case, QuickMark).

NOTE

You can tell WordPerfect to insert a QuickMark whenever you save a document. Choose **Preferences** from the Edit menu, double-click on **Environment**, and check the **Set QuickMark on Save** box.

Do It

To create a named bookmark:

1. Place your insertion point where you want the Bookmark.

2. Choose **Bookmark** from the Insert menu, or click the right mouse button on one of the scroll bars and choose **Bookmarks** from the QuickMenu (see Figure 10.14).

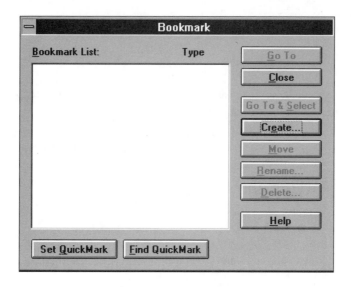

Figure 10.14 *The Bookmark dialog box.*

3. Choose **Create** from the Bookmark dialog box (see Figure 10.15).

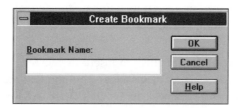

Figure 10.15 *The Create Bookmark dialog box.*

NOTE

You get different choices in the Position list if you have text selected or if you're in a column or table when you choose **Go To**.

4. Enter a name in the Bookmark Name box and choose **OK**.

NOTE

If your insertion point is in front of text when you create a bookmark, a sample of that text is inserted in the Bookmark Name text box. You can use that text if it's descriptive enough for you, or you can replace it with another name.

Do It

There are two ways to find a Bookmark—through the Bookmark dialog box or by using the Go To feature. To find a bookmark with Go To, use the instructions I gave you in the previous section and choose the bookmark you want from the Bookmark drop-down list.

To find a bookmark through the Bookmark dialog box:

1. Choose **Bookmark** from the Insert menu, or click the right mouse button on one of the scroll bars and choose **Bookmarks** from the QuickMenu.

2. Move the selection bar to the bookmark you want to find.

3. Click on the **Go To** button (or press **Enter**).

Not much more to it. A QuickMark stays put until you replace it by setting another QuickMark. Named bookmarks stay where they are until you delete or move them. A bookmark can be deleted or moved just like any other code (there's also a **Move** option in the Bookmark dialog box).

FROM HERE ...

Now that you can use Find and Replace, Go To, and Bookmarks, you can get where you want to go with ease. Combine these features with all the techniques you learned earlier for moving your insertion point, and you'll be able to find the most obscure nooks and crannies in your document.

In the next chapter, you'll learn about WordPerfect's proofreading tools. Before a document is complete, you have to make sure everything's spelled correctly and that your grammar will pass muster. And as a final finishing touch, you can use the Thesaurus to fine-tune those word choices.

WordPerfect 6.1 for Windows

CHAPTER 11

Proofreading Tools

(What? A Mistake?)

Let's talk about:

- ❖ Checking spelling
- ❖ Using QuickCorrect
- ❖ Checking grammar
- ❖ Using the Thesaurus

Without WordPerfect, proofreading can be a really tedious task. You print your document and try to read through it carefully as your eyes slowly glaze over. You puzzle over some unfamiliar words and try to find your dictionary in that pile of books and wonder how the heck you look something up when you don't know how to spell it in the first place. As a last resort, you call your mom to ask about the grammar in that one really funny-looking sentence.

With WordPerfect's proofreading tools, you can let that dictionary molder away in the corner and give your mom some peace and quiet.

In Chapter 1, you got a little taste of WordPerfect's spell checking abilities. In this chapter, we'll explore more spelling options, check out QuickCorrect, and also take a look at Grammatik, the grammar checker that comes with WordPerfect. Finally, we'll look at the Thesaurus, a great writer's tool that helps you find synonyms and antonyms.

WARNING

All of these tools still don't totally take the place of proofing the document yourself. As you saw in Chapter 1, a word can be spelled correctly and still be wrong for the document. And electronic grammar checkers are, at their best, fallible and subject to human interpretation. They give you choices, but you make the final decisions. If your document is important, don't assume that it's perfect just because you've spell checked and used Grammatik. These tools catch a lot of errors and make your proofing job much easier, but in the end, it's still up to you to make sure it's right.

A WORKING TOOL

Type the following paragraph to use in this chapter, "misteaks" and all, and leave it on your screen:

```
Please accept my resination starting right no1. I can't work for
Ms. Crowe. They makes too many misteaks. This upset me me alot.
fFrankly tHis is bad place to work for perfektunist like me. I
ampride of my work.


Sincerly, Sarita Sarelli
```

USING THE SPELL CHECKER

WordPerfect's Spell Checker can check your whole document or specified portions of it. It can even check text that you've entered in a text box inside a dialog box.

When you spell check a document (or a section), WordPerfect checks your text against its main dictionary. It can also check special supplementary dictionaries that you can create and edit.

Do It

To start a Spell Check session:

❖   The easiest way to start a spell check is by clicking the **Spell Check** button on the Toolbar. ▣ You can also start a spell check by choosing **Spell Check** from the Tools menu or pressing **Ctrl+F1**.

❖   The Spell Checker stops at the first word that's not in its dictionary, and the dialog box shown in Figure 11.1 is displayed, with the name of your current document in the Title Bar.

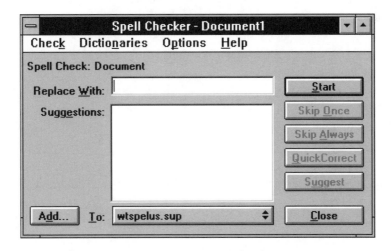

Figure 11.1 *The Spell Checker dialog box.*

❖ By default, the spell check begins automatically. If the default option has been changed, you may have to choose **Start** (or press **Enter**) from the Spell Checker dialog box. If you don't want to spell check the entire document, you can make a selection from the Check pull-down menu shown in Figure 11.2.

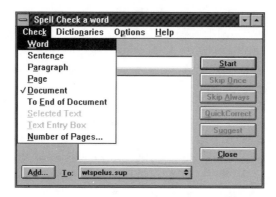

Figure 11.2 *The Check pull-down menu.*

As you can see, you have a lot of choices. These options are really useful if you add text to your document and don't want to check the whole document again. You can check the current word, sentence, paragraph, page, the entire document, or just the text from your insertion point position to the end of the document.

If your insertion point is in a block of selected text when you open Spell Checker, the Selected Text option is available. If it's in a text entry box (in a dialog box), the Text Entry Box option is available. Finally, you can choose **Number of Pages** to check a specified number of pages, starting with the current page.

During a Spell Check

When you start the spell check, WordPerfect stops at the first word it finds that's not in its dictionaries and waits for you to do something. The misspelled word (or at least the word WordPerfect thinks is misspelled) is selected, and there's usually a list of words in the Suggestions list box. In Figure 11.3, The Spell Checker has stopped and selected *resination*, and there are three alternatives in the Suggestions box.

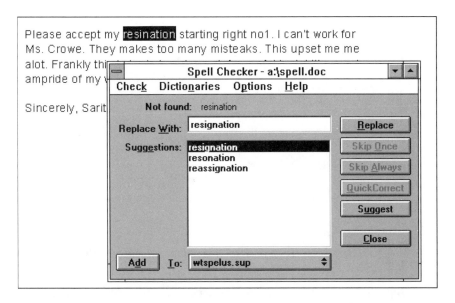

Figure 11.3 *The Spell Checker dialog box during a spell check.*

What do you do? That all depends on what you want to do about the word:

❖   If the word you want is in the **Suggestions** list box, click on it (you may have to use the scroll bar to move through the list if you can't see all the words). The word you select is displayed in the **Replace With** box.

❖   Choose **Replace** to replace the word in your document with the word in the **Replace With** box. For this example, make sure *resignation* appears in the **Replace With** text box, and choose **Replace**.

❖   Choose **Skip Once**, **Skip Always**, or **Add** if the word is spelled correctly but doesn't happen to be in WordPerfect's dictionary. Peoples' names often fall into this category, as well as words that might be specific to your profession.

> ❖ **Skip Once** causes the Spell Checker to ignore the word, but if it finds it again in the document, it stops. *Snowe* is a good example of a word where you would choose **Skip Once**. It's a person's name, and it's spelled correctly, but it's so close to the spelling of a real word that you want to make sure the Spell Checker stops if it sees it again, just in case it's really supposed to be *snow* the next time.

❖ **Skip Always** ignores the word during the current spell check session. Suppose you're writing a letter to Mr. Bartesque. You know you'll never write to him again, so you don't want to add his name to your supplementary dictionary. There's no possibility of his name being mistaken for a regular word, so choose **Skip Always** to bypass any occurrences.

❖ **Add** is an option you will probably use a lot (or at least you should). When you choose **Add**, the word is added to the supplementary dictionary that you choose (more on how you do that in a bit). In the sample text, you would choose **Add** when the Spell Checker stops at *Sarita* and *Sarelli*. She no doubt signs her name to every letter, and she wouldn't want the Spell Checker to stop every time it encounters her name (she has enough to worry about already).

❖ Use the **QuickCorrect** button to replace a word with its associated QuickCorrect entry (QuickCorrect is covered a little later in the chapter).

❖ **Suggest** is an interesting one. You can select one of the words in the **Suggestions** list, which places that word in the **Replace With** box, and then choose **Suggest**. You'll get a list of suggested words that go along with the word you've chosen. Why would you want to do that? Watch what happens when the Spell Checker stops at *misteaks*. Mistake is in the **Suggestions** list, but the plural isn't. Just click on **mistake** and choose **Suggest**, and you'll get a list that now includes the word you want: *mistakes*.

❖ Unless you specify otherwise, Spell Checker stops at duplicate words, words with irregular capitalization, and words with numbers in them. In the sample text, *no1* should be *now*, *THis* should be *This*, the duplicate *me* needs to be deleted (notice that Spell Checker handles this automatically), and *fRanKly* should be *frankly*.

❖ Did you notice Spell Checker did not stop at *alof*? It just automatically corrected it. You'll learn how this amazing feat was accomplished a little later when we talk about **QuickCorrect**.

❖ You can manually edit a word at any time by clicking in the document window. This temporarily pauses the spell check. Do this when you get to *ampride*. Spell Checker suggests it should be two words, but Spell Checker doesn't know the second word is not used correctly in this sentence, so the correct alternative isn't in the **Suggestions** list. Just move your insertion point past the *m* and press the **Spacebar** (leave *pride*, we'll need that later). When you've paused a spell check, the **Replace** button changes to **Resume**. Just click on **Resume** when you're ready to continue. You can also edit a word manually by typing the correct entry in the **Replace With** text box.

NOTE

Don't forget to save your document every time you do a spell check. The changes you make during a spell check can be gone like the wind if anything happens to your computer before you save.

Choosing a Supplementary Dictionary

When you choose **Add** during a spell check, Spell Checker adds the word to whichever supplementary dictionary you select from the **Add To** pop-up list.

WordPerfect comes with two supplementary dictionaries: *Document Dictionary* and *WTSPELUS.SUP*. You can also create additional dictionaries. For example, a law firm might have a separate supplementary dictionary for each case that contains the names of all the parties and any other specific terms.

Editing a Supplementary Dictionary

Words get added to a supplementary dictionary whenever you choose **Add** during a spell check. But you can also add your own words and do some other neat tricks by editing the supplementary dictionary.

Do It

1. Choose **Supplementary** from Spell Checker's Dictionaries menu. The Supplementary Dictionaries dialog box is displayed, as shown in Figure 11.4. It lists the Document Dictionary, WTSPELUS.SUP, and any other supplementary dictionaries you have.

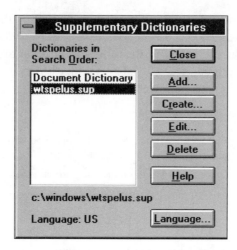

Figure 11.4 *The Supplementary Dictionaries dialog box.*

2. Select the dictionary you want to edit and choose **Edit**. The Edit dialog box for the dictionary you selected is displayed, as shown in Figure 11.5. The Key Words list includes all of the words that you've added to the dictionary. The Skip Word list contains any words or phrases that you've told Spell Checker to skip.

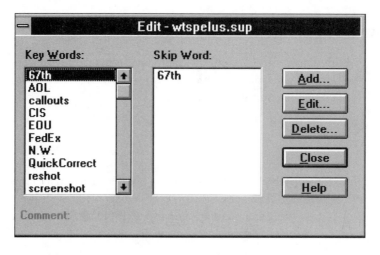

Figure 11.5 *The Edit dialog box for WTSPELUS.SUP.*

NOTE

Go through your supplementary dictionaries from time to time and check for unwanted or misspelled words. It's easy to sit there like a zombie and click that **Add** button during a spell check—you can add a misspelled word without even noticing it.

3. You can delete a word from the dictionary by highlighting it in the **Key Words** list and choosing **Delete**. If the word you delete has a replacement word attached to it, the replacement is automatically deleted, too.

4. Choose **Add** to add a word or phrase to the dictionary. The Add Word/Phrase dialog box is displayed, as shown in Figure 11.6.

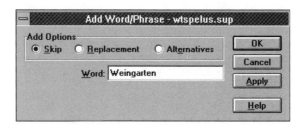

Figure 11.6 *The Add Word/Phrase dialog box.*

❖ Type a word or phrase in the **Word** text box. In Figure 11.6, I've entered my last name.

❖ Choose **Skip.** Press **Enter** or choose **OK** to add the word to the dictionary. From now on this word is skipped when you do a spell check.

❖ Or choose **Replacement** if you want to specify a word or phrase that will replace the word during a spell check. When you choose **Replacement**, a Replacement text box opens up below the Word text box. This feature is terrific if you type the same word or phrase over and over. You can enter an abbreviation in the Word text box and the entire phrase in the Replacement text box. In Figure 11.7, I've set it up so that every time I type **SS**, those letters are replaced by **Sarita Sarelli** when I run a spell check.

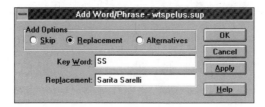

Figure 11.7 *Enter the word you want to use as a replacement in the Replacement text box.*

❖ If you choose **Alternatives**, you can create your own list of alternative words or phrases that show up in the **Suggestions** box when you run Spell Checker. You can even add a comment that appears every time Spell Checker sees a particular word or phrase.

A keyword can have either a replacement word or a list of alternatives. It can't have both.

NOTE

Changing Spell Checker's Options

There's one last item on the Spell Checker menu that's worth a mention—Options. The choices on the Options menu are shown in Figure 11.8, and they let you refine what happens during a spell check.

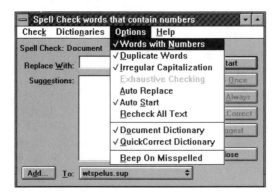

Figure 11.8 *Spell Checker's Options menu.*

❖ **Words with Numbers**, **Duplicate Words**, and **Irregular Capitalization** are checked by default. You can disable them, but I don't recommend it as a general rule. It's too easy to accidentally hit a number key in the middle of a word, type the same word twice in a row, or hold down that **Caps** key just a tad too long. I figure I need all the help I can get during a spell check. The only time I might disable **Words with Numbers** would be in a document with a lot of codes that combine letters and numbers (like parts codes or serial numbers).

❖ **Auto Replace** works hand-in-hand with the replacement feature in the supplementary dictionaries. If you've added a word or phrase that has a replacement word or phrase attached to it, choosing **Auto Replace** means that Spell Checker won't stop there during a spell check—it automatically takes care of the replacement.

❖ **Auto Start** automatically spell checks the document when you open speller.

❖ The **Document Dictionary** can be disabled if you're not using a document-specific dictionary. If you only use WTSPELUS.SUP or your own supplementary dictionaries, you don't need the document dictionary.

❖ **QuickCorrect Dictionary** (which is checked by default), instructs Spell Checker to use your QuickCorrect options during the spell check.

❖ **Recheck All Text** spell checks the entire document. So what, you say? If you've already performed a spell check on a document, subsequent spell checks check only new or changed text unless this option is checked.

❖ **Beep on Misspelled** is for those of you with short attention spans who can't stay awake during a spell check (just kidding—sort of). With this option checked, you'll hear a beep every time Spell Checker stops at a word or phrase.

❖ **Exhaustive Checking** is an option available only when you're doing a spell check in a language other than English

NOTE

When you change any of these options, they stay changed until you change them again. It's not just for the current spell check session. This document's about as spell checked as it can get, but it still has problems. I think it needs to go through the grammar mill.

QUICKCORRECT

The QuickCorrect feature will automatically correct your typing errors, expand abbreviations, and fix spacing and capitalization problems as you type. WordPerfect has already included a whole bunch of the most common typing and spelling errors in the QuickCorrect dictionary, and you can edit the list to fit your specific needs.

Do It

To edit the **QuickCorrect** dictionary:

1. Choose **QuickCorrect** from the Tools menu (or press **Ctrl+Shift+F1).**

2. Type the word or phrase you want to replace in the **Replace** box. QuickCorrect will highlight the word if it's already on the list and allow you to edit or delete the entry (see Figure 11.9).

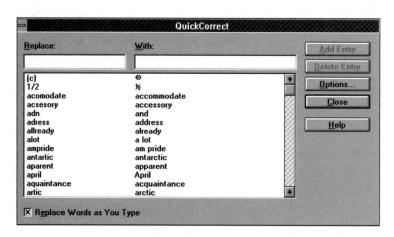

Figure 11.9 *The QuickCorrect dialog box.*

3. **Tab** over to the With box (don't press **Enter** or you'll be dumped back into the document).

4. Type the replacement word, and choose **Add** (or **Enter**—it's okay to use it here). Choose **Close** when you've finished editing the list.

You can also change the defaults for how QuickCorrect handles sentence problems. While in the QuickCorrect dialog box, choose Options and select or deselect to suit your needs. Then choose **OK** and **Close** to return to your document (see Figure 11.10).

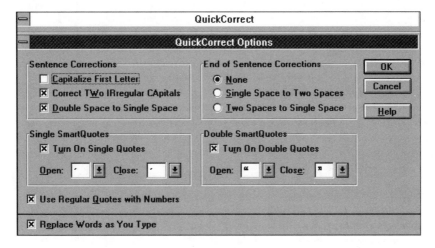

Figure 11.10 *The QuickCorrect Options dialog box.*

CHECKING GRAMMAR

WordPerfect comes with Grammatik 6, its own built-in grammar checker. After you use Spell Checker, you can check your documents for correct grammar.

Do It

To check the grammar in your document:

1. Make sure the paragraph you typed earlier (and just spell checked) is on your screen.

2. Choose **Grammatik** from the Tools menu, or press **Alt+Shift+F1**. The Grammatik dialog box is displayed, with the name of your current document in the Title Bar, as shown in Figure 11.11.

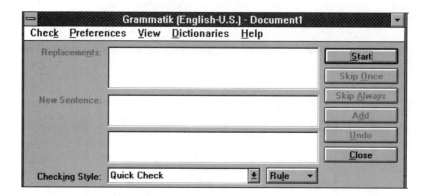

Figure 11.11 *The Grammatik dialog box.*

By default, Grammatik immediately begins to check the whole document. If you have a block of text selected when you choose Grammatik, the default changes to **Selected Text**. And if you're in a dialog box, the default changes to **Text Entry Box.** The Check pull-down menu also gives you the option to check the current sentence or paragraph, or check from the insertion point to the end of the document.

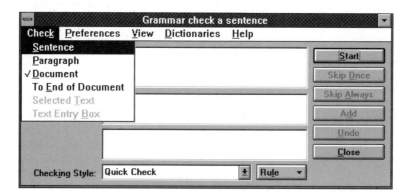

Figure 11.12 *Grammatik's Check pull-down menu.*

The **Preferences** pull-down menu provides options for predefined Checking Styles to tailor proofreading for that document, and **Environment** options to specify how you want Grammatik to work for you. We'll talk about that a little bit later.

During a Grammatik Session

When you start a Grammatik session, Grammatik checks your document against a built-in set of rules for grammar and writing style. (Later I'll show you how you can tell Grammatik which set of rules you want to use.) Grammatik stops at the first questionable word or phrase, gives you some options, and waits for you to make a choice. We'll move through the paragraph and take a look at how Grammatik works.

In the sample paragraph, the first place Grammatik stops is on *accept.* Figure 11.13 shows the Grammatik dialog box at this point. Grammatik tells you which rule class it's using, gives a short explanation, and displays any suggested alternatives in the replacement box.

Grammatik will even give you a grammar lesson. Move your mouse pointer over any of the underlined words or phrases in the explanation box. You can tell when this will work because a question mark bubbles out of the mouse pointer. Just click the left mouse button to display a Help window for the rule class, word, or phrase. Close the Help window when you're done reading.

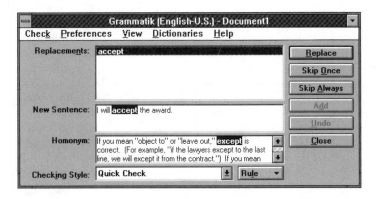

Figure 11.13 *The Grammatik dialog box during a grammar check.*

❖   *Please accept* is actually correct grammar, but since *except* can also be used as a verb, Grammatik can't be sure which you really mean. This is a good example of the inherent shortcomings of a grammar checker. It can only check against a set of rules. It can't read your mind.

❖ Because *Please accept* is correct, choose **Skip** to move on to the next problem, choose **Next Sentence** to ignore any other possible problems in that sentence, or choose **Ignore Phrase** if you don't want Grammatik to stop on the particular phrase again during this session.

❖ You can turn off all the rules for this Grammatik session by selecting **Turn Off** from the Rule drop-down list. Turning off rules can save you time and frustration. It can get really annoying when Grammatik keeps stopping on words and phrases you know are correct. Turning off a rule is better than throwing a shoe at your monitor.

❖ The next problem Grammatik finds is what it thinks is a spelling error: *Crowe*. By default, Grammatik checks for spelling errors using the same main dictionary as Spell Checker, and any supplementary dictionaries you might have created. (It stopped on *Crowe* because we didn't add it to a dictionary.) You probably won't want Grammatik to recheck the spelling if you've already spell checked the document. I'll show you how to disable spelling before you start a session when we get to the **Preferences** section.

❖ What's next? Hey, a real error! Grammatik stops at *makes*, as shown in Figure 11.14. In this case, Grammatik's suggested replacement, *make*, is correct. Choose **Replace**.

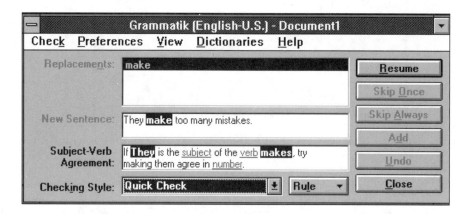

Figure 11.14 *Grammatik flags* makes *as an error in subject-verb agreement.*

What's this? We're done? Judging from Figure 11.15, I guess that's it.

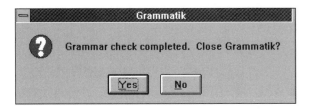

Figure 11.15 *This dialog box is displayed at the end of a Grammatik session.*

❖ Choose **No** for now so the Grammatik window stays on your screen.

But what about the last three sentences? Grammatik didn't even stop. *This upset me a lot* should be *This upsets me a lot*, *this is bad place* should be *this is a bad place*, *for perfectionist* should be *for a perfectionist*, and *I am pride of* should be either *I am proud of* or *I take pride in*. These examples show, once again, that Grammatik won't catch everything. It can't possibly know, for example, whether you meant for *upset* to be in the present or past tense.

Grammatik (and any grammar checker) can help, and you can maximize its usefulness to you by adjusting the options covered in the next section, but, as you've seen from this short sample, it's not magic. Are you getting tired of me repeating that yet? Good. Remember it.

Changing How Grammatik Works for You

Click on **Preferences** and select **Environment**. The Environment dialog box is displayed, as shown in Figure 11.16.

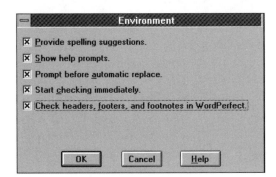

Figure 11.16 *The Environment dialog box.*

❖ **Provide spelling suggestions** can be toggled on or off. When it's off, Grammatik won't stop when it finds a mistake in spelling.

❖ The **AutoReplace** feature works here just like it does with Spell Checker. Choose **Prompt before automatic replace** if you want to verify the replacement text.

❖ You can choose to Start checking immediately, as well as Check headers, footers and footnotes.

❖ **Show help prompts** will display help information in the title bar.

Choosing a Writing Style

You can turn Grammatik into a more useful tool by setting its options to reflect your writing style as closely as possible. Click on **Preferences** and choose **Checking Styles.** The dialog box shown in Figure 11.17 appears

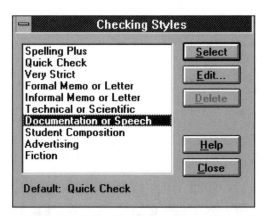

Figure 11.17 *The Checking Styles dialog box.*

There are 10 writing styles to choose from. In addition, you can create custom writing styles as needed. The selection you make here determines what set of rules Grammatik will use. You can adjust and edit these styles to suit your preferences. You might want to choose different styles for different kinds of documents. For example, you could use the *Documentation or Speech* style for your annual report, and *Fiction* for that short story you're writing during your lunch hours.

Editing a Writing Style

If you like a particular writing style but it still flags too many correct choices, you can edit it so it flags only the rules you want it to.

Do It

1. In the Checking Styles dialog box, move the selection bar to the style you want to edit and choose **Edit**. Figure 11.18 shows the Edit Rules - Quick Check dialog box. An **x** next to a rule means that rule will be used during a Grammatik session.

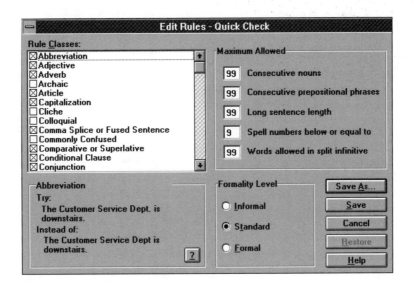

Figure 11.18 *Settings for the Quick Check style.*

2. Click on a selection to turn a rule on or off. You can also use the **Up** or **Down Arrow** key on your keyboard to move to a rule, and then press the **Spacebar** to toggle the selection on or off.

    Notice that the **Standard** radio button is selected under Formality Level. Grammatik checks your document based on the level selected. For example, *can't* would be acceptable for an informal or standard document, but Grammatik would question its use in a formal document.

❖ Click on the question mark in the Abbreviation area for an explanation of how Grammatik handles abbreviations.

❖ The Maximum Allowed options tell Grammatik where you want to start flagging certain parts of speech. For example, the *99* next to *Consecutive Nouns* means that Grammatik will stop whenever it sees more than 99 nouns in a row.

3. Change any of the numbers you want.

4. Choose **Save** or **Save As** to save the edited writing style.

Grammatik has some grammar lessons included in its Help screens. Just choose **Writing** from the Grammatik's Help Contents window. You'll get a list of topics to choose from. There's even a reading list.

NOTE

USING THE THESAURUS

Between Spell Checker, Grammatik, and a little judicious proofreading of your own, everything in your document is correct. But have you always used the most effective words to get your points across? For that finishing touch, use WordPerfect's Thesaurus.

Do It

To start the Thesaurus:

1. Place your insertion point anywhere in the word you want to look up.

2. Choose **Thesaurus** from the Tools menu, or press **Alt+F1**.

The Thesaurus dialog box is displayed, with the name of your current document in the Title Bar. Type **work** in the Word text box and click on **Look Up**.

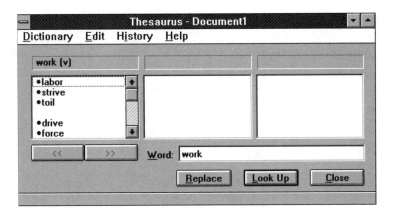

Figure 11.19 *The Thesaurus dialog box.*

The word is identified at the top of the column by its speech part. Notice that it says *(v)* after work. That means that the words in the list are all verbs. Since work can also be a noun, scroll down the list to find where the nouns begin (the v at the top changes to an *n* when you get to that point). If the word has any antonyms (opposites), they're shown at the bottom of the list. Just scroll all the way to the bottom to see them.

Maximizing the Thesaurus window can save you a lot of scrolling and make it easier to work with Thesaurus. Just click on the **Maximize** button in the upper-right corner of the window.

Replacing a Word

If you see a word you like better than the one in your document, Thesaurus can make the replacement for you:

1. Choose the word you want in one of the word lists. Notice that the selected word appears in the Word text box.

2. Choose **Replace**.

Looking Up a Word

You can look up additional words while the Thesaurus dialog box is open:

1. Type the word you want to look up in the Word text box, or double-click on the word in your document to select it.

2. Choose **Look Up**. If the word is a headword, a new list of words is displayed.

If there isn't a list of words in the first column, that means the word you want to look up isn't a headword. A *headword* is a word that has a list of related words in the Thesaurus. In the word lists, headwords have bullets next to them. You can double-click on any headword to get a list for that word.

When you try to look up a word that's not a headword, a *Word not found* message appears in the lower-left corner of the Thesaurus window. When you open Thesaurus, part of the window is often hidden at the bottom of the screen, so you might not see this message. You can fix that by either maximizing the Thesaurus window (which I recommend) or moving the window up a bit.

❖ The History menu has a list of all the words you've looked up during the current session. Choose any of the words to open up its list.

❖ You can keep looking up as many words as you want while the Thesaurus window is open.

❖ The Thesaurus is a great tool for playing what if. If you want to find a more precise word for a particular situation, just look it up. If you don't find what you're looking for right away, try looking up some of the other headwords on the list. You can often find just the right word by probing down a few layers in Thesaurus.

FROM HERE ...

This chapter gave you a set of tools to check and fine-tune your writing. Just remember that none of them takes the place of your own proofreading efforts. Have I repeated that often enough yet? You'll avoid a lot of errors if you spell check every single document (and don't forget to save after spell checking).

Then spell check whenever you make changes (remember, you don't have to check the whole document—you can easily check just the portion of the document that you've changed). Use Grammatik if it aids in your writing efforts. Edit the rule classes so that it's a help rather than a hindrance. And remember Thesaurus for those agonizing word choices.

After all of this heavy-duty proofreading stuff, it's time for some fun. In the next section, you'll get to cut loose and play around a little (or a lot). The fun starts in the next chapter, where we look at all the different ways you can change the way your text looks. There's even a terrific feature, TextArt, that lets you change text into all sorts of strange shapes and styles.

WordPerfect 6.1 for Windows

SECTION III

DRESSING UP
FONTS AND
GRAPHIC ELEMENTS

CHAPTER 12

A Look at Fonts

(Typecasting and Character Development: The Secret World of Fonts)

Let's talk about:

- ❖ What are fonts?
- ❖ Using the Font Toolbar
- ❖ Using the Font dialog box
- ❖ Inserting special characters
- ❖ Adding drop caps to text
- ❖ Having fun with TextArt

Let's make this a multiple choice quiz. My trusty *Webster's Dictionary* gives me two definitions for font. Which one do you think applies here?:

1. "A receptacle for baptismal or holy water."
2. "An assortment of printing type of one size and style."

If you chose 2, step to the head of the class. (If you chose 1, go back to the beginning of the book and read every chapter twice.) Yes, we are talking about the text that you see on your screen and on the printed page. *Font* is just a fancy word for the size and shape of your text.

There's one more term you need to be familiar with before we move on: *point size*. The point size just tells you how tall the font is. A point is 1/72 of an inch, so a 12-point font (which is a standard size for business documents) would be 12/72 of an inch tall. You'll often see a font listed something like this:

Century Gothic Regular 12 pt

Century Gothic is the name of the font (WordPerfect calls this the *font face*) and describes a particular typestyle. *Regular* is what WordPerfect refers to as the *font style*. The same font can come in several different styles. For example, Century Gothic comes in regular, bold, italic, and bold italic; and *12 pt* is the point size. There. Now you know how to decipher a font listing. You'll see a lot of in this chapter. Figure 12.1 shows an assortment of fonts, styles, and point sizes.

Century Gothic Bold 8 pt   C G Times Regular 12 pt

Commercial Script Normal 18 pt

Old Town Normal 30 pt

Times New Roman 40 pt

Arial Regular 58 pt

Figure 12.1 *An assortment of fonts.*

Can I Do All of This?

Yes, depending on your printer's capabilities. WordPerfect comes with about two billion fonts (I might be exaggerating just slightly), and you might have even more that come with your printer. You can do everything you see in Figure 12.1 and much, much more. You can change fonts whenever you want, and you can enhance their appearance by adding attributes like bold, double underline, and shadows.

NOTE

You can buy more fonts that come either on disks that you install or cartridges that you insert in your printer, but unless you have really specialized needs, the fonts you get with WordPerfect should be plenty. I used to use extra fonts, but I never need them anymore.

Just keep in mind what I mentioned in Chapter 7 (when we played with bold, italic, and underline) about the ransom note school of design. With all of these riches at your disposal, it's easy to get carried away with too many different sizes and styles. Be judicious—try to stick to one or two typestyles for a document, and be consistent and careful with sizes and attributes. (If you really are writing a ransom note, don't pay any attention to this advice.)

Special Font Power Tools

WordPerfect makes it simple to change fonts and everything associated with them. You've already used some font power tools. Did you know that when you used the bold, italic, and underline Toolbar buttons in Chapter 7, you were actually changing font attributes?

Power Bar Buttons

There are two more buttons for changing the font face and the font size:

❖ The **Font Face** button lists all of your available fonts. Just click to choose one (note that the last four fonts you used are at the top of the list).

❖ The **Font Size** button lists several common point sizes. Again, just click to choose the one you want.

Font Toolbar

Remember in Chapter 3 when I showed you all of the different Toolbars that come with WordPerfect? The Font Toolbar, displayed in Figure 12.2, makes it possible to do most of your fancy font work without getting near a dialog box. And if you do need to go to the Font dialog box, there's a button for that too.

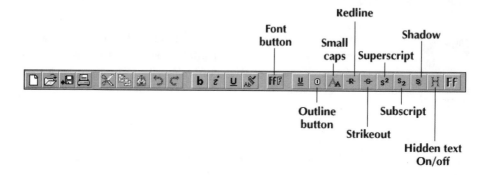

Figure 12.2 *The Font Toolbar.*

❖ Switch to the Font Toolbar now by clicking the right mouse button anywhere on the Toolbar and choosing **Font**. Keep the Font Toolbar displayed for the rest of this chapter, and use it when you're doing a lot of work with fonts—it can be a real timesaver.

Where do I Put the Font Code?

The same rules apply whether you're changing a font's face, size, or appearance. You can insert the code before you start typing or apply it to text that's already there. There are just a few things to know:

❖ The code stays right where you put it. Font codes aren't affected by Auto Code Placement.

❖ The code affects everything from the insertion point location forward. So, if you insert a code to change your font size to 16 point, all of the text after the code will be 16 points until you change it to something else.

❖ If you want the font change to affect a particular section of text, select the text before you insert the code. Using the 16 point example, if you select text before you choose the font size, WordPerfect inserts a 16 point code in front of the text and a code for whatever size you were using before that at the end of the selected text.

Knowing these rules, all you have to do is put your insertion point where you want it (or select a block of text) and choose a font face, size, or attribute from the Power Bar or Toolbar. If you want to do several things at once, use the Font dialog box.

Using the Font Dialog Box

The Font dialog box makes it easy to change a lot of font settings at once. Everything's in one place—just make the selections you want and choose **OK**.

❖ Click on the **Font** button.

❖ If the Font Toolbar is not active, you can double-click on the **Font Face** or **Font Size** button on the Power Bar, press **F9**, or choose **Font** from the Format menu.

The Font dialog box is displayed, as shown in Figure 12.3.

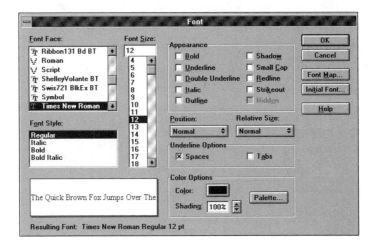

Figure 12.3 *The Font dialog box.*

❖ Choose a font from the **Font Face** list.

❖ Choose a size from the **Font Size** list or type a number in the Font Size text box. The Font Size list only includes whole numbers, so if you want an odd point size (like 12.5), you have to enter it yourself.

❖ If the font face you choose comes in more than one style, make a choice from the **Font Style** list.

❖ Choose any of the Appearance options you want.

❖ Choose **Superscript** or **Subscript** from the Position pop-up list. Superscript characters appear slightly smaller and above the regular text[1] (like the number at the end of the word *text*). Subscript characters appear slightly smaller and below the regular text (like H_2O).

❖ Make a choice from the Relative Size pop-up list to increase or decrease the font size relative to your current font instead of picking a specific size. You can choose from **Fine**, **Small**, **Normal**, **Large**, **Very Large**, and **Extra Large**. This can be handy if you want to make a section of text slightly larger or smaller than the rest but don't know exactly what size to pick.

Take some time to play with the different choices.

NOTE

As you make selections in the Font dialog box, the Resulting Font box shows you how the font will look with those settings. The full font name displays just below the Resulting Font box. Keep an eye on this area as you make changes—you'll always have a good idea of the final result before you leave the Font dialog box.

There are a few more options on the Font dialog box that need a little extra explanation.

Underline Options

By default, when you use the *Underline* or *Double Underline* attributes, WordPerfect underlines the spaces between words, but spaces created by tabs aren't underlined. You can change either of these options by checking or unchecking the **Spaces** and **Tabs** boxes in the Underline Options area. Figure 12.4 shows text with these options at different settings.

By default, WordPerfect underlines spaces between words

But you can tell it not to

Chapter 1   My Book   The tab on this line is not underlined.

Chapter 1   My Book   On this line it is.

Figure 12.4 *Text with different underline options.*

Color Options

You can use this option to change your text to different colors. You can get some great effects by playing with these settings. Just remember that if you don't have a color printer, none of these changes will translate to the printed page—you're stuck with boring old black and white.

NOTE

Until you become a WordPerfect wizard, ignore the **Font Map** button. It has to do with editing and customizing font settings and changing how fonts interact with your printer. You have enough to deal with for now.

Initial Font

When you start a new document, WordPerfect uses whichever font has been selected as the Printer Initial Font for the printer you're using. You can override that for a particular document by choosing **Initial Font** from the Font dialog box and selecting the font you want. You can also choose **Document** from the main Format menu and then choose **Initial Font** from the cascading Document menu. The Document Initial Font dialog box is displayed, as shown in Figure 12.5.

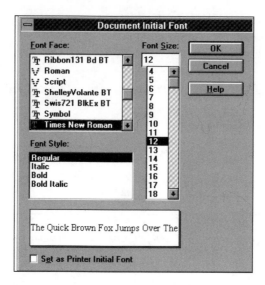

Figure 12.5 *The Document Initial Font dialog box.*

The initial font is used for your document text (until you insert a new font code) and for areas like headers, footers, footnotes, and graphics captions (again, unless you choose another font for those areas).

❖   The **Font Face**, **Font Size**, and **Font Style** lists work exactly the way they do in the Font dialog box. Make the choices you want and choose **OK**.

❖   If you want the font you choose to be the initial font for all documents you create from now on, check the **Set as Printer Initial Font** box.

Redline and Strikeout

These two items are in the Appearance area, which I mentioned earlier, but I want to tell you a little about what they do. *Redline* and *strikeout* are features that are usually used for editing documents. The terms come from the old printing days, where an editor would draw a line through (strike out) text that was supposed to be deleted, and add new text in red pencil (redline). The whole process is called *redlining*.

When you choose **Strikeout**, the text has a line through it, as if it's been crossed out. **Redline** actually makes the text red on your screen. Unless you have a color printer, however, redlined text usually prints with a shaded box around it.

NOTE

There's a feature called **Compare Document** that can take the place of manual redlining in most cases. You can make your changes, save the document with a different name, and then use **Compare Document** to compare and mark the differences. **Compare Document** is found on the File menu.

Using Special Characters

In addition to all of the regular font choices, WordPerfect comes with a bunch of special characters (everything from musical notes to the entire Greek alphabet) that act just like text and can be inserted anywhere in a document. It's really simple. Figure 12.6 uses a couple of these special characters.

You can ✂ through the red tape and learn WordPerfect in no ☺ at all.

Figure 12.6 *Special characters can be inserted anywhere in a document.*

Do It

To insert a special character:

1. Place your insertion point wherever you want the special character to be.

2. Choose **Character** from the Insert menu or press **Ctrl+W**. The WordPerfect Characters dialog box is displayed, as shown in Figure 12.7.

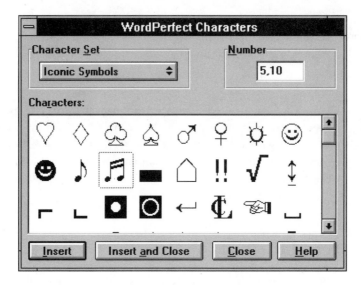

Figure 12.7 *The WordPerfect Characters dialog box.*

NOTE

This keyboard shortcut, **Ctrl+W**, is a good one to remember. It gives you instant access to all of the special characters.

Notice the numbers in the upper-right corner of the dialog box in Figure 12.7. Every WordPerfect character has its own number. The first number identifies the character set, and the number after the comma identifies the character itself. In Figure 12.7, the musical notes in the Iconic character set are selected, and the number in the box is 5,10. That means that the Iconic symbols are set number 5, and the musical notes are the tenth character in that set. If you happen to know the character set and number for a particular symbol (they're all listed in the manual that came with your WordPerfect software), you can enter it in the Numbers box.

3. Select **Character Set** to choose the set in which your character is located.

4. Next, select **Characters**. As you use the mouse or the arrow keys to move around in the display, you will notice a dotted box surrounding the

currently selected character. Highlight the character you need, and then click on **Insert and Close** to return to your document. However, if you need to insert more than one character at the same insertion point, double-click the mouse, click on **Insert**, or press **Enter** to put the character in your document and remain in the dialog box.

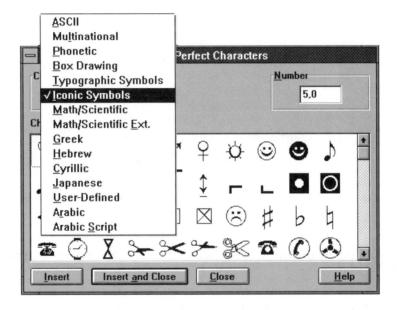

Figure 12.8 *Each of these character sets includes a group of special characters.*

WordPerfect Characters act just like regular characters. If you choose a larger font size for your text, any special characters that are included in the text also change size.

NOTE

What's a Drop Cap?

Use the Drop Cap feature to enlarge the first character, letters, or words of a paragraph. Drop caps are commonly used at the beginning of book chapters, and can be an effective way to enhance announcements or stationery.

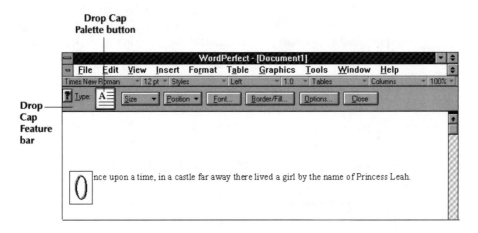

Figure 12.9 *Be creative with Drop Cap.*

Do It

To create a drop cap:

1. Choose **Drop Cap** from the Format menu or press **Ctrl+Shift+C**, then begin typing. If you have already typed the item you want drop capped, just place the insertion point anywhere within the paragraph, then select **Drop Cap**. The Drop Cap feature will automatically enlarge the first character of that paragragh.

2. Click the **Drop Cap Palette** button ⒜ from the feature bar to choose one of the various styles and sizes offered. It's here that you would also come to turn off the drop cap feature by clicking the **NO CAP** button.

3. You may customize the Drop Cap by clicking the **Size**, **Position**, **Font**, or **Border/Fill** buttons.

4. Click the **Option** button if you want the Drop Cap feature to affect more than just one letter.

5.   Click **Close** when you are finished editing your Drop Cap.

Introducing TextArt

TextArt is a terrific feature that lets you perform amazing stunts and contortions on your text with the greatest of ease. Instead of spending a lot of time talking about it, take a look at Figure 12.10 to see what I mean. I did all of these in about two minutes. Really. I've used other programs that can do similar things with text, but *none* of them is as easy (or so much fun).

TextArt is really a graphics feature, so I should wait until the next chapter to show it to you, but it does relate to text and fonts, and it's just too cool for words—I couldn't wait!

Figure 12.10 *A small taste of TextArt's possibilities.*

Do It

To use TextArt:

1.   If the Font Toolbar is still on your screen, switch back to the 6.1 WordPerfect Toolbar. Hey look, TextArt has its own button 🔳 .

2.   Click on the **TextArt** button (or choose **TextArt** from the Graphics menu). The TextArt window is displayed, as shown in Figure 12.11.

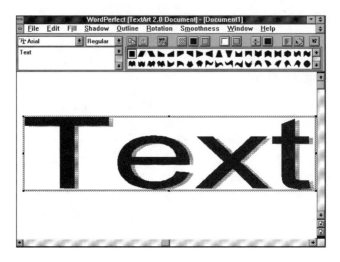

Figure 12.11 *The TextArt window.*

3. Type your text in the box. (For now you can use the sample word *Text* that's already there if you want.)

4. When you click on one of the shapes, the text in the preview box changes to match the shape you've chosen, as shown in Figure 12.12.

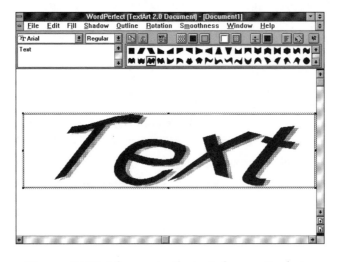

Figure 12.12 *Like magic, the text changes its shape.*

What can you do to the text besides change its shape?

❖ Create TextArt in any of your available fonts by choosing a font from the Font drop-down list.

❖ Make the text bold, italic, or bold and italic by choosing an option from the Font Attribute drop-down list.

❖ Change the thickness or color of the text's outline by clicking on the **Text Outline Width** or **Text Outline Color** button (or choosing **Width** or **Color** from the Outline menu).

❖ Choose different patterns and colors to fill the text by clicking on the **Text pattern**, **Text pattern foreground color**, or **Text pattern background color** button. (You can also choose **Pattern**, **Foreground Color**, or **Background Color** from the Fill menu.

❖ Add a shadow behind the text in your choice of color. Click on the **Shadow position** button to display a palette of shadow options and click on the one you want. (You can also choose **Type** from the Shadow menu.) To change the shadow's color, click on the **Shadow color** button or choose **Color** from the Shadow menu.

❖ Adjust the rotation angle of the text by clicking on the **Rotate** button, and then dragging one of the rotation handles.

❖ Adjust the smoothness of the text edges by making a choice from the Smoothness menu.

Go ahead—play around in here for a while. Choose different shapes and options and observe the results. And when you're done …

Exiting TextArt

Nothing to it. When you're finished with your masterpiece (for the moment anyway), just click anywhere outside the image box. The TextArt menus disappear, and the TextArt becomes part of your WordPerfect document.

It might not be the size you want, and it might not be in the right location, but it is a regular WordPerfect graphics box that you can size and move around just like any other graphics box. The only problem is, you haven't learned how to do that yet. Patience, patience. We'll take care of that in the next chapter.

NOTE

You can't save a TextArt object as a separate document. If you want to use a piece of TextArt in another document, select it and copy it to the Clipboard.

FROM HERE …

With what you learned in this chapter, you can really start to wow your friends and colleagues with your expertise and ability to turn out professional-looking documents. Not only can you change fonts at will, you can use special characters and drop caps to add some flair. And you can perform incredible feats with text, twisting it into every shape imaginable at the touch of a button.

There's more to come. In the next chapter, you'll learn how to include graphic images (pictures) in your documents. And you don't even have to be an artist—WordPerfect graciously provides the pictures.

CHAPTER 13

Working with Graphics

(Warning: This Chapter Contains Graphic Images)

Let's talk about:

- ❖ Creating an image box
- ❖ Moving and sizing a graphics box
- ❖ Editing a graphics box

You got a little taste of graphics in the last chapter, with TextArt. TextArt actually turns your text into a graphic image, then places that image inside a graphics box when you bring it into WordPerfect.

As you'll see in this chapter, the possibilities with graphics boxes are almost unlimited. You can use graphics to get your newsletters, reports, and memos noticed. You can even turn that boring old set of numbers into a pie chart that dramatically makes your point. This chapter doesn't tell you everything you can do with graphics in WordPerfect—there's just too much. It does cut right through the confusion and gets you going quickly. And I'll point you in the right direction for further exploration.

Let's get one thing straight right at the start—a graphics box is a graphics box is a graphics box. Got it? You can eliminate a lot of confusion by realizing that all graphics boxes in WordPerfect are the same. It doesn't matter whether you call it an image box, equation box, TextArt, or a text box—it's the same animal and you treat it the same way.

The only thing that's different is its contents, and you do have different editing options depending on what's in the box. If you try to edit the contents of a box that has TextArt, you'll be taken back to the TextArt dialog box. If you edit a box that has text in it, you use a special text editor to change the text, and there are specific options for editing images.

It's easy to be overwhelmed by all of the choices on the menus and the Toolbar. There's a button for an Image and one for TextArt. On the Graphics menu, you can choose from **Image**, **Text Box**, **Equation**, **Custom Box,** or **TextArt**. So why all the choices if there really isn't any difference between them?

Just think of the different box styles as shortcuts. Each type of graphics box comes with its own default style and set of options, but you can change anything about any of the box types. You can even create your own custom styles. For example, an Image box has single borders all the way around, and WordPerfect initially assumes that you will put a graphic image (or picture) into it, but you can put text, an equation, a table (or any other WordPerfect object) into an image box. Figure 13.1 shows an image-style box with its default options, and Figure 13.2 is the same box with a couple of options changed.

Figure 1 Just Horsing Around

Figure 13.1 *By default, an image-style box has no borders or shading, and the caption (if you use one) is displayed at the bottom left.*

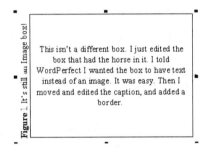

Figure 1 It's still an Image box!

This isn't a different box. I just edited the box that had the horse in it. I told WordPerfect I wanted the box to have text instead of an image. It was easy. Then I moved and edited the caption, and added a border.

Figure 13.2 *This is still an image-style box—I didn't have to do anything special to change it.*

I'm belaboring this point now to make it easier for you down the road. When you see buttons for different types of boxes or a list of different box styles, just think of them as starting points. Once you place a graphics box in a document, you can move it or change its size, borders, contents, and other options too numerous to mention here.

As we work through this chapter, I'll talk about image boxes and text boxes, and refer to other box styles. Each style gives you different options while you're creating it—just remember you use the same methods for editing and working with a graphics box, whatever it's called.

The next section gives you a running start with graphics. We'll take advantage of the shortcut button WordPerfect provides for creating an image box.

CREATING AN IMAGE BOX

WordPerfect makes it really easy to bring an electronic image (often called *clip art*) into a document.

Do It

1. Click on the **Image** button 🖼 on the Toolbar. You can also press **F11**, or choose **Image** from Graphics menu. The Insert Image dialog box, as shown in Figure 13.3, contains a list of all of the graphics that are included with WordPerfect.

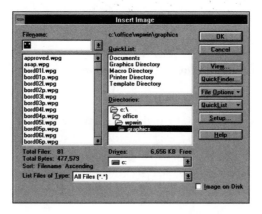

Figure 13.3 *The Insert Image dialog box.*

As you can see by scrolling through the file list, there's quite a selection (including a lot of fancy borders). These images were copied to your graphics directory when you installed WordPerfect. They all have an extension of WPG, which stands for *WordPerfect Graphic*. You can list and retrieve the files for any other clip art you have on your computer by switching to the appropriate directory. (If you don't know how to do that, see Chapter 15, "Managing Files and Directories.")

2. Select the file you want to use and choose **OK**. or double-click on the filename. For this example, choose **DRAGN.WPG**.

NOTE

If you're not sure which file you want, choose **View** from the Insert Image dialog box to open up the Viewer, as shown in Figure 13.4. You can see what the different images look like by moving the selection bar in the file list. When you find the one you want, just choose **OK** in the Insert Image dialog box.

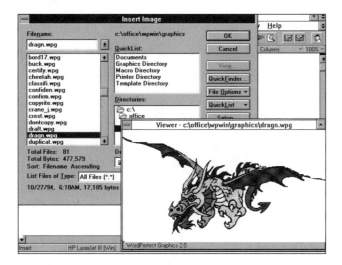

Figure 13.4 *The Insert Image dialog box with Viewer open.*

As soon as you choose **OK**, the image you selected is placed in your document, as shown in Figure 13.5. Notice that there are little black boxes around the box—they're called *handles*—that appear whenever you select a graphics box, and you'll use them later to change the size of the box. There's also a special Graphics Feature Bar just below the Power Bar (or below the Ruler if it's visible)—we'll get to all of its options later too.

Figure 13.5 *DRAGN.WPG in a default image box.*

3.   Choose **Close** from the Feature Bar. The handles disappear, and the graphics box is part of your document. We'll play with it in a bit.

The image on the screen started out as a default image box. By the end of this chapter, we'll move and transform it. You'll change its borders, its size, what's inside, and just about everything else. Read on.

Dragging to Create an Image Box

You can tell WordPerfect where to position your box and how big to make it before choosing its contents by using the **Drag to Create** feature.

Do It

1.   Choose **Drag to Create** from the Graphics menu. If you see the box that gives you information about Drag to Create, just choose **OK**. A check mark is placed in front of the **Drag to Create** command and this option remains in effect until it's deselected by choosing **Drag to Create** from the Graphics menu again.

2.   Click on the **Image** button on the Toolbar. You can also press **F11**, or choose **Image** from the Graphics menu. The mouse pointer looks like a hand holding a box.

3.   Move the mouse pointer to the location of your screen where you want to begin creating your image box, then press the left mouse button and drag diagonally until the box is the desired size, as shown in Figure 13.6.

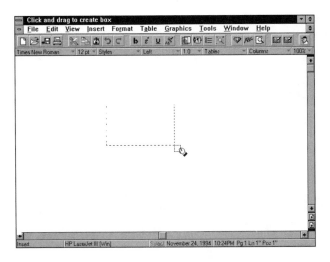

Figure 13.6 *Dragging to create a box.*

4. Release the mouse button—the Insert Image dialog box appears so you can choose the image to place in the box.

You can use the Drag to Create feature to position and size any of the graphic box types. Using Drag to Create, you're just making the size and position choice before choosing the contents.

NOTE

Creating a Custom Box

In addition to the Image, Text, and Equation boxes available from the Graphics menu, WordPerfect provides several other box styles in the Custom Box dialog box. Remember, only their default attributes—which can all be changed—differentiate one box style from another. The predefined box styles are just shortcuts that save you from having to specify all of your box's attributes.

Do It

1. Choose **Custom Box** from the Graphics menu. The Custom Box dialog box appears, as shown in Figure 13.7.

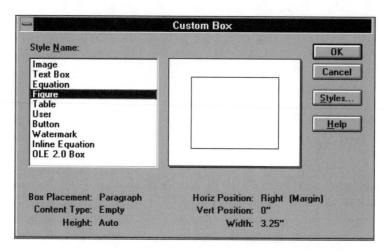

Figure 13.7 *The Custom Box dialog box with the Figure style highlighted.*

2. Move the selection bar to choose the box style you want to use. Notice the border style in the preview section of the dialog box to the right of the Style Name list. The attributes for the selected style are displayed at the bottom of the dialog box.

3. Click on **OK** to accept your choice and place the box in the document. After placing a custom box in the document, you need to add something to it, such as text, an image, an equation, or whatever. You may also want to add a caption, borders, and change other elements of the box. The easiest way to do this is by editing the box using the Feature Bar, as you'll see later in the chapter.

Selecting and Deselecting Boxes

Selecting a box is the first step for almost anything you want to do with a graphics box. You select the box and then you do something to it. Then when you're done, you deselect the box.

Do It

1. Click on the graphics box you want to select. You can tell that a box is selected when it has handles (the little black boxes) around it. There isn't a super simple keyboard shortcut for selecting a graphics box. If you only have one graphics box in your document, choosing **Edit Box** from the Graphics menu (or pressing **Shift+F11**) selects the box. But if there's more than one box, you have to specify the box number after you choose **Edit Box**.

NOTE

If you haven't gotten a mouse yet, **do it now**. I'll tell you keyboard shortcuts for editing graphics, but a mouse is the only way to fly with graphics. The next two sections really show you what I mean. Without a mouse, you don't have a simple way to move and size your graphics on the screen. And lots of other options that can be changed in a snap with the mouse require going through layers of dialog boxes with the keyboard.

2. Click anywhere outside a graphics box to deselect it.

Moving a box and changing its size are probably the two things you'll want to do right away with almost every box you create, so let's get right to it. You'll be pleased to find that it's really easy.

MOVING A GRAPHICS BOX

Okay, this is really complicated, so listen up:

1. Select the box you want to move and place your mouse pointer anywhere inside the box. The mouse pointer will turn into a four-headed arrow.
2. Drag the box wherever you want it and release the mouse button.
3. Deselect the box.

Yeah, that's all there is to it. While you drag, the handles disappear and you'll see a dashed outline of the box, as shown in Figure 13.8.

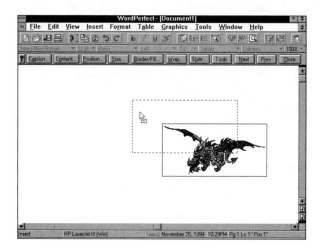

Figure 13.8 *A graphics box being dragged to a new location.*

Make sure you don't grab a handle by mistake. You can tell you've got a handle because the mouse pointer is a two-headed instead of a four-headed arrow. The handles are for resizing the box, as you'll see shortly. If you accidentally resize or move a box, just use **Undo** before you do anything else.

NOTE

SIZING A GRAPHICS BOX

Changing a box's size is as easy as dragging a handle.

1. Select the box you want to resize.

2. Move your mouse pointer over one of the handles. Notice that the pointer turns into a two-headed arrow.

3. Drag the handle in the direction you want to make the box larger or smaller. Drag a corner handle if you want to change the height and width at the same time. While you drag, the handles disappear and a dashed border shows you the new dimensions.

4. When the box is the size you want, release the mouse button.

5. Deselect the box.

Figure 13.9 shows what a little draggin' did to our dragon.

Figure 13.9 *That's a big dragon!*

DELETING A GRAPHICS BOX

Yeah, sometimes you just want to get rid of the box altogether. No problem. There are two ways to delete a graphics box. I recommend the first one—it's easier, and you don't have to worry about deleting the wrong box.

1. Select the box you want to delete and press the **Delete** key, or

2. When you create a graphics box, a box code is inserted in Reveal Codes. You can delete the box code just like any other WordPerfect code. Turn on Reveal Codes, place your insertion point before the box code and press **Delete** (or after the code and press **Backspace**). If you have more than one graphics box in your document, make sure you're deleting the right code.

EDITING A GRAPHICS BOX WITH THE FEATURE BAR

Use the Feature Bar to make most editing changes to a graphics box. The Feature Bar is displayed when you first create a graphics box. When I told you how to create image boxes, I had you close the Feature Bar after you created the box. But you can leave the Feature Bar on your screen—instead of closing the Feature Bar, just click anywhere outside the graphics box. The graphics box is deselected, and the Feature Bar stays on your screen.

❖ If you only have one graphics box in your document, choosing an item from the Feature Bar automatically selects the graphics box and activates the features you have chosen. If you have more than one graphics box in your document, you must select the box you want before you choose an option from the Feature Bar.

❖ To open the Feature Bar if it's not on your screen, select a graphics box, click the right mouse button anywhere inside the box, and choose **Feature Bar** from the QuickMenu. You can also choose **Edit Box** from the main Graphics menu, but you can't have a box selected when you use this technique.

The following sections go through the options on the Feature Bar in sequence. Before you continue:

❖ Make sure the Feature Bar is visible.

❖ Select the graphics box that contains our friendly dragon.

To choose a Feature Bar option with the keyboard, hold down **Alt+Shift** while you press the underlined key for that option. For example, to choose **Caption**, press **Alt+Shift+A**.

Adding a Caption

1. With the graphics box selected, choose **Caption** from the Feature Bar. The Box Caption dialog box appears, as shown in Figure 13.10.

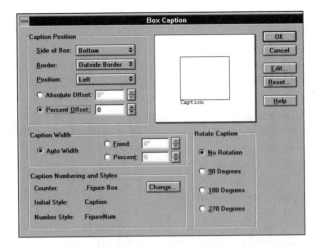

Figure 13.10 *The Box Caption dialog box.*

Don't worry about all of the confusing-looking options. I'll go over most of them, but if you want a default caption below the box, the only option you need to deal with is the **Edit** button.

2. Choose **Edit**. The Box Caption dialog box closes and your insertion point moves below the box. Notice that the Title Bar tells you that you're in the Caption Editor. This is another one of those special areas that's not really part of your main document text.

To accept the default options for the caption, you can bypass the Box Caption dialog box by choosing **Create Caption** from the Graphics QuickMenu. This takes you right to the Caption Editor where you can type your text.

NOTE

3. Type whatever text you want for your caption. Press **Backspace** to delete the default text if you don't want it included (that's the text that says Figure 1 for this box). This text is actually a code, so the whole thing disappears at once when you press the **Backspace** key.

That's really all you have to do to create a caption. Anytime you want to edit the caption, choose **Edit Caption** from the Graphics QuickMenu or from the Box Caption dialog box.

NOTE

As you try different options, the sample display area shows you what the results will be. If you don't know what an option does, just try it out before you leave the dialog box.

Before we leave captions, take another look at the Box Caption dialog box (you can refer back to Figure 13.10). Here are a few other things you can do with your captions:

❖ You can change the position of a caption by changing the selections in the Caption Position area. **Side of Box** lets you place the caption on the top, bottom, right, or left of the box. **Border** lets you place the caption inside, outside, or on the border. **Position** lets you align the caption with the left or right edge of the box, or center it between the box margins.

❖ You can rotate the caption. Figure 13.11 shows a caption placed on the left side of the box, centered between the margins, and rotated 90 degrees.

Figure 13.11 *You can change the position and placement of the caption.*

❖ You can adjust the width and change the numbering style used for the caption. Normally, you can use the default settings in these areas.

❖ You can delete the caption by choosing **Reset**. When you choose **Reset**, all of the caption options return to their defaults, and the caption text is deleted.

Changing the Box Contents

I told you before that you could put whatever you want in a graphics box. Here's how you do it.

Do It

Follow these steps if you just want to replace the current graphics image with another one.

1. Choose **Content** from the Feature Bar or the QuickMenu. The Box Content dialog box is displayed, as shown in Figure 13.12. Notice that the Content drop-down box displays Image as the contents.

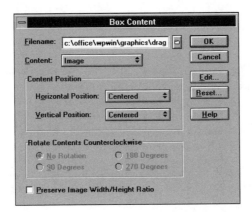

Figure 13.12 *The Box Content dialog box.*

2. Click on the file folder button next to the Filename text box.

3. Choose the image you want from the Select File dialog box and choose **OK**. (You can choose **View** to open the Viewer if you want to preview the image before you select it.) Then choose **OK** again in the Box Contents dialog box. Choose **Yes** when you're asked if you want to replace the current box contents.

The new image is displayed in the box, as shown in Figure 13.13.

Figure 13.13 Same box, same caption, different image.

Do It

Follow these steps to change the box contents entirely.

1. From the Box Content dialog box, choose an option from the Content drop-down list. A box can have the following contents:

   ❖ **Empty:** this isn't really contents, but sometimes you might want to use an empty graphics box as a placeholder in a document.

   ❖ **Image:** a graphics image.

   ❖ **Text:** this can be regular text, columns, or a table. You can type the text directly in the box as you did earlier or retrieve a previously created file.

   ❖ **Equation:** WordPerfect comes with a full-featured Equation Editor. When you choose **Edit** after choosing this option, you are taken into the Equation Editor where you can create your equation.

   ❖ **Image on Disk:** use this option to reduce the size of your documents that use graphics. Instead of retrieving the graphics image into your document, this option just tells WordPerfect to find the image when you print.

2. If you chose text or equation, choose **Edit** to insert text or an equation into your box.

What else can you do from the Box Content dialog box?

❖ You can change the position of the contents within the box.

❖ If the box contains text, you can rotate the text within the box.

❖ Choose **Preserve Image Width/Height Ratio** to make sure that the contents stay in proportion when you resize the box.

NOTE

Here's one more item you might see on the Contents drop-down list: **OLE Object**. This means that the image or object was created or edited in another program. OLE stands for *object linking and embedding*, and it's a way that Windows can link data between programs. Anything that you create in TextArt ends up as an OLE Object in WordPerfect. In addition, anything that you create or edit in WP Draw (see the following warning) becomes an OLE Object. I'm telling you all this mainly so you don't get freaked out when you see that strange-looking word. You don't really have to do anything about it.

WARNING

This is actually part caution, part enticement. WordPerfect comes with its own drawing program, WP Draw, that you can use to create your own drawings and make all sorts of fancy changes to the WordPerfect images (and any other clip art images you might have). That's the good part. The caution is that it's really easy to end up in WP Draw by mistake when you're working with graphics boxes. For example, choosing **Edit** from the Box Content dialog box opens WP Draw. So does double-clicking on a graphics box. If you see a Title Bar that says WP Draw, and that's not where you want to be, just choose **Exit** from its File menu (just the way you would exit any other program). Chapter 27 contains a short introduction to WP Draw.

Box Position—Changing the Anchor Type

You already moved your box with the mouse. The **Position** option lets you make precise position settings and decide how you want the box to move in relation to its surrounding text. Let's get into the dialog box and I'll explain what that means.

1. Choose **Position** from the Feature Bar or the QuickMenu. The Box Position dialog box is displayed, as shown in Figure 13.14. Depending on the type of box you have selected, the options you see might look different than those in Figure 13.14.

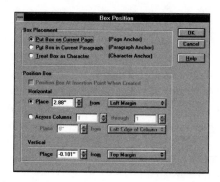

Figure 13.14 *The Box Position dialog box.*

2. Choose one of the Box Placement options.

3. Enter selections in the Position Box area (the options vary depending on the box type).

So what was that all about? Did you notice the word *anchor* next to each of the Box Placement choices? You can anchor (or attach) a graphics box to a page, a paragraph, or a character. Here's what happens with each option:

❖ **Page:** the box stays on the current page no matter what else you do to the page. You can add or delete text and the box stays put—it's anchored in an absolute position on the page.

❖ **Paragraph:** the box acts just like a text paragraph (or it can be part of a paragraph that contains text). If you insert a hard return in front of the box, it moves down. If you insert a hard page break, the box moves to the next page.

❖ **Character:** the box is treated just like a text character (no matter how big the box is). If you add text on the same line in front of the box, the box wraps when it reaches the right margin.

Changing the Size

You changed the size of a box with the mouse by selecting a box and dragging the handles. If you want to specify precise dimensions, you can use the Size dialog box.

1. Choose **Size** from the Feature Bar or the QuickMenu. The Box Size dialog box is displayed, as shown in Figure 13.15.

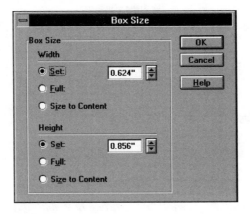

Figure 13.15 *The Box Size dialog box.*

2. Choose the settings you want:

    ❖ Choose **Set** and type a number in the text box to specify a size.

    ❖ Choose **Full** if you want the box to take up all of the space between the margins. If you choose **Full** for both Width and Height, the box fills the page. If the box is inside a column or table, the box will fill the column borders or the current cell.

    ❖ Choose **Size to Content** to allow the size to adjust automatically depending on the contents of the box. If you want your image to stay in proportion, make sure you choose **Size to Content** for either Height or Width. If you specify set measurements for both Height and Width, you can end up with a distorted image.

Adding Borders and Fills

You can have a lot of fun with this option. This is where you can change and customize the borders and add shading or fill patterns inside the box.

1. Choose **Border/Fill** from the Feature Bar or the QuickMenu. The Box Border/Fill Styles dialog box is displayed, as shown in Figure 13.16.

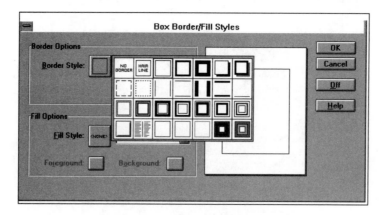

Figure 13.16 *The Box Border/Fill Styles dialog box, with the Border Style palette open.*

2. Choose the kind of border you want from the Border Style palette. In Figure 13.16, the palette is opened so you can see the choices.

3. If you want shading or a fill pattern, make a choice in the Fill Options area.

❖ You can specify one of the percentage fill options from the drop-down list. These fill the box with a shaded background. The higher the percentage fill, the darker the shading. *Tip:* 10% Fill is usually just about right if you have text in the box (you don't want the fill so dark that you can't see the text).

❖ You can also choose from 29 predefined fill patterns on the Fill Style palette. Figure 13.17 shows you the Fill Styles palette.

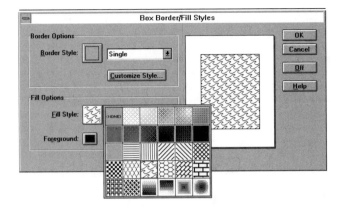

Figure 13.17 *You can choose any of these patterns to fill your box.*

In Figure 13.18, I changed the border style and added a fill pattern.

Figure 13.18 *This box uses the Shadow border style and the Waves fill pattern.*

NOTE

Remember to use the sample display area to preview your choices. As you move the selection bar through different options in the drop-down lists, you can see what the option will look like.

NOTE

Any selections you make in this dialog box apply to all four borders, and you're limited to WordPerfect's predefined options. Choose **Customize Style** if you want to really let loose. From the Customize Border dialog box, you can change the style of each line separately, adjust where a shadow will appear and how it will look, add rounded corners, and a whole lot more. You can even change the settings for any of the line styles. For example, if you don't like the width that WordPerfect chose for Extra Thick Single lines, you can change it.

Changing How Text Wraps Around the Box

By default, text flows around the borders of a box on the left or right, depending on where there's more room. If your graphics box is at the left margin, the text would flow around the right side, and vice versa. The box in Figure 13.19 uses the default wrap options. The way the text flows is called *text wrap*.

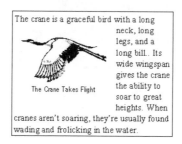

The crane is a graceful bird with a long neck, long legs, and a long bill.. Its wide wingspan gives the crane the ability to soar to great heights. When cranes aren't soaring, they're usually found wading and frolicking in the water.

The Crane Takes Flight

Figure 13.19 *The wrapping type for this box is square, and text is wrapped around the largest side.*

To change the text wrap:

1. Choose **Wrap** from the Feature Bar or the QuickMenu. The Wrap Text dialog box is displayed, as shown in Figure 13.20.

Figure 13.20 *The Wrap Text dialog box, set to its default options.*

2. Select one of the radio buttons to choose a Wrapping Type. The pictures next to each option show you what the results will be—they're a little cryptic, so I'll explain:

❖ **Square** follows the borders of the box.

❖ **Contour** actually wraps text around the shape of whatever's in the box. This one's the most fun, as you can see from Figure 13.21. When you choose this option, the box borders disappear.

❖ **Neither Side** means that text won't appear to the left or right of the box. It wraps from above the box to below, not around it.

❖ **No Wrap** prints text right through the box—it doesn't wrap at all. Be careful with this because your text can easily get lost behind an image.

3. Choose one of the Wrap Text Around options. Depending on which Wrapping Type you choose, some of these options might be dimmed. The little pictures for this one are pretty self-explanatory.

Figures 13.21 through 13.23 show the same image and text as Figure 13.19 with different wrap options.

Figure 13.21 *Contour text wrap around largest side.*

Figure 13.22 *Wrapping type is set to Neither Side.*

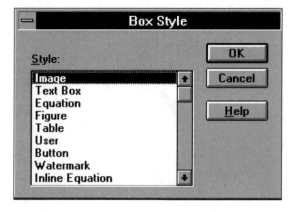

The crane is a graceful bird with a long neck, long legs, and a long bill.. Its wide wingspan gives the the ability to soar to great heights. When cranes aren't soaring, the usually found wading and frolicking in the water. When these birds try to catch fish in lakes and rivers, they

The Crane Takes Flight

Figure 13.23 *This is set to No Wrap—the text displays right through the box.*

Changing the Box Style

You can change the default style options for a box. Remember, these options don't have anything to do with what's in the box—they just affect things like borders and fill and the location of the caption.

NOTE

If you've already changed the lines, fill, or caption placement, picking a different style option might not have any effect. Any custom choices you make take precedence over the default style.

1. Choose **Style** from the Feature Bar or the QuickMenu. The Box Style dialog box is displayed, as shown in Figure 13.24.

Figure 13.24 *The Box Style dialog box.*

2.   Choose the style you want, then choose **OK**.

As you can see, this dialog box doesn't give you any visual cues to tell you what the different choices do. Because of this, and because these options aren't as flexible as the other editing choices, as a general rule it's easier to change the specific settings you want. For example, if you want to change the border lines, do it through the Box Border/Fill Styles dialog box instead of here.

There is, however, one really useful option here. By choosing **Watermark**, you can reduce the intensity of any image so that it displays as background behind your text. In Figure 13.25, I took our graceful crane and chose **Watermark** from the Box Style dialog box. That's all I did. (Okay, I also made him a little larger and moved him to the center of the text.)

> The crane is a graceful bird with a long neck, long legs, and a long bill. Its wide wingspan gives the crane the ability to soar to great heights. When cranes aren't soaring, they're usually found wading and frolicking in the water. When these birds try to catch fish in lakes and rivers, they|

Figure 13.25 *The crane appears as background for the text.*

ROADMAP

There's a special Watermark feature that you can use to "stamp" text or images on every page. I'll talk about it in the next chapter.

Using the Image Tools Palette

The **Tools** button only appears on the Feature Bar if your box contains an image and a box is selected. This button is the gateway to changing the appearance of the image within a box. I'll describe and show some of the possibilities, but the best way to find out what you can do is just to play with the Image Tool palette.

1. Choose **Tools** from the Feature Bar or **Image Tools** from the QuickMenu. The cute little Image Tools Palette shown in Figure 13.26 pops up next to the selected box.

Figure 13.26 *The Image Tools palette.*

2. Choose a tool by clicking on its icon.

3. Make any changes you want with the tool.

These instructions are purposely vague because the choice of tools and the possible variations are almost unlimited. To see what each tool does, move your mouse pointer over its icon and look at the Help Prompt on the Title Bar.

Figure 13.27 shows an image as it originally appears, and Figures 13.28 through 13.30 give you an idea of some of the possible mutations you can put it through.

Figure 13.27 *CHEETAH.WPG as it originally appears in a figure-style box.*

Figure 13.28 *You can flip the image from right to left with the Mirror Vertical tool. Notice that the cheetah is now facing to the left instead of right.*

Figure 13.29 *Use the move and scale tools to move and size the image with the box.*

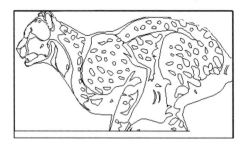

Figure 13.30 *I used scale to make the image bigger, then used an option from the Fill Attributes tool to turn the image into an outline.*

Moving Between Graphics Boxes

If you have more than one graphics box in your document, you can use the **Next** and **Previous** buttons on the Feature Bar to move between them. **Next** selects the box after the currently selected box. **Previous** selects the box that precedes it.

This option can be especially helpful if you've layered boxes on top of each other. It can be hard to click in just the right place to select the box you want. **Next** and **Previous** let you cycle among all of the boxes in your document, even if they're hidden behind several layers.

FROM HERE ...

This chapter gave you a taste of what you can do with graphics, but it's only the beginning. As you sharpen your skills, you'll continually discover more and more facets to this powerful feature. When you are comfortable with the basics of working with graphics boxes, take a look at WP Draw. You will be amazed with what you can do there (Chapter 27 introduces you to this program).

In the next chapter, you'll learn how to add graphics lines and borders to your text, and how to place a watermark image on every page (just like a header or footer).

CHAPTER 14

Working with Borders, Graphics Lines, and Watermarks

(Head for the Border, or What's My Line?)

Let's talk about:

- ❖ Creating page borders
- ❖ Creating paragraph borders
- ❖ Adding graphics lines
- ❖ Moving and sizing graphics lines
- ❖ Editing graphics lines
- ❖ Adding a watermark

❖   Editing a watermark

Want to place a quick border around every page of a document? Or around one paragraph to make it stand out from the rest? Or highlight a section of text by adding a vertical or horizontal line? Or stamp *Top Secret* on every page without using a messy stamp pad that gets ink all over your fingers? You can do all of the above in about the time it took me to write this paragraph.

As we go through this chapter, a lot of it will seem familiar to you. You can apply a lot of the same options to borders, lines, and watermarks that you can to graphics boxes. In some places you might wonder why you would want to use one of these features when you could just create a graphics box. I'll point out the benefits of using each feature as we get to it.

Before you continue, open LONGDOC.WPD (that's the document you created several chapters ago) or any other document that's more than a page long.

BORDERS

The Borders feature is a handy way to put a border around pages, paragraphs, and columns. You can use any of the line styles and fill patterns that are available for graphics boxes. There are two main differences between borders and graphics boxes:

1.   When you turn a border on, it stays on until you turn it off. That means you can create a border once and have it appear around every page of your document. To do the same thing with a graphics box, you would have to create a separate graphics box on each page, or put the graphics box in a header or footer.

2.   Graphics boxes can be customized in many more ways than borders. As you've seen, you can change their size, move them around, and do all sorts of other things to them. You have more limited options with borders— they're either around a page, a paragraph (or paragraphs), or columns.

It's easy to see how the first difference can be an advantage, but why would you want fewer options in a feature? In a word, to make your life easier. Okay, that was five words, but who's counting?

To get a full-page border around a page with a graphics box, you have to create a box, choose border options, adjust the height and width so the box fills the page, and change the text wrap options so your text can print in the same location as the box. To do the same thing with a border, you just turn the border on and decide which line and fill styles you want to use. Simple.

Having just told you why you want to use the Borders feature instead of graphics boxes, there's one exception: If you want to use one of the fancy clip art borders that comes with WordPerfect (or use other clip art for your border), you have to use a graphics box. You can't use clip art with the Borders feature.

NOTE

Do It

1. Make sure your insertion point is on the page where you want the border to start.

Auto Code Placement moves page border codes to the top of the current page.

NOTE

2. Choose **Page** from the Format menu, then choose **Border/Fill** from the cascading Page menu. The Page Border dialog box is displayed, as shown in Figure 14.1. This dialog box works just like the Box Border/Fill Styles dialog box you used to select border options for graphics boxes. You can make choices from the Border Style and Fill Style palettes (you open the palette by clicking on the button next to the item) or use the drop-down lists. I'd much rather use a palette—it's easier to pick from a picture than a name on a list. From the keyboard, press the **Tab** key until the **Border Style** or **Fill Style** button is selected, then press the **Spacebar** to open the palette.

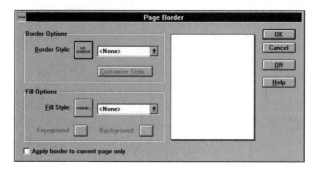

Figure 14.1 *The Page Border dialog box.*

3. Choose the Border Style you want.

4. Choose a Fill Option if you want any shading or fill inside the border.

5. If you want the border to appear only on the current page, check **Apply Border to Current Page Only**. For now, go ahead and uncheck it so you can see what happens.

6. Choose **OK** when you've changed all of the options you want.

Choose **Customize Style** to change settings for individual lines, add a drop shadow, adjust the spacing between the text and the lines, or round the corners of the borders.

NOTE

Figure 14.2 shows page 1 of LONGDOC.WPD with a page border added.

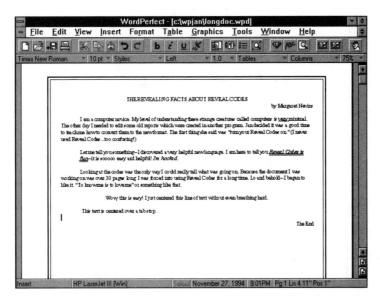

Figure 14.2 *I've added the Thick/Thin 2 border style to LONGDOC.WPD.*

Now, press **Alt+PageDown** to move to page 2. Hey, there's a border on this page too! The border is on every page until you turn it off.

Do It

To turn off a page border:

1. Place your insertion point on the page where you want the border to stop.

2. Choose **Page** from the Format menu, then choose **Border/Fill** from the cascading Page menu.

3. Choose **Off**.

NOTE

This doesn't just turn the border off for the current page—it cancels it for the rest of the document. There's no way to suppress a border for just one page like there is for headers, footers, and watermarks.

Do It

To create a paragraph border:

1. Place your insertion point anywhere in the paragraph where you want the border to start. If LONGDOC.WPD is on your screen, place your insertion point in the paragraph that begins with *Let me tell you something.*

2. Choose **Paragraph** from the Format menu, then choose **Border/Fill** from the cascading Paragraph menu. The Paragraph Border dialog box is displayed. Except for the title, it's exactly like the Page Border dialog box in Figure 14.1.

3. Choose the Border Style you want.

4. Choose a Fill Option if you want any shading or fill inside the border.

5. For this example, let's apply the border to just the one paragraph, so make sure **Apply Border to Current Paragraph Only** is checked.

6. Choose **OK** when you've changed all the options you want.

Figure 14.3 shows LONGDOC.WPD with a single border around one paragraph.

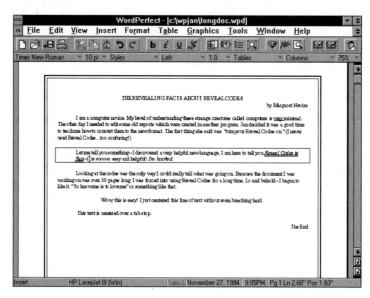

Figure 14.3 *I've added a single paragraph border to the second paragraph.*

Turning Off a Paragraph Border

If the paragraph border extends for more than one paragraph, you can turn it off by moving your insertion point into the paragraph where you want the border to stop and choosing **Off** from the Paragraph Border dialog box. If you apply a paragraph border to existing text, you don't have to worry about turning the border off. WordPerfect just places the border around the selected paragraph or paragraphs.

ROADMAP

You can also create borders around columns. You use pretty much the same techniques, but I'll cover column borders a little more in Chapter 18 when I show you how to use columns.

GRAPHICS LINES

Graphics lines are like graphics boxes in a lot of ways. You can drag them wherever you want, drag handles to change their size, and change the style of the line. The main difference is that there isn't anything inside a line. The careful addition of a line here and there can add clarity and definition to your documents.

There are two kinds of graphics lines: *horizontal* and *vertical*. The only difference is that one goes from left to right and the other goes from top to bottom. In fact, as you'll see, you can easily change a horizontal line to vertical, and vice versa.

Do It

If you just want a single line that stretches from the top to the bottom margin or from the left to the right margin, WordPerfect makes it really easy for you: choose **Horizontal Line** or **Vertical Line** from the Graphics menu. Or press **Ctrl+F11** for a horizontal line, or **Ctrl+Shift+F11** for a vertical line.

Voila! The lines appear on your screen. The vertical line is at the left margin, and the horizontal line is on the line where your insertion point is located. I'll show you a little later how you can move, size, or edit the lines.

Do It

If you want to specify a location, size, line style, or any number of other settings for your line, you can create a custom line.

It really doesn't matter whether you start with the line on your page and then edit it, or choose your settings first by creating a custom line. A line can be edited at any time, so do it whichever way works best for you.

1. Choose **Custom Line** from the Graphics menu. The Create Graphics Line dialog box is displayed, as shown in Figure 14.4.

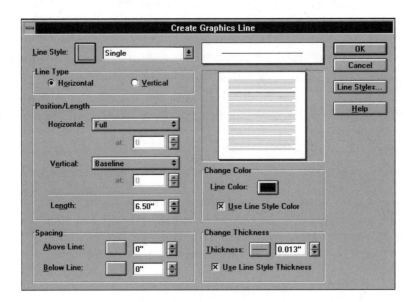

Figure 14.4 *The Create Graphics Line dialog box.*

2. Make a choice from the Line Style palette (or the **Line Style** drop-down

list). These are the same choices you have for borders and graphics boxes.

NOTE

The **Line Styles** button (just below **Cancel**) lets you customize the line styles.

3. Choose **Horizontal** or **Vertical** from the Line Type area.

4. Make selections in the Position/Length area to specify the location and size of the line.

5. Make any changes you want to the spacing, color, and thickness of the line.

6. When you've changed all of the settings you want, choose **OK**.

Depending on whether you choose a horizontal or vertical line, you have different options for Position and Spacing.

Position and Spacing Options for Horizontal Lines

Following are the horizontal positions:

❖ **Full:** the line takes up all the space between the left and right margins. The Length setting automatically changes when you choose **Full**.

❖ The line can be **Left**, **Right**, or **Centered** in relation to the left and right margins.

❖ **Set:** the line begins at whatever position you enter in the **at:** text box. The position is measured from the left edge of the page. **Set** gives you precise control over the placement of lines.

Following are the vertical positions:

❖ **Baseline:** this positions the line where the bottom of a line of text would be at your insertion point location.

❖ **Set:** you can choose **Set** and then enter a measurement in the **at:** text box to place the line a precise distance from the top edge of the page.

❖ **Length:** enter a specific measurement for the line.

Following is the spacing option:

❖ You can move the line a certain distance above or below the baseline by entering an amount in the **Above Baseline** or **Below Baseline** text box.

Position and Spacing Options for Vertical Lines

Following are the horizontal positions:

❖ The line can be at the left or right margin or centered between the margins. It can also be positioned after a specific column.

❖ **Set:** you can choose **Set** and then enter a measurement in the **at:** text box to place the line a precise distance from the left edge of the page.

Following are the vertical positions:

❖ **Full:** the line takes up all of the space between the top and bottom margins. The length setting automatically changes when you choose **Full**.

❖ You can align the line with the top or bottom margin, or center it between the top and bottom margins.

❖ **Set:** the line begins at whatever vertical position you enter in the **at:** text box. The position is measured from the top of the page.

❖ **Length:** enter a specific measurement for the line.

Following is the spacing option:

❖ Enter a number in the **Border Offset** text box to move the line a specified distance from the left or right margin. If the line is at the left margin, the line moves to the left of the margin. If the line is at the right margin, it moves to the right.

Figure 14.5 shows LONGDOC.WPD with a horizontal line above the title and a vertical line next to *The End.*

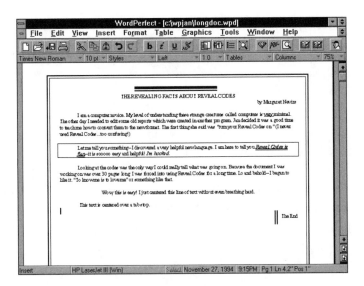

Figure 14.5 *I changed the position, line style, and length for these lines.*

Moving a Graphics Line with the Mouse

1. Select the line you want to move.

2. Place your mouse pointer on top of the line until the pointer turns into a four-headed arrow.

3. Drag the line wherever you want it and release the mouse button.

Not much else to say about this.

NOTE

Selecting a line can be a little trickier than selecting a box, since a line is a much smaller target. Watch your mouse pointer as you move over the line. When it changes from the I-beam shape to an arrow, that's when you can click to select the line.

Sizing a Graphics Line with the Mouse

You change the size of a graphics line by dragging a handle, just like you do with graphics boxes.

1. Select the line by clicking anywhere on it.

2. Move your mouse pointer over one of the handles. Notice that the pointer turns into a two-headed arrow.

3. Drag the handle in the direction you want to make the line longer or shorter. You can also drag a handle up or down (for a horizontal line) or left or right (for a vertical line) to make the line thicker or thinner.

4. When the line is the size you want, release the mouse button.

5. Deselect the line.

Editing a Graphics Line

When a graphics line is selected, you can click the right mouse button on the line to bring up a QuickMenu. Choose **Edit Vertical Line** or **Edit Horizontal Line** (the option that is displayed on the QuickMenu depends on which kind of line is selected). The Edit Graphics Line dialog box is displayed. It's just like the Create Graphics Line dialog box—you can change anything you want about the line.

You can also choose **Edit Line** from the Graphics menu. If you have more than one graphics line in your document, this brings up the Edit Graphics Line dialog box for whichever line code is just past your insertion point.

NOTE

If you only have a few graphic lines in your document, the easiest way to access the Edit Graphics Line dialog box is to double-click on the appropriate Graph Line code in Reveal Codes.

Deleting a Graphics Line

You can delete a graphics line by selecting it and pressing **Delete,** or by deleting its code in Reveal Codes.

WATERMARKS

A watermark (which can include text or graphics) prints in a lighter shade so it appears as background behind your document text. In the last chapter, I showed you an example of a graphics box that used the Watermark style. Using the Watermark feature lets you stamp text or an image on every page or selected pages of a document, just like a header or footer. In fact, the Watermark feature works almost exactly like headers and footers.

Figure 14.6 shows LONGDOC.WPD with one of the 30 watermarks that come with WordPerfect, but any text or clip art can be used as a watermark. You could even have your company logo as a background on every page of your letters and memos.

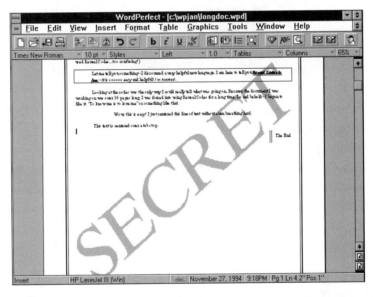

Figure 14.6 *I stamped LONGDOC.WPD with a "SECRET" watermark.*

Do It

Creating a watermark is sort of a combination between creating a header or footer and a graphics box. You'll see what I mean in a minute.

1. Make sure your insertion point is on the page where you want the watermark to begin.

2. Choose **Watermark** from the Format menu (or choose **Watermark** from the QuickMenu that you get by clicking near the top of a page). The Watermark dialog box is displayed, as shown in Figure 14.7.

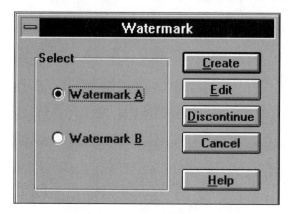

Figure 14.7 *The Watermark dialog box.*

3. Choose **Watermark A** or **Watermark B** (in this case, accept the default, which is **Watermark A**).

4. Choose **Create** (or press the **Enter** key). The Watermark window opens—you can tell because the Title Bar says *Watermark A* after the document name, and a Feature Bar is displayed. Is this starting to sound familiar? So far, it's just like a header or footer, right?

5. At this point you'll use the **Image** button to select an image, the **File** button to retrieve a text file, or type the text you want directly into the Watermark window. For this example, choose **Image**. The same Insert Image dialog box that you already used for creating graphics boxes is displayed.

6. Choose the image you want, then choose **OK**. For now, choose **SECRET.WPG**. The image you selected is displayed in the Watermark editing screen, and the Graphics Feature Bar temporarily replaces the Watermark Feature Bar, as you can see in Figure 14.8. At this point you can make any changes you want to the image using the techniques you learned in the last chapter.

Figure 14.8 *You're still in the Watermark editing screen, and the Graphics Feature Bar is active.*

7. Choose **Close** to close the Graphics Feature Bar.

8. Click on the **Pages** button to tell WordPerfect whether you want the watermark to appear on every page, odd pages, or even pages.

9. When you are done, choose **Close** from the Feature Bar to leave the Watermark editing screen and return to your document text.

10. Press **Alt+PageDown** to move your insertion point to the beginning of the second page. Notice that your watermark is also on that page.

Discontinuing a Watermark

To turn off a watermark in the middle of a document, just move your insertion point to the page where you want the watermark to stop. From the Watermark dialog box, select **Watermark A** or **Watermark B** and choose **Discontinue**.

Suppressing a Watermark

If you want to keep a watermark from appearing on the current page, choose **Suppress** from the Format, Page menu. In the Suppress dialog box, check **Watermark A** or **Watermark B** and choose **OK**.

Editing a Watermark

To edit a watermark:

1. Make sure your insertion point is on a page where the watermark you want to edit appears.

2. Choose **Watermark** from the Format menu (or from the QuickMenu at the top of the page).

3. From the Watermark dialog box, choose **Watermark A** or **Watermark B**, then choose **Edit**.

4. To edit an image in the Watermark editing screen, choose **Edit Box** from the Graphics menu. This opens the Graphics Feature Bar and gives you access to all of the options for editing graphics boxes.

5. When you're done, choose **Close** from the Graphics Feature Bar and again from the Watermark Feature Bar.

FROM HERE ...

Between graphics boxes, graphics lines, borders, and watermarks, you have a heavy-duty arsenal for decorating your documents. You can add just the right touch to emphasize your message and make it stand out from the crowd.

In the next chapter, we'll get into managing and keeping track of your files. This might seem like a boring subject, but it's not—trust me. Have you ever had a file that you just knew was somewhere in your computer, but you couldn't find it? If that or any other file mishap has ever happened to you, read on. Learning to organize your files can be fun. Okay, it may not be truly exciting, but it will make your life (at least the part of it that involves your computer) a whole lot easier.

SECTION IV

FILE MANAGEMENT
AND PRINTING

CHAPTER 15

Managing Files and Directories

(I Know That File Was There The Last Time I Looked!)

Let's talk about:

- ❖ Understanding files, directories, and drives
- ❖ Changing directories
- ❖ Copying, moving, and renaming files
- ❖ Deleting files
- ❖ Printing file lists
- ❖ Creating directories
- ❖ Creating and using a QuickList
- ❖ Creating and using a QuickFinder Index

The more work you do on your computer, the more important it is to organize your files so you can find what you want when you want it. There's an easy way to avoid having to deal with file management—just don't create any files and you won't have to bother with any of this stuff. If that's not an option, you should probably continue reading this chapter.

Windows comes with its own file management tool called *File Manager*. If you've used it and feel comfortable with it, go right ahead and keep using it. With the exception of QuickList and QuickFinder, everything in this chapter can be accomplished through File Manager. But even if you use File Manager, take a look at the tools WordPerfect provides. You can handle most (if not all) of your file management chores without ever leaving WordPerfect. Plus, WordPerfect has some nifty tricks and tools that simplify the job of working with files and cut down the time it takes to locate the right file and get where you want to go.

WHAT IS FILE MANAGEMENT?

When you pay your bills, do you throw all of the receipts in a shoe box? And then throw the unmarked shoe box into a closet that's filled with a bunch of other shoe boxes and other stuff? If that's your system, how easy is it to find that one bill from the TV repair place from three years ago? (That's a rhetorical question—you don't have to answer.) You know what the solution is: Organize all of those receipts with separate folders for utilities, rent, etc. Well, it's the same deal with your computer files. The key is to put your files into groups that make sense to you so you don't waste time rummaging through that metaphorical messy closet whenever you need to work on something.

UNDERSTANDING FILES, DIRECTORIES, AND DRIVES

You've been working with files and directories throughout this book. Every time you save a document, you're creating or updating a file. The program that starts WordPerfect is in a file. Every time you insert an image into a graphics box, you're opening a file. And that document or that image has to go to or come from somewhere, and that somewhere is called a *directory*. And your directories are all stored on a *drive*, which can be a hard disk drive or a floppy disk drive.

Since we're talking about WordPerfect here, let's get right to it and use some WordPerfect file listings to make all of this clear and show you how to move between files and directories.

You can do file management in WordPerfect through any dialog box that contains directory and file listings—WordPerfect calls them *directory dialog boxes*. For example, you get one of these directory dialog boxes whenever you choose **Open** or **Save As** from the File menu or create a figure box.

Figure 15.1 shows the Open File dialog box with WPWIN and its subdirectories.

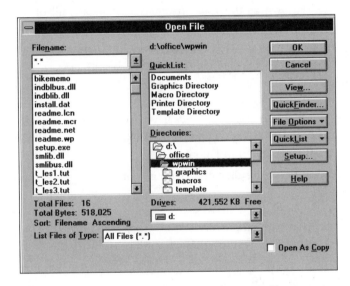

Figure 15.1 *All directory dialog boxes contain the same file management options. Everything that we'll do in this chapter is accessed from a dialog box like this.*

In Figure 15.1, look just below the Title Bar where it says D:\OFFICE\WPWIN. That's the directory path. As you can see, I'm working from my D:\ drive. If you did a default installation of WordPerfect your files will be on your C:\ drive.

Deciphering Paths

When you see a file listed, it often looks something like this:

```
C:\OFFICE\WPWIN\GRAPHICS\DRAGN.WPG
```

❖   **C:** is the drive name. Anytime you see a letter followed by a colon in a directory listing or in a filename, that's the name of the drive. If you have one hard drive, it's always **C**. If you have more than one hard drive (or if your hard drive is broken down into sections or if you're on a network), the drives will be lettered from D on up. If you have one floppy drive, it's A. Your second floppy drive is B. (Lettering schemes can be rearranged, but most computers are set up something like this.)

❖   **C** is also known as the *root directory*. That means all of the directories on the C drive branch off the C:\ directory.

❖   **OFFICE**, **WPWIN**, and **GRAPHICS** are directories. They're also *subdirectories*, because they're under other directories. A subdirectory always has a parent and can sometimes have a child. The parent is the directory just above the subdirectory—WPWIN is the parent of GRAPHICS. A directory can only have one parent, but it can have many children. GRAPHICS is a child of WPWIN, but so are WPDOS, MACROS, and TEMPLATE (seen in Figure 15.1).

❖   **DRAGN.WPG** is the filename. The filename is always at the very end of the path.

Every file is part of a path, and every subdirectory has a parent. You just learned the important part. The rest of this chapter gets into the gory details of maneuvering through paths and making sure your files and directories are organized the way you want.

Switching Directories

Take another look at Figure 15.1. The **Filename** list on the left includes all of the files in the current directory. The name of the selected directory is displayed just below the Filename in the Title Bar: D:\OFFICE\WPWIN.

You can also tell which directory is selected by looking at the file folder icons next to the directory names in the **Directories** list (just to the right of the **Filename** list). An open file folder means that the directory is open. You'll see open file folders for the selected directory and any directories above it. All other subdirectories have closed file folders next to them.

NOTE

If you don't see the Directories listing in a window to the right of the filename list, click on the **QuickList** button and choose **Show Directories** or **Show Both** from the drop-down list on that menu.

❖ To open the file list for another directory, double-click on the directory name or move the selection bar to the directory name and choose **OK**. Figure 15.2 shows what happened when I double-clicked on GRAPHICS. I now have a list of the files in D:\OFFICE\WPWIN\GRAPHICS.

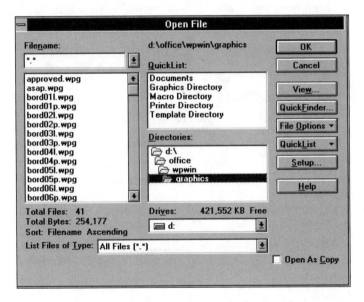

Figure 15.2 *GRAPHICS is now the selected directory.*

❖ You can always move backward through your directories by double-clicking on a directory above the current one. For example, if you want to move back to the main WordPerfect directory, just double-click on **WPWIN**.

NOTE

You can save a file to a specific directory or drive by choosing the drive and opening the directory you want (look for the open folder symbol) before you enter the filename. As you begin to organize your directories, pay attention to this step every time you save a file. It's really easy to save files to the wrong directory without thinking about it.

Changing Drives

If you want to find or open a file on a floppy disk, or if you have more than one hard drive, you need to switch drives. To switch to a different drive, just choose the letter you want from the Drives drop-down list, as shown in Figure 15.3.

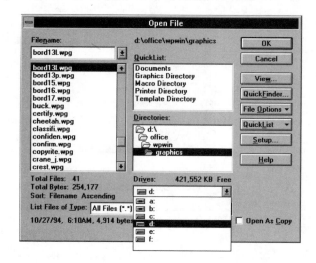

Figure 15.3 *The Drives drop-down list.*

NOTE

The dialog boxes that you use for file management have other purposes. For example, the dialog box we've been using so far is the one you use for opening files. If you're using the dialog box for something other than the function described on its Title Bar, choose **Cancel** instead of **OK** to close the dialog box. For example, if you choose **OK** in the Open File dialog box, WordPerfect thinks you're saying it's okay to open a file. It seems like **Cancel** would cancel whatever you've done, but it won't. If you've copied a file, it stays copied—**Cancel** just closes the dialog box.

Copying, Moving, and Renaming Files

On my computer, WordPerfect is installed on my D: drive. If you did a default installation, yours is on C:. That's why some of the screens in this section may look different from yours.

It's easy to move or copy a file from one directory to another or give a file a different name. There's a file called CHEETAH.WPG in C:\OFFICE\WPIN\GRAPHICS. Let's copy it to C:\OFFICE\WPWIN\WPDOCS and rename it.

Do It

1. From any directory dialog box, open the directory that contains the file you want to move, copy, or rename. Figure 15.4 shows the Open File dialog box with the files in the D:\OFFICE\WPWIN\GRAPHICS directory in the Filename list.

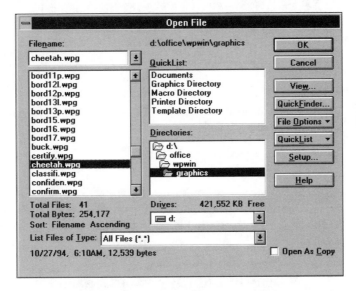

Figure 15.4 *D:\OFFICE\WPWIN\GRAPHICS is the selected directory.*

2. Select the file you want from the Filename list (*don't* double-click). You can also type the filename in the Filename text box. In Figure 15.4, **CHEETAH.WPG** is selected.

3. Choose **File Options** (that's the fifth button down on the right side of the dialog box). Figure 15.5 shows the File Options drop-down list.

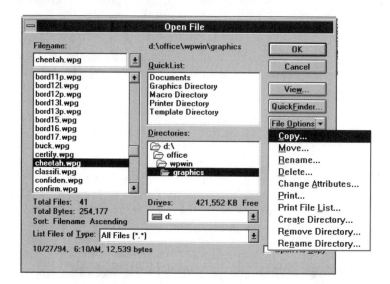

Figure 15.5 *The File Options drop-down list.*

NOTE

There's a QuickMenu that has all of the items on the File Options drop-down list. To open the QuickMenu, just click the right mouse button anywhere in the Filename list area.

4. Choose **Copy**, **Move**, or **Rename**. For this example, choose **Copy**. Figure 15.6 shows the Copy File dialog box. The file you chose (and its full path) appears in both the **From** and **To** text boxes. If the **From** text box lists the file you want to copy, move on.

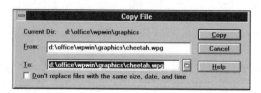

Figure 15.6 *The Copy File dialog box.*

5. If you know the exact name of the directory you want to copy the file to, type the name in the **To** text box. In this case, you could just replace GRAPHICS with **WPDOCS** in the path name.

NOTE

Notice that the whole path is selected in the **To** text box. If you just start typing, the whole path is deleted and you'll have to start from scratch. If you want to leave part of the path the way it is, make sure you click in the text box or press one of the Arrow keys on your keyboard to deselect the text before you type anything. Then you can change just the parts you want. In this example, select **GRAPHICS**, then type **WPDOCS**.

If you're not sure of the exact path, you can choose it from a directory listing by clicking on the file folder icon next to the **To** text box. This opens the Select Directory dialog box, shown in Figure 15.7. Change to the correct directory or drive the same way you did in the Open File dialog box. When the directory you want is selected (displayed in the Directory Name text box), choose **OK**.

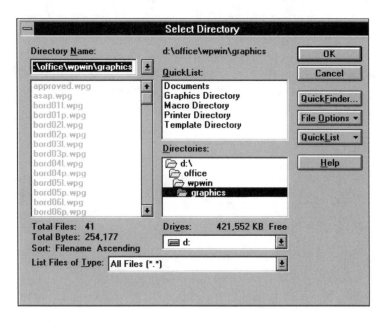

Figure 15.7 *The Select Directory dialog box.*

6. When you've completed the From and To information, click on the **Copy**, **Move**, or **Rename** button (depending on which action you're performing).

NOTE

If you don't include a filename in the **To** text box, WordPerfect moves or copies the file to the new directory and keeps the same filename. If you want to move or copy the file and give it a new name at the same time, just replace the current information in the **To** text box with the path and filename. For now, type **\MYCHEE** after C:\OFFICE\WPWIN\WPDOCS.

That's it. The file is copied to the new directory. Take a look in the WPDOCS directory to make sure it's there. That'll also give you some more practice moving between directories.

❖   The dialog boxes and procedures are exactly the same for copy, move, and rename. They just have slightly different results. With copy, the file stays put in its current directory and a copy is placed in the new directory. With move, the file is taken out of the current directory and moved to the new directory.

❖   You can use these options to move and copy files between directories, to move and copy files from your hard disk to a floppy disk, or to rename a file in the same or a different directory.

Deleting Files

Deleting a file is just as easy as moving or copying it. It's more permanent, though—make sure the file you select is one you really want to delete before you proceed.

Do It

1. From any directory dialog box, open the directory that contains the file you want to delete.

2. Select the file you want from the Filename list (don't double-click).

3. Choose **Delete** from the **F**ile Options drop-down list or the Filename QuickMenu. The dialog box shown in Figure 15.8 is displayed.

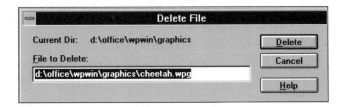

Figure 15.8 *This dialog box makes you confirm that you really want to delete the file.*

WARNING

Stop!! Don't hit that **Enter** key without paying attention. The Delete File dialog box pops up for a purpose. Always take a moment to double-check the filename in this dialog box. It's really easy to choose **Delete** with the wrong file selected, and this is your only chance to back out. Notice that **Delete** is the default choice here—if you press the **Enter** key, it's just like saying *OK, go ahead and nuke this file.*

4. If you're sure you want to delete the file, choose **Delete** (or press **Enter**) in the Delete File dialog box. If you decide not to delete the file, choose **Cancel**.

Creating Directories

Creating directories is an important part of file management. Once you decide how you want your directories organized, you need to create directories for all of your different file categories. In my case, I create a new directory for every book I work on. Then, depending on what's involved, I may create subdirectories for different areas that relate to the project.

Do It

1. From any directory dialog box, open the directory that will be the parent of the one you want to create. For example, if I want to create a new subdirectory under C:\BOOKS, I should have the BOOKS directory open, as shown in Figure 15.9.

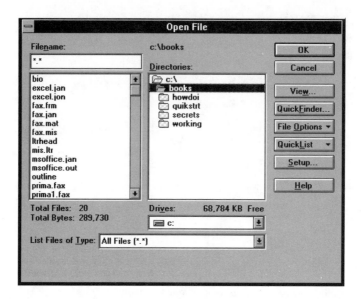

Figure 15.9 *I'm ready to create a subdirectory under C:\BOOKS.*

2. Choose **Create Directory** from the File Options drop-down list or the Filename or Directory QuickMenu. The Create Directory dialog box is displayed, as shown in Figure 15.10.

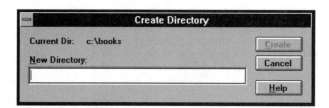

Figure 15.10 *The Create Directory dialog box.*

3. Type a name in the **New Directory** text box and choose **Create**. The name of the new directory is displayed in the Directories list under its parent.

Removing Directories

WARNING

You can *really* get into trouble with this one if you space out. WordPerfect helpfully warns you before it proceeds, but it's not difficult to delete a directory and all of the files in it. Pay attention to the dialog boxes that prompt you for responses. Read what they say before clicking or pressing a key.

Now that the warning is out of the way, I'll tell you how to remove directories. You might create a directory by mistake. Or you might have a directory that's full of files you don't need anymore. Just be sure you really don't need any of those files before you continue.

Do It

1. From any directory dialog box, open the directory that you want to remove. Make sure the name of the directory is displayed below the Title Bar.

2. Choose **Remove Directory** from the File Options drop-down list or the QuickMenu. Figure 15.11 shows the Remove Directory dialog box.

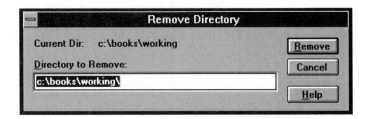

Figure 15.11 *The Remove Directory dialog box.*

3. If you're *sure* the directory shown is the one you want to remove, choose **Remove**. Otherwise, choose **Cancel**.

4. If there are files in the directory, you'll see the dialog box shown in Figure 15.12.

Figure 15.12 *This is your last warning before all files are deleted along with the directory.*

5. Choose **Yes** if you're still sure you want to remove the directory. If you proceed, the directory and everything in it will be deleted.

There are ways to recover deleted files and directories, but they should only be used as a last resort. (I didn't even want to tell you about them until *after* I gave you all of those warnings.) Anyway, DOS versions 5 and up include an undelete feature, and there are other undelete utilities available.

NOTE

Remember how I told you at the beginning that you can use any directory dialog box for file management? Well, instead of trying to figure out which dialog box to open every time you want to copy a file or create a directory, just pick one that you always use to do your file housekeeping. The Open File dialog box is a good one because it has both a Toolbar icon and a shortcut key (**Ctrl+O**). I think of **Ctrl+O** as my file management key.

Selecting Groups of Files

Almost everything that you can do to one file can be done to a group of files: You can move, copy, delete, rename, or print several files at once. You just select the files before you choose the command.

❖ To select files that are next to each other in a Filename list, drag the mouse pointer over the files you want to select. You can also hold down the **Shift** key while you press the **Up Arrow** or **Down Arrow** key.

❖ To select files that aren't together, hold down the **Ctrl** key while you click each file. Keep doing that until all of the files you want are selected. Figure 15.13 shows a file list with several files selected.

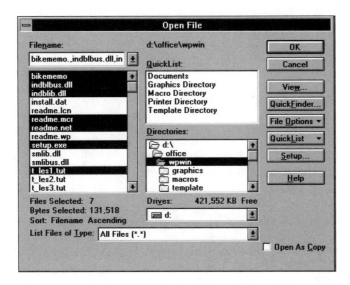

Figure 15.13 *The Open File dialog box with files selected.*

❖ Once the files are selected, choose the command you want from the File Options drop-down list or the QuickMenu.

Printing from a Directory Dialog Box

In the next chapter, we'll talk about all sorts of printing options. Most of them, however, have to do with printing one file (or part of a file) at a time. If you want to send several files to the printer at once, you can do it from a directory dialog box:

❖ Select the files you want to print and choose **Print** from the File
    Options drop-down list or the QuickMenu.

You can also print a list of all of the files in a directory:

❖ From any directory dialog box, choose **Print File List** from the File
    Options drop-down list or the QuickMenu.

❖ You can also print a directory list by choosing **Print Directory List**
    from the Directories Quick Menu.

Viewing Files

In Chapter 13, you opened the Viewer to look at images before you brought
them into a graphics box. The Viewer also works for text files.

❖ From any directory dialog box, select a file and choose **View** to open
    the Viewer, as shown in Figure 15.14.

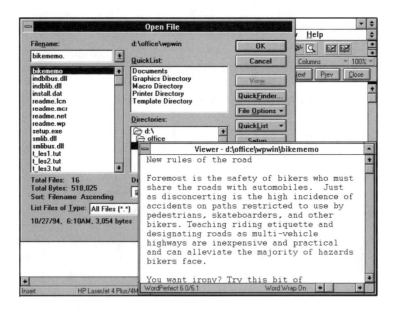

Figure 15.14 *The selected file is displayed in the Viewer window.*

Just select different files by clicking on them or using the arrow keys. This can be a great way of browsing through a directory. Close the Viewer window by double-clicking on its control-menu box.

Changing the Appearance of the Directory Dialog Box

By default, directory dialog boxes just show the filenames in the **Filename** list box, and they're listed in alphabetical order. If you want to see more information in the **Filename** list box or change the order of the list, choose **Setup** to customize your directory dialog boxes. In Figure 15.15, I changed the setup so you can see the size of each file and the date and time it was last updated. I also changed the order to show the files sorted by date, with the ones I created most recently listed at the top.

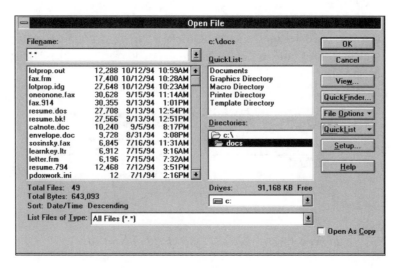

Figure 15.15 *You can change the information that appears in the directory dialog box.*

NOTE

Any change that you make in Setup is permanent until you change it again. And the change affects all of your directory dialog boxes.

CREATING AND USING A QUICKLIST

As I've mentioned once or twice, I'm really lazy. For that reason, the *QuickList* is a feature close to my heart. As easy as it is to get to the directory you want by clicking a few times, QuickList makes it even easier. It's a shortcut method of accessing directories you use a lot. For example, if I put all of my WordPerfect documents in D:\WPWIN\WPDOCS, I can set up a QuickList entry called *My Documents* that takes me right there, instead of wading through three directory levels. You can even have a QuickList entry that takes you to a particular file. We'll create a QuickList entry so you can see what I mean.

Do It

To add a QuickList entry:

1. Choose **Add Item** from the QuickList drop-down list or from the QuickList QuickMenu. The Add QuickList Item dialog box is displayed, as shown in Figure 15.16.

Figure 15.16 *The Add QuickList Item dialog box.*

2. Type the full path name (include a filename if you want the QuickList entry to point to a specific file) in the **Directory/Filename** text box, or click on the file folder icon and choose the directory you want from the Select Directory dialog box.

3. In the **Description** text box, type the name you want for the QuickList entry. You're not limited to a regular eight-character filename, and there can be spaces between the words. For example, you could have a QuickList item called *Third Quarter Reports*.

4.   Choose **OK**.

Using the QuickList

The descriptive QuickList name is just a shortcut that points to the directory or file it stands for. Choosing a QuickList item is the same as choosing the directory or file.

By default, your directory dialog boxes show both **QuickList** and your **Directories** list. You may change this by choosing **Show QuickList** or **Show Directories** from the QuickList drop-down box. When you choose **Show QuickList,** the QuickList list extends and replaces the Directories list.

Figure 15.17 shows the Open File dialog box with both the QuickList and the Directories list visible. Notice that *My Documents* is selected in the QuickList; you can tell what directory it points to by looking in the Filename text box.

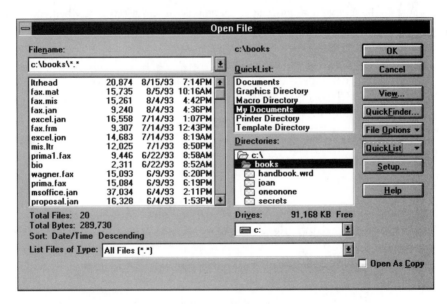

Figure 15.17 *This default Open File dialog box shows both the QuickList and Directories list.*

❖   To move to a QuickList directory, double-click on the name or select the name and choose **OK**.

CREATING AN INDEX AND USING THE QUICKFINDER

Has this ever happened to you? You just created a document, and you can't find it anywhere. You know you saved it, but you can't remember which directory you saved it to. All you know is that it has the word *antediluvian* in it. Now what? QuickFinder to the rescue!

You can create a QuickFinder Index to do almost any kind of search—it can search your whole hard drive or any selected group of drives or directories, files, file segments, or file summaries for any word, Word form, phrase, or combination of words. After the index is set up, the search takes just a couple of moments.

NOTE

Setting up an index for your whole hard drive could take quite a while (mine took about 40 minutes), depending on how much you have on your hard drive and how fast your computer is. Do it at a time when you're not in a rush to get any work done on your computer. Start the index and go take a walk—the fresh air'll do you good.

In this section, we'll index a few directories, just to give you a taste of this powerful feature. I'll create an index for the chapters in this book so that I can instantly find anything I've talked about.

Do It

To create an index:

1. Choose **QuickFinder** from one of the directory dialog boxes. The QuickFinder dialog box is displayed, as shown in Figure 15.18.

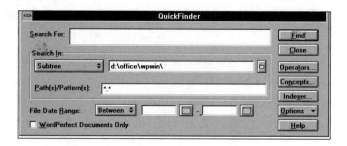

Figure 15.18 *The QuickFinder dialog box.*

2. Choose **Indexer**. If you haven't already selected a directory for your indexes, a dialog box displays, asking which directory you want your QuickFinder indexes in. Select the directory and choose **OK**. The QuickFinder File Indexer dialog box is displayed, as shown in Figure 15.19.

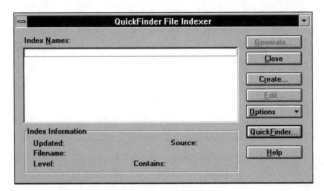

Figure 15.19 *The QuickFinder File Indexer dialog box.*

3. Choose **Create**.

4. Enter a name for the index, as shown in Figure 15.20, then choose **OK**.

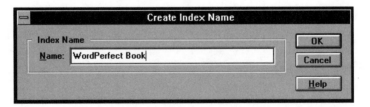

Figure 15.20 *The name should be descriptive, just like a QuickList name. I'm calling this index WordPerfect Book.*

5. Choose **Browse** from the Create Index dialog box. The Filename, Directories, and Drives lists in this dialog box are the same as in any directory dialog box.

6. Choose the files or directories you want to index and choose **Add**.

7. If you want to index any subdirectories that belong to the selected directory, check the **Include Subtree** box. Figure 15.21 shows the Create Index dialog box with C:\WPWBOOK in the **Directories to**

Index box. The */s* after the directory name means that the subdirectories will be indexed. You can continue adding directories and/or files to the **Directories to Index** list by selecting them and choosing **Add**.

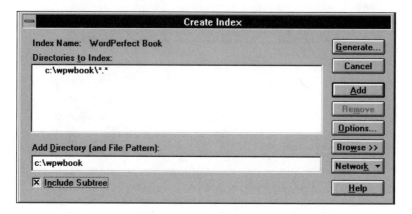

Figure 15.21 *The Create Index dialog box.*

8. Choose **Generate** when you're ready to create the index. A Generate dialog box lets you know how the index is progressing—it'll tell you how long the process has taken so far, and what portion of it is done.

9. When the index is complete, choose **Close** to return to your document.

Searching an Index

Now that the index is created, I can use it to find anything in the directories that I included in the index. Let's do a quick search and see what happens:

Do It

1. Choose **QuickFinder** from the File menu or from any directory dialog box.

2. If you want to limit the search to files with a specific name or extension, enter the information in the **Path(s)/Pattern** text box. For example, to search only files with a WPD extension, you would enter ***.WPD**. The asterisk is a wildcard that stands for any number of characters. ***.*** means

any filename with any extension.

3. Enter text in the **Search For** text box. In Figure 15.22, I entered the words *file* and *management*, which means that QuickFinder will find any file that contains both of those words anywhere in the document. You can expand your search by selecting **Concepts.** The Concept Builder dialog box that opens up when you click on this button allows you to use Word Forms, the WordPerfect Thesaurus, and typographical or phonetic word variations.

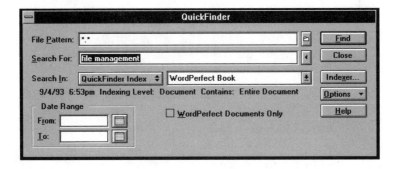

Figure 15.22 *The QuickFinder dialog box with search criteria entered.*

You can refine your search further by selecting **Operators** to open the Search Operators dialog box—this allows you to use search operators and switches to do a more complex search.

NOTE

4. If you have more than one index, choose the index you want to search from the **QuickFinder Index** pop-up list.

5. If you want to limit the search to files created between certain dates, enter the dates in the **From** and **To** text boxes. (If you click on one of the little calendar icons, you can choose the date from the visual display of a monthly calendar.)

6. Choose **Find** to start the search.

When the search is complete, all of the files that were found show up in the Search Results dialog box, as shown in Figure 15.23. From this dialog box, you can open or view any of the files on the list. Chap15 was the only one found since this is the only document that has the words "file management."

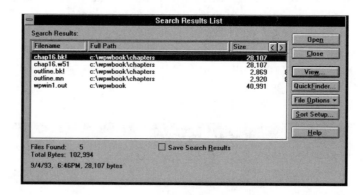

Figure 15.23 *The Search Results dialog box.*

That was a quick introduction to QuickFinder. There's a lot more you can do with it—lots of ways to refine your indexes and your searches, especially with the Search Operator and Concept Builder features that are new with WordPerfect 6.1. And you can quickly update the indexes so they're always current. As you work with QuickFinder, explore its different options. Don't forget to use WordPerfect's Help feature as a resource.

FROM HERE ...

Now that you can manipulate files and directories with ease, you have no excuse for dumping all your files in one directory. Get organized—manage those files. And use QuickList to put frequently used directories at your fingertips. But if you do happen to lose a file, just call on your QuickFinder index to save the day.

In the next chapter, we get into printing big time. You'll learn how to select the right printer, print selected pages of a document, cancel a print job, and much more. Stay tuned.

CHAPTER 16

Printing

(The Paperless Office? Yeah, Right!)

Let's talk about:

- ❖ Selecting a printer
- ❖ Printing the full document
- ❖ Printing selected pages
- ❖ Printing multiple copies
- ❖ Canceling a print job
- ❖ Printing an envelope

You've worked hard—your document looks great, and you want to show it off. You could have everyone crowd around your computer and stare at the screen, but your mom in Missoula doesn't drive. Hey, I've got it! How about printing it out and mailing her a copy?

You printed the document you created in Chapter 1, but that was just a quick introduction to printing. It's time to fulfill the promise I made to tell you more about WordPerfect's printing capabilities. By the end of this chapter, you'll be in total control of your print jobs.

SELECTING A PRINTER

Before you can print, WordPerfect has to know what kind of printer you have. And if you have more than one printer, you need to tell WordPerfect which one you want to use.

Do I Need to Select a Printer?

When you install WordPerfect, you tell it what kind of printer you have, and if you only have one printer that's all there is to it (until you buy a new printer). How do you know if you need to select a printer? The Print dialog box (which you can open by clicking on the **Print** button on the Toolbar, selecting **Print** from the File menu, or pressing **Ctrl+P**) displays the current printer selection. Take a look at Figure 16.1.

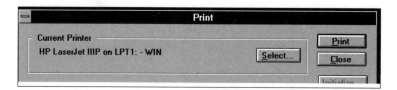

Figure 16.1 *The Print dialog box tells you which printer is currently selected.*

If the name in the **Current Printer** box is the printer you actually have and want to print to, you can move right ahead to printing. If there's no printer listed, or if you want to choose a different printer, you have to make a selection.

NOTE

If you use more than one printer, glance at the Current Printer box every time you print to make sure you're sending to the right printer.

Do It

To select a printer:

1. Choose **Select** from the Print dialog box. The Select Printer dialog box is displayed, as shown in Figure 16.2.

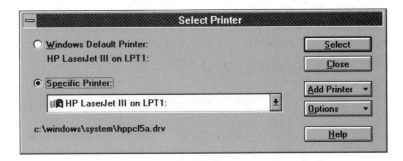

Figure 16.2 *The Select Printer dialog box.*

2. Select one of the radio buttons on the left side of the dialog box.

   ❖ **Windows Default Printer** selects whichever printer is your current Windows default printer (shown below and to the right of the radio button).

   ❖ **Specific Printer** allows you to choose from any of your available printers. Highlight the printer you want and choose **Select** (or double-click on your printer selection).

That's it, but there's a little more to explain about the process. Like, what are all those printers on the list in the Select Printers dialog box? And, why do some of them have a little Windows logo next to them and some have a WordPerfect logo?

About Printer Drivers

The information that WordPerfect (or any other program) needs in order to print a document is contained in a file called a *printer driver*. Windows comes with its own printer drivers. When you installed Windows and told it what kind of printer or printers you have, it installed the appropriate drivers for those printers. WordPerfect also has its own printer drivers that can be installed when you install WordPerfect, or at a later time.

The Select Printer dialog box contains a list of all of the Windows and WordPerfect printer drivers that you've added to your system. You can tell which kind of driver it is by the Windows or WordPerfect logo.

Why are there two kinds of printer drivers and which should you use?

❖ If you use the Windows drivers, all of your documents will be compatible with any other Windows program. If you do most of your work with Windows programs, you should probably select a Windows driver.

❖ Use the WordPerfect drivers if you use WordPerfect on other platforms (like OS/2 or UNIX)—Windows drivers aren't compatible between platforms. (I'm not even going to explain that sentence—if you work on different platforms, you know what it means. And if you don't, you don't need to know what it means.)

❖ WordPerfect has drivers for more printers than Windows does. If you have a printer that's not supported by Windows, there might be a WordPerfect driver for it.

Whichever kind of driver you use, you'll be able to do everything I talk about in this chapter.

This might seem obvious, but you can't select a printer unless it's installed on your computer. If the printer you want doesn't appear on the list in the Select Printer dialog box, see Appendix A for information about installing printer drivers.

WHAT CAN MY PRINTER DO?

WordPerfect comes with a printer test document that's designed to give you an idea of your printer's capabilities. The document is called PRINTST.WPD—if you used the default directory settings when you installed WordPerfect, it's in C:\OFFICE\SHARED\WPC20.

Do It

To print the test document:

1. Open PRINTST.WPD (if you need help getting to the right directory, refer to the last chapter).

2. Click on the **Print** button on the Toolbar (you can also choose **Print** from the File menu or press **Ctrl+P**).

3. Choose **Print** from the Print dialog box—since Full Document is the default selection, you don't have to do anything else.

USING THE PRINT DIALOG BOX

You make all of your printing choices (except selecting the printer) through the Print dialog box, shown in Figure 16.3. (The instructions for opening the Print dialog box are included in the previous section, "What Can My Printer Do.")

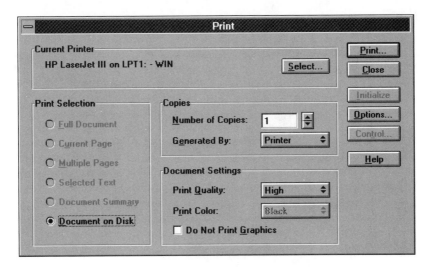

Figure 16.3 *The Print dialog box.*

Printing the Whole Document

This is the easiest one—you don't have to do anything but click on the **Print** button or press **Enter**. Full Document is always the default, so all you have to do is open the document you want to print, open the Print dialog box, and choose **Print**.

Printing the Current Page

This isn't much harder than printing the whole document. If you want to print the current page, just select the **Current Page** radio button before you click on the **Print** button.

Printing Selected Pages

Let's say you have a 50-page document, and you make corrections on pages 5 and 9, change the section from pages 21 through 28, and add three pages at the end. You don't want to reprint the whole document, and moving to and printing the changed pages one at a time would be a pain. WordPerfect's **Multiple Pages** option is the answer. You can specify exactly what portion of your document you want to print:

Do It

1. From the Print dialog box, choose **Multiple Pages** and then choose **Print**. The Multiple Pages dialog box is displayed, as shown in Figure 16.4.

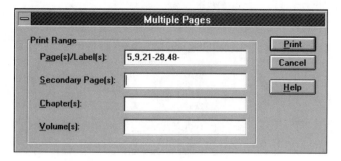

Figure 16.4 *The Multiple Pages dialog box.*

2. In the **Page(s)/Label(s)** text box, specify the pages or labels you want to print.

ROADMAP

To learn more about labels, see Chapter 18, "Columns, Labels and Subdivide Page."

3. If you've used secondary, chapter, or volume numbering, you can enter selections in those text boxes.

4. Choose **Print**.

Figure 16.4 is set up to print the pages I used in my example at the beginning of this section:

❖ **5,9** means that pages 5 *and* 9 will be printed. The comma is like saying *and.*

NOTE

WordPerfect accepts spaces in place of commas, but I find it easier to see my choices with commas. Strictly a matter of preference.

❖ **21-28** means that pages 21 *through* 28 will be printed. The hyphen is like saying *through.*

❖ **48-** means that page 48 and all of the pages that follow it will be printed. You can use a hyphen before or after a number to print a range from the beginning or to the end of a document. **48-** prints from page 48 to the end; **-10** prints from the beginning through page 10.

❖ Notice that the example in Figure 16.4 uses a combination of ranges. You can print exactly what you want by stringing together different page ranges.

Printing More than One Copy

If you need more than one copy of a document, you can do it through WordPerfect instead of printing the document and waiting in line at the copy machine. And you don't have to send the print job twice.

From the Print dialog box, type a number in the **Number of Copies** text box (or use the incrementing arrows or the **Up** and **Down Arrows** on your keyboard) to increase or decrease the number in the text box).

By default, multiple copies are generated by the Printer. If you want them generated by WordPerfect, choose **WordPerfect** from the **Generated By** pop-up list. What's the difference?

Suppose you specify two copies in the **Number of Copies** text box. If WordPerfect generates the document, it assembles two complete copies of the document before it sends them to the printer. This means that, for a ten-page document, you'd get all ten pages of one copy before the other copy starts printing. If you tell WordPerfect to have the printer generate the copies, WordPerfect sends the job to the printer right away and the printer takes care of the rest. For that same ten-page document, you would get two copies of the first page, then two copies of the second page, and so on.

Letting the printer generate copies can speed up your print job.

NOTE

Document Settings

You probably want your finished document to look as good as possible. Why would you want to print in anything other than the highest quality you can get? Well, as you're working on a document, you might print out several draft copies, and you don't really care what they look like—you just want them fast. That's what the **Document Settings** area is all about—letting you print at different qualities to save time. It's also where you choose your print color if you have a color printer.

The Print Quality pop-up list has three choices: **High**, **Medium**, and **Draft**. *High* gives you the best output your printer's capable of, but it takes the longest. *Draft* is the lowest quality, but it's the fastest and is usually adequate for drafts.

Medium is, well, medium. Your printer might not be able to print at all three quality settings. If you don't notice any difference, don't bother changing the settings.

You can speed up printing even more by checking **Do Not Print Graphics**. If you're just printing a draft so you can proofread it, you might not care about seeing your graphics boxes and lines. This option can save a lot of time, especially if you have a lot of graphics in your document.

Printing a Document that is Not on Your Screen

Use the **Document on Disk** option to print documents without having to open them first. This can be a real timesaver. If you're in the middle of working on a document, and your boss pops in and says, "Say, could you print out that report we put together last month?" you can smile and say, "Right away!"—and *mean* it!

Do It

1. From the Print dialog box, choose **Document on Disk**, then choose **Print**. The Document on Disk dialog box is displayed, as shown in Figure 16.5.

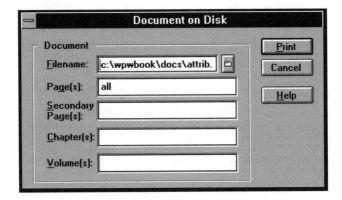

Figure 16.5 *The Document on Disk dialog box.*

2. Enter the name (and full path, if it's not in your current directory) of the file you want to print in the Filename text box. (Or open the Select File dialog box by clicking on the file folder icon, and pick the file you want.)

3. If you don't want to print the whole document, enter page or label ranges in the appropriate text boxes. (This works just like the Multiple Pages dialog box we talked about a little earlier.)

4. Choose **Print**.

Changing Printing Options

Choose **Options** from the Print dialog box for more choices about your print job. Figure 16.6 shows the Print Output Options dialog box.

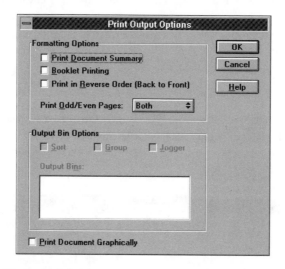

Figure 16.6 *The Print Output Options dialog box.*

❖ If you use the Document Summary feature, you can check this option to have the summary printed along with your document. (If your current document doesn't have a summary, this option is dimmed.)

❖ If you've used Labels or Subdivide Page (see Chapter 18) to set up your document as a booklet, check **Booklet Printing** before you print.

❖ If you want the document to come out of the printer with the last page first, choose **Print in Reverse Order**.

❖ Choose **Odd** or **Even** from the **Print Odd/Even Pages** pop-up list to print only the odd or even pages of your document.

❖ **Output Bin Options** lets you tell WordPerfect how the document will come out of the printer. Unless your printer has more than one bin, this option is dimmed.

❖ If your printer has trouble with reverse text (white-on-black), choose **Print Document Graphically**.

❖ **Print Document Graphically** sends your document to the printer without downloading fonts.

When you've made all of your selections in the Print Output Options dialog box, choose **OK** to return to the Print dialog box, then choose **Print** to send your document to the printer.

CANCELING A PRINT JOB

You just sent that 200-page job to the printer, and your boss (who just happens to be the president of the company) wants her memo printed *now*. You don't want to jeopardize that raise you're in line for by telling her she has to wait half an hour or so. What's a person to do?

Don't fret—there's an easy way out of this jam.

❖ Once you've sent a job to the printer, you can choose **Control** from the Print dialog box to open the WordPerfect Print Job dialog box, shown in Figure 16.7. Choose **Cancel** from this dialog box to stop the job.

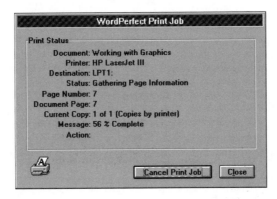

***Figure 16.7** The WordPerfect Print Job dialog box.*

Depending on the speed of your computer, you might not be able to cancel the job before WordPerfect sends it to the printer. If you see the WP Print Process dialog box shown in 16.8, it means it's too late to cancel the job through WordPerfect. At that point, you'll have to cancel the job at the printer. Refer to your printer manual for instructions.

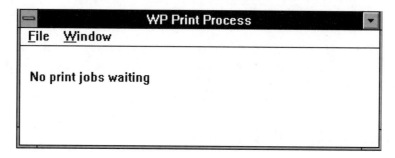

Figure 16.8 *The WP Print Process dialog box.*

PRINTING AN ENVELOPE

With WordPerfect's envelope feature, it's a snap to address an envelope and send it to the printer. You don't have to do any fancy formatting; just enter the mailing and return addresses and WordPerfect takes care of the rest. It can even pull an address out of the document on your screen.

Do It

1. If you want to use the address from a document (like a letter), open the document.

2. Choose **Envelope** from the Format menu. The Envelope dialog box is displayed, as shown in Figure 16.9. If there's more than one address in your document, you can select the address you want before you open the Envelope dialog box. The address you select will be inserted in the Mailing Addresses box.

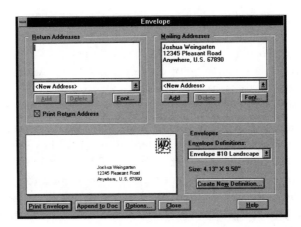

Figure 16.9 *The Envelope dialog box. The address from my letter is displayed in the Mailing Addresses box.*

3. Type your return address in the **Return Addresses** text box. You can save a mailing or return address by choosing **Add** after you enter the address. The next time you want to use the address, you can choose it from the drop-down list below the **Return Addresses** or **Mailing Addresses** text box.

4. If you didn't pull a mailing address from your document, type an address in the **Mailing Addresses** text box.

NOTE

As you type in either the Return or Mailing Addresses area, watch what happens in the preview display. It shows you where your text will be placed.

5. When you've entered all of the address information and the preview display looks the way you want, choose **Print Envelope**. (Make sure you insert an envelope in your printer first!) If you don't want to print the envelope right now, choose **Append to Doc** instead of **Print Envelope**. This adds the envelope information to the end of your current document and allows you to save the envelope with the document and print it whenever you want.

That's about it, but there are a few more settings you can change:

❖ Choosing **Font** in either the Return Address or Mailing Address area takes you to a Font dialog box where you can tell WordPerfect how you want the address printed. You can print the return and mailing addresses in different fonts.

❖ By default, WordPerfect is set to print on a #10 envelope (that's standard business size). The Envelope Definitions area shows which envelope form is selected. If you want to use a different envelope definition, you can choose from one of WordPerfect's predefined forms by picking it from the Envelope Definitions drop-down list. You can also choose **Create New Definition** to set up a custom envelope definition.

❖ Choose **Options** to open the Envelope Options dialog box shown in Figure 16.10. From this dialog box, you can change the positions for the return and mailing addresses. You can also tell WordPerfect to print a bar code above or below the mailing address by clicking on one of the radio buttons in the USPS Bar Code Options area.

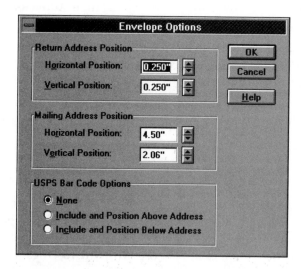

Figure 16.10 *The Envelope Options dialog box.*

NOTE

A bar code converts the zip code into symbols that the post office uses to sort mail more quickly. Sometimes you can get a discount on bulk mailings if you use bar codes.

FROM HERE ...

At this point, you should feel in control of your print jobs. You can select which printer you want to use. You can print the whole document or any part of it, and you can change the number of copies and the print quality. You even know how to print a document without opening it first. And printing envelopes will never be a hassle again.

Coming up, you get an introduction to WordPerfect's powerful Tables feature. At its most basic, it's a quick way to set up rows of text and numbers without using tabs. At its most powerful, a table can contain complex formatting and mathematical formulas.

SECTION V

TABLES AND COLUMNS

CHAPTER 17

Working with Tables

(Yes, You're Still in the Right Book—This Isn't a Lesson in Basic Carpentry)

Let's talk about:

- ❖ What is a table?
- ❖ Creating a table
- ❖ Editing a table's structure
- ❖ Formatting a table
- ❖ Using Sum to total a column of numbers
- ❖ Saving and deleting a table
- ❖ Data fill
- ❖ Creating a chart from a table

WordPerfect tables make it easy to create charts, forms, and any other document that you want formatted in columns and rows. You could do a lot of the same things by setting tabs or using the Columns feature (which you'll learn about in the next chapter), but in most cases, tables are even easier and much more versatile.

You can change where a table is positioned on the page, adjust the width of table columns by dragging the mouse, and click a button to change the way numbers are formatted—and that's just the beginning.

The Tables feature has its own set of spreadsheet features you can use to perform all sorts of complex calculations. If you've used a spreadsheet program like Lotus 1-2-3, Quattro Pro, or Excel, you'll be pleased to find that WordPerfect includes a lot of the same functions and capabilities. Depending on your needs, the Tables feature might keep you from having to buy a separate program to set up your spreadsheets.

This chapter introduces you to tables. You'll learn how to create a simple table, format it, and use a formula to total a column of numbers. And you'll get a glimpse of the powerful spreadsheet features—just enough to point you in the right direction. When you're comfortable with table basics, use WordPerfect's Help screens and your manual to venture deeper into table territory.

ANATOMY OF A TABLE

Before you create a table, there's just one thing you should know—what exactly *is* a table anyway? Glad you asked. A table is just a bunch of rows and columns that can contain text or numbers. You can even include graphic images and lines inside a table. You only need to know three words to work with tables: *row*, *column*, and *cell*. Figure 17.1 shows you how it works.

Column A	Column B	Column C	
Cell A1	Cell B1	Cell C1	Row 1
Cell A2	Cell B2	Cell C2	Row 2
Cell A3	Cell B3	Cell C3	Row 3
Cell A4	Cell B4	Cell C4	Row 4

Figure 17.1 *A sample table.*

A table is made up of rows and columns. The boxes that the rows and columns make when they meet are called *cells*. As you can see, *rows* go across and are identified by numbers, *columns* go down and are identified by letters, and cells get their names from their column and row location. So, a cell that's in the second row (row 2) of the far left column (column A) is named cell A2 (the column always comes first in the name).

Did I say you only needed three words? So I lied—there's one more: *cell address.* That's what you call the cell location. In the example I used in the previous paragraph, A2 is the cell address. Okay class, the vocabulary/anatomy lesson is over. Time to build a table (no, no, put away those hammers and nails—not *that* kind of table).

CREATING A TABLE

Okay, who's already noticed the **Tables** button on the Power Bar? You get a purple jelly bean. The rest of you, move your mouse pointer to the Tables button. The QuickTip tells you this is the Table QuickCreate button, and the Help Prompt on the Title Bar says *Click and drag to create a table.* That button's not called QuickCreate for nothing, as you'll soon see.

NOTE

This feature's another strong pro-mouse argument. Creating a table and working with a lot of its features are much simpler with a mouse.

1. Position your mouse pointer over the **Tables** button and hold down the left mouse button. The title box will initially say No Table.

2. Drag the mouse down over the table grid—as you drag, notice that the numbers in the title box tell you how many columns and rows are selected (the column number is first, just like in the cell address). In Figure 17.2, I have 3 columns and 4 rows selected.

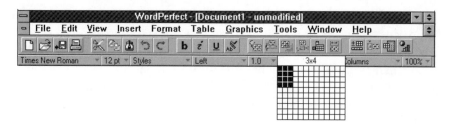

Figure 17.2 *Just drag the mouse down to select as many columns and rows as you want.*

3. When you've selected the correct number of columns and rows, release the mouse button. For this example, release the mouse button when you have a table that is 3 columns by 4 rows. Your screen should look like Figure 17.3.

Figure 17.3 *When you release the mouse button, the empty table is displayed on your screen.*

You can create a table with the keyboard by pressing **F12** or choosing **Create** from the Table menu. Just enter the number of columns and rows you want in the text boxes in the Create Table dialog box and choose **OK**.

NOTE

If you're creating a really large table, it can be faster to use the Create Table dialog box. A table can have up to 32 columns and 32,765 rows—it would take a lot of dragging to create a table that size.

NOTE

It's a good idea to plan your table in advance, but don't worry too much about whether you have the right number of rows or columns. It's so easy to add and delete rows and columns (and change everything else about the table) that you can just sort of rough it out and work out the details as you go along.

Entering Text in a Table

Once you've created the basic table structure, you can type in any of the cells just like you would anywhere else in your document. When you first create a table, your insertion point ends up in cell A1. If you want to enter text in that cell, just start typing. Otherwise, click in the cell where you want to enter text (or use the **Arrow** or **Tab** key to move to a cell). Table 17.1 lists keyboard shortcuts for moving around a table.

NOTE

Since the **Tab** key works differently in tables, what do you do if you want to use a regular tab? Simple—just press **Ctrl+Tab.**

Table 17.1 *Keyboard shortcuts for moving your insertion point in a table.*

Keystroke	Where it takes you
Tab	One cell to the right (if you're in the far right cell of a row, it takes you to the first cell of the next row)
Shift+Tab	Cell to the left
Alt+Down Arrow	Down one row
Alt+Up Arrow	Up one row
Home, Home	First cell in the current row
End, End	Last cell in the current row
Alt+Home	First line of text in a cell (useful if there are several lines in a cell)
Alt+End	Last line of text in a multi-line cell

NOTE

You can always tell which cell your insertion point is in by looking at the Status Bar. Don't be confused by the Title Bar—it shows which cell your mouse pointer's on. Try it: with your insertion point in cell A1, move your mouse pointer around the table and watch the Title Bar. The Title Bar keeps changing depending on where the mouse pointer is, but the Status Bar continues to say cell A1.

Do It

1. Enter text in the table (use Figure 17.4 as an example).

2. Use the **Tab** key to move to the next cell, or click in the cell you want.

NOTE

As you're entering text in a table, it's usually easier to press the **Tab** key than to reach for the mouse.

Category	1993	1994
Salaries	152334	380952
Telephone	1890	2590
Meeting and Seminar Refreshments	250	18620

Figure 17.4 Enter your text as shown here.

Did you notice that the bottom row got bigger when you typed **Meeting and Seminar Refreshments**? The height of a cell increases automatically when text wraps to the next line. Also, I purposely had you type the numbers without commas or any kind of formatting—we'll fix them later.

TABLE TOOLS

We're about to start messing with the table's format. To make that task easier, it's time to drag out WordPerfect's arsenal of table tools:

❖ First, there's the old familiar QuickMenu. You get the Tables QuickMenu by clicking your right mouse button anywhere on the document screen when your insertion point's in a table. Figure 17.5 shows the Tables QuickMenu.

Category	1993	
Salaries	152334	
Telephone	1890	
Meeting Refreshments	250	

Paste

Format...
Number Type...
E**x**pert...
Lines/Fill...

Insert...
Delete...
Si**z**e Column to Fit
Split Cell...

Su**m**
Ca**l**culate
Ro**w**/Column Indicators
Fo**r**mula Bar

Figure 17.5 *The Tables QuickMenu.*

NOTE

If you don't get this QuickMenu when you click the right mouse button, check to make sure your insertion point's actually inside the table.

❖ Figure 17.6 shows the Tables Toolbar, which automatically appears as soon as you create a table.

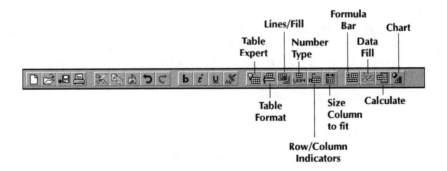

Figure 17.6 *The Tables Toolbar.*

Both of these tools give you quick access to most of the Tables features.

INSERTING ROWS AND COLUMNS

Do It

Let's add a title row at the top of the table:

1. Place your insertion point anywhere in Row 1.

2. Choose **Insert** from the Table menu or QuickMenu. The Insert Columns/Rows dialog box shown in Figure 17.7 is displayed.

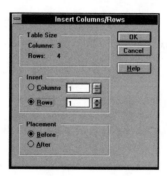

Figure 17.7 *The Insert Columns/Rows dialog box.*

3. Choose **OK** (or press **Enter**) to insert one row above your insertion point location. You don't have to make any selections in the box, because **Rows, 1,** and **Before** are the defaults.

Use this dialog box to add columns or rows:

❖ Choose **Columns** or **Rows**.

❖ Enter the number you want to add in the appropriate text box (or click the **Up** or **Down Arrow** next to the text boxes).

❖ Choose **Before** to add a column to the left of your insertion point or a row above the insertion point.

❖ Choose **After** to add a column to the right of your insertion point or a row below the insertion point.

After you choose **OK**, your table should look like Figure 17.8.

Category	1993	1994
Salaries	152334	380952
Telephone	1890	2590
Meeting and Seminar Refreshments	250	18620

Figure 17.8 *The new row appears above the row where your insertion point was located.*

NOTE

There are two quick and easy keystroke shortcuts for adding one row at a time: **Alt+Insert** adds a row above your insertion point, and **Alt+Shift+Insert** adds a row below your insertion point. One more tip: You can delete the current row by pressing **Alt+Delete**.

NOTE

To view row and column indicators (which display the row number and column letter), simply click the **Row/Column Indicators** button on the Tables Toolbar.

Adding a Row as You Type

The procedure described above is the best way to add rows or columns *except* in one situation. You can add a row at the end of a table by pressing the **Tab** key with your insertion point in the very last cell.

Do It

1. Move your insertion point to the last cell.

2.   Press the **Tab** key. A new row is created at the bottom. Leave the row empty for now—we'll use it later to add up the columns of numbers.

This feature means that you can keep entering text and adding rows on the fly without having to go through the Insert Columns/Rows dialog box every time. It only works at the end of a table, though—you can't use this technique to add rows in the middle of a table (or to add columns anywhere). If you want to disable Auto Row Insert, choose **Format** from the Table menu, select the **Table** radio button, and check **Auto Row Insert.**

Joining Cells

The top row is broken down into three cells, just like all of the other rows, but we want a title that spans all of the columns. To do that, we need to turn the three cells into one. Sounds complicated, but it's not.

Do It

1.   Select the cells you want to join by dragging the mouse pointer across them, or by using the **Shift** key in combination with the **Arrow** keys. For this example, select cells A1 through A3.

2.   Choose **Join Cells** from the QuickMenu. You can also choose **Join** from the Table menu, then choose **Cell** from the cascading Join menu.

3.   Type the text shown in the top row of Figure 17.9. Cells A1 through A3 are now one big cell called A1, as you can see in Figure 17.9.

Department Budget		
Category	1993	1994
Salaries	152334	380952
Telephone	1890	2590
Meeting and Seminar Refreshments	250	18620

Figure 17.9 *The cells in the top row are joined to create one cell.*

You can also split a cell into more than one row or column by choosing **Split Cell** from the Tables QuickMenu (or **Split**, then **Cell**, from the Table menu). If you want to split a group of cells (for example, you could select several cells in one row and split them into two columns) you have to use the Table menu. When cells are selected, **Split Cell** is replaced by **Join Cells** on the QuickMenu.

Changing Column Widths

Let's increase the width of the first column so *Meeting and Seminar Refreshments* fits on one line.

The fastest way to get *Meeting and Seminar Refreshments* on one line is to select **Size Column to Fit** from the Table Toolbar or QuickMenu. The column will expand to include the entire line.

Another way to increase your column is to use the Ruler Bar. Figure 17.10 shows what the Ruler Bar looks like when your insertion point is inside a table. The downward-pointing arrows are for the column width, and the arrows that point in are for the column margins. You only see margin markers for the column where your insertion point is located (in Figure 17.10, the insertion point is in column B, so the margin markers you see are for that column). You can drag the column markers to increase or decrease the width of a column, or drag the margin markers to change the margins within a column.

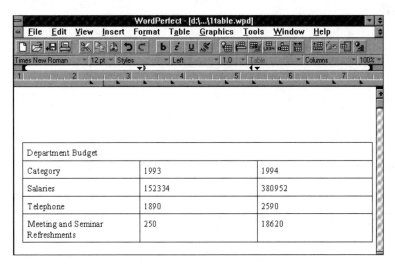

Figure 17.10 *Notice the column and margin markers on the Ruler Bar.*

NOTE

You can drag to change column widths even if the Ruler Bar isn't turned on. Just position the mouse pointer over a column line until the mouse pointer changes into a double arrow.

Do It

Drag the arrow to the left or right to change the size of the column:

1. If the Ruler Bar isn't visible, activate it.

2. Position your mouse pointer on the downward-pointing arrow on the Ruler between columns 1 and 2.

3. Drag the mouse to the right to increase the width of the column, then release the mouse button. As you drag, a dashed line appears to help you see where you are.

NOTE

You can change column widths with the keyboard by placing your insertion point anywhere in the column and pressing **Ctrl+<** to make the column narrower, or **Ctrl+>** to make the column wider. You can hold down the **Ctrl** key and keep tapping the < or > key until the column is the right width.

You might have to experiment a little to get the right width. If the text isn't all on one line when you release the mouse button, or if you dragged too far and the column's too wide, just try it again.

Using the **Size Column to Fit** option or the Ruler to change column widths is quick and easy, but there might be times when you want to enter more precise measurements for column width (or change the widths for several columns at one time). You can do that through the Table or Column Format dialog box, which we'll talk about in a bit.

USING THE TABLE EXPERT

The easiest way to format your table is to use one of the 40 predefined styles included with WordPerfect. Just choose **Expert** from the Table menu or

QuickMenu, or click the Table Expert button on the Tables toolbar. You can preview the different styles by clicking on their names in the Available Styles list. If you don't want the style to affect any cells you might add to the table, select **Apply Style on a Cell by Cell Basis**. Select **Clear Current Table Settings Before Applying** to get rid of any existing formatting before applying the style. Once you choose a style and select the options you want, just click **Apply.**

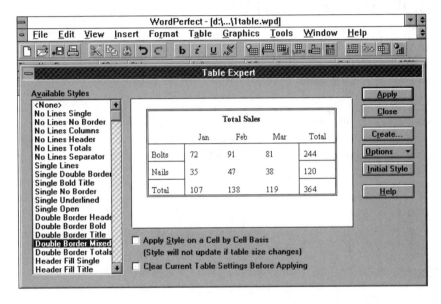

Figure 17.11 *Choose a style in the Table Expert dialog box.*

You can also create your own styles. Just format your table however you want—add borders, lines, and other stuff (using the techniques covered in the next section)—then, with your insertion point anywhere in the table, follow the steps below to give your style a name so that you can easily reapply it to any other table.

1. Open the Table Expert dialog box and choose **Create**.
2. Enter a name in the Create Table Style dialog box.
3. Choose **OK**.

That's all there is to it. The style you just created appears at the end of the Available Styles list in the Table Expert dialog box. Use the same techniques to apply it to a table that you would use for any of the predefined styles.

NOTE

If you want to use a particular style (either one you've created or one of WordPerfect's) as the default for all of your tables, choose **Initial Style**, then choose **Yes**.

ADDITIONAL FORMATTING TECHNIQUES

When you're entering text in a table, you can use most of the formatting techniques you've already learned. You can press **Shift+F7** to center text on a line, or use the **Bold**, **Italic**, or **Underline** button to change the appearance of a portion of text.

But what if you want *all* of the text in one column centered? Or you want to change all of your headings to bold text, and be sure that any text you add to those cells will also be bold? The Format dialog boxes give you options for making changes to the whole table or any part of it.

NOTE

If you want to apply the same formatting to a group of cells, select the cells before you choose **Format**.

Whether you want to format one cell, a row, a column, or the entire table, you get to the Format dialog boxes the same way.

In the following sections, I'll go over the various options for formatting cells, rows, columns, and tables. For all of them, you'll use one of these procedures to open a Format dialog box:

❖ Click on the **Table Format** button on the Tables Toolbar.

❖ Choose **Format** from the Tables QuickMenu.

❖ Press **Ctrl+F12** or choose **Format** from the Table menu (if you don't have a mouse, these are your only options).

The options for formatting tables, columns, and cells are related, so I'll discuss them first. Then I'll discuss the row options separately.

Selecting in Tables

You'll often select a group of cells before you edit a table's structure or format. For the most part, selecting in tables works the same as in your document text, but there are a few things to be aware of.

Pay attention to the shape and direction of your mouse pointer before you start selecting. If it's shaped like an I-beam, dragging selects only the text in the cells, not the cells themselves. When you move the mouse pointer near any of the cell borders, the I-beam turns into an arrow. To select cells, make sure the mouse pointer is an arrow (but not the double-headed arrow you get when the mouse pointer's *on* a cell border—that's used for changing the column width).

Now that you know what to look for, I can give you a few selecting shortcuts:

❖   Double-click when you see an upward arrow to select an entire column.

❖   Double-click when you see a left-pointing arrow to select an entire row.

❖   Triple-click when you see either of the arrows to select the entire table.

If you're using the keyboard, **Shift+F8** turns cell selection on. **F8** (the regular select key) just selects cell contents.

Using the Cell Format Dialog Box

Options that you choose in the Cell Format dialog box apply to the cell where your insertion point is currently located, or to the group of cells that you select before you open the dialog box.

Do It

1. Place your insertion point in the cell you want to format, or select a group of cells.

2. Open the Format dialog box using any of the techniques described in "Additional Formatting Techniques" earlier in this chapter. The Format dialog box is displayed with the **Cell** radio button selected, as shown in Figure 17.12.

WARNING

The dialog boxes for cell, column, row, and table don't actually have different names. The only way you can tell which one is active is by looking at which radio button is selected. Double-check the radio buttons before you change any settings, or you could end up changing the whole table when you only meant to change a cell.

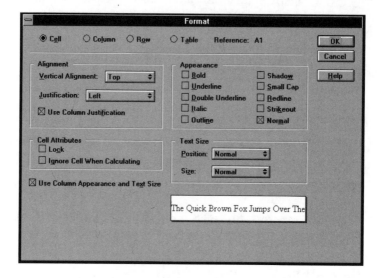

Figure 17.12 The Cell Format dialog box.

❖ Choose **Top, Bottom,** or **Center** from the Vertical Alignment pop-up list to align text or numbers vertically in a cell.

❖ The **Justification** options are the same ones you already learned about: **Left, Right, Center, Full,** and **All.** There's also a **Decimal Align** option that lines numbers up on their decimal points (it's just like the decimal-aligned tabs you used earlier).

❖ Change the text appearance by choosing one or more of the check boxes in the Appearance area.

❖ Choose **Subscript** or **Superscript** from the Position pop-up list if you want the text to appear above or below the baseline.

❖ Choose one of the size options to change the size of your text in relation to your base font.

❖ Choose **Lock** from the Cell Attributes area if you don't want what's in the cell to be changed. When a cell is locked, you can't enter or edit text in that cell.

WARNING

Don't think that locking a cell protects you from any changes being made. Anyone who knows how to format a table can just go in and unlock it. The main purpose of locking a cell is to keep anyone from *accidentally* changing its contents.

❖ Choose **Ignore Cell When Calculating** from the Cell Attributes area if you don't want a cell's contents included in any formulas or calculations. You should do this for any cells that have numbers that are just part of the text (like dates or part numbers).

NOTE

Use Column Justification and **Use Column Appearance and Text Size** are checked when you first open the dialog box. Unless you specify otherwise, cells use whatever settings are in effect for the columns in which they are located.

Using the Column Format Dialog Box

The Column Format dialog box contains a lot of the same options as the Cell Format dialog box. The main difference is that any options you select here apply to the entire column where your insertion point is located (or to a selected group of columns).

Do It

1. Place your insertion point anywhere in the column you want to format (you don't have to select the whole column). If you want to format more than one column at a time, select at least a part of each column before you proceed.

2. Open the Format dialog box and make sure the **Column** radio button is selected. The Column Format dialog box is displayed, as shown in Figure 17.13.

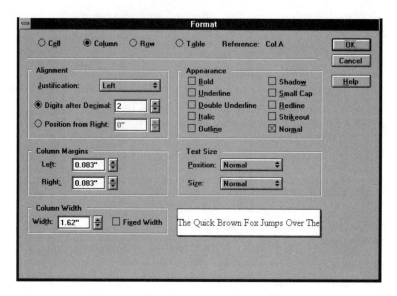

Figure 17.13 *The Column Format dialog box.*

❖ The **Justification**, **Appearance**, and **Text Size** options are the same as those in the Cell Format dialog box.

❖ You can make precise margin adjustments (instead of using the Ruler Bar) by entering settings in the **Column Margins** text boxes.

❖ You can enter a precise width setting in the **Column Width** text box.

If you want several columns to have the same width or the same margin settings, use this dialog box instead of adjusting the widths with the Ruler Bar. Doing this through the dialog box is much faster and more exact—with the Ruler Bar, not only do you have to adjust each column separately, but it can be difficult to end up with the same settings for several columns.

Using the Table Format Dialog Box

A lot of the choices here will look familiar from working with cells and columns. If you want a particular setting to apply to the whole table, make the selection from the Table Format dialog box.

Do It

1. Your insertion point can be anywhere in the table.

2. Open the Format dialog box and make sure the **Table** radio button is selected. The Table Format dialog box is shown in Figure 17.14.

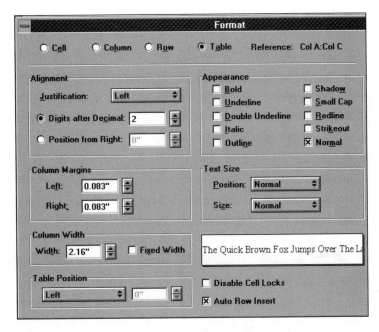

Figure 17.14 *The Table Format dialog box.*

❖ You can adjust the alignment, column margins, column width, appearance, or text size for the whole table.

❖ Choose **Left**, **Right**, **Center**, **Full**, or **From Left Edge** to tell WordPerfect how you want the table placed on the page. **Left**, **Right**, and **Center** align the table in relation to the left and right margins. If you choose **Full**, WordPerfect adjusts the column widths to make the table fill all the space between the margins. If you choose **From Left Edge**, enter a number in the text box to specify where you want the table to start on the page.

WARNING

If you set the position to full, you lose control over your column widths and may end up with some unpredictable results. If you add or delete a column, WordPerfect makes adjustments so the table always fills all of the available space between the margins. As a general rule, don't choose **Full** for any table where you want your column widths to stay put.

Using the Row Format Dialog Box

The Row Format dialog box has options that apply specifically to rows. One of the most useful Table features, the ability to create header rows that repeat on every page of a table, is hidden away at the bottom of this dialog box.

Do It

1. Place your insertion point anywhere in the row you want to format. If you want to format more than one row, select a portion of each row.

2. Open the Format dialog box and make sure the **Row** radio button is selected. The Row Format dialog box is shown in Figure 17.15.

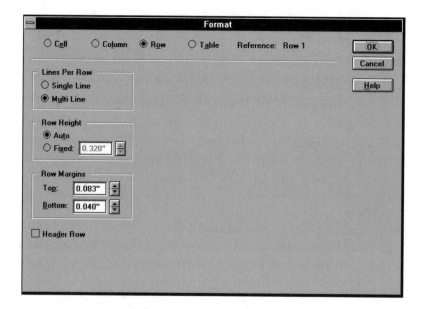

Figure 17.15 *The Row Format dialog box.*

❖ By default, you can enter as many lines of text as you want into a row, and the height of the row automatically expands to fit the text. You can specify a specific row height by entering a number in the **Fixed** text box, and you can limit text entry to one line by choosing **Single Line**.

❖ Use **Row Margins** to adjust the top and bottom margins for the row or rows.

❖ When you check the **Header Row** check box, the row where your insertion point is located (or the multiple rows that you selected) repeats at the top of every page if the table continues beyond a page break.

Do It

Now that you understand the different formatting options, make the following changes to the table you created:

1. Center all of the headings. *Hint:* use column formatting for the first column and cell formatting for the top two rows.

2. Make the top row a header row. *Hint:* use the Row Format dialog box.

3. Center the text in the top row, change the text size to **large**, and change the appearance to **bold**. *Hint:* use the Cell Format dialog box.

4. Tell WordPerfect to ignore the cells containing the dates during calculations. *Hint:* try the Cell Format dialog box.

When you're done, your table should look like Figure 17.16.

Department Budget		
Category	1993	1994
Salaries	152334	380952
Telephone	1890	2590
Meeting and Seminar Refreshments	250	18620

Figure 17.16 *The sample table with formatting applied.*

The table is starting to look pretty good. Just a few more touches and it will be ready to go.

Changing the Number Type

This is where you see why I had you type the numbers without any commas or dollar signs. You can type your numbers as plain vanilla text and use the Number Type feature to format them.

Do It

1. Depending on what you want to do, position your insertion point as follows:

    ❖ To select a number type for one cell, your insertion point should be in that cell.

    ❖ To select a number type for a column, your insertion point can be anywhere in the column.

    ❖ To select a number type that will apply to the whole table, your insertion point can be anywhere in the table.

    ❖ To select a number type for a group of cells, select the cells.

    For our sample table, select cells **B3 through C6**. (Yes, I know that includes a row with nothing in it, but we're formatting it now so it'll be all set when we do our calculations.)

2. Choose **Number Type** from the Tables Toolbar or the Tables QuickMenu. The Number Type dialog box is displayed, as shown in Figure 17.17. You can also press **Alt+F12** or choose **Number Type** from the Table menu.

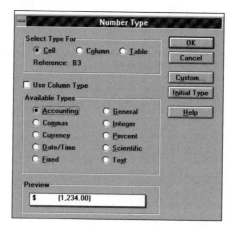

Figure 17.17 *The Number Type dialog box.*

3. Choose one of the Select Type For radio buttons: **Cell** affects only the cell or selected cells; **Column** affects a column or selected columns; **Table** affects the entire table. For the sample table, choose **Cell**.

4. Select the number type you want and choose **OK**. For the sample table, we'll choose the **Accounting** type, which formats the numbers as currency and lines up the dollar signs to the left.

5. Select the **Initial Type** button if you would like your changes to be the default number format for future tables.

Before you leave this dialog box, take a little time to play with the different choices and see what they do in the Preview box.

NOTE

When you choose **Text**, WordPerfect treats whatever you put in the cell as regular text and doesn't include it in any calculations. Changing the number type to **Text** for the cells containing dates would have had the same effect as choosing **Ignore Cell When Calculating**. The main difference between the two options is that you can use **Ignore Cell When Calculating** even if the number is formatted as a type that is normally included in calculations.

Take a look at Figure 17.18. We're almost there!

Department Budget		
Category	1993	1994
Salaries	$ 152,334.00	$ 380,952.00
Telephone	$ 1,890.00	$ 2,590.00
Meeting and Seminar Refreshments	$ 250.00	$ 18,620.00

Figure 17.18 *The sample table with numbers formatted as Accounting type.*

Changing the Border and Line Styles

You can change the borders, lines, and fill patterns for tables just like you did with graphics boxes. If you wanted, every cell could have a different line style (of course, that would look pretty silly, but it's technically possible).

When you change lines or borders, the changes affect the cell that your insertion point is in or the group of cells that is selected.

Do It

1. Place your insertion point in the cell you want or select a group of cells.
2. Choose **Lines/Fill** from the Tables Toolbar or **Lines/Fill** from the QuickMenu (or press **Shift+F12)**. The Table Lines/Fill dialog box is displayed, as shown in Figure 17.19.

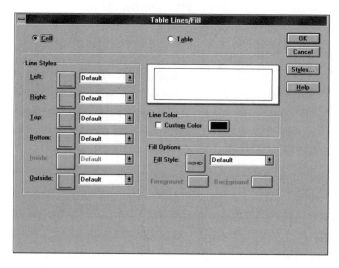

Figure 17.19 *The Table Lines/Fill dialog box.*

3. Choose **Cell** if you want your choices to affect just one cell or selected cells. Choose **Table** if you want your choices to affect the entire table.
4. Choose a line style from the line style palette or drop-down list next to the line you want to change.

NOTE

If you have a group of cells selected, the line style positions apply to the entire selection. For example, choosing **Outside** would affect all of the outside lines for the currently selected block of cells.

In Figure 17.20, I selected the entire table and changed the outside lines to the **Gray Mat** style. Then I changed the bottom lines for the first and second rows to **Double**.

If you want a table without any lines, select the whole table, then choose **None for Inside and Outside Lines**.

Department Budget		
Category	1993	1994
Salaries	$ 152,334.00	$ 380,952.00
Telephone	$ 1,890.00	$ 2,590.00
Meeting and Seminar Refreshments	$ 250.00	$ 18,620.00

Figure 17.20 The sample table with a line-style change.

If you use a thick line style (as I did in Figure 17.20), you might have to adjust your column margins and line height. I had to increase the line height for the first and last rows and increase the column margin for the last column so the text wouldn't be crowded.

I think this table's just about done. Just one more thing: we need to total up the columns.

PERFORMING CALCULATIONS ON A COLUMN OR ROW OF NUMBERS

This serves as a brief (and I hope tantalizing) introduction to all of the wonderful mathematical calculations you can perform in tables. You can insert complex formulas of your own, or use the predefined functions to create forms and reports. You can even insert formulas in floating cells, which can be part of your text and reference formulas in tables.

Do It

To add a column or a row:

1. Place your insertion point in the cell just below or to the right of the numbers you want to add up. For the sample table, place your insertion point in cell B6.

2. Choose **Sum** from the Table menu.

Voila! The numbers are totaled, just like that, as shown in Figure 17.21. With your insertion point in cell B6, take a look at the Status Bar—instead of the number in the cell, it displays *SUM(B2:B5)* after the cell address. When you chose **Sum**, WordPerfect inserted a predefined formula in the cell.

Department Budget		
Category	1993	1994
Salaries	$ 152,334.00	$ 380,952.00
Telephone	$ 1,890.00	$ 2,590.00
Meeting and Seminar Refreshments	$ 250.00	$ 18,620.00
TOTAL	$ 156,467.00	

Figure 17.21 *Sample table with the numbers in column B totaled with* **Sum**.

WARNING

Make sure your insertion point is in the right place before you choose **Sum**. If there's anything in the cell, the Sum calculation replaces it.

If you change any of the numbers in cells that are part of a formula, choose **Calculate** from the Table Toolbar or from the Quickmenu. Choose **Calc Table** to calculate all formulas in the current table, or **Calc Document** to calculate the formulas in all tables in your document.

How about automating the calculation so that each time you change a number in the formula it automatically totals with the correct new number? If you would like this option, then go back to the Calculate dialog box. See the **Automatic Calculation Mode** radio buttons? Click on either **Calculate Table** or **Calculate Document**. Now change a number (within a formula), move your insertion key, and watch your total change.

Sum is one of almost 100 spreadsheet functions that you can use in your table formulas. *Functions* are predefined math formulas. For example, there's a function called PV that can calculate the periodic interest rate from specified cells, and another called MAX that can find the largest number in a list. To learn more about using functions and formulas in tables, refer to the section on "Tables: Spreadsheet and Floating Cell" in your WordPerfect manual. To get quick on-line help for formulas and functions when you're in a table, choose **Formula Bar** from the QuickMenu or the Tables menu, click on **?**, and choose **Help**. This gives you a list of specific Help topics that apply to the spreadsheet features—just choose the one you want.

Copying a Formula

Once you define a formula, you can copy it to different cells. Let's copy the total from cell B6 to C6.

Do It

1. Place your insertion point in the cell you want to copy from (B6).

2. Choose **Copy Formula** from the Formula Bar or the Table menu. The Copy Formula dialog box, shown in Figure 17.22, is displayed.

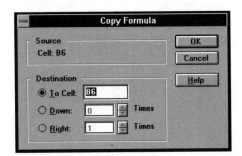

Figure 17.22 *The Copy Formula dialog box.*

The Source Cell is displayed at the top of the dialog box (in this case, B6). You can copy a formula to a specific cell or to adjacent cells to the right of or below the current cell. If you choose **Down** or **Right**, enter a number in the appropriate text box to tell WordPerfect how many times you want to copy the formula.

3. Choose **Right**, accept the default value of **1**, and choose **OK**. The completed table is displayed in Figure 17.23. Good work!

Department Budget		
Category	1993	1994
Salaries	$ 152,334.00	$ 380,952.00
Telephone	$ 1,890.00	$ 2,590.00
Meeting and Seminar Refreshments	$ 250.00	$ 18,620.00
TOTAL	$ 156,467.00	$ 404,156.00

Figure 17.23 *The completed table.*

SAVING A TABLE (OR PART OF ONE)

When you save a WordPerfect document, any tables in the document are saved along with it, so you don't have to do anything special unless you want to save only part of a table or to save the table as a separate file. To save part of a table (for example, a couple of rows or columns), just select the cells you want before saving. You'll get a dialog box that asks if you want to save the **Entire File** or **Selected Text**. If you choose **Selected Text**, WordPerfect takes you to the Save As dialog box, where you can give your selection a name.

DELETING A TABLE (OR PART OF ONE)

Now that you've created this masterpiece, I'll tell you how to tear it apart, or even get rid of the whole thing. (If you want to keep the sample table, be sure you save it before you proceed.)

Deleting an Entire Table or Its Contents

Do It

1. Select the entire table. *Hint*: triple-click when the mouse pointer looks like a left or up arrow.

2. Choose **Delete** from the Tables QuickMenu or the Tables menu, or just press the **Delete** key. The Delete Table dialog box shown in Figure 17.24 is displayed.

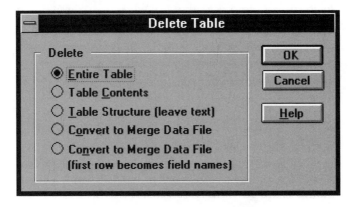

Figure 17.24 *The Delete Table dialog box.*

3. Make a selection:

    ❖ Choose **Entire Table** to delete the table and its contents.

    ❖ Choose **Table Contents** to delete any text or formulas in the table, but retain the structure and formatting. You can clear everything in the table and start from scratch.

    ❖ Choose **Table Structure (leave text)** to remove all of the table structure and formatting but leave the text. When the table structure is deleted, WordPerfect inserts tabs between the columns.

    The last two choices have to do with merge files, which are covered in Chapter 22. Just note for now that it is possible to convert a table to a merge data file.

WARNING

Don't delete a table or its structure unless you're absolutely sure that's what you want. If you do either of these by mistake, choose **Undo** or **Undelete** right away.

4.   Choose **OK**.

Deleting Columns, Rows, or the Contents of Selected Cells

If your insertion point is in one cell, or if you have anything less than the entire table selected, you get the dialog box shown in Figure 17.25 when you choose **Delete**.

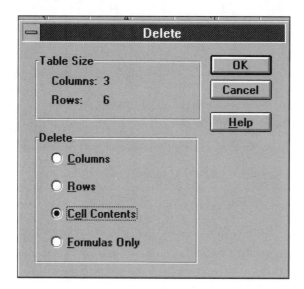

***Figure 17.25** The Delete dialog box.*

❖   Choose **Columns** to delete a column or selected columns.

❖   Choose **Rows** to delete a row or selected rows.

❖   Choose **Cell Contents** to delete the contents of a cell or selected cells.

❖   Choose **Formulas Only** to delete the formulas of your selection.

DATA FILL

If you're creating a list of incremental numbers or dates, this option can automate the process and fill in the blanks for you. It's easy. In the example shown below I wanted to create a table that lists numbers going across by 5s up to 50. Instead of typing **5**, **10**, **15**, and so on, I can easily type the first two figures and let **Data Fill** do the rest.

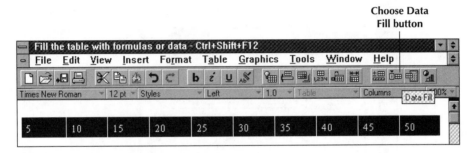

Figure 17.26 *Table data created using Data Fill.*

Do It

1. Create your table, and type in the first two numbers (at least two cells with values need to be input to establish a pattern).

2. Select the cells that contain the incrementing pattern of values you want to repeat and extend the selection to include the cells in which you want to continue the pattern. In this example 10 columns must be highlighted.

3. Choose **Data Fill** from the Table Toolbar or the Table menu (or press **Ctrl+Shift+F12**).

CREATING A CHART FROM A TABLE

Once a table is complete you can then create a chart. From the example shown in this chapter we've completed a table comparing 1993 and 1994 department budgets. Now let's take this data (no need to retype the information) and create a chart.

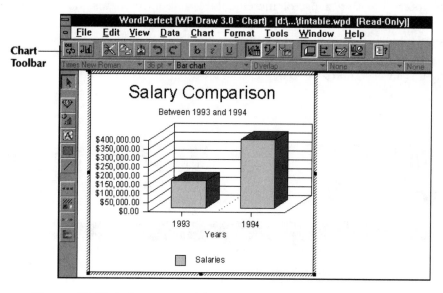

Chart —
Toolbar

Figure 17.27 *A chart created from our Department Budget Table.*

Do It

1. Create a table with data you want to appear in a chart.

2. The top row (Row 1) and the first column (Column A) will be the data labels. In my example I selected rows 2 and 3 to be included in this chart. Row 2 and column 1 gave me my *x*- and *y*-axis, and the second row shows the salary between 1993 and 1994 (additonal rows may be included).

3. With the insertion point in the table (or with your selection highlighted), choose **Chart** from the Tables Toolbar or the Table menu.

4. Now you are in **Chart Editor**. Here you can change the legends, add a title, and create the chart appearance you desire (lines, bars, pie chart, etc.). These options are available by choosing **Chart** from the Menu bar, or by selecting one of the various chart buttons.

5. To return to your table, just click your mouse outside of the chart area.

FROM HERE ...

As you've seen, Tables is an extremely powerful and multifaceted feature. And we hardly even scratched the surface in terms of the spreadsheet capabilities! As you work with tables, you'll continue to discover new uses. Several of the templates included with this book use tables—take a look at them to get an idea of what's possible.

In the next chapter, we'll take a look at the Columns feature—another way of formatting text in rows and columns. And you'll learn how to set up a list of names and addresses so they'll print on mailing labels.

CHAPTER 18

Columns, Labels, and Subdivide Page

(Dividing Up Your Page)

Let's talk about:

- ❖ Types of columns
- ❖ Creating newspaper columns
- ❖ Creating parallel columns
- ❖ Editing columns with the Ruler Bar
- ❖ Creating mailing labels
- ❖ Subdividing pages

In the last chapter, you learned about tables, one of WordPerfect's most powerful tools. But WordPerfect doesn't stop with just one feature for dividing a page into columns and rows—Columns, Labels, and Subdivide Page all give you different ways of breaking a page into smaller parts.

UNDERSTANDING COLUMN TYPES

There are two main types of columns: *newspaper* and *parallel*. Newspaper columns come in two flavors: regular and balanced. Parallel columns can be defined as regular or block protected.

❖   **Newspaper-style columns** get their name from (you guessed it) newspapers. Newspaper articles are usually laid out in two or more columns, and the text wraps from the bottom of one column to the top of the next. Newsletters are another common application for newspaper-style columns. With regular newspaper-style columns, the text flows to the bottom margin before it wraps to the next column. This can result in uneven column lengths, as shown in Figure 18.1.

Figure 18.1 *Newspaper Columns with uneven column lengths.*

❖   **Balanced Newspaper columns** are just like regular newspaper columns. The only difference is that WordPerfect adjusts the columns so they are all the same length. Figure 18.2 shows the same text as Figure 18.1 with Balanced Newspaper columns turned on.

Figure 18.2 *The same text with balanced newspaper columns.*

❖ **Parallel columns** are arranged in rows, as shown in Figure 18.3. A new row starts below the longest column in the previous row.

	Cranial Nerves
Olfactory	Conducts impulses from nose to brain. Controls sense of smell.
Facial	Conducts impulses from taste buds of tongue to brain and from brain to face muscles. Controls sense of taste and contraction of muscles of facial expression.
Acoustic	Conducts impulses from ear to brain. Controls hearing and sense of balance.
Spinal Accessory	Conducts impulses from brain to some shoulder and neck muscles. Controls shoulder movements and turning movements of head.

Figure 18.3 *An example of parallel columns.*

❖ **Parallel with Block Protect** is exactly the same as parallel. The only difference is that block protect codes are placed around every row, so that if an entire row won't fit on the page, it wraps to the next page.

Working with Newspaper Columns

As with most other WordPerfect features, you can apply column formats before or after you enter your text. For newspaper-style columns, it's usually easier to type your text first and then turn on the columns feature with a couple of mouse clicks. Of course there are several ways to refine your columns, but it really can be that easy.

To see how newspaper columns work, enter some text, or open a document that contains a little over half a page of regular text.

Do It

The Power Bar is the quickest and easiest way to define two to five columns. If you don't have a mouse, or if you want to make more refinements to your column definition, use the Columns dialog box (instructions follow this section).

1. Place your insertion point where you want the columns to begin. Using Figure 18.1 as an example, I placed my insertion point in the first text paragraph, since I didn't want the heading to be part of the first column.

2. Click on the **Columns** button on the Power Bar.

3. Click on the number of columns you want (or click on **Columns** and then click on your selection). Figure 18.4 shows the button options; I've selected **2 Columns**.

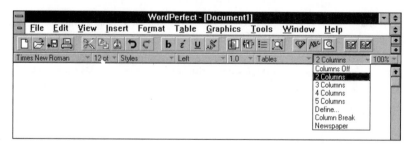

Figure 18.4 *The pulled-down Columns Define button.*

As soon as you release the mouse button, your text reformats into columns. Any text you add is automatically part of the column format.

Do It

To define columns using the columns dialog box:

1. Place your insertion point where you want the columns to begin.

2. Select **Define** from the Columns Power Bar button pull-down list, or select **Columns** from the Format menu and choose **Define** from the cascading Columns menu. The Columns dialog box is displayed, as shown in Figure 18.5.

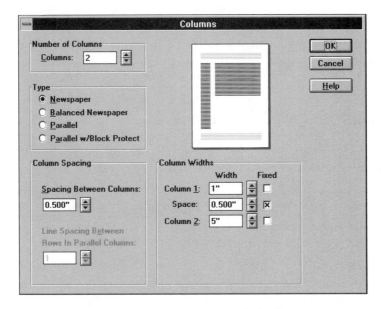

Figure 18.5 *The Columns dialog box.*

3. Enter the number of columns you want in the **Columns** text box, or use the **Up** and **Down Arrows**.

4. Select one of the **Type** radio buttons.

5. Adjust the measurements in the Column Spacing and Column Widths areas if necessary.

6. When you're done, choose **OK**.

By default, WordPerfect leaves a 0.5-inch gutter between each column, and the columns all have the same width.

❖ Enter a number in the **Spacing Between Columns** text box to specify the amount of space you want between columns.

❖ Enter a number in the appropriate **Column Width** or **Space** text box to increase or decrease the width of a particular column or adjust the spacing between specific columns.

❖ Choose **Fixed** for any column or spacing measurement to make sure the setting stays the same even if you make changes to the other columns. Unless you check **Fixed**, WordPerfect adjusts the column and spacing measurements so that they fill all of the space between the margins. In Figure 18.5, I decreased the width of Column 1 to 1", and this automatically increased the width of Column 2 to 5".

Working with Parallel Columns

There are two main differences between creating parallel columns and newspaper columns:

❖ You have to create parallel columns through the Columns dialog box. They can't be defined through the Power Bar (although you *can* use the Power Bar to access the dialog box).

❖ With parallel columns, it's easier to define them before you enter your text. Don't worry about getting the column widths and margins exactly right, though—you can adjust them later with the Ruler Bar.

In most cases, anything that you would use parallel columns for can be done more easily in a table. Because each cell in a table is treated as a separate unit, it's easier to edit text in tables.

NOTE

Do It

To create parallel columns:

1. Follow the procedures described above to access and choose your options in the Columns dialog box. Notice that there's one additional option for parallel columns: you can adjust the line spacing between rows.

2. Enter your text for the first column.

3. Press **Ctrl+Enter** or choose **Column Break** from the **Columns** button on the Power Bar to force text to the next column.

4. Continue entering text, pressing **Ctrl+Enter** or choosing **Column Break** each time you want to move to the next column or start a new row from the rightmost column.

Turning Columns Off

Once you turn columns on, everything you type is in column format. When you press **Ctrl+Enter**, instead of getting a hard page break, you just force your text to the next column. (To insert an actual hard page break while you are in Column mode, press **Ctrl+Shift+Enter**.) If you want to enter text that's not in column format, you need to turn columns off.

1. Place your insertion point where you want the columns to end.

2. Choose **Columns Off** from the **Columns** button on the Power Bar, or choose **Columns** from the Format menu and choose **Off** from the cascading Columns menu.

Once you've defined columns in a document, you can turn them on and off as many times as you want. Just open the Columns dialog box and choose **OK** to turn columns on. Your current definition is already in there, so you don't have to make any changes.

Adding a Border

You can easily add a border around your columns, and you can customize the borders in any way you want. For newspaper columns, column borders work like page borders—they begin on the page that you specify and continue on every page until you turn them off. For parallel columns, the border applies to the current column group unless you specify otherwise.

1. Place your insertion point on the page where you want the border to start.

2. Choose **Columns** from the Format menu, then choose **Border/Fill** from the cascading Columns menu. The Column Border dialog box is displayed, as shown in Figure 18.6.

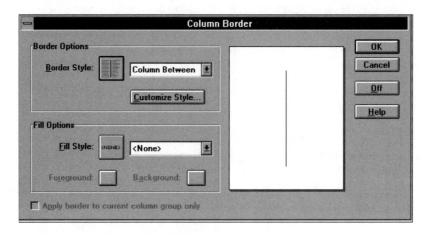

Figure 18.6 *The Column Border dialog box.*

3. Choose a border style from the Border Style palette or drop-down list. In Figure 18.6, you can see that I've chosen **Column Between**, which places a vertical line between each column.

4. If you want shading or a pattern, choose a fill pattern from the Fill Style palette or drop-down list.

5. Choose **OK** when you've made all of your selections. Figure 18.7 shows the sample text with the border applied.

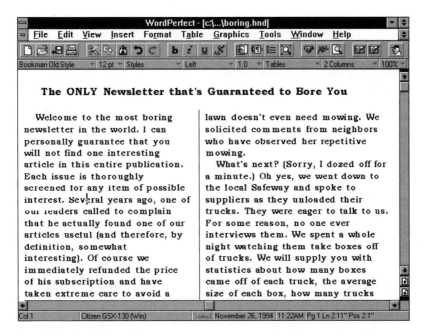

Figure 18.7 *You can place a vertical line between columns.*

To customize your borders by adding a shadow, rounding the corners, or modifying the style for particular lines, choose **Customize Style** from the Column Border dialog box.

Adding Text and Moving Among Columns

You don't have to do anything special to add text—any text that you add between a column definition code and a column off code is part of the column format. You can use any of the formatting techniques you've already learned. You can change fonts and justification; you can even insert a table or a graphics box (see Figure 18.8 for an example).

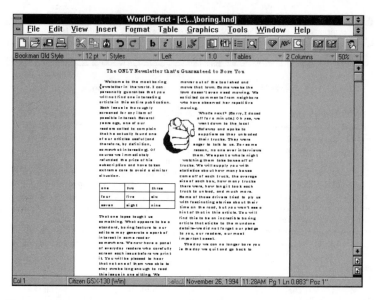

Figure 18.8 *A two-column document with table and graphics box.*

To move your insertion point into a particular column, just click anywhere in that column. Don't forget the Status Bar—it displays information about your column location.

There's a quick keyboard shortcut for moving between columns: press **Alt+Right Arrow** to move your insertion point one column to the right, or **Alt+Left Arrow** to move one column to the left.

Adjusting Columns with the Ruler Bar

You can always edit your column widths and the spacing between columns by going back into the Columns dialog box, but it's much easier with the Ruler Bar. You just drag a marker to make changes, just like you did with document margins and table column widths.

When there are columns, you can only make changes with the Ruler Bar when none of your document is selected—or all of it is.

A reminder—changes you make using the Ruler Bar apply only to the current row and all rows following in that section of your document.

NOTE

LABELS

Now that you've written your newsletter, you need to print mailing labels before you can ship it off to your readers. The most difficult part of this procedure will be reading the number on your box of labels (oh yeah, you do have to remember to buy the labels first). Once you know what kind of labels you want to use, all you have to do is pick your label format from a list.

WordPerfect comes with more than 130 predefined label formats for everything from standard address labels to labels for floppy disks, video cassettes, and name tags. If you can buy the label in a store, WordPerfect probably includes a label definition for it. And if WordPerfect doesn't have the label definition you need, you can create your own or edit one of the predefined formats.

Let's add a label definition and type a few labels so you can see how easy it is. Then I'll go over a few concepts to help you understand how labels work.

Do It

To select a label definition:

1. Place your insertion point where you want the labels to start.

2. Choose **Labels** from the Format menu. The Labels dialog box is displayed, as shown in Figure 18.9. I've chosen **Avery 5160 Address** labels, a very common format for mailing labels.

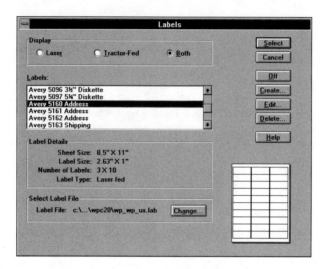

Figure 18.9 *The Labels dialog box.*

3.   Select the label definition you want from the Labels list and choose **Select**.

The first label is displayed on your screen and WordPerfect inserts Labels Form and Paper Sz/Typ codes, as shown in Figure 18.10.

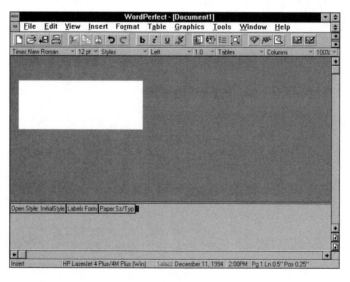

Figure 18.10 *The first label is displayed on screen.*

Do It

To enter text on labels:

1. Enter the text for the label.
2. Press **Ctrl+Enter** to move to the next label.

Repeat steps 1 and 2 until you've entered the text for all of your labels. Every time you press **Ctrl+Enter**, a new label page appears on your screen. Figure 18.11 shows several labels entered. I've set the zoom to **Page Width** to see all of the labels across the page.

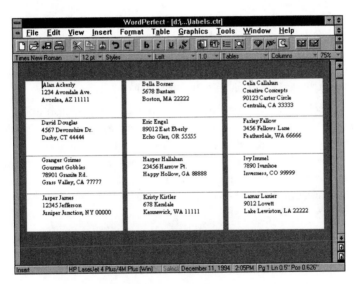

Figure 18.11 *I've entered text for several labels.*

You can also use the merge feature to merge a previously created address list with a labels form. See Chapter 20 for instructions on creating a form file.

Understanding Logical Pages

Did you notice that when you pressed **Ctrl+Enter** to move to the second label, the Status Bar told you you were on page 2? The whole sheet of labels will print on one *physical* page, but each label is considered a separate, *logical* page. The logical page concept means that you can apply page formatting features to labels and have them affect each label. For example, you could create a header or a page border that appears on every label.

NOTE

If you choose **Current Page** in the Print dialog box, the whole physical page (or sheet of labels) will print. To print just one label, use the **Multiple Pages** option.

Understanding the Labels Dialog Box

Take a look back at Figure 18.9. Notice that the **Both** radio button is selected. WordPerfect has label definitions for both laser and tractor-fed printers, and by default it displays all of the definitions for both kinds of printers. This makes for a pretty long list. If you only use one printer, select the appropriate radio button (**Laser** or **Tractor-Fed**) to limit the size of the list.

When the selection bar is on a label definition, information about the labels is displayed in the Label Details area, and a visual representation is displayed in the preview box. In Figure 18.9, you can see that an entire sheet of Avery 5160 labels is 8.5 x 11 inches, each label is 2.63 inches wide and 1 inch high, there are 3 columns and 10 rows, and the labels are laser fed (which means these labels are manufactured to print on a laser printer). The preview box shows the layout for a page of labels.

NOTE

If you don't see an exact definition for the labels you have, you can often substitute another definition that matches your labels. For example, your labels might not be Avery, but they could have the exact same dimensions as the Avery 5160 labels.

Creating Your Own Label Definition

To create a custom label definition, choose **Create** from the Labels dialog box to display the Create Labels dialog box shown in Figure 18.12.

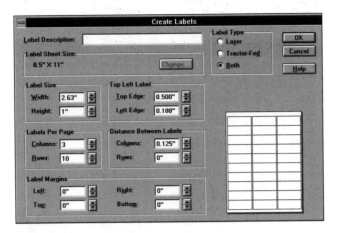

Figure 18.12 *The Create Labels dialog box.*

Before you create labels, move the selection bar to the definition that most closely matches your labels. The Create Labels dialog box uses the options for the currently selected label format. It's usually easier to use a current definition as a starting point.

As a general rule, forget that the **Edit** button on the Labels dialog box even exists. WordPerfect lets you edit any of the predefined label formats, but once you overwrite a format you can't get the original settings back. It's much safer to highlight the labels you want to edit and use **Create**. That way, you'll create a new definition that's based on the original format, but the original format is still intact if you ever want to go back to it.

Label Formatting Tip

In Figure 18.11, the text starts at the top of each label. Since most of the addresses in this example only have three lines, there is a lot of white space at the bottom of the label. You can center each label vertically on its logical page.

1. Place your insertion point anywhere in your first label.

2. Choose **Page** from the Format menu, then choose **Center** from the cascading Page menu. The Center Page(s) dialog box is displayed, as shown in Figure 18.13.

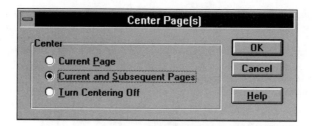

Figure 18.13 *The Center Page(s) dialog box.*

3. Choose **Current and Subsequent Pages** to center all of your addresses vertically within each label.

Figure 18.14 shows the labels as they appear after inserting the Cntr Pgs code at the top of the document. I also dragged the left margin marker on the Ruler Bar to move the text a little to the right.

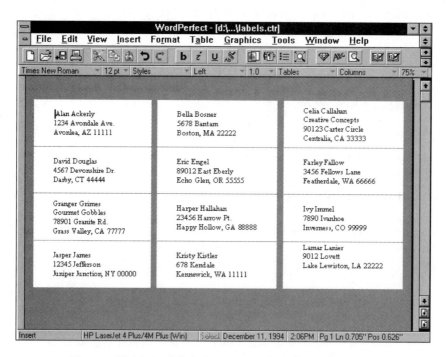

Figure 18.14 *Each label is centered on its logical page.*

Deleting Label Definitions

You can delete a label definition by highlighting the label in the Labels list box and choosing **Delete**. WordPerfect displays a dialog box that asks if you're really sure you want to delete the label form. If you're sure, choose **OK**.

Be very careful with this. The individual label forms are all contained in one file that doesn't take up much space on your hard disk, so there's really no need to delete labels. Don't do it unless you know *absolutely positively for sure* that you'll never use that label definition *anytime ever.*

SUBDIVIDE PAGE

This feature is kind of a subdivision of labels. It uses the same logical page concept, but it's easier to use than labels for creating booklets, programs, invitations, and similar documents.

Instead of selecting or creating a label definition, you just tell WordPerfect how many sections you want the page divided into.

Do It

To subdivide the current page (and all pages following your insertion point):

1. Choose **Page** from the Format menu, then choose **Subdivide Page** from the cascading Page menu. The Subdivide Page dialog box is displayed, as shown in Figure 18.15.

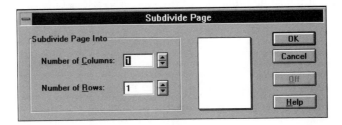

Figure 18.15 *The Subdivide Page dialog box.*

2.   Enter the number of columns and rows you want and choose **OK**.

This is similar to the Create Table dialog box, but here you are telling WordPerfect to divide the whole physical page into the specified number of logical pages. For example, if you choose 2 columns and 2 rows, the page is divided into 4 equal sections.

When you choose **OK**, your document is shown in the logical page format you chose. Enter text or graphics, using any of WordPerfect's formatting features.

As with labels, press **Ctrl+Enter** to move (and force any text following your insertion point) to the next logical page. All following physical pages are subdivided unless you end the Subdivide Page feature by choosing **Off** from the Subdivide Page dialog box—be careful that your insertion point is on the page *after* the last page you want to be subdivided .

FROM HERE ...

It just keeps getting better and better. Not only do you have the power of tables to work with, you know how to use columns for those occasions when tables aren't quite what you need. And you can whip out a sheet of mailing labels in a flash. You know what logical pages are all about, and you can subdivide a physical page to create invitations and brochures.

The next chapters begin a journey into new and exciting territory—the world of automation tools. In a way, all of WordPerfect's features are automation tools, but the features in the next section are specifically designed to speed up and automate word processing tasks. The first, macros, is one of the most powerful, and at the same time, one of the easiest to use.

SECTION VI

AUTOMATION TOOLS

CHAPTER 19

An Introduction to Macros

(I'm Tired of Typing the Same Thing Over and Over—I Thought Computers Were Supposed to Make My Life Easier)

Let's talk about:

- ❖ What is a macro?
- ❖ Recording a simple text macro
- ❖ Editing a macro
- ❖ Pausing during macro recording
- ❖ A look at the macros included with WordPerfect

What is a macro? An excellent question. Great minds have pondered that question down through the centuries (well, for at least ten years or so). At its most basic, a macro is a shortcut that uses one command to replaces several keystrokes, commands, or actions. You can use macros to eliminate repetitive typing or to replace any series of actions that you perform on a routine basis.

In this chapter, you'll create a simple recorded macro—sort of like turning on a tape recorder and letting WordPerfect record everything you do. You'll learn how to create, play back, and edit a macro. I'll even show you how to pause in the middle of recording a macro.

But WordPerfect macros are much more than a simple recording device. The macros feature includes a complete programming language that can be used to perform almost any task imaginable. For example, you could use the different programming commands to set up a complete data-entry system with its own custom menus and dialog boxes. You can even write macros that control other programs.

We won't get quite that fancy. The goal of this chapter is to help you understand the basics of macros. When you're ready, take a look at WordPerfect's *Online Macros Manual*, especially the modules on Macros Basics and Programming Basics. You can access the online manual by choosing **Macros** from the main Help menu.

RECORDING AND PLAYING A SIMPLE MACRO

Don't underestimate a macro just because it's simple—even the most basic text macro can save you untold hours of typing the same thing over and over. Let's say you write ten letters a day. At the end of every one of them you type **Sincerely**, then you press the **Enter** key three times, type your name, press the **Enter** key again, and type your title. That can get pretty tedious, especially when there's no reason to do it. WordPerfect macros can take the tedium out of typing.

Let's give it a try. We'll start with the signature macro I just described.

Do It

To record a macro:

1. Choose **Macro** from the Tools menu, then choose **Record** from the cascading Macro menu (or press **Ctrl+F10**). The Record Macro dialog box is displayed, as shown in Figure 19.1.

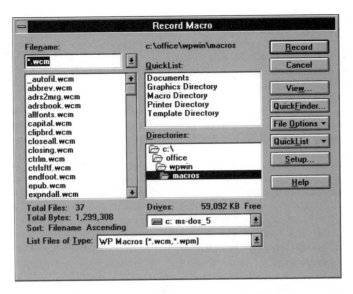

Figure 19.1 *The Record Macro dialog box.*

2. Enter a name for the macro in the **Name** text box. For now, call your macro **sig** (for signature line).

You can use up to eight characters for the macro name, but you don't have to add an extension. WordPerfect automatically supplies a WCM extension for macros. If you create a macro with a different extension, you will have to type in your extension when you run the macro.

NOTE

3. Choose **Record** (or press **Enter**). Notice that the words *Macro Record* are shown at the lower-left corner of the Status Bar; a Macro Bar with buttons including **Stop**, **Play**, and **Pause** buttons is displayed just above your document window; and your mouse pointer turns into the universal *no* symbol (a circle with a diagonal line through it). While you're recording a macro, you can use your mouse to make selections from menus and dialog boxes, but you can't use it to move your insertion point or select text—you have to use the keyboard.

4. Type the text for the signature line just as you normally would. Type **Sincerely,** followed by three hard returns, your name, another hard return, and your title. Figure 19.2 shows my document screen during macro recording with the text entered.

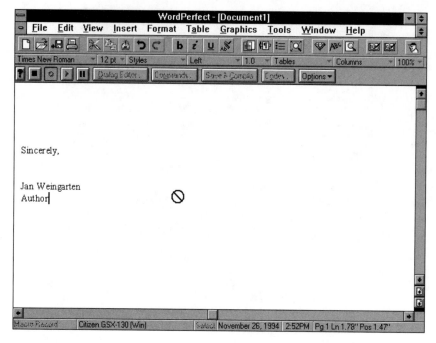

Figure 19.2 *I've entered the text for the signature macro.*

WARNING

If you begin typing before the Macro Bar appears, some of your text may not be successfully recorded into your macro.

5. When you've finished entering text, choose **Macro** from the Tools menu and **Record** from the cascading Macro menu to turn off the recording. (You can also click on the **Stop** button in the Macro Bar, or press **Ctrl+F10**.)

Notice that your pointer turns back into an I-beam, the Macro Bar disappears, and *Macro Record* is no longer shown in your Status Bar. Since the text you typed was just for the purpose of creating the macro, go ahead and close the document without saving.

You just recorded your first macro! Let's prove it by playing it back.

Do It

To play a macro:

1. Choose **Macro** from the Tools menu, then choose **Play** from the cascading Macro menu (or press **Alt+F10**). The Play Macro dialog box shown in Figure 19.3 is displayed.

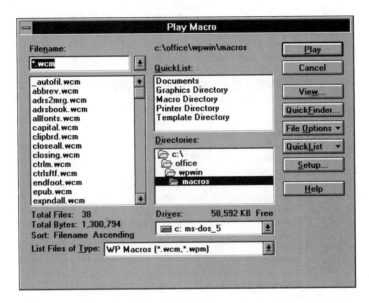

Figure 19.3 *The Play Macro dialog box.*

2. Enter the name of the macro in the Name text box. In this case, it would be **sig.wcm**. You can also choose the macro you want to play from the list below the Filename text box.

3. Choose **Play** (or press **Enter**).

The text you just typed should magically appear on your screen. Now, whenever you want a signature line, all you have to do is play the macro.

The keyboard is much quicker than the mouse for playing macros. To play back a macro with the keyboard, just press **Alt+F10**, type the macro name (without the WCM extension), and press **Enter**. Since the whole idea behind macros is saving time, there's no point in wading through a bunch of menus.

NOTE

There is a nifty way of accessing Macros directly from the Menu. Notice that the cascading Macro menu lists the last four macros you played, as shown in Figure 19.4—since **sig.wcm** was the last macro played, it's shown next to the number 1. You can replay the macro by clicking on its name or by typing **1** (if the cascading menu is displayed).

Tools	
Spell Check...	Ctrl+F1
Thesaurus...	Alt+F1
Grammatik...	Alt+Shift+F1
QuickCorrect...	Ctrl+Shift+F1
Language...	

Play... Alt+F10	**M**acro	▶
Record... Ctrl+F10	**T**emplate Macro	▶
Pa**u**se		
Edit...	Me**r**ge...	Shift+F9
	Sort...	Alt+F9
Macro Bar	**O**utline	
1 sig.wcm	**H**ypertext	
2 ctrlm.wcm		
3 capital.wcm	L**i**st	
4 transpos.wcm	Inde**x**	
	Cross-**R**eference	
	Table of **C**ontents	
	Table of **A**uthorities	
	Ge**n**erate...	Ctrl+F9
	O**b**ject Exchange	▶

Figure 19.4 *The cascading Macro menu.*

NOTE

Template macros are macros assigned to templates—they are always available with a certain template, and can be included in the design of a template. For more on templates, see Chapter 23.

Editing a Macro

A macro file can be edited like any WordPerfect file, but, as you'll see, there are a few things to watch out for. We'll edit the macro you just created to change *Sincerely* to *Yours Truly*.

Do It

To open a macro file:

1. Choose **Macro** from the Tools menu, then choose **Edit** from the cascading Macro menu.

2. Enter the name of your macro in the Filename text box, as shown in Figure 19.5. You can also select the macro you want to edit from the Filename list. Or, if the macro has been recently played, click on the arrow to the right of the Filename text box to show a drop-down list of recently played macros.

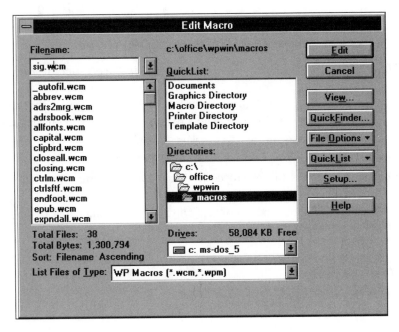

Figure 19.5 *The Edit Macro dialog box.*

3. Choose **Edit**. Your macro appears in a new document window, as shown in Figure 19.6.

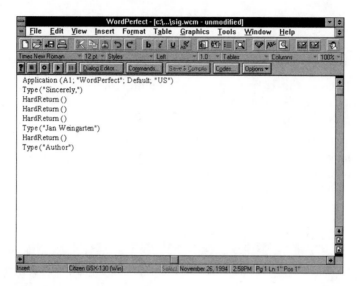

Figure 19.6 *Your sig.wcm macro as it appears in the document window.*

❖ The lines that start with the word *Type* tell WordPerfect that the text between the quotation marks and parentheses should be inserted in the document when the macro is played. Notice that *Sincerely*, my name, and the word *Author* are all inside quotation marks.

❖ HardReturn() is the macro code that tells WordPerfect to insert a hard return in the document when the macro is played. You pressed the **Enter** key three times between *Sincerely* and your name, so there are three HardReturn codes.

Do It

To change the text in the macro:

1. Move your insertion point past the first quotation mark on the second line of the macro.

2. Delete the word *Sincerely*, and type **Yours Truly,** but make sure you leave the quotation marks.

3. Choose **Save and Compile** from the Macro Bar to update the macro file.

4. Choose **Close** from the File menu to clear the document from your screen.

It's easy to edit a text macro. Just add or change any of the text between the quotation marks.

WARNING

Be very careful not to change anything else in the macro file, unless you really know what you're doing. Except for the text between quotation marks, everything else is a code or command. For this macro, make sure you *only* change text inside the quotation marks. If you change something else by mistake, just close the document without saving it or save the macro with a different name. A macro is just a regular file—you can use the **Save As** button on the Macro Bar to give it a different name.

Naming Macros

A macro ends up in a regular document file. You can give a macro any valid filename that's up to eight characters long. When you create a macro, WordPerfect gives the macro an extension of wcm. If you ever use the **Save As** command from the File menu to rename a macro, make sure you include a wcm extension if you want WordPerfect to automatically recognize the file as a macro.

In addition to regular filenames, you can also name a macro with the **Ctrl** or **Ctrl+Shift** keys in combination with any of the number or letter keys on your keyboard (with some exceptions—see the warning below). To do this, just press **Ctrl** or **Ctrl+Shift** plus the number or letter you want instead of typing a filename in the Record Macro dialog box. For example, to create a macro called *Ctrl+1*, open the Record Macro dialog box and place your insertion point in the Name text box. Hold down the **Ctrl** key while you press the **1** key, then release both keys. The name shows up in the text box as **ctrl1.wcm**.

The advantage of using **Ctrl** or **Ctrl+Shift** macros is that they're much faster to play. Instead of pressing **Alt+F10**, typing a macro name, and pressing **Enter**, you can just press **Ctrl** or **Ctrl+Shift** with the letter or number to play the macro. To play the macro named **Ctrl+1**, all you have to do is press **Ctrl+1**.

WARNING

WordPerfect uses all of the **Ctrl+letter** combinations and several of the **Ctrl+Shift** key combinations for its own shortcuts, and WordPerfect's keyboard shortcuts take precedence over any macros that you create. For example, **Ctrl+B** is a shortcut for inserting a bold code, and **Ctrl+S** activates the Save feature. WordPerfect allows you to name a macro **Ctrl+S**, but when you press **Ctrl+S** to play the macro, you'll actually save your document. You can safely use any of the keyboard numbers (keypad numbers won't work) in combination with the **Ctrl** key for macro names, and you can use **Ctrl+Shift** with any keyboard number or letter except the following: B, C, D, O, P, Q, R, S, V, and Z. (You can change the keyboard layout if you want to use more of the **Ctrl**+key combinations for your own purposes or assign different values to any other keys. See Appendix B for more information.)

Pausing While You Record a Macro

You might need to pause to do something else while you're in the middle of recording a macro. To do this, choose **Macro** from the Tools menu, then choose **Pause** from the cascading Macro menu shown in Figure 19.4 (or you can just click on the **Pause** button on the Macro Bar).

When **Pause** is checked (when this happens, the **Pause** button on the Macro Bar appears to be pressed, as shown in Figure 19.7), you can do whatever you want in WordPerfect and it won't be recorded as part of your macro (except for your first selection of the **Pause** feature—see the note below). Pause is a toggle, so when you're ready to start recording again, just choose **Pause** again (or press **Return**.)

NOTE

Recording a macro that pauses once or several times can be useful—you can use the pause(s) to enter something special that changes, like your work title (if you moonlight) or a nickname. Just select **Pause** or press **Enter** to start the macro up again. (See Chapter 20, "Using Merge," for more advanced methods of doing this).

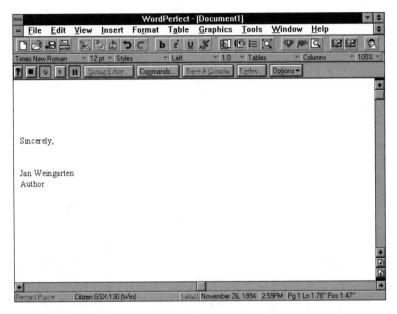

Figure 19.7 *The Macro Bar with Pause activated.*

A Look at the Macros Included with WordPerfect

WordPerfect comes with a whole bunch of useful macros that are all ready to play. They're automatically installed in your macro directory when you install WordPerfect.

All macros in the Macros directory, including all the ones written by WordPerfect or you or anybody else, are listed below the Filename text box in the Play Macro dialog box (shown in Figure 19.3). All you have to do is press **Alt+F10** to open the Play Macro dialog box, scroll up or down the list of macro files, click on the name of the macro and click on **Play** (or press **Enter**) to play it. Easier still—double-click on the macro name to select and play it.

None of this will be very useful to you, though, if you don't know what the macros do.

Here's a hint—try clicking on one of the macro names listed below the text box. If you select a macro that was included with WordPerfect 6.1 (or one of your own macros that you've added a description to), a very brief description of the macro appears at the bottom of the dialog box.

NOTE

The macros played most recently can be found easily with a click on the drop-down list arrow to the right of the Filename text box, as shown in Figure 19.8.

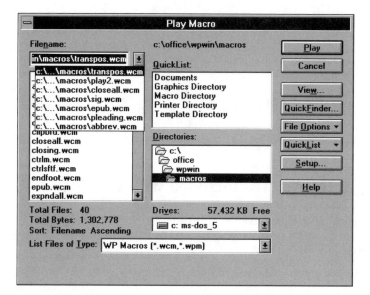

Figure 19.8 *All recently played macros are listed in a drop-down list below the Filename text box in the Play Macro dialog box.*

As you move the selection bar to different filenames, notice that a brief description is displayed at the bottom of the dialog box. For example, in Figure 19.9, **allfonts.wcm** is highlighted, and the description at the bottom says that it creates a list of all font faces available. You can get an idea of what's available by browsing through this list, and playing the predefined macros is a good way to see how powerful macros can be. The descriptions in the Select File dialog box are *really* succinct, so I'll help you out by describing some of the more useful macros.

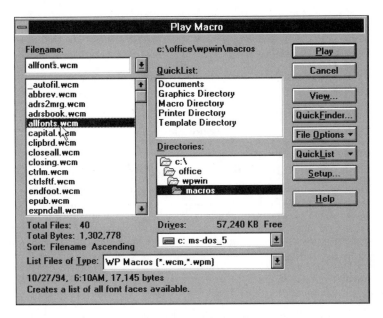

Figure 19.9 *The Play Macro dialog box, showing a brief description of*
***allfonts.wcm** .*

❖ **allfonts.wcm** creates a list of all of your available fonts and displays
the list on screen. You can print the file if you want to see what all of
your fonts look like on the printed page. This macro can take a while to
run, especially if you have a slow computer. You can amuse yourself by
watching its progress on the Status Bar.

❖ **capital.wcm** capitalizes the first letter of the word that your insertion
point is on.

❖ **clipbrd.wcm** displays the Clipboard Viewer. This is useful if you can't
remember what you've cut or copied to the Clipboard.

❖ **closeall.wcm** closes all of your open document windows. It displays a
dialog box that allows you to save changes to any of the documents
before they're closed.

❖ **endfoot.wcm** converts any endnotes in your document to footnotes.

❖ **filestmp.wcm** inserts the name of your document in a header or footer
and gives you options for including the full path name.

❖ **fontdn.wcm** decreases the current font by two point sizes. If you select text before you run the macro, the change applies to the selected text. Otherwise, it applies to all text from the insertion point location onward.

❖ **fontup.wcm** is Fontdn in reverse—it increases the current font by two point sizes. Both of these are really handy when you just want to bump the size up or down a bit without having to choose a specific point size.

❖ **footend.wcm** converts any endnotes in your document to footnotes.

❖ **pagexofy.wcm** keep track of how many pages you have in your document and inserts the current page number and the ending page number in a specified location. You would commonly use this macro in a header or footer. For example, the second page of a ten-page document would say *Page 2 of 10*. If you add or delete pages from the document after you've used this macro, run the macro again to adjust the page numbers.

❖ **parabrk.wcm** displays a dialog box with a selection of fancy symbols that you can use to separate paragraphs. You can choose from symbols like diamonds, snowflakes, or fleur-de-lis, or you can create your own custom symbols.

❖ **pgborder.wcm** lets you select from a list of graphics borders that you can place around a page of text. It displays a dialog box with a **Preview** button that lets you view the different borders before you select the one you want.

❖ **reverse.wcm** allows you to display and print selected text in white on a black background. The dialog box also gives you options for changing the text and background colors. Note that some printers aren't capable of printing reverse text.

❖ **transpos.wcm** transposes the two characters to the left of the insertion point. For example if your insertion point is just past the letters *ab* when you run the macro, it transposes them to read *ba*.

❖ **watermrk.wcm** leads you through the process of creating a watermark. It gives you a choice between adding text or a graphic image. If you choose **Graphics**, it displays a dialog box with a **Preview** button that lets you view the different watermark graphics before you select the one you want. If you choose **Text**, the macro gives you an opportunity to change the font and point size after you type the text you want.

NOTE

WordPerfect's Help system includes an online macro manual. To see brief descriptions of all the macros included with WordPerfect, choose **Macros** from the Help menu and **Additional Help** from the WP Online Macros Manual contents window. Then choose **WordPerfect Macros** from the Additional Help window. As you dig deeper into the world of macros, you'll find the macro manual a valuable resource—it contains a comprehensive reference of all macro commands and features.

ROADMAP

WordPerfect allows you to edit the Toolbar and the Power Bar to create new buttons with your macros on them. See the section on "Creating and Editing Toolbars" in Appendix B.

FROM HERE ...

You've learned how to create and edit simple macros, and I've introduced you to the macros that are included with WordPerfect. The best way to get familiar with macros is by playing with them. Just start creating and using macros for tasks you do on a regular basis. Pretty soon you'll wonder how you ever got along without them. Whenever you create a macro, familiarize yourself with the macro codes by looking at the macro in the editing screen. And when you're ready to start experimenting with more complex macros, start by looking at the *Online Macros Manual.*

The next chapter continues the automation theme by teaching you how you can use the merge feature to streamline the task of creating form letters and similar documents.

CHAPTER 20

Using Merge

(Turn On Your Signal and Merge Into the Fast Lane)

Let's talk about:

- ❖ Understanding data and form files
- ❖ Creating a data file
- ❖ Creating a form file
- ❖ Performing the merge
- ❖ Stopping a merge
- ❖ Setting up a keyboard merge

Have you ever gotten one of those form letters that sounds like it was meant just for you, but you know the same letter went to several thousand other people? Ever wonder how they include your name and all of that specific information without making it look like it's pasted in? Well, they probably have a program like WordPerfect that lets them merge a list of names, addresses, and other variable information into a form letter.

UNDERSTANDING DATA AND FORM FILES

You need to have two files before you can perform a merge: a data file and a form file.

The *data file* contains the list of variable information—using the form letter example, the data file would be the list of names and addresses. The *form file* is the letter itself—you insert codes into the form file to tell WordPerfect where the information from the data file should go when the two are merged.

This will all make sense after you've created your own data and form files.

Creating a Data File

You're going to create a data file that contains the following information:

```
Charity Chambers
Casual Corner
300 Cherry Lane
Chehalis, WA 98111
Charity
$92,000

Mary Masterson
400 Juniper Alley
Jumping Frog, GA 98778
Mary
$84,000,000
```

```
Kim Klaster
Kustom Karpets
500 Kiplinger Korner
Kalamazoo, KY 88888
Kim
$150,000
```

The data file is made up of fields and records. A *field* is one piece of information. For example, "Kim Klaster" is one field. A *record* is a group of related fields—all of the information for Kim is one record.

Do It

1. Choose **Merge** from the Tools menu (or press **Shift+F9)**. The Merge dialog box is displayed, as shown in Figure 20.1.

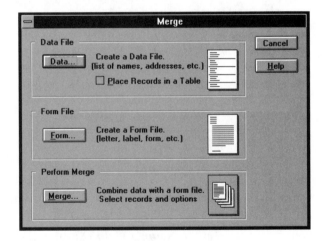

Figure 20.1 *The Merge dialog box.*

2. Choose **Data**. The Create Merge dialog box shown in Figure 20.2 may display. If it does, make sure **New Document Window** is selected, then choose **OK**.

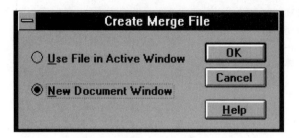

Figure 20.2 *The Create Merge File dialog box.*

At this point, the Create Data File dialog box shown in Figure 20.3 should be on your screen. Use this dialog box to name your fields.

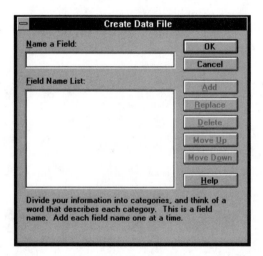

Figure 20.3 *The Create Data File dialog box.*

3. Enter your field names in the **Name a Field** text box, choosing **Add** (or pressing **Enter**) after each one. Field names should be descriptive enough to remind you what information to enter for each record. For this example, use the following field names:

```
Full Name
Company
Street Address
City, State, Zip
Salutation
Amount Won
```

Every time you choose **Add** (or press **Enter**), the name you just typed is displayed in the Field Name List. When you're done, the Create Data File dialog box on your screen should look like Figure 20.4.

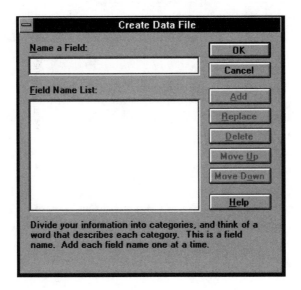

Figure 20.4 *The completed Field Name List.*

4. Choose **OK** when your Field Name List is complete. The Quick Data Entry dialog box is displayed, with all of the fields you entered, as shown in Figure 20.5.

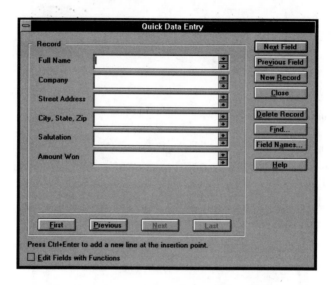

Figure 20.5 *The Quick Data Entry dialog box.*

This is where you enter the specific information for each record. All you have to do is type in the appropriate text box and press **Enter** to move to the next field. When you press **Enter** from the last field (in this example, Amount Won), the current record is entered in your document and the text boxes clear so you can enter the information for the next record.

Enter all of the information for *Charity*. Her name in the **Full Name** text box, the name of her company in the **Company** text box, etc. You can move to any field by clicking in its text box. You can also choose **Next Field** to move your insertion point one field down, or **Previous Field** to move up one field. And of course, just like in any dialog box, you can press **Tab** or **Shift+Tab** to move between the fields and buttons.

When you've entered all of the data for *Charity*, choose **New Record** (or press **Enter** if your insertion point is in the last field) and continue until you have completed all three records. Notice that there's no company name for *Mary Masterson*. Just leave her **Company** text box blank.

In Figure 20.6, I've moved the Quick Data Entry dialog box over so you can see part of document screen. As you complete each record, it gets "dumped" into your document. Figure 20.6 shows two complete records, with the last one being entered in the dialog box.

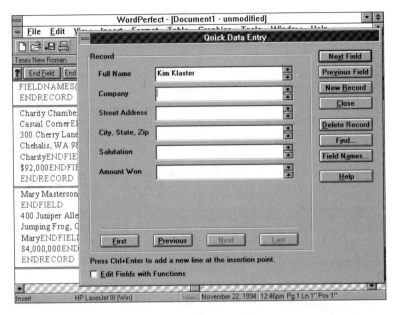

Figure 20.6 *Each record appears in your document when you finish entering the information.*

When you're done entering records, choose **Close**. The dialog box shown in Figure 20.7 asks whether you want to save the data file.

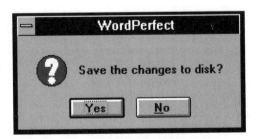

Figure 20.7 *You should save your data file at this point.*

You don't have to save right now, but it's a good idea. You wouldn't want to have to recreate what you just did, would you? And that's just what could happen if the power went out before you had a chance to save. Anytime WordPerfect gives you an opportunity to save, take it.

❖ Choose **Yes** and enter a filename in the Save Data File dialog box. For this example, name your file **LOTTERY.DAT**.

NOTE

It's a good idea to use consistent extensions for your data and form files. It makes them easier to find in your file lists. I use DAT for data files and FRM for form files. The rules for naming merge files are exactly the same as for any other file—you don't have to use an extension if you don't want to.

At this point your document screen should look like Figure 20.8.

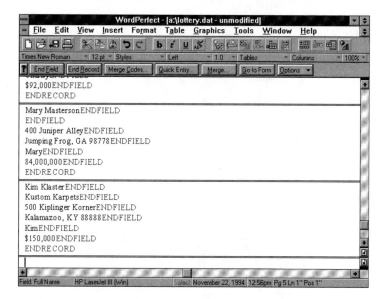

Figure 20.8 *The completed data file.*

Notice that the first record contains the field name information. Every field ends with an ENDFIELD code, and every record ends with an ENDRECORD code and a hard page break (the double lines). Place your insertion point at the beginning of the second line in *Mary Masterson's* record—the one with the ENDFIELD code all by itself—and take a look at the Status Bar. The Status Bar tells you that this line is for the Company field. Even though *Mary* doesn't have a company, the ENDFIELD code has to be there as a placeholder. In a data file, every record has to contain the same number of fields, and the fields always have to be entered in the same order.

Hey, there's another one of those cool feature bars (just above the field names record). This one takes the work out of working with data files, and we'll even use it to help create the form file. Figure 20.9 shows the Merge Bar.

Figure 20.9 *The Merge Bar for data files.*

❖ The first two buttons, **End Field** and **End Record**, insert those codes directly into your document at your insertion point location. You can edit a data file manually by entering text and inserting ENDFIELD and ENDRECORD codes in the right places, but I don't recommend doing it this way. It's too easy to forget to put in an ENDFIELD code, or to put a code in the wrong place. Use the **Quick Entry** button instead—you'll avoid errors (and it's *much* easier).

❖ The **Quick Entry** button takes you back into the Quick Data Entry dialog box, where you can edit, delete, and add records. To edit a particular record, just place your insertion point anywhere in that record and choose **Quick Entry**. From the Data Entry dialog box, you can choose **New Record** to add a new record just below the record your insertion point is in. If you want the new record added at the end of the list, choose **Last** to move to the end of the list before you choose **New Record**. Likewise, **First** will put you at the top of the list. You can also delete records from this dialog box (make sure your insertion point is in the record you want to delete before you choose **Delete Record**).

❖ The **Merge Codes** button displays the Insert Merge Codes dialog box, which allows you to use programming commands to control the merge. The Merge feature contains its own programming language that is almost as complex as the macro language.

❖ **Go to Form** is the button we'll use to create the form file a little later.

❖ The **Options** button lets you sort the data file (sorting is covered in the next chapter) or print it as a list. Because there is a hard page break between each record, you would get one record on every page if you use the regular print feature. You can also choose to display the merge codes as markers or hide them completely. This can be useful if you want to print your mailing list for proofreading—all of those ENDFIELD and ENDRECORD codes can be distracting on a printout. The final option is for removing the Merge Bar from the screen.

When you create a data file, you can choose to have the fields and records arranged in a table format. Just choose **Place Records in Table** before you choose **Data** from the Merge dialog box. Figure 20.10 shows the mailing list in a table. Notice that you don't see the ENDFIELD and ENDRECORD codes. With this format, each row is a record, and each cell is a field. The field names display as column headings in the first row. How you choose to display your data files is just a matter of preference—they both work the same way.

Full Name	Company	Street Address	City, State, Zip	Salutation	Amount Won
Charity Chambers	Casual Corner	300 Cherry Lane	Chehalis, WA 98111	Charity	$92,000
Mary Masterson		400 Juniper Alley	Jumping Frog, GA 98778	Mary	$84,000,000
Kim Klaster	Kustom Karpets	500 Kiplinger Korner	Kalamazoo, KY 88888	Kim	$150,000

Figure 20.10 *The data file in table format.*

Okay, you have your data file, and you know how to edit it. It's time to create the form file.

Creating a Form File

A form file is just a regular document with codes wherever you want to enter variable information from the data file. Take a look at the following letter:

```
Charity Chambers
Casual Corner
300 Cherry Lane
Chehalis, WA 98111


Dear Charity,


We are pleased to inform you that you are the lucky winner of
$92,000. Please contact the Lottery Office by 5 p.m. on November
15 to claim your winnings.
```

```
Sincerely,


Marla Millions
Lottery Administrator
```

What's the variable information? Well, the name and address for a start. Instead of Charity's name and address, we need a code that tells WordPerfect to use the information from the data file when we run the merge. We also need codes instead of the salutation (otherwise all the letters would say *Dear Charity*) and the amount. Let's do it.

There are two ways to create a form file: from the Merge dialog box or the Merge Bar. They're just two different ways of getting to the same place.

Creating a Form File from the Merge Dialog Box

1. Choose **Form** from the Merge dialog box (see Figure 20.1). If necessary, choose **OK** from the Create Merge File dialog box to open the Create Form File dialog box shown in Figure 20.11.

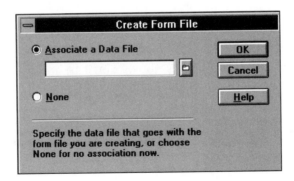

Figure 20.11 *The Create Form File dialog box.*

2. If you want the form file linked to a particular data file, enter the filename in the **Associate a Data File** text box (or click on the file icon and choose the file from the Select File dialog box). If you don't want to link the form file, choose **None**. Choose **OK** when you are done.

As you'll soon see, there are definite advantages to associating a data file with the form file. For this reason, I recommend that you create your data file first (even though WordPerfect doesn't require you to create the files in any order). If the data file doesn't exist, you can't use the Associate option.

Creating a Form File from the Merge Bar

This is the simplest option if your data file's still on screen.

1. Choose **Go to Form** from the Merge Bar.
2. Choose **Create** from the Associate dialog box, shown in Figure 20.12.

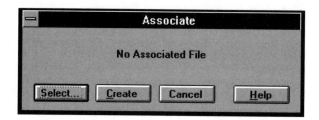

Figure 20.12 *The Associate dialog box.*

Entering Text in the Form File

After you follow either set of steps above, you'll be in an empty document window with the Merge Bar shown in Figure 20.13.

Figure 20.13 *The Merge Bar for form files.*

These steps are specific to the sample letter, but they'll familiarize you with procedures you can use in any form file.

1. Make sure your insertion point is at the top of the document.

2. Choose **Date** from the Merge Bar (this inserts a DATE code that prints the current date when you perform the merge) and press the **Enter** key twice. This is where you would usually type in the person's name and address. Instead of an actual name and address, we'll use merge codes.

3. Choose **Insert Field** from the Merge Bar. The Insert Field Name or Number dialog box is displayed, as shown in Figure 20.14. Notice that the **Field Names** list contains all of the fields from LOTTERY.DAT. This takes all the guesswork out of inserting field codes in your form file.

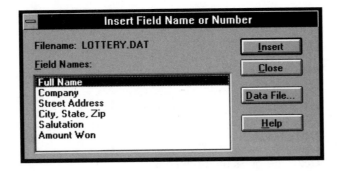

Figure 20.14 *The Insert Field Name or Number dialog box.*

4. Move the selection bar to the field you want (in this case, the first field to insert would be **Full Name**) and choose **Insert**. As you can see in Figure 20.15, WordPerfect inserts a FIELD code followed by the name of the field, and the Insert Field Name or Number dialog box stays on screen so you can continue inserting fields.

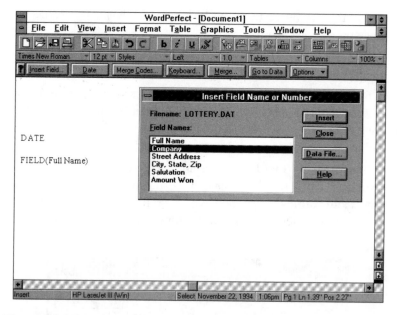

Figure 20.15 *You continue inserting Field Names from the dialog box.*

5. Press the **Enter** key to move to the next line and repeat step 4 to insert FIELD codes for *Company, Street Address,* and *City.* Press the **Enter** key twice to move to the salutation line.

6. Type **Dear** and press the **Spacebar**.

7. Insert the Salutation FIELD code from the Insert Field Name or Number dialog box, then type a **comma** and press the **Enter** key twice.

8. Type: We are pleased to inform you that you are the lucky winner of.

9. Make sure you press the **Spacebar** after the word *of,* then insert the **Amount Won** FIELD code and type an **exclamation mark**.

10. Enter the rest of the text:

```
Please contact the Lottery Office by 5 p.m. on November 15 to
claim your winnings.
    Sincerely,


    Marla Millions
    Lottery Administrator
```

11. Choose **Close** from the Insert Field Name or Number dialog box. Your screen should look like Figure 20.16.

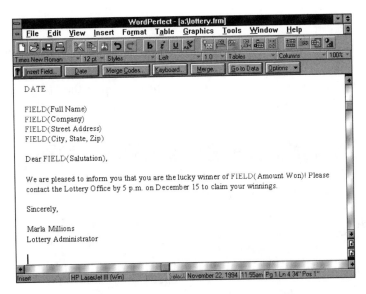

Figure 20.16 *The completed form file.*

12. Save the file as **LOTTERY.FRM** and leave it on your screen.

NOTE

Be sure you spell check and proofread your form file before you perform a merge. Otherwise you could end up with the same error repeated on every letter. If you do discover a mistake after performing a merge, just close the merged file without saving and run the merge again. That's much easier than making corrections on each letter.

That's it. You just created a data file and a form file. All that's left is to bring them together.

Performing the Merge

This is a piece of cake if you start with your data or form file on screen (and it's even more of a piece of cake if you've associated the data and form files). It's not hard if you start from a blank screen—it just means that you have to specify which data and form files you want to use.

For these steps, I'm assuming that LOTTERY.FRM is still on-screen.

Do It

1. Choose **Merge** from the Merge Bar. You can also choose **Merge** from the Tools menu or press **Shift+F9.**

2. Choose **Merge** from the **Perform Merge** area in the Merge dialog box. The Perform Merge dialog box is displayed, as shown in Figure 20.17.

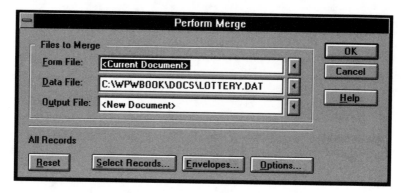

Figure 20.17 *The Perform Merge dialog box.*

3. The Form File text box shows *<Current Document>*. That means the merge will use the document on your screen unless you specify another file by choosing **Select File** from the drop-down list.

4. The Data File text box shows **LOTTERY.DAT** with its full directory path. That's the file that's associated with the LOTTERY.FRM file on your screen, but you can use another data file by choosing **Select File** from the drop-down list.

5. The default for **Output File** is **<New Document>.** That means WordPerfect will put the merged records into a new document window. You can also choose to send the completed merge directly to the printer or to a file on disk. One of the options for Output File is **<Current Document>**, but that would add the merged records to the end of the document on your screen.

6. If you want to create envelopes at the same time, choose **Envelopes**.

7. Choose any merge options you want. I'll cover envelopes and options in the following sections. The **Select Records** button, which lets you pull specific records during a merge, is discussed in the next chapter, which covers sorting and selecting.

8. When you're ready to run the merge, choose **OK** from the Perform Merge dialog box.

Quick as a flash (it might take a few flashes if you're using a long data file), the merged documents are displayed on your screen, with the insertion point at the bottom of the last record. Press **Alt+PgUp** to take a look at your other records. You should have three letters, with all of the right information in the right places. At every point you inserted a code in the form file, you now have the specific information for each addressee.

Now let's take a look at Mary Masterson's letter. Remember, we left the Company field of her data record blank. So how come there's no blank line after Mary Masterson's name? Explanation coming right up!

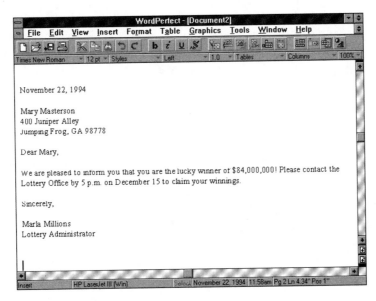

Figure 20.18 *The merged record for Mary Masterson.*

Changing Merge Options

The Perform Merge Options dialog box lets you control the results of the merge. Before you run a merge, you can choose **Options** from the Perform Merge dialog box. The Perform Merge Options dialog box is displayed, as shown in Figure 20.19.

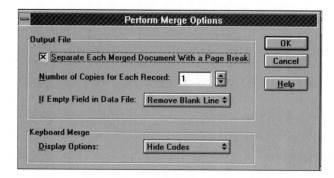

Figure 20.19 *The Perform Merge Options dialog box.*

Notice that the default for **If Empty Field in Data File** is **Remove Blank Line**. That's why you didn't end up with a blank line in Mary's record. If you actually want the blank line to appear, choose **Leave Blank Line** from the pop-up list.

This dialog box contains a couple of other useful options:

❖ By default, every record begins on a new page. If WordPerfect didn't do it that way, you could end up with more than one letter on a page. But what if you want to merge your data file to a list instead of letters? Just deselect **Separate Each Merged Document With a Page Break** before you run the merge, and you're all set.

❖ If you want to merge more than one copy of each record, enter a number in the **Number of Copies for Each Record** text box.

❖ The options for keyboard merges are also included in this dialog box. They'll be discussed a little later when I tell you how to do a keyboard merge.

In most cases, you don't need to save the completed merge file. You can always recreate it by merging the form and data files—saving the completed merge is usually a waste of disk space.

Creating Envelopes During a Merge

You could merge your data file with your letter form file, then create a separate envelope form file and merge your data file to it, but once again WordPerfect provides you with a shortcut. Why go through the merge process twice when it can all be done at once?

Before you run the merge, choose **Envelopes** from the Perform Merge dialog box. This brings up an Envelope dialog box similar to the one you used in Chapter 16, but we'll use it a little differently. Instead of entering a name and address in the **Mailing Addresses** box, we'll insert field codes.

1. If necessary, enter a return address.

2. Place your insertion point in the Mailing Addresses text box.

3. Choose **Field** to display the Insert Field Name or Number dialog box.

4. Move the selection bar to the field you want and choose **Insert**.

5. Repeat steps 3 and 4 until you've entered all of the fields shown in Figure 20.20.

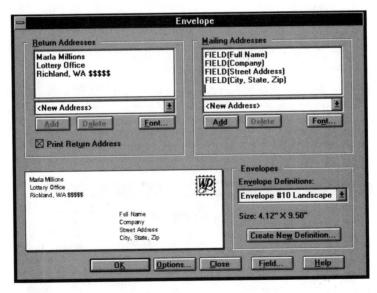

Figure 20.20 *The Envelope dialog box with the name and address fields inserted.*

6. Choose **OK** to close the Envelope dialog box.

When you perform the merge, an envelope is created for each record at the end of the merged file.

Keyboard Merges

A keyboard merge doesn't use a data file at all. Instead, you insert KEYBOARD commands in the form file. When you perform the merge, WordPerfect pauses whenever it sees a KEYBOARD code and lets you enter information directly from the keyboard.

Keyboard merges are great when you use the same basic document over and over, but you want to enter different information each time. To see how this works, let's recreate the lottery letter as a keyboard form file.

Creating the Keyboard Form File

1. Make sure your insertion point is at the top of a blank document window, and select **Merge** from the Tools menu (or press **Shift+F9**).

2. Choose **Form**.

3. Choose **New Document Window** from the Create Merge File dialog box.

4. Choose **None** from the Create Form File dialog box. (You don't want to link a data file with a keyboard form file.)

5. Choose **Date** from the Merge Bar to insert the DATE code and press the **Enter** key twice.

6. Choose **Keyboard** from the Merge Bar. The Insert Merge Code dialog box is displayed, as shown in Figure20.21,

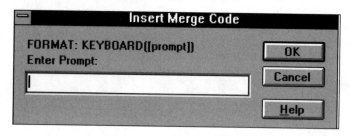

Figure 20.21 *The Insert Merge Code dialog box.*

7. Enter information in the **Enter Prompt** text box. The instructions you enter will display when the merge is run. For this example, type **Type the name and address information here**, then choose **OK**. WordPerfect inserts a KEYBOARD code followed by the prompt you entered.

8. Enter the rest of the information for the letter, inserting KEYBOARD codes instead of text, as shown in Figure 20.22.

DATE

KEYBOARD(Type the name and address information here)

Dear KEYBOARD(Enter the salutation here),

We are pleased to inform you that you are the lucky winner of KEYBOARD(Enter the amount won)! Please contact the Lottery Office by 5 p.m. on December 15 to claim your winnings.

Sincerely,

Marla Millions
Lottery Administrator

Figure 20.22 *The completed keyboard form file.*

9. Save the completed file as **LOTTERY.KBD**.

Performing a Keyboard Merge

1. Access the Merge dialog box using any of the techniques you've learned, and choose **Merge**.

2. If the form file is on your screen when you choose Merge, it should say **<Current Document>** in the Form File text box. Otherwise, enter the name of the file in the Form File text box (or choose it from the Select File dialog box).

3. Make sure the Data File text box says **<None>**.

4. Make sure the Output File text box says **<New Document>**.

5. Choose **OK** to begin the merge.

The merge pauses at the first KEYBOARD code and displays a Merge Message dialog box that contains the prompt you entered when you created the form file (see Figure 20.23).

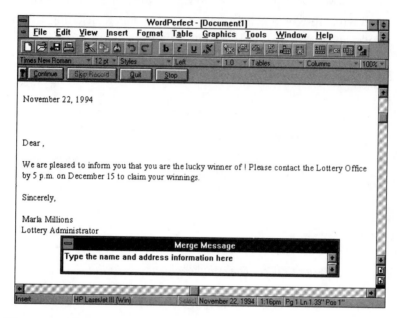

Figure 20.23 *The merge pauses and prompts you to enter information.*

6. When you've entered the requested information, choose **Continue** from the Feature Bar to move to the next KEYBOARD code. Repeat this step until you've entered all of the variable information for the document.

When there aren't any more KEYBOARD codes, the Feature Bar disappears. At this point, you can save or print the document.

You can stop a keyboard merge at any time by choosing **Quit** or **Stop** from the Feature Bar. **Quit** leaves all of your text on-screen, including any KEYBOARD codes you haven't used. **Stop** deletes everything on your screen beyond the last KEYBOARD prompt you've answered.

FROM HERE ...

As you work with merges, you'll find them to be invaluable. Once you create a data file, you can merge it with any number of form files. For example, you could use the same mailing list to create letters, labels, envelopes, and a phone list. Use keyboard merges to speed up data entry. Create the form file once, and enter KEYBOARD codes wherever there's variable information. When you run the merge, the prompts remind you what to type.

In the next chapter, you'll expand your ability to control groups of data. You'll learn how to sort information in text files, data files, and tables. And you'll use Select to pull just the information you want out of a file.

CHAPTER 21

Sorting and Selecting

(Feeling Out Of Sorts? Read This Chapter to Take Care of the Problem)

Let's talk about:

- ❖ Basic sorting concepts
- ❖ Performing a simple line sort
- ❖ Sorting paragraphs
- ❖ Sorting a data file
- ❖ Sorting a table
- ❖ Creating selection statements
- ❖ Selecting records during a merge

You can sort just about any kind of WordPerfect file any way you want. You can sort alphabetically, numerically or in reverse order. You can sort information in lists, paragraphs, tables, parallel columns, and data files. You can sort the entire document or just a selected portion of it. A sort can be as simple as alphabetizing the names in a list, or as complex as sorting all of the names in a data file by city and limiting the sort to only those records for people whose last names begin with *S* and are also company presidents.

You control all of this by telling WordPerfect which *fields* to sort on. WordPerfect looks at text and data files in terms of fields and records. Depending on the type of sort, the fields and records are defined differently:

❖ For a **Line** sort, every line that ends with a hard return is a record, and fields are separated by tabs or indents.

❖ For a **Paragraph** sort, every paragraph that ends with two or more hard returns is considered a record, and fields are separated by tabs or indents.

❖ A **Merge Record** sort uses a data file. Every record ends with an ENDRECORD code, and every field ends with an ENDFIELD code.

Tables and columns are broken down as follows:

❖ When you sort tables, each row is considered a record, and you specify which column of cells to sort on.

❖ When you sort parallel columns, each row of columns is considered a record, and you specify which column to sort on.

Sounds like a lot of confusing stuff to remember, but we'll get off to a quick start with a simple line sort. Once you see how easy it is, you'll be off and running.

Performing a Simple Line Sort

This sort will show you how easy sorting can be. Type the following list exactly as shown, including the uppercase letters:

Orange

apple

watermelon

blueberry

pineapple

cherry

cantaloupe

Apple

orange

What a mess! How could you possibly find anything in that list? I'll tell you how:

1. With your insertion point anywhere in the document, choose **Sort** from the Tools menu or press **Alt+F9**. The Sort dialog box is displayed, as shown in Figure 21.1.

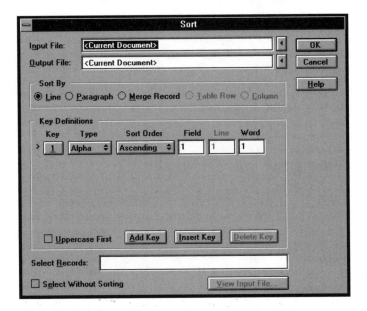

Figure 21.1 *The Sort dialog box.*

2. Choose **Sort**. The Sort dialog box disappears, and your list should look like Figure 21.2. Notice that the words starting with uppercase letters sort after their lowercase counterparts (*Apple* is after *apple*, and *Orange* is after *orange*).

apple
Apple
blueberry
cantaloupe
orange
Orange
pineapple
watermelon

Figure 21.2 The list is in alphabetical order.

You should always save your file before you perform a sort or check **Allow Undo** in the Sort dialog box Options drop-down list. Since the sorted data replaces whatever was on your screen, you'll want to be able to go back to the original in case the sort doesn't turn out quite the way you expected. **Allow Undo** will let you use the **Undo** feature to return the document to its presorted condition. I highly recommend you use this option.

Understanding the Sort Dialog Box

Wow, that was quick. It looked like there were a lot of choices to make in the Sort dialog box, but you didn't have to make any because we took advantage of all of the default options. Let's take another look at Figure 21.1 to see what happened:

❖ The defaults for **Input File** and **Output File** are both <Current Document>. That means the sort uses the information that's on your screen and sorts the results back to the screen. You can choose to sort from a file on disk, or send the results of the sort to a file, but most of the time you'll just accept these defaults.

❖ **First word in a line** is selected in the Defined Sorts list. WordPerfect has already created definitions for the most commonly used sorts. When you choose Sort, WordPerfect tries to determine what kind of file you're using. If you have more than two hard returns anywhere, it selects **First**

word in a paragraph. If you have a data file on your screen, it selects **First word in a merge data file**. In most cases it chooses correctly, but you should double-check to make sure the correct option is selected before you perform a sort.

❖ By default **Uppercase First** is not checked. That's why the words in our sorted list appear with the lowercase word before its uppercase counterpart. Select or deselect this option prior to performing the sort.

Creating a Customized Sort Definition

You've seen how easy it is to perform a simple sort using the default options—let's try something a little more daring. Suppose you belong to a choir and you want a list that's sorted according to the parts everyone sings, and in each part you want the names listed alphabetically. Type the list as shown in Figure 21.3.

Sarah Maria Weingarten	Soprano
April Lawrence	Alto
Jan Weingarten	Soprano
Jennifer Sue Jordan	Soprano
Evan Abernathy	Tenor
Mason Barker	Bass
Patsy Jordan	Soprano
Bill Jordan	Bass
Barbara Benson	Alto

Figure 21.3 *The choir list, ready to be sorted.*

You should have only one tab marker between the name and part fields. Remember that WordPerfect uses tabs or indents to separate fields, so make sure you have only one tab set between the two fields before continuing.

1. Choose **Sort** from the Tools menu (or press **Alt+F9**) and then choose **Edit**.

2. Make sure the **Line** radio button is selected.

3. Enter the Key Definitions information as shown in Figure 21.4. The Key Definitions area is potentially the most intimidating, but it doesn't have to be. A *key* is just the way you tell WordPerfect what part of the record you want to use for the sort. By default, there's one key defined, and it performs an alphabetical sort in ascending order on the first word in the first field. In order to sort on anything else (for example, the second word in the last field), you have to edit the key definitions. Just click in the appropriate **Field** or **Word** text box to enter a number, and use the **Add Key** button to add the additional two keys.

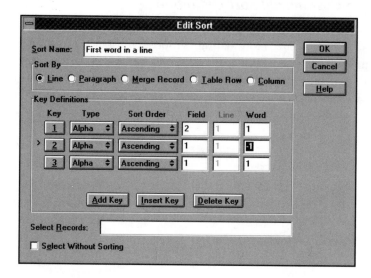

Figure 21.4 *Key definitions for sorting the choir list.*

I bet you'd like me to tell you what you just did. If you think of the keys as your sort priorities, it's easy.

❖ Your top priority is to sort singers according to the parts they sing, so Key 1 is set up to sort the parts field. The parts list is one tab stop over from the margin, so it's Field 2. There's only one word in the field, so the sort is on Word 1.

❖ Next, you want the singers grouped by last name, so that's your second priority (or Key 2). The singers are in Field 1 (at the left margin), and you want to sort on the last word in the field. You can't sort on Word 2, since some of the singers have middle names. You use a minus sign to count backward from the end of a field, so you enter **-1** in the Word text box for Key 2.

❖ Finally, you want to sort by first name. That's the last (or lowest) priority—Key 3. The singers' first names are the first word in the first field.

You can define up to nine sort keys. Once you've defined all of your sort keys, choose **OK** to perform the sort. Figure 21.5 shows the sorted list. All of the singers are grouped according to part, and in each part they're listed alphabetically by first and last name.

Barbara Benson	Alto
April Lawrence	Alto
Mason Barker	Bass
Bill Jordan	Bass
Jennifer Sue Jordan	Soprano
Patsy Jordan	Soprano
Jan Weingarten	Soprano
Sarah Maria Weingarten	Soprano
Evan Abernathy	Tenor

Figure 21.5 *The sorted choir list.*

The next few sections talk about sorting paragraphs, tables, and data files. Each type of sort gives you different options for defining sort keys, but you use the same methods to define the keys regardless of the sort type.

Paragraph Sorts

You can use paragraph sorts to sort any information that's separated by two or more hard returns. Figures 21.6 and 21.7 show examples of two instances where you might use a paragraph sort. The first example doesn't look like what you would normally think of as paragraphs, but it qualifies because most of the records contain more than one line and each group is separated by two hard returns. A paragraph sort keeps all of the information grouped according to record. The second example shows a group of more typical paragraphs.

Evan Abernathy	Tenor	Going on vacation in September
Mason Barker	Bass	Not available on Wednesdays or Saturdays
Barbara Benson	Alto	Consult before scheduling the concert
Jennifer Sue Jordan	Soprano	Starting new job
Patsy Jordan	Soprano	Needs a ride to Federal Way concert

Figure 21.6 *You would use a paragraph sort for this example.*

Beeley, John, & Wheely, Marie. *Teaching Your Car to Drive Itself.* Baltimore: Decisive Books, 1989.

Corrigan, Chip. *How to Build a Robot for $999 or Less.* New York: Cooper Publishing Co., 1992.

Steele, Bart. *Artificial Intelligence for Household Appliances.* New York: Future World Publishers, 1993.

Zanders, Flora, & Flanders, Zed. *Building Electric Cats: Pets for the 21st Century.* Los Angeles: Escapade Books, 1990.

Figure 21.7 *This example would also use a paragraph sort.*

Paragraph sorts work almost exactly like line sorts: the only difference is that you can specify which line you want to sort on when you define your keys.

If a paragraph or line sort doesn't turn out right, double check to make sure you don't have more than one tab or indent between any of the fields. It's easy to let an extra tab sneak in there, and it can really throw a sort out of kilter.

Sorting Data Files

The ability to sort data files means that you can add records to your mailing lists without worrying about putting them in the right place. Just add them at the end of the list and then sort the list. It also means you can group the list by cities, zip codes, or any other criteria.

Figure 21.8 shows LOTTERY.DAT sorted according to the amount of winnings, with the amounts in descending order, and Figure 21.9 shows the Sort dialog box set up to perform the sort.

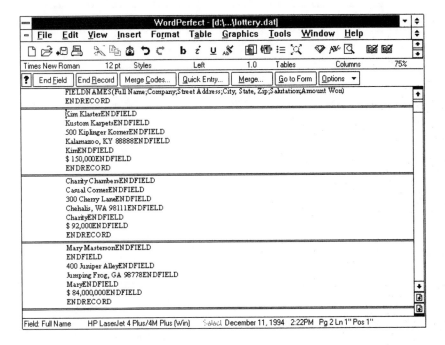

Figure 21.8 *LOTTERY.DAT sorted by winnings.*

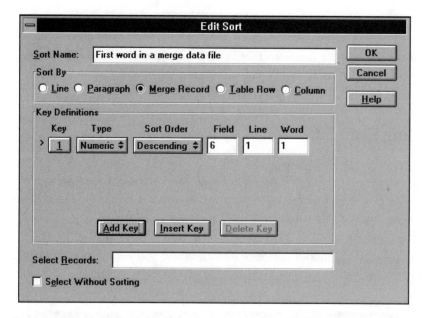

Figure 21.9 *The Sort dialog box set up to sort LOTTERY.DAT by winnings.*

I made the following changes to the Key Definition for Key 1:

❖ I changed the type to **numeric** so that the numbers would sort properly.

❖ I changed the sort order to **descending** so that the largest number would be first.

❖ I specified **Field 6** in the Field text box. (Just count the ENDFIELD codes in a record to figure out which field you want to sort on; in this case the Amount Won field is the sixth field down.)

Sorting Tables

WordPerfect can sort information that's in table format, but a table sort can be a little trickier than some of the sorts we've done so far. Because tables can contain complex formatting, headers, split and joined cells, and many other elements, the results of a table sort can be unpredictable. Figure 21.10 shows the table we created in Chapter 18, with a joined row added at the bottom.

Department Budget		
Category	**1994**	**1995**
Salaries	$ 152,334.00	$ 380,952.00
Telephone	$ 1,890.00	$ 2,590.00
Meeting Refreshments	$ 250.00	$ 18,620.00
TOTAL	$ 156,468.00	$ 404,157.00
Note: 1994 figures are pending approval by VP		

Figure 21.10 *Table with joined rows.*

Figure 21.11 shows the same table after a default sort.

Category	**1994**	**1995**
Department Budget		
Meeting Refreshments	$ 250.00	$ 18,620.00
Note: 1994 figures are pending approval by VP		
Salaries	$ 152,334.00	$ 380,952.00
Telephone	$ 1,890.00	$ 2,590.00
TOTAL	$ 156,468.00	$ 404,157.00

Figure 21.11 *This table has been sorted using the default options.*

Not a pretty sight. When I told WordPerfect to sort the table, it took me at my word and put every single row into alphabetical order according to the first word in the first column, and it took any formatting contained in the row along with it.

What's the answer? Always save before you try a table sort in case the sort goes south on you. But the real solution is to select the rows you want sorted before you perform the sort. Figure 21.12 shows the table (pre-sorting) with the middle three rows selected. Figure 21.13 shows the table after sorting. Notice that only the selected rows were affected—everything else stayed put. No problem.

Remember, you can select a portion of your document before performing any type of sort. This can be useful if you have a list or a group of paragraphs you want to sort that are part of a larger document.

Department Budget		
Category	**1994**	**1995**
Salaries	$ 152,334.00	$ 380,952.00
Telephone	$ 1,890.00	$ 2,590.00
Meeting Refreshments	$ 250.00	$ 18,620.00
TOTAL	$ 156,468.00	$ 404,157.00
Note: 1994 figures are pending approval by VP		

Figure 21.12 *The table with three rows selected.*

Department Budget		
Category	**1994**	**1995**
Meeting Refreshments	$ 250.00	$ 18,620.00
Salaries	$ 152,334.00	$ 380,952.00
Telephone	$ 1,890.00	$ 2,590.00
TOTAL	$ 156,468.00	$ 404,157.00
Note: 1994 figures are pending approval by VP		

Figure 21.13 *The middle three rows are sorted—the rest of the table is unaffected.*

Sorting Dates

What do you do if you have a field that contains dates entered like *10/12/92?* How can you organize the dates by year, then sort them by months and days within each year? There's a trick to this, and it has to do with the way WordPerfect recognizes words. In addition to spaces, it sees forward slashes and hyphens as word separators. So, in a field with the date shown above, the month would be word 1, the day word 2, and the year word 3. You would define Key 1 to sort on word 3, Key 2 on word 1, and Key 3 on word 2.

Gluing Words Together

Here's another tricky situation. What if you want to sort on the last name, but you have the following names in your list: *John Foxworthy Jr., Sarah Maria Weingarten, M.D.,* and *J. Carswell III?* You can't sort on word 2 because of *Sarah's* middle name and the *J. Carswell* business. If you sort on the last word by specifying **word -1**, the list sorts according to *Jr., M.D.,* and III instead of their last names.

Here's the simple answer to the tricky situation: hard spaces. A hard space "glues" words together so that WordPerfect treats them as one word during a sort. To insert a hard space between *Foxworthy* and *Jr.,* press **Ctrl+Spacebar** instead of pressing the **Spacebar** by itself. With a hard space, *Foxworthy Jr.* is considered one word, so a sort on **word -1** can work.

Selecting Records

You can create what's called a *selection statement* to pull specified records out of a document. Using the choir list (see Figure 21.3), suppose you want to create a list that just contains the sopranos. Here's what you do.

1. With the file on screen (or a portion of the file selected), open the Sort dialog box and choose **Edit**.

2. Make sure the correct radio button is selected (in this case, it would be **Line**).

3. Define any keys you want to use in the selection statement. For this example, you just need to change Field to **2**.

4. Enter the selection statement in the Select Records text box. The statement to select only the sopranos would read: **key 1 = soprano**. Figure 21.14 shows the Sort dialog box with Key 1 defined and the selection statement entered.

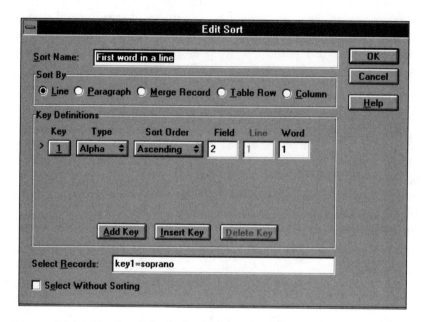

Figure 21.14 *The Sort Edit dialog box, ready to select all of the sopranos.*

It's pretty simple—you defined Key 1 as Field 2, and you told WordPerfect to pull all of the records in Key 1 (Field 2) that are equal to soprano. Notice that the selection statement isn't case sensitive. You can enter your selection criteria in uppercase or lowercase. The equal sign is a selection operator. Table 21.1 lists some of the selection operators and examples of how they could be used in selection statements.

Table 21.1 *Selection Operators*

Operator	Meaning	Valid selection statement
OR	or	key 1 = soprano OR key 2 = Weingarten would select all records where key 1 is *soprano or* key 2 is *Weingarten.*
AND	and	key 1 = soprano AND key 2 = Weingarten. The records must meet both criteria. This would select only the records where key 1 is *soprano and* key 2 is *Weingarten.*
<>	not equal to	key 1 <> soprano would select all records in which key 1 is *not soprano.*
>	greater than	key 1 > 90210 would select records containing zip codes greater than 90210.
<	less than	key 1 < 90210 would pull all the records with zip codes less than 90210.
>=	greater than or equal to	key 1 >= Castle would select records that contain *Castle* and any other names that appear after it in the alphabet.
<=	less than or equal to	key 1 <= Castle would select records that contain *Castle* and any other names that appear before it in the alphabet.

5. Choose **Select Without Sorting** to pull the records without changing the sort order. If this box isn't checked, the selected records will be sorted based on your key definitions. Figure 21.15 shows the file after selecting records. Only the records that contain the word *soprano* in Field 2 remain.

Sarah Maria Weingarten	Soprano
Jan Weingarten	Soprano
Jennifer Sue Jordan	Soprano
Patsy Jordan	Soprano

Figure 21.15 The list with sopranos selected.

There's a special global select key you can use to select records containing a word or number without restricting the selection process to a particular field. The statement *key g = dinosaur* would select all records that contain the word *dinosaur*, regardless of the field in which the word appears. You don't have to define keys in order to write a selection statement using key g.

Selecting Records During a Merge

If you want to perform a merge on just the records meeting certain criteria, you could write a selection statement to pull out the records you want to use in the merge, and then perform the merge (a two-step process), but there's a much better way to do this. Just choose **Select Records** from the Perform Merge dialog box, shown in Figure 21.16, and have WordPerfect select the records you want as part of the merge process.

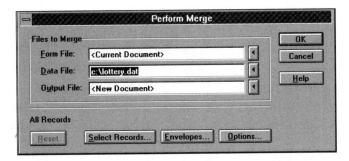

Figure 21.16 *Choose* **Select Records** *before you perform the merge.*

After you choose **Select Records**, the Select Records dialog box, shown in Figure 21.17, is displayed.

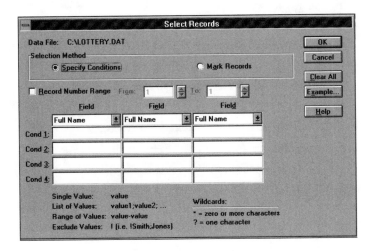

Figure 21.17 *The Select Records dialog box.*

If you want to merge only the 50th through the 150th records, check the **Record Number Range** check box, and enter **50** in the From text box and **150** in the To text box.

Select fields to which you want conditions to apply from the Fields drop-down lists. Each drop-down list contains all of the field names for your data file. You can define up to four separate conditions to use during the merge. The best way to begin understanding how this works is to choose **Example** from the Select Records dialog box. This displays the Example Select Records dialog box, shown in Figure 21.18.

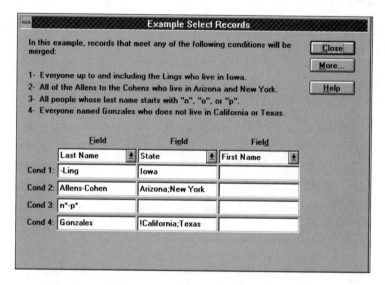

Figure 21.18 *The Example Select Records dialog box.*

This dialog box shows different example conditions and explains what they mean. To see more examples of valid conditions, choose **More** to display the dialog box shown in Figure 21.19.

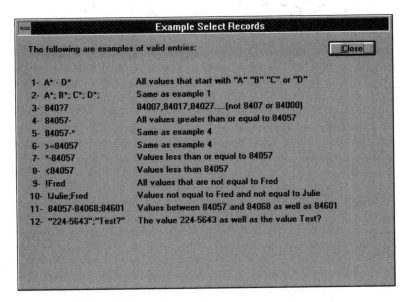

Example Select Records

The following are examples of valid entries:

1-	A* - D*	All values that start with "A" "B" "C" or "D"
2-	A*; B*; C*; D*;	Same as example 1
3-	840?7	84007,84017,84027....(not 8407 or 84000)
4-	84057-	All values greater than or equal to 84057
5-	84057-*	Same as example 4
6-	>=84057	Same as example 4
7-	*-84057	Values less than or equal to 84057
8-	<84057	Values less than 84057
9-	!Fred	All values that are not equal to Fred
10-	!Julie;Fred	Values not equal to Fred and not equal to Julie
11-	84057-84068;84601	Values between 84057 and 84068 as well as 84601
12-	"224-5643";"Test?"	The value 224-5643 as well as the value Test?

Figure 21.19 Additional examples of conditions.

When you've assigned all of the conditions you want, choose **OK** to close the
Select Records dialog box, then choose **OK** again to perform the merge.

FROM HERE ...

So, have you sorted it all out yet? I hope so, because I'm not going to talk about
sorting anymore. We covered sorting lines, paragraphs, tables, and data files,
and you learned how to write a selection statement to pull specific records out
of a file. Enough sorting already!

Coming up ... styles. No, *not* the new fall fashions—WordPerfect Styles, a
powerful tool that can help you achieve consistency in your formatting.

CHAPTER 22

Working with Styles

(You'll Always be in Style With WordPerfect Styles)

Let's talk about:

- ❖ Why use styles?
- ❖ Using the predefined styles
- ❖ Paired verses open styles
- ❖ QuickStyle—creating a style from existing text
- ❖ Creating a style from scratch
- ❖ QuickFormat
- ❖ Saving a style file
- ❖ Retrieving a style file
- ❖ Editing a style

Isn't it great to be in style? You're lookin' good, and you know you haven't forgotten any of those ever so essential accessories. Well, you can give your WordPerfect documents that same secure, stylish feeling with the Styles feature. A style is just a way of applying formatting in a consistent manner. You put all of the formatting codes into a style, and then you apply the style to a section of text.

WHY USE STYLES?

So far, styles sound kind of like macros, don't they? Well, in a way they are. You could write a macro that contains formatting codes and then run the macro whenever you want to apply the formatting to a section of text. So why create a style? Here's the scoop. Styles have one *big* advantage over macros for formatting text—they let you change your mind. And, in matters of style, it's always important to change with the times.

Say you write a macro that centers and bolds text for a heading, and you apply that macro to headings throughout a document. Everything's great—until you decide that you really want all of those headings to be at the left margin and in a different point size. Oh, and you want a conditional end of page code attached to each heading to make sure you don't end up with headings dangling by themselves at the bottom of a page.

Hmmm, what to do? You could write another macro that does all of the new stuff and deletes the old codes. The macro could even search through your document to find the old formatting codes. But there would be quite a few steps involved. And besides, you've used the same macro to format 50 other documents. You'd have to open each document and run the new macro.

Here's the beauty of styles—if you edit a style, every place you've applied that style is automatically updated to reflect the change. Using the example above, if you had used a style instead of a macro, all you would have to do is edit one style—delete the formatting codes you no longer want and add the new codes. That's it. Convinced?

You've already used some of WordPerfect's predefined styles. When you created bulleted and numbered lists, WordPerfect used styles to format the lists. When you created graphics boxes, you picked from a set of predefined box styles, and you chose your borders from a list of border styles. WordPerfect uses styles in many of its features to ensure consistency and at the same time allow flexibility. You can change the appearance of a graphics box, a border, or a list just by editing a style.

In this chapter, I'll show you how to use the styles that come with WordPerfect, and then you'll learn how to create your own styles.

Using WordPerfect's Predefined Styles

WordPerfect, thoughtful as ever, gives you several predefined styles that you can use "out of the box." Let's take a look.

❖ Click on the **Styles** button on the Toolbar. You can also press **Alt+F8** or choose **Styles** from the Format menu. The Style List dialog box is displayed, as shown in Figure 22.1. Notice that the selection bar is on **<None>**. By default, none of the styles are applied to your text.

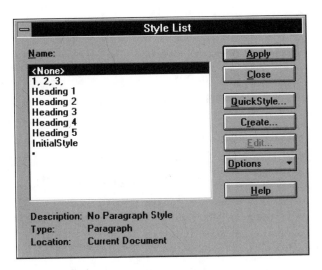

Figure 22.1 *The Style List dialog box.*

❖ You can always turn off a style (whether it's one of WordPerfect's or one you've created) by choosing **<None>** from the Style List.

❖ To apply one of the styles, just highlight the one you want and choose **Apply**. You can also apply a style by double-clicking on the style name.

❖ The styles supplied by WordPerfect include several numbering, bullet, and heading formats. If a description was included when the style was created, the description is displayed just below the list box when the style name is highlighted.

❖ Move your selection bar through the Style List and notice that there are descriptions for the various styles. Let's apply the style called 1, 2, 3 to create a list.

NOTE

If the 1,2,3 style doesn't appear on your Style List, do the following: Close the Style List dialog box if it's open. Choose **Bullets & Numbers** from the Insert menu, choose the **Numbers** style, and choose **OK**. Then close the document on your screen without saving. The next time you open the Style List dialog box, the 1,2,3 style will be included.

Do It

To apply a style:

1. Place your insertion point where you want the list to begin.
2. Open the Style List dialog box.
3. Double-click on **1, 2, 3** (or highlight 1, 2, 3 and choose **Apply**). The number 1 is inserted in your document, followed by an indent.
4. Type **Feed the cat** and press **Enter**.
5. Repeat steps 2 and 3, type **Feed the dog** and press **Enter**.
6. Repeat steps 2 and 3 and type **Buy dog food**.

Great feature. But turning on the same style over and over again can become rather tedious. Let's edit the style to make it more user friendly. And while we're at it, let's make a few more changes

Usually with a list, you want the number to be followed by a period, and that's the WordPerfect default for this numbering style. But what if you need something different? Let's edit the 1, 2, 3 style to add a colon after the number.

To edit the 1, 2, 3 style:

1. Open the Style List dialog box.
2. Select **1, 2, 3**.
3. Choose **Edit**. The Styles Editor dialog box is displayed, as shown in Figure 22.2.

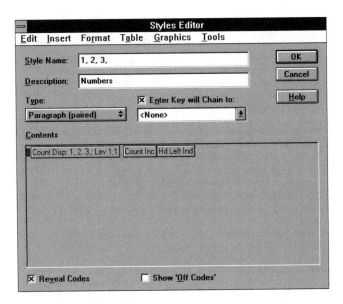

Figure 22.2 *The Styles Editor dialog box for the 1, 2, 3 style.*

4. Place your insertion point after the Count Disp code in the contents box and replace the period with a colon. The 1, 2, 3 style uses counters to increment the numbers when you press **Enter**. Count Disp tells WordPerfect to display the number in your document. All you are doing here is telling WordPerfect to add a colon whenever it inserts a number.

5. Change the style's Description to **Number + Colon**.

6. *Now for the most important step.* Make sure **Enter Key will Chain to** is checked and then choose **<Same Style>** from the drop-down list.

7. Choose **OK** to close the Styles Editor dialog box, then choose **Close** to close the Style List dialog box.

8. And like magic, the periods following the numbers in your list have all changed to colons.

9. Now press **Enter**. The number *4* appears on the next line, followed by a colon and an indent.

10. Type **Get dressed** and press **Enter**. The number *5* appears on the next line, followed by a colon and an indent. Uh oh, we're done with the list, but there's a number on the last line, and each time you press **Enter** you'll get another number.

11. Turn the style off by opening the Style List dialog box and choosing **<None>**. Either double-click on **<None>** or select it and choose **Apply**. Notice that the number *5* disappears. Any text you enter from this point does not contain the style formatting.

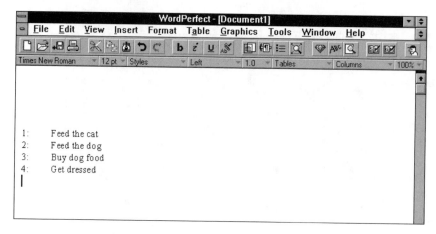

Figure 22.3 *A list using the 1, 2, 3 style.*

Pretty simple, huh? You edited the style, and the style in your document automatically changed. Now, whenever you use the 1, 2, 3 style in this document, you'll get a colon after the number.

That's all there is to applying and turning off a style—you'll learn more about edting styles as we go on.

Creating a Style

A style doesn't have to be complicated—you can create a style that does something as simple as insert a font change. In fact, a simple style can be one of the most useful. If you're formatting a document and playing around with different fonts and attributes, use styles. That way, when you change your mind, you can change your document just by editing a style, and you can easily experiment with different effects.

We'll start creating styles in just a minute. But first, a few words about an essential concept: *style types.*

Style Types

There are three types of styles: character, paragraph, and document.

❖ **Character styles** apply formatting to small blocks of text. You might use a character style for a font or attribute change within a paragraph.

❖ **Paragraph styles** usually apply formatting to paragraphs of text (although they can also be used for blocks of selected text). For example, you might use a paragraph style to change justification and margins for particular paragraphs.

❖ **Document styles** affect larger chunks of your document. You might use a document style to insert a paper size code or add page borders.

Character and paragraph styles are both what are called *paired styles*. That means that paired codes are inserted into your document when you apply a character or paragraph style, and any text between the beginning and ending codes is part of the style. There are two types of paragraph styles: paired and paired-auto. The only difference between the two is that paired-auto styles automatically update when you change the formatting of the paragraph that contains the style. Document styles are *open styles*. That means the style takes effect at your insertion point location and remains in effect until it encounters another style or code that changes it. As we create styles, you'll see the difference and learn when you would use the various style types.

Using QuickStyle

The easiest way to create a style is to use the QuickStyle option to build your style from existing text. You can use QuickStyle to create paragraph or character styles. Enough talk. Let's do it.

Let's use a really simple example of text that's centered and has a font change applied to it:

❖ Press **Shift+F7** (center).

❖ Select **Font** from the Format menu, and choose the **Ribbon131 Bd BT** font.

❖ Set the font size at **30** and choose **OK**.

❖ Type **Gloucester Heights Gazette**.

You should have a line of text that looks like Figure 22.4. If you turn Reveal Codes on you should see the codes shown in Figure 22.4.

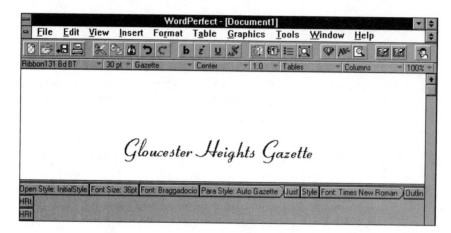

Figure 22.4 *Text with center and font codes.*

Do It

1.   Place your insertion point anywhere in the line of text.

2.   Open the Style List dialog box.

3.   Choose **QuickStyle**. The QuickStyle dialog box appears, as shown in Figure 22.5.

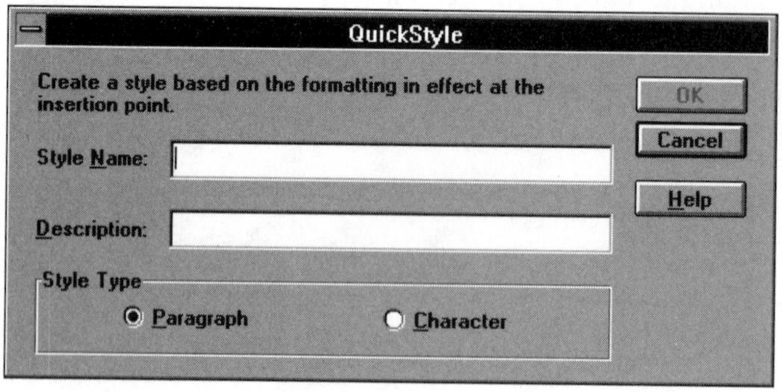

Figure 22.5 *The QuickStyle dialog box.*

4. Enter a name in the Style Name text box. For this example, type **Gazette**.

5. If you want, type a description in the Description text box. For this example, type **Masthead**.

6. Choose **Paragraph** or **Character** from the Style type box. For now, go ahead and accept the default, which is **Paragraph**. This option creates a style that includes all of the formatting codes and font attributes applied to the text. If you choose **Character**, only the font attributes for the text at the insertion point location are included in the style.

7. Choose **OK**. Notice that your new style is on the Style List. You can apply it to text or edit it like any other style.

Let's see what happened when you used QuickStyle. Highlight the **Gazette** style in the Style List and choose **Edit**. You should see the Styles Editor dialog box, shown in Figure 22.6.

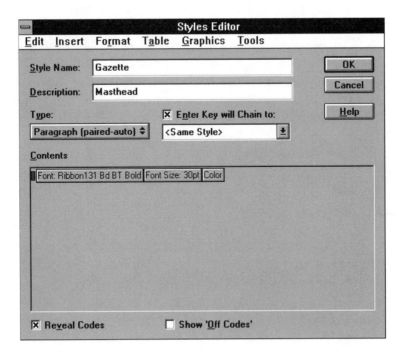

Figure 22.6 *The style you just created.*

The Contents box contains the formatting and attribute codes for the paragraph. After you take a look at the codes, go ahead and choose **Cancel** to close the Styles Editor.

Creating a Style from Scratch

With QuickStyle, you can copy text formatting to a character or paragraph style. But you can also create your own style from scratch in the Styles Editor.

1. From the Styles List dialog box, choose **Create**.

2. Enter a name in the Style Name text box. The style name can be up to 12 characters, and it can include spaces.

3. Enter a description in the Description text box (the description is optional, but I suggest that you add one to help identify your styles in the Style List).

4. Choose the appropriate option from the Type pop-up list.

5. Place your insertion point in the Contents box and add any formatting codes you want to include in the style. Use the Styles Editor menu bar to select codes to insert in the style. You can also insert codes using most of the shortcut keystrokes you've learned. For example, pressing **Ctrl+B** inserts a bold code in the style. While you're creating a style, you don't have access to the Toolbar, Power Bar, or main pull-down menu.

NOTE

Since the **Enter** and **Tab** keys work differently in a dialog box, you have to press **Shift+Enter** to insert a hard return in your style and **Ctrl+Tab** to insert a tab.

6. Use the Enter Key Will Chain To drop-down box if you want to change the way the **Enter** key works when you use the style:

   ❖ Notice that by default the **Enter Key Will Chain to** box is checked, and the selected option is **<Same Style>**. This is the option we selected when we edited the *1, 2, 3* style. It toggles the style off and back on every time you press **Enter**. When **Enter** is pressed, the style turns off, moves past the insertion point past the ending style code, and turns the style off.

❖ If you select **<None>**, pressing the **Enter** key in a character or paragraph style moves the insertion point past the ending style code and turns the style off.

❖ You can have the **Enter** key turn on a different style by choosing that style from the drop-down list.

❖ If you want the **Enter** key to act like it normally does (inserting a hard return without turning off the style), deselect the **Enter Key Will Chain To** check box.

7. Choose **OK** when you're finished creating the style.

8. Choose **Apply** or **Close** to exit the Style List dialog box.

Deleting a Style

If you just want to get rid of the style code from one particular spot, turn on reveal codes, find the code and delete it. But if you've used a style throughout your document and want to quickly delete all references to it:

1. Open the Style List dialog box and highlight the style you want to delete.

2. Choose **Delete** from the Options drop-down list. The Delete Styles dialog box is displayed, as shown in Figure 22.7.

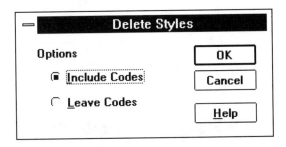

Figure 22.7 *The Delete Styles dialog box.*

3. Choose **Include Codes** to delete the style and any formatting codes that are included with it. Choose **Leave Codes** to delete the style and leave the formatting codes in the document.

4. Choose **OK**.

WHAT HAPPENS TO STYLES?

When you create a style, where does it go? When you close the current document, can you still use the style?

To talk about what happens to styles, we have to get into templates a little bit. You'll learn all about templates in the next chapter. For now, all you need to know is that you use a template every time you create a document, whether you realize it or not. Every new document uses a standard template that contains formatting and style options. You can also choose from several predefined templates that perform specified functions. Templates are like patterns you can use to build documents. They can contain styles, macros, and many other elements.

When you create or edit a style, the style is saved with either the default template or the current document. By default, it's saved with the current document. This means that any changes you make to the style (or any new styles you create) apply only to the current document. If you want the changes to apply to other documents, you need to save the style to a template. (You can also save a list of styles to a file that can be retrieved into another document—I'll talk about that later.)

To use the numbered list example, if you want a colon after the number *every time* you use the *1, 2, 3* style, you have to copy the style to the default template.

Copying a Style to the Current Template

1. Open the Style List dialog box and highlight the style you want to copy.

2. Choose **Copy** from the Options drop-down list. The Styles Copy dialog box is displayed, as shown in Figure 22.8.

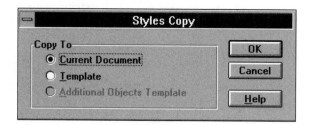

Figure 22.8 *The Styles Copy dialog box.*

3. Choose **Template**.

4. You are prompted with **Overwrite current styles?** Choose **Yes** and then choose **OK** to return to the document screen. The style is then saved to your default or supplemental template.

Saving a Style List

If you create a bunch of styles in one document, you can save all of the styles in a file so they can be used in other documents.

1. Open the Style List dialog box. Don't worry about which style is highlighted—this feature applies to the whole list of styles.

2. Choose **Save As** from the Options drop-down list. The Save Styles To... dialog box is displayed, as shown in Figure 22.9.

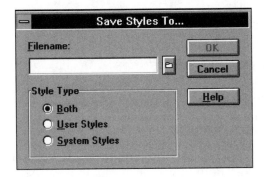

Figure 22.9 *The Save Styles To... dialog box.*

3. Enter a name for the Style List in the Filename text box. The filename should include the complete directory path , otherwise they'll go to your default template directory. Also, I suggest that you give your style files a consistent extension (I use STY).

4. If you want the style file to include the styles created by WordPerfect as well as styles you've created, choose **Both**. If you only want to save the styles you've created, choose **User Styles**. If you only want to save the WordPerfect-created styles, choose **System**.

5. Choose **OK**.

Retrieving Styles

You can retrieve styles from a file or from another document. Suppose you're working in a document and you remember that you created a set of styles in a similar document, but you didn't save the styles to a separate file. No problem.

1. Open the Style List dialog box.

2. Choose **Retrieve** from the Options drop-down list. The Retrieve Styles From... dialog box is displayed, as shown in Figure 22.10.

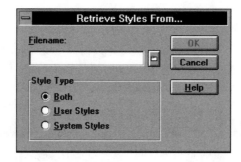

Figure 22.10 *The Retrieve Styles From... dialog box.*

3. Enter the name of the document or style file that contains the styles you want to use. You can click on the file icon and choose from the Select File dialog box.

4. To retrieve styles created by WordPerfect as well as styles you've created, choose **Both**. If you only want to retrieve styles you've created, choose **User Styles**. If you only want to retrieve the WordPerfect-created styles, choose **System Styles**.

5. Choose **OK**.

QUICKFORMAT

There one other quick trick for applying formatting or styles to text. Have you noticed the QuickFormat button on the Toolbar? If you have, you've probably been wondering when I'd get around to it. The time has come.

The **QuickFormat** button is an easy way to copy a paragraph style or font and attribute codes from one part of a document to another. You can turn on a style in one paragraph, then use QuickFormat to copy the style to several other paragraphs. Or you can add font and attribute codes (like bold, underline, or font changes) to a section of text and use QuickFormat to quickly copy the formatting to additional sections of text.

1. Place your insertion point anywhere in the paragraph that contains the formatting or style you want to copy. If you only want to copy the formatting from a portion of a paragraph, select the text first.

2. Click on the **QuickFormat** button on the Toolbar or choose **QuickFormat** from the Format menu.. The QuickFormat dialog box, shown in Figure 22.11, is displayed.

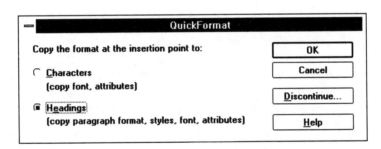

Figure 22.11 The QuickFormat dialog box.

3. Chose **Characters** if you want to copy only the text formatting codes. Choose **Headings** to copy any paragraph formatting attached to the paragraph, as well as text formatting codes.

4. As soon as you make a choice, an icon attaches itself to your mouse pointer. If you chose **Characters,** it's a paintbrush; if you choose **Headings,** it's a paint roller. Move the pointer to the area where you want to apply the formatting or style.

5. If you chose **Characters,** drag the mouse pointer to select the text you want to affect. When you release the mouse button, the text is deselected, and the new formatting or style takes effect. If you chose **Headings,** all you have to do is click anywhere in the paragraph to which you want to apply the style.

In either case, notice that the **QuickFormat** icon remains attached to your mouse pointer when you're done. Until you turn **QuickFormat** off, you can apply the formatting or style to as many paragraphs or blocks of selected as you want..

6. When you've applied the formatting or style to the locations you want, click on the **QuickFormat** button to turn off the feature.

If you have text selected when you choose **QuickFormat**, you won't see the QuickFormat dialog box. WordPerfect assumes you just want to copy the font and attribute codes.

INITIAL STYLE

If you've been paying attention to the Reveal Codes window, you've probably noticed a code that appears at the beginning of every document. If you haven't noticed it, open Reveal Codes and take a look. At the very top of your document, you'll see a code that says [Open Style: InitialStyle]. The InitialStyle contains all of your default formatting. You can't delete this code, but you can change what's included in it. It's a style that can be edited like any other style.

Any codes that you put in the InitialStyle affect your whole document, including special areas like headers, footers, footnotes, and endnotes. For example, if you change the font in the InitialStyle, all of your headers and footers would use that font (unless you change the font code in the header or footer).

NOTE

The InitialStyle style is an open style, which means that it takes effect from its position in the document (in this case, the beginning) and remains in effect until it encounters a code that tells WordPerfect to do something else. For example, if you change your left margin in the InitialStyle, the margin change applies to all of your text until you insert another left margin code in the document.

You can edit the InitialStyle style by double-clicking on it in Reveal Codes. You can also highlight **InitialStyle** in the Style List dialog box and choose **Edit**. Either way, you end up in the Styles Editor dialog box, shown in Figure 22.12.

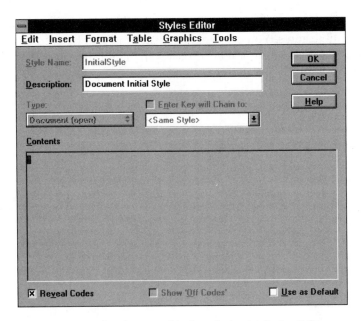

Figure 22.12 *The InitialStyle style in the Styles Editor.*

Notice that the Style Name text box and the Type pop-up list are dimmed. Also notice the Use as Default check box in the lower-right corner of the dialog box. If you check this box, the codes that you include in InitialStyle will apply to all of the documents you create from now on.

Use InitialStyle to customize your document formats. For example, if you want all of your documents to have 1.25-inch left and right margins, edit the InitialStyle style to include the margin codes and check the **Use as Default** check box. From that point on, every document you create will have the new margins.

FROM HERE ...

You can use styles to help you achieve consistent formatting in your documents. If you've used styles, you can make changes throughout a document just by editing a style. You can create a style from text you've already formatted by using QuickStyle, and you can apply a style or formatting codes to selected text with QuickFormat.

The next chapter talks about templates, which are one of WordPerfect's most powerful features. You can build templates that can be used as patterns for documents that you use on a regular basis. The templates included on the disk that accompanies this book demonstrate some of the possibilities.

CHAPTER 23

Working with Templates

(Don't Worry. We're Not Talking Templates of Doom Here.)

Let's talk about:

- ❖ What are templates?
- ❖ Using templates
- ❖ Creating a template
- ❖ Editing a template

Has this ever happened to you? You create a form to use for your memos. You plan to create your memos by retrieving the form, filling in the information for the memo, and saving the document with a different name. But every once in a while you forget to save with a different name, and your form ends up with a bunch of unwanted text in it. So you have to delete all of the text to get your form back the way it was.

If you use the same basic pattern for documents that you create on a regular basis, WordPerfect templates can save you a lot of time. You can create a document template that contains all of the formatting and fixed text. To use the template, just open it, add whatever information you want, and save it as a WordPerfect document. With the templates feature, you can't accidentally save something on top of the original form. The template itself remains unchanged, so you can use it again and again.

What's the difference between templates, macros, and styles? Each of these features allows you to automate the process of document creation. Macros and styles can both include formatting codes, text, tables, and almost any other WordPerfect element. You've already seen how powerful these two features can be.

So what do templates give you that macros and styles don't? When you open a template, you have access to everything that's associated with that template, including styles, macros, Toolbars, menu bars, abbreviations, and keyboard layouts.

Templates are an integral part of WordPerfect. Every time you create a new document and choose **Create a blank document** from the New Document dialog box, you're really opening a template called STANDARD.WPT. This template controls the options that are available to you. Everything that you see on the screen (and some things you don't see) is part of a template. The Toolbar, Power Bar, and initial styles are all attached to STANDARD.WPT. When you make a change to the initial style and specify that you want to use the style as a default, WordPerfect saves the changes to STANDARD.WPT so that they're applied to all of your new documents.

If you choose a different option from the New Document dialog box, you're actually choosing a template.

WordPerfect comes with more than 75 predefined templates, along with a guide that explains how they work.

ROADMAP

Included with this book is a disk containing 20 additional templates, which are described in Appendix C.

USING TEMPLATES

When you install WordPerfect, the predefined templates are installed in C:\OFFICE\WPWIN\TEMPLATE, unless you specify another directory during the installation. To use a template:

1. Choose **New** from the File menu, or press **Ctrl+T**. The New Document dialog box, shown in Figure 23.1, is displayed.

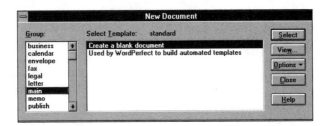

Figure 23.1 *The New Document dialog box.*

2. Choose **Fax** from the Group list. The available fax templates display in the Select Template list, as shown in Figure 23.2.

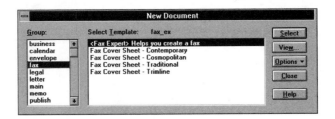

Figure 23.2 *Choose from this list of fax templates.*

3. Select **Fax Cover Sheet - Traditional**.

NOTE

You can choose **View** to get a preview of the template before you choose it.

4. Choose **Select.** The Personalize Your Templates information box, shown in Figure 23.3, is displayed.

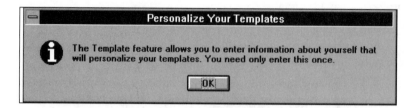

Figure 23.3 *The Personalize Your Templates information box.*

5. WordPerfect lets you personalize templates the first time you use them. Click on **OK** (or press **Enter**) and you'll see the Enter Your Personal Information dialog box shown in Figure 23.4. Fill in the information in the appropriate text boxes. You only have to do this once and the information is available for all of the templates requiring it.

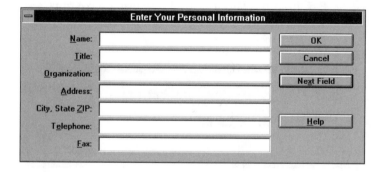

Figure 23.4 *The Enter Your Personal Information dialog box.*

6. Choose **OK**. The Template Information dialog box is displayed, as shown in Figure 23.5.

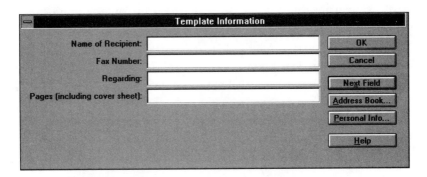

Figure 23.5 *The Template Information dialog box.*

7. Enter the requested information and choose **OK** (or press **Enter**). The information you entered has been inserted in the fax form.

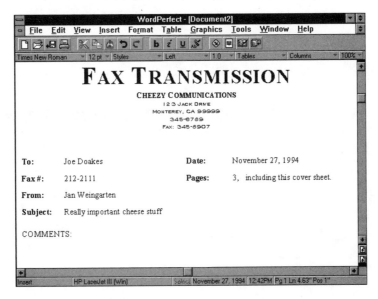

Figure 23.6 *The filled-in fax form.*

What if you correspond with this person several times a month? You'd get pretty tired of typing the same name and address over and over again. WordPerfect has a solution for that situation. Several of the predefined templates include the option of using names and addresses from an electronic address book. Use Address Book and you'll never have to type the same address again.

Create a new fax document, but this time, instead of filling in the information in the Template Information dialog box, click on **Address Book** to open the Template Address Book dialog box, shown in Figure 23.7.

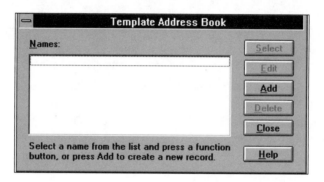

Figure 23.7 *The Template Address Book dialog box.*

To create an entry for the address book, choose **Add**, fill in the appropriate information in the Edit Address dialog box shown in Figure 23.8, and choose **OK**.

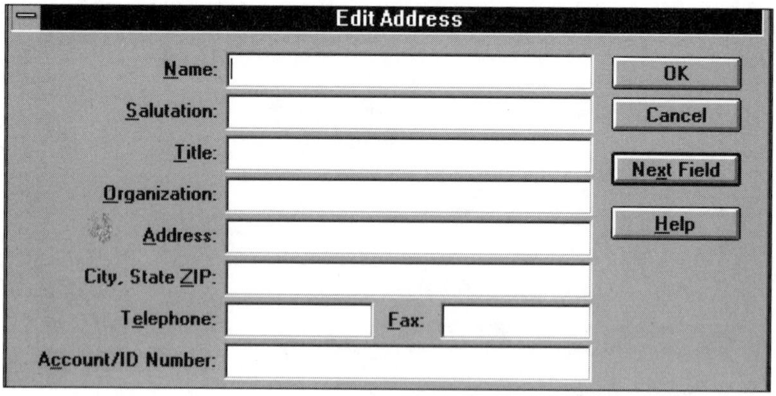

Figure 23.8 *Create an address book entry using this dialog box.*

Once you've created address book entries, you can insert information into a template by choosing **Address Book**, highlighting the appropriate name, and choosing **Select**. You can edit an entry by highlighting the name and choosing **Edit** from the Address Book dialog box.

Since a template can be just about anything, I can't give you specifics about filling out a template. Just follow the instructions on screen—fill out any appropriate text boxes and make choices in any dialog boxes that display. In most cases, once you've completed all of the dialog boxes, you will be left with a document on screen that you can complete in any way you want.

Using the fax template as an example, the information that you enter in the Template Information dialog box is inserted in the fax document. Once the dialog boxes have disappeared, your insertion point is placed at the end of the document, ready for you to type any notes or additional information.

A template is a regular WordPerfect document. You can make any changes you want—edit the text, change the formatting, etc. When you open a template, notice that the Title Bar doesn't display a document name. The template information is brought into a new WordPerfect window, and the template itself remains unchanged. When you've added text and made all of the changes you want, save just like you would any WordPerfect document.

Creating a Template

To create a template:

1. Choose **New** from the File menu or press **Ctrl+T**.

2. Open the Options drop-down list and choose **New Template**. The dialog box closes and you're left at a blank WordPerfect screen. [Template1] appears as the name of your template in the Title Bar, and the Template Feature Bar is displayed, as shown in Figure 23.9.

Figure 23.9 *The Template Feature Bar.*

3. Insert any text or formatting you want included in the template. Here's what the Feature Bar buttons do:

❖ **Insert File** allows you to use an existing document as the basis for your template.

❖ **Build Prompts** lets you insert prompts for the information to be inserted at a specified point.

❖ You can copy objects (styles, macros, etc.) that were created in another template by using the **Copy/Remove Object** option.

❖ Choose **Associate** to tie objects to certain editing windows. For example, use it if you want a particular Toolbar to display when you're working in a table. **Associate** also launches a macro at a certain point. For example, you could specify that a particular macro will play right after you've printed the document.

❖ Choose **Description** to create or edit the description for the template.

4. When the template is complete, choose **Exit Template** from the Feature Bar and answer **Yes** when WordPerfect prompts you to save the template. Choose the appropriate option when asked to save the Entire File or just the Selected Text.

5. Insert any text or formatting you want included in the template. When the template is complete, choose **Exit Template** from the Feature Bar and answer **Yes** when WordPerfect asks if you want to save the template.

The Save Template dialog box shown in Figure 23.10 appears.

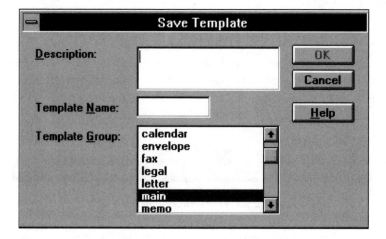

Figure 23.10 *The Save Template dialog box*

6. Type a descriptive name for the template inthe Description text box. When you choose New from the File menu, your description is what appears in the Template List in the New Document dialog box.

7. Enter a filename in the Template Name box.

8. Make a choice from the Template Name box.

NOTE

You can create a new group by choosing **Options, New Group** from the New Document dialog box.

NOTE

Some predefined templates have automated capabilities called Document Experts to simplify complicated tasks for you. If available, the Expert will be listed at the top of the selected template styles box.

NOTE

If you're not going to attach a lot of fancy stuff to your template, you can turn a regular WordPerfect document into a template just by saving it with a WPT extension. This is probably the easiest way to create a template. Just create the document the way you normally would and save it as a template. Be sure you save the document in your templates directory.

Editing a Template

You can edit WordPerfect's predefined templates, the templates included with this book, or templates that you've created yourself. It doesn't matter where the template came from; the procedure to edit it is the same.

1. Choose **New** from the File menu or press **Ctrl+T**.

2. Highlight the template you want to use.

3. Open the Options drop-down list and choose **Edit Template**. The template and the Template Feature Bar are displayed on your screen.

4. Make any changes you want and choose **Exit Template**.

Deleting a Template

1. From the Templates dialog box, highlight the template you want to delete.
2. Open the Options drop-down list and choose **Delete Template**.
3. Answer **Yes** at the *Delete Selected Document Template?* prompt.

FROM HERE ...

The Templates feature has almost unlimited potential. As you work with WordPerfect's templates and the templates included with this book, you'll begin to see the possibilities. A template can be as simple as a memo form. And the sky's the limit—you can associate a template with macros, styles, Toolbars, menus, and different keyboard layouts. Start small—use the predefined templates, edit them to suit your needs, and create simple templates for your everyday tasks. Templates will soon become an indispensable tool for you.

This chapter completes the section on automation tools. The next section covers organizational and referencing tools. You'll learn about features that will help you work with large documents, and I'll show you how to manipulate several documents at one time. In the next chapter, "Lists and Outlines," you'll see how easy it is to create bulleted lists and organize your thoughts with the outline feature.

ORGANIZATIONAL AND REFERENCING TOOLS

CHAPTER 24

Lists and Outlines

(Make a List and Check It Twice. Then Make an Outline That's Really Nice.)

Let's talk about:

- ❖ Creating a bulleted or numbered list
- ❖ Using the Outline feature bar
- ❖ Creating a simple outline
- ❖ Changing the outline definition
- ❖ Collapsing and expanding the outline

493

If only I could organize my thoughts as easily as WordPerfect can organize my lists and outlines! With WordPerfect's Outline feature, I never have to remember which number comes next or which level I'm supposed to be in (but I still have to come up with the ideas to put in the outline—maybe they'll have a solution for that by version 7.0). I can collapse the outline to see only the major headings. I can use the Outline feature bar to quickly move text between outline levels. When I move an entire "family" of outline text to a new location, it automatically renumbers. But before we get to all the fancy outline stuff, there's an even easier feature for creating a quick bulleted or numbered list.

CREATING A BULLETED OR NUMBERED LIST

Bullets can add pizzazz to what might otherwise be a boring list. Take a look at Figure 24.1. I want to use this list in a presentation to get people all excited about WordPerfect. How exciting does this look? In my opinion, not very.

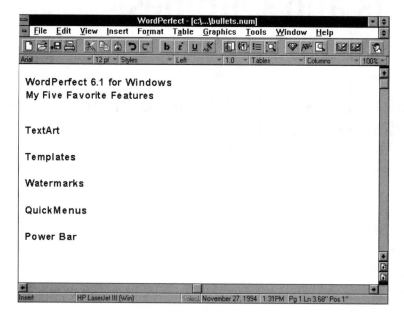

Figure 24.1 *A boring list.*

Go ahead and type the list as shown in Figure 24.1, and follow along as we spiff it up.

1. Select the lines to which you want to add the bullets. In Figure 24.2, I've selected the lines that contain the featured items. Notice that I only selected part of the first and last lines. You don't have to select the entire line—as long as a portion of the line is selected, you can apply bullets or numbers to it.

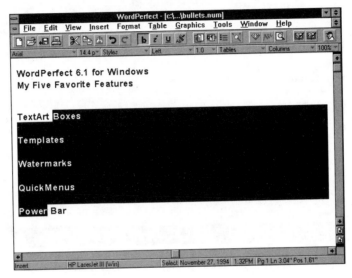

Figure 24.2 *List with items selected.*

2. Choose **Bullets & Numbers** from the Insert menu.

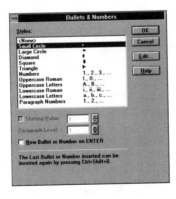

Figure 24.3 *The Bullets & Numbers dialog box.*

3. Click on the bullet or number style you want and choose **OK**. For Figure 24.4, I chose **Square**.

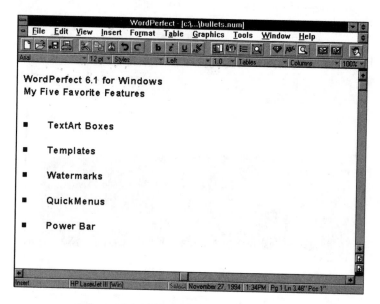

Figure 24.4 *The list with bullets added.*

Those bullets sure do pack a wallop—maybe my audience will actually stay awake during the presentation!

That's all there is to it. You can change the bullet or number style as easily as you set it up in the first place. For example, suppose you change the heading to read *My Five Favorite Features,* and you want the items numbered instead of bulleted. Just select at least a portion of each line again, open the Bullets & Numbers dialog box, and choose the style you want. Figure 24.5 shows the new, numbered list.

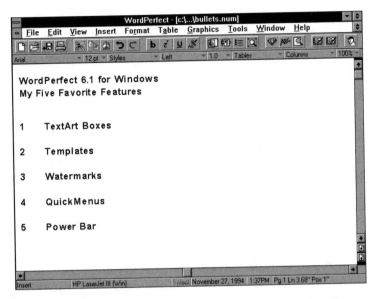

Figure 24.5 *The same list with numbers instead of bullets.*

Getting Rid of Bullets

If you decide you don't want the bullets or numbers anymore, no problem. Just select the list and choose **<None>** from the Bullets & Numbers dialog box.

Changing the Bullet Style

Changing the bullet style is as simple as getting rid of the bullets. Just select the list and choose a different style from the Bullets & Numbers dialog box. If you select a number style and you want to start the list with something other than the number 1, choose **Starting Value** and enter the number you want in the text box.

Adding Items to a Bulleted List

Once you've chosen a bullet or number style, it's easy to add items to the list. Just place your insertion point on the line where you want to add the item, and press **Ctrl+Shift+B** to add a bullet or number in the currently selected style followed by an indent.

Creating a Bulleted List as You Type

The first example showed you how to add bullets or numbers to a list after you've entered the text, but it's just as easy to apply the bullet or number style before you type.

1. Place your insertion point where you want the list to begin.

2. Choose a bullet or number style from the Bullets & Numbers dialog box.

3. Check the **New Bullet or Number on ENTER** check box if you want a new bullet or number inserted automatically every time you press the **Enter** key.

4. Choose **OK**. The first bullet or number appears on your screen followed by an indent code.

5. Type the text for the first item and press **Enter**. In Figure 24.6, I've typed one item and pressed the **Enter** key.

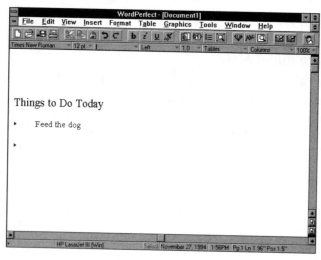

Figure 24.6 *You can create a bulleted list as you type.*

If you want more control over the bullets, don't check the **New Bullet or Number on ENTER** check box. With this option checked, you get a bullet or number *every* time you press the **Enter** key. And, you would have to select **<None>** each time you want to turn it off. What if you want two hard returns between each entry? Or you want to add a line of unbulleted text between entries? Can't do it. So, for more control, follow all of the instructions above except number 3. As you type your list, press **Ctrl+Shift+B** on each line where you want to add a bullet or number.

OUTLINES

Okay, bullets and numbers are pretty cool for a quick list, but what about a real outline? Creating your outline can be as simple as turning on the Outline feature and typing your text, but the feature contains enough power to manipulate your outlines in almost any way you could desire.

Understanding Outline Levels

An outline usually contains items grouped according to their relation to a main topic. A main topic could have several subordinate topics, and each subordinate topic could have its own set of subcategories. In outline terminology, each group or subgroup is a *level,* and an entry along with all of its subordinate levels is considered a *family.* In a standard outline, subordinate levels are indented under their parents, as shown in Figure 24.7.

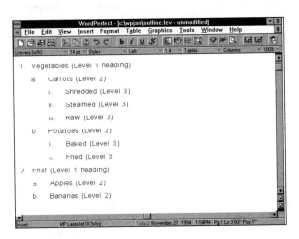

Figure 24.7 *An outline with three levels.*

Vegetables is a major category, so it's a first level item at the left margin. *Carrots* and *potatoes* are level 2 items that are part of the *vegetables* family. The different carrot classifications belong to the *carrots* family, as well as the *vegetables* family. The family concept will become important when you start moving outline groups around.

The second level items are indented one tab stop under the first level items. As you add levels, each level is indented one tab stop to the right and given a different numbering style. Figure 24.7 uses the default outline definition, but you can choose from several predefined definitions or create your own. We'll talk about the different styles later, but I wanted you to have a basic understanding of outline levels before you create your own outline.

Do It

To create a simple outline:

1. Place your insertion point where you want the outline to begin and choose **Outline** from the Tools menu. Notice that the Outline feature bar is displayed and there are funny symbols in the left margin. I'll explain the symbols later. (You might have to scroll over to the left to see them.) The number 1 appears at your left margin, followed by an indent.

2. Type the text for your first item. In Figure 24.8, my insertion point was two lines below the first paragraph when I turned **Outline** on, I then typed the text for that line and pressed **Enter** to move to the next line.

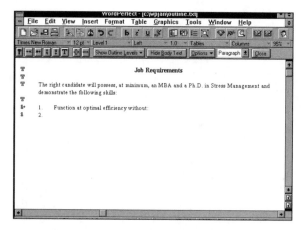

Figure 24.8 *The Outline feature bar and symbols are displayed when you turn Outline on.*

3. Press the **Enter** key. When the Outline feature bar is turned on, pressing **Enter** moves you to the next line and inserts a new number. Notice that the number is at the first level. Outline automatically adds new numbers at the current level. To change a number to the next level, press the **Tab** key or click the **Right Arrow** button on the Outline feature bar. To change the level of an item to the previous level, press **Shift+Tab** or click the **Left Arrow** button.

4. Press **Tab** to change the second line to level two.

5. Continue entering text and changing levels as necessary until you have created the outline shown in Figure 24.9.

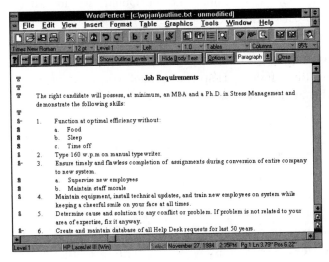

Figure 24.9 *The completed outline.*

Outline Symbols

Now it's time to talk about those funny-looking symbols. They're just there to let you know what's happening and make it easier to work with the outline. If you look at the Ruler Bar, you can see that the symbols are way over in the left margin and are not part of your document text. They won't print, and they won't be visible once you turn off the Outline feature bar. But they're really useful while you're working in an outline.

You can quickly tell which level you're on by looking at the number. If there's a plus sign next to the number, that means there are subordinate levels or text lines attached to the level. A *T* tells you the line is a text line that's not included in the outline.

You can also use the symbols to quickly select entire outline families. Just click on a level symbol to select the current line and any subordinate levels belonging to it. If you click on a *T* symbol, you'll select the entire text paragraph.

Using the Outline Feature Bar

The Outline feature bar is displayed when you choose **Outline** from the Tools menu. You can edit your outline with the Outline feature bar closed, but the Outline feature bar's tools (including the margin symbols we just talked about) simplify the process.

Move your mouse pointer over the Outline feature bar buttons and look at the Title Bar—those friendly Help prompts tell you what each button does. But I'll explain them a little more anyway.

NOTE

You can activate the Outline feature bar at any time by choosing **Outline** from the Tools menu.

All of the functions on the Outline feature bar can be accessed by pressing an **Alt+Shift+letter** combination. With the Outline feature bar visible, press **Alt+Shift+F10** to pull down the Outline feature bar menu, as shown in Figure 24.10. This shows you which keystroke combinations to use for the various Outline feature bar options.

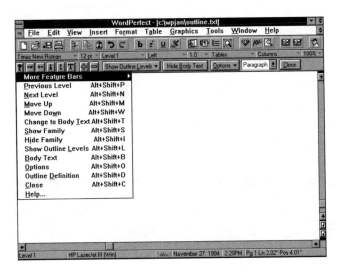

Figure 24.10 *The Outline feature bar with the menu pulled down.*

Changing Levels

❖ Use the **Left Arrow** button on the Outline feature bar to move an item or a selected family back one level. For example, if you want *Supervise new employees* to be a level one item, place your insertion point anywhere in that line and click the **Left Arrow** button.

❖ You can move any item back one level by pressing **Shift+Tab** with your insertion point at the beginning of the text.

❖ Use the **Right Arrow** button to move an item or a selected family to the next level.

❖ You can move any item to the next level by pressing **Tab** with your insertion point at the beginning of the text.

Moving Items and Families

The **Left Arrow** and **Right Arrow** buttons change outline levels, but they don't affect the item's or family's location in the outline. You can use the **Up Arrow** and **Down Arrow** to rearrange the order of your items and/or families.

Just place the insertion point in the item you want to move, or select a family. In Figure 24.11, I clicked on the symbol to the left of the number 3 to select the entire family.

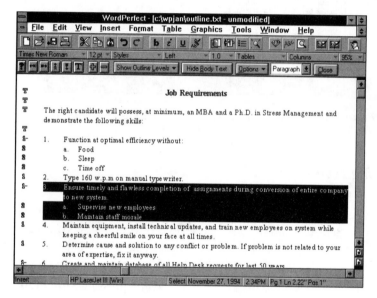

Figure 24.11 *An entire outline family is selected.*

With the family selected, I'm going to click on the **Up Arrow** to move the whole family up. In Figure 24.12, you can see that the level one item in the selected group is now number 2 in the list, and its kids followed right along. The *Type 160 w.p.m.* item got bumped down to number 3.

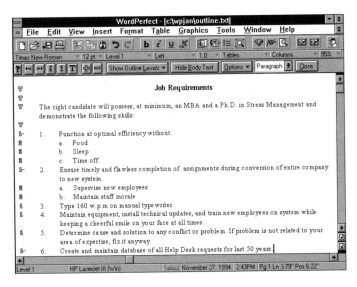

Figure 24.12 *I moved the entire family up.*

Adding Body Text to an Outline

When you created your outline, you saw that every time you pressed **Enter**, WordPerfect added a new number. That's fine if you want the next entry to be part of the outline. But what if you want to enter some plain old body text in the middle of your outline? Easy. Use that cool looking **T** button on the Outline feature bar (or press **Alt+Shift+F10**) to toggle back and forth between outline and regular text. This feature will also convert a selected block from an outline item to regular text, or regular text to an outline item.

NOTE

When you press the **Enter** key twice during outline creation, you automatically get a blank text line.

Collapsing and Expanding the Outline

When you're working on an outline, sometimes it helps to be able to see only certain portions of it. For example, you might want to hide everything but the level 1 headings to make sure you've covered all of your major points. With the plus (+), minus (-), and numbered **Show** buttons, you're in the driver's seat. You can display as much or as little of your outline as you want.

❖ Click on the - button to hide all of the levels below the one your insertion point is in in the current family.

❖ Click on the + button to show all of the levels of the current family.

❖ Use the **Show Outline Level** button to display a specified number of outline levels. For example, if you click on **1**, only the level 1 items are visible; if you click on **8**, all of the outline levels are visible.

❖ Choose **Hide Body Text** if you only want to see the outline items. This is a toggle switch, so choose it again when you want the text shown.

Ending an Outline

Until you end an outline, any text that you type is considered part of the outline style. To turn off an outline, choose **End Outline** from the Options menu on the Outline feature bar. Choosing **End Outline** doesn't close the Outline feature bar. To do that, choose **Close**.

Resetting the Numbering

Whenever you turn off an outline or create a new one, the numbering is reset to 1. If you want your outline to start with a different number, choose **Outline** from the Tools menu to open the Outline feature bar. Then choose **Set Number** from the Options menu, enter a starting number in the Paragraph Number text box, and choose **OK**.

Changing Outline Definitions

There are seven predefined outline styles that use different formatting and numbering methods (including two separate legal numbering definitions). There's even one called *Headings* that doesn't use numbers at all—it formats section headings for reports and similar documents.

To change the definition of the current outline, place the insertion point anywhere in the outline. Open the Outline Definition drop-down list. It's the one to the right of the **Options** button. The current definition displays in the box next to the **Down Arrow** (since we haven't changed from the default definition, yours probably still says *Paragraph*). Just choose the definition you want and the whole outline changes.

You can edit any of the outline definitions by choosing **Define Outline** from the **Options** button on the Outline feature bar, selecting the definition you want to change, and choosing **Edit**. You can also create new definitions by choosing **Create**. You might want to hold off on creating your own definitions until you feel pretty comfortable working with styles.

FROM HERE ...

You can use bulleted or numbered lists to add emphasis to your reports and presentations without breaking a sweat. And if you have ideas to organize, WordPerfect can help you put them in order. You can do your thinking on screen, moving families and levels around as much as you please.

In the next chapter, we'll make short work out of long documents. You'll learn to generate a table of contents or an index, cross reference items in different locations, and use the Master Document feature to manage those extra-long documents.

CHAPTER 25

Working with Long Documents

(Wanna Write a Book?)

Let's talk about:

- ❖ Creating a table of contents
- ❖ Creating an index
- ❖ Cross referencing
- ❖ Using a master document
- ❖ Working with footnotes

Does this scenario seem familiar to you? Your report is proofed, spell checked, and ready to go. You've carefully checked your table of contents to make sure the page numbers are correct. And you triple-checked every place in the document where you cross-referenced another page or a figure. That was a lot of work, but it's done, and it's perfect. But wait—you find out that the chart on page two has to come out—the figures aren't ready to be released. Now all of your carefully checked page numbers are wrong. Major bummer.

Unless, of course, you used WordPerfect's automated referencing features to mark all of your table of contents and cross-referencing entries. If you did, all you have to do is regenerate and you can go home. Another last-minute change? Just smile and say, "No problem."

TABLE OF CONTENTS

Creating a table of contents involves three steps:

1. Marking the text you want to include in the table of contents.
2. Defining the table of contents. This means telling WordPerfect how you want the table of contents formatted and where it should be located.
3. Generating the table of contents. This is where WordPerfect actually builds the table of contents by finding all of the codes you inserted when you marked the text.

Planning the Table of Contents

Before you start marking or defining, you have to decide how many levels you want. Do you want to mark only the major chapter headings? In that case, you would only have one level. You can have up to five levels in a table of contents. Think about how detailed you want your table to be, and decide ahead of time which headings will belong to which levels. Consistency is important—you don't want some of your section headings to be level 1 and some level 3. (If all this level stuff doesn't make sense yet, it will as soon as you start marking.)

Marking Text for the Table of Contents

You can mark text as you're typing, or you can go back and mark everything at the end. As with most of WordPerfect's features, the choice is yours.

1. Choose **Table of Contents** from the Tools menu. The Table of Contents feature bar is displayed, as shown in Figure 25.1.

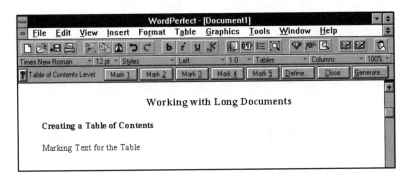

Figure 25.1 *The Table of Contents feature bar.*

2. Select the text you want to include in the table of contents. In Figure 25.2, I've selected **Working With Long Documents.** Notice in the Reveal Codes window that **Select** is turned on *after* the bold and large codes.

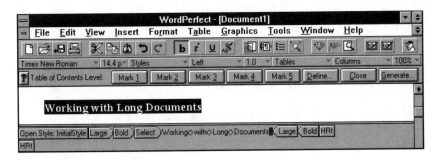

Figure 25.2 *Text selected for marking.*

NOTE

It's a good idea to turn on Reveal Codes when you are marking text. If you include formatting codes in your selection, they'll be included in the table of contents. In Figure 25.2, I moved my insertion point past the bold and large codes before I started selecting.

3. Click on the **Mark** button for the level you want. Figure 25.3 shows my example marked for a level 1 entry. Notice the mark text codes are placed at the beginning and end of the selected text.

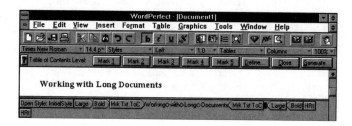

Figure 25.3 *Text marked as a level 1 entry.*

4. Repeat steps 2 and 3 for every entry you want included in the table of contents. Just select the text and click on one of the **Mark** buttons.

If you have created styles to format your section headings, you can include the codes to mark text within the styles. For an example of how this works, take a look at any of the predefined Heading styles. Just choose **Styles** from the Tools menu, select a Heading style in the Style List, and choose **Edit**. Studying WordPerfect's predefined styles is a good way to get ideas and learn more.

Defining the Table of Contents

You can define the table of contents before or after you mark the text.

1. If the Table of Contents feature bar isn't visible, choose **Table of Contents** from the Tools menu.

2. If you want the table of contents pages to be separated from the rest of your document, press **Ctrl+Enter** to create hard page breaks before and after the table. Then move your insertion point into the blank page you just created.

3. Type any title text you want on the table of contents page and place your insertion point exactly where you want the table to begin.

4. Choose **Define** from the feature bar. The Define Table of Contents dialog box is displayed, as shown in Figure 25.4.

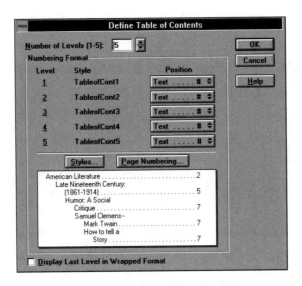

Figure 25.4 *The Define Table of Contents dialog box.*

5. In the Number of Levels text box, specify how many levels your table of contents contains. In Figure 25.4, I chose **5** levels, and the preview box shows me an example of how each level will appear.

6. For each level, choose a numbering style from the Position pop-up lists. Notice that the preview box changes to show you the effects of different choices.

7. To change the way the page numbers are formatted in your table of contents, choose **Page Numbering** and make any changes you want in the Page Number Format dialog box. Unless you want to include volume, chapter, or secondary page numbers in the table, you probably don't need to use this option.

8. When you've made all of your selections, choose **OK**, then choose **Close** from the Feature Bar. WordPerfect inserts a place marker in your document, along with the codes shown in Figure 25.5.

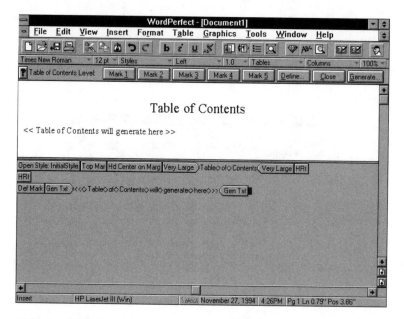

Figure 25.5 *You can see where the table of contents will appear.*

To make sure your pages are numbered correctly, insert a new page number code at the beginning of the first page after the table of contents. If your table of contents is at the beginning of the document, and you want the first text page to be page 1: Choose **Numbering** from the Format, Page menu; choose **Value** from the Page Numbering dialog box; enter the number **1** in the New Page Page Number text box; and choose **OK** to return to your document.

Generating the Table of Contents

Once you've marked all of your text and defined the table, all that's left is to generate. This is the easiest part—you just give WordPerfect the go-ahead, and it does the rest.

1. With your insertion point anywhere in the document, choose **Table of Contents** from the Tools menu.

2. Choose **Generate**. The Generate dialog box is displayed, as shown in Figure 25.6.

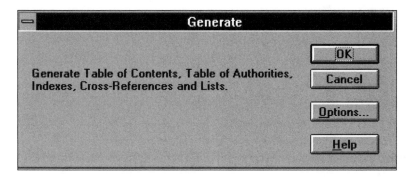

Figure 25.6 *The Generate dialog box.*

3. You can combine steps 1 and 2 by pressing **Ctrl+F9**. There isn't a separate Generate option for each referencing feature—when you choose **Generate**, any text that you've marked for a table of contents, table of authorities, index, cross-reference, or list is also generated.

4. Choose **OK**. Figure 25.7 shows a completed table of contents.

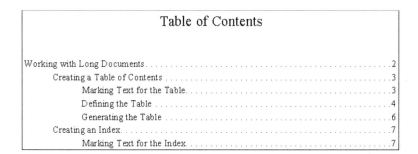

Figure 25.7 *A sample table of contents with three levels.*

Whenever you add new headings to your document, remember to mark them for the table of contents. And, when you make any change to the document that might affect pagination, be sure to regenerate. This applies to all of the referencing tools in this chapter.

NOTE

INDEX

Just like a table of contents, you create an index by marking items, defining the index, and generating. See, you already know what to do (but I'll give you a few pointers anyway).

Do It

To mark index entries:

1. Choose **Index** from the Tools menu. The Index feature bar is displayed, as shown in Figure 25.8.

Figure 25.8 *The Index feature bar.*

2. Select the text you want to mark.

3. Click in the **Headings** text box.

4. If you want to use the selected text as a main heading, choose **Mark**.

   ❖ The text in the Heading box doesn't have to be the same as the selected text. For example, you might want *cross-referencing* to be indexed under *cross-reference*. Just type whatever you want in the Heading text box or choose an entry from the drop-down list box, then choose **Mark**.

   ❖ If you want to mark the text as a subheading, click in the Subheading text box and change the text if necessary, then choose **Mark**.

5. Repeat steps 2 through 4 to mark the rest of your index entries.

SHORTCUT

Use **Find** to help locate the text you want to mark. That can really speed up the indexing process.

Do It

To define an index:

1. Place your insertion point on the page where you want the index to begin (an index is usually located at the end of the document). If you want the index to start on a new page, press **Ctrl+Enter** to insert a page break.

2. If the **Index** feature bar isn't visible, choose **Index** from the Tools menu.

3. Type any title text you want on the index page and place your insertion point exactly where you want the index to begin.

4. Choose **Define** from the feature bar. The Define Index dialog box is displayed, as shown in Figure 25.9.

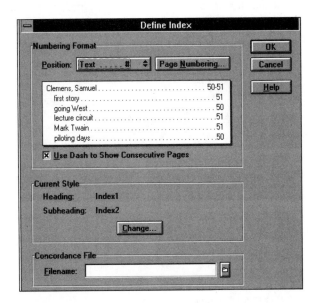

Figure 25.9 *The Define Index dialog box.*

5. Choose a numbering style by using the **Text** and **Page Numbering** buttons. Notice that the preview box changes to show you the effects of different choices.

6. By default, entries that appear on consecutive pages are separated by a dash (for example, **2-5**). If you want to show all of the page numbers, deselect the **Use Dash to Show Consecutive Pages** box. With this box deselected, the example above would appear as **2,3,4,5**.

7. If you're using a concordance file, enter the name of the file in the Filename text box (or click on the **File** button to select the file from the Select File dialog box).

8. Choose **OK**. WordPerfect inserts a place marker and definition codes similar to those for a table of contents.

NOTE

A concordance file is a WordPerfect document that contains a list of words or phrases you want to include in an index. It can be a time saver because it eliminates the need to search for mark entries in your document. But be careful. A concordance file will mark *every* occurance of the items in the list. You should still check your document carefully to make sure items are marked the way you want them.

Do It

To generate an index:

1. Choose **Generate** from the Index feature bar.

2. Choose **OK**.

All of the entries appear in alphabetical order, followed by page numbers in the format you selected.

CROSS REFERENCING

Suppose I'm writing a report about the *Ballard Garlic Festival,* and I want to reference a chart that appears on another page:

The Ballard Garlic Festival was a huge success (see chart on page 5).

Without a lot of hassle, how do I make sure that I'm always referencing the right page, no matter how the text gets moved around? By designating the chart I want to refer to as a *target,* tying the *reference* sentence to the target, and (of course) generating. Using the example above:

1. Choose **Cross-Reference** from the Tools menu to display the Cross-Reference feature bar, shown in Figure 25.10.

Figure 25.10 *The Cross-Reference feature bar.*

2. Place your insertion point on the target (in this case, *the chart*).

3. Enter a name for the target in the Target text box. (The name doesn't really matter; it's just used to tie the target to the reference.) For this example, I'm naming the target **chart**.

4. Choose **Mark Target** to place a referencing code at the target location.

5. Return to the sentence that contains the reference, and place your insertion point right where you would type the page number. By default, the reference is tied to the page that the target is on. You can choose from several reference types (for example, you can tie a reference to a particular footnote number) by making a selection from the Reference drop-down list on the Cross-Reference feature bar.

6. Choose **Mark Reference**. Word Perfect inserts a question mark at the reference location. When you generate, the question mark is replaced with the correct page number for the target.

7. Choose **Generate** to generate all references in the document (including tables of contents, indexes, etc.), then close the Feature Bar.

MASTER DOCUMENT

The Master Document feature is a great way of breaking a gargantuan project into manageable chunks (called *subdocuments*). A book is a perfect example for this feature. As you write each chapter, you save it as a separate document. But at the end, you want to be able to create a table of contents and index that treats the entire book as one piece. Easy. You just create a master document that links all of the chapters together. And guess what? I'm going to tell you how.

Do It

To assemble a master document:

1. Open the file you want to use as the master document, or open a new document.

2. Place the insertion point where you want to insert the first subdocument.

3. Choose **Master Document** from the File menu, then choose **Subdocument** from the cascading Master Document menu. The Include Subdocument dialog box is displayed, as shown in Figure 25.11.

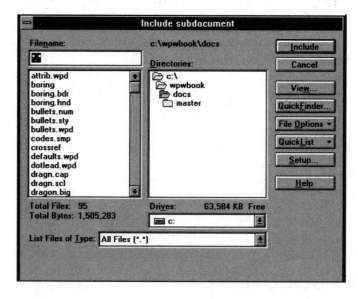

Figure 25.11 The Include Subdocument dialog box.

NOTE

There's nothing special about a subdocument. It's just any old document that you choose to include in a master document.

4. Select the file you want and choose **Include**. (If necessary, use the Drives and Directories boxes to move to the directory that contains the file.) The appearance of the subdocument link depends on the view mode. In Draft view, the link displays as a shaded comment containing the subdocument's entire filename. In Page or Two Page view, the link appears as an icon in the left margin. To see the subdocument filename, click on the icon. In Figure 25.12, which is in Page view mode, you can see that the filename of the subdocument displays in a little bubble when you click on the icon. Just click anywhere to hide the display again.

Figure 25.12 *Click on the link icon to display the subdocument information.*

5. Repeat steps 3 and 4 to continue adding subdocuments. If you want the subdocument to begin on a new page, press **Ctrl+Enter** before inserting the subdocument link.

6. Save the master document using any valid filename.

The master document now contains links to the subdocuments. You can continue working on and saving all of the subdocuments as separate files. When you're ready to put the whole thing together, you can expand and print the master document.

A master document can contain its own text and formatting, as well as the subdocument links. In fact, you could place all of your page and document formatting codes (like top and bottom margins, page numbering, and headers and footers) at the top of the master document instead of formatting all of the subdocuments individually.

Expanding the Master Document

If you want to view or print the entire master document, you must first expand it. This opens all of the subdocuments so you can work with them in one place.

1. With the master document on your screen, choose **Master Document** from the File menu, then choose **Expand Master** from the cascading Master Document menu. The Expand Master Document dialog box, shown in Figure 25.13, is displayed.

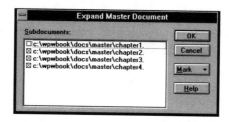

Figure 25.13 The Expand Master Document dialog box.

2. Select the subdocuments you want to expand by checking or unchecking the boxes. You can choose **Mark All** or **Clear All** from the Mark drop-down list to select or deselect all of the documents at once. Why would you want to expand some documents and not others? Well, maybe you just want to do the final formatting for the first three chapters. If you have a lot of subdocuments, it can take quite a while to expand all of them (depending on the speed of your computer).

3. Choose **OK** when you've selected the documents you want to expand.

All of the subdocuments are expanded and retrieved into your master document. Figure 25.14 shows page one of the expanded document, with the bubble display telling me which subdocument I'm in.

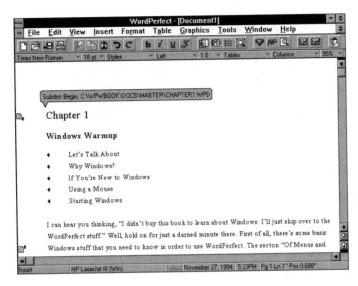

Figure 25.14 *The expanded master document.*

Notice the down arrow next to the link icon. That tells you it's the beginning of a subdocument. At the end of each subdocument, there's an icon with an up arrow. You can use the **Find** feature to search for Subdoc Begin and Subdoc End codes.

You can make any changes you want in the expanded document. When you condense the master document, you'll have an opportunity to save the changes back to the individual files.

Condensing the Master Document

When you're done working with the expanded document, you can condense it to remove the subdocuments. Don't worry—you're just removing them from the master document file, not from your disk. Your original documents are unaffected.

1. With your insertion point anywhere in the master document, choose **Master Document** from the File menu and **Condense Master** from the cascading Master Document menu. The Condense/Save Subdocuments dialog box is displayed, as shown in Figure 25.15. Notice that each subdocument is listed twice. You can choose to condense or save any or all of the subdocuments by selecting and deselecting the check boxes. The Mark drop-down list contains options to **Condense All**, **Clear Condense**, **Save All**, or **Clear Save**.

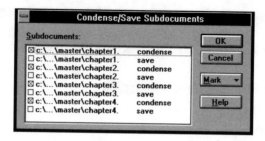

***Figure 25.15** The Condense/Save Subdocuments dialog box.*

Make sure you check the boxes you want before you choose **OK**. If you don't save a particular subdocument before condensing, any changes you made to it while it was expanded will be lost.

2. Choose **OK** to condense the master document.

The documents disappear from your screen, with just the link icons remaining.

Saving a Master Document

If you try to save an expanded master document, you'll get a dialog box that warns you that the document is expanded and asks if you want to condense it first. Unless you have a particular reason for saving the document in its expanded form, say **Yes**. The Condense/Save Subdocuments dialog box that we just looked at is displayed, and you can make your choices and condense the document.

FOOTNOTES AND ENDNOTES

You wouldn't want to be accused of plagiarism, so it's very important to give proper credit where it's due. Yes, I'm talking about the ubiquitous footnotes and endnotes that you had to use in those incredibly dry school papers you were forced to write (or maybe you're still writing them). If you're a teacher who assigns those incredibly dry papers, you have my apology (yeah, right).

Anyway, it might be hard to dig up all of those obscure references, but creating the footnotes in WordPerfect is a snap. The only difference between footnotes and endnotes is that footnotes appear at the bottom of each page, and endnotes appear at the end of the document. I'll lead you through the creation of a footnote in this section. If you want to create endnotes, you'll follow exactly the same steps, except you'll choose **Endnote** instead of **Footnote** from the Insert menu.

Do It

To create a footnote:

1. Place your insertion point just past the text you want to footnote. In Figure 25.16, my insertion point is at the end of the sentence.

I think that I shall never see a frog as lively as a flea. |

Figure 25.16 The insertion point is placed where I want the footnote reference.

2. Choose **Footnote** from the Insert menu, then choose **Create** from the cascading Footnote menu. The Footnote/Endnote feature bar is displayed, and your insertion point is in the Footnote window, as shown in Figure 25.17.

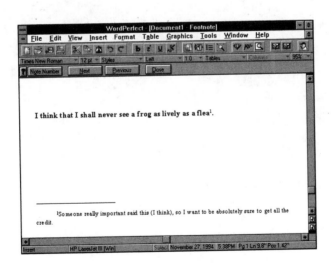

Figure 25.17 You enter text for the footnote in the Footnote editing window.

3. Type the text for your footnote.

4. Choose **Close** from the feature bar.

The footnote is tied to the reference text—it prints at the bottom of whatever page the sentence ends up on. As you add more footnotes, they are automatically numbered in sequence.

Changing Footnote Options

It's easy to change the position and style of your footnotes. Just move the insertion point to where you want the change to begin and choose **Options** from the Footnote menu. Make any changes and choose **OK.**

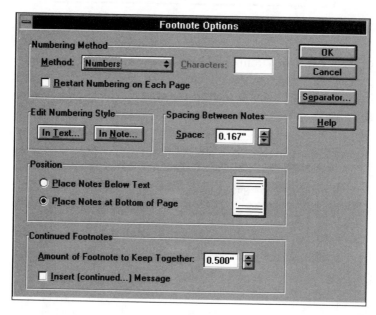

Figure 25.18 *The Footnote Options dialog box.*

Editing a Footnote

1. Choose **Footnote** from the Insert menu, the choose **Edit** from the cascading Footnote menu.

2. Enter the number of the footnote you want to edit in the Edit Footnote dialog box and choose **OK**. Your insertion point moves into the Footnote editing window, and the feature bar is displayed.

3. Make any changes you want and choose **Close** to return to your document window.

The **Next** and **Previous** buttons on the feature bar let you cycle between all of the footnotes in your document. The **Note Number** button restores the note number if you accidentally delete it while editing the note.

SHORTCUT

You can also edit a footnote just by placing the insertion point in the footnote text at the bottom of the page. When you do it this way, the Footnote feature bar is not activated.

Deleting a Footnote

When you delete a footnote's number in your document text, the footnote itself is automatically deleted, and any other footnotes in your document are renumbered to fill in the gap. And of course, you can always delete a footnote through Reveal Codes.

Changing the Numbering for Footnotes

You can start renumbering your footnotes at any point in a document.

1. Place your insertion point where you want the new numbers to start.

2. Choose **Footnote** from the Insert menu, then choose **New Number** from the cascading Footnote menu. The Footnote Number dialog box is displayed, as shown in Figure 25.19.

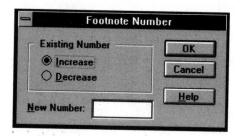

Figure 25.19 *The Footnote Number dialog box.*

3. You can enter a new starting number in the **New Number** text box, or bump the existing number up or down a notch by checking the **Increase** or **Decrease** radio buttons.

FROM HERE ...

Even though WordPerfect can't take all of the work out of writing long documents, it can sure make it easier to organize and format them. Once you mark your targets and references, and mark and define your tables of contents and indexes, you can edit and move things around all you want without worrying about what ends up on which page. Just regenerate to update all of your marked text whenever you make changes that might affect the pagination. And footnotes and endnotes may not be any more fun to write, but they're painless to create.

Now that you can work with really long documents, how about learning how to juggle nine documents at once? Yes, that's right, WordPerfect allows you to work with nine open documents at the same time. Why would anyone want to do that, you might ask. For the answer to that riveting question, you'll have to read the next chapter.

CHAPTER 26

Working with Multiple Documents

(Yes, I really LIKE working on 10 projects at the same time!)

Let's talk about:

- ❖ Opening multiple documents
- ❖ Switching between documents
- ❖ Arranging document windows
- ❖ Sizing document windows
- ❖ Minimizing documents
- ❖ Cutting and pasting between documents
- ❖ Switching between applications

Now that you can do just about anything you want to a WordPerfect document, what's left? Doing stuff to several documents at once! WordPerfect lets you have up to nine documents open at the same time. And now for the answer to the burning question I left you with at the end of the last chapter—why would anyone *want* to juggle nine documents (or even two)?

When you're working on a project, it's often helpful to be able to refer to another portion of it. I had Chapter 25 (the previous chapter) open while I wrote this chapter. That way, I was able to quickly switch to it and double-check the question I asked you at the end. Switching back and forth between open documents is much quicker and easier than closing the document you're working on, opening the one you want to look at, closing it, and reopening the first one.

Being able to open more than one document at a time also means that you can switch gears in midstream without losing momentum. If your boss runs in and asks you to make a quick change to the report you completed yesterday, you don't have to quit what you're doing. Just leave your document on screen, and open his report in a new document window. When you finish and close his document, your document's sitting right where you left it. No wasted steps.

Last, but most definitely not least, having several documents open makes it easy to move and copy information between them. Suppose you used a table in last month's report, and now you want to include it in another document. Just open both documents—as you'll soon see, you can even arrange it so you can see both of them at once. Using the same techniques you've already learned for cutting and pasting, just copy the table from one document to the other.

OPENING MULTIPLE DOCUMENTS

Whenever you open a document, it is displayed in a document window. By default, the current document window is maximized, which means that it takes up all of the space in the WordPerfect window. When you open another document (or start a new one), it also is displayed in its own maximized window. Let's work through this together so you can see what I mean.

Do It

To open multiple documents:

1. Open any document by clicking on the **Open** icon on the Toolbar and choosing any document you've already created from the file list. (You can also Press **Ctrl+O**, or choose **Open** from the File menu.)

2. Without closing the first document, use the procedures in step 1 to open a second document.

3. Click on the **New Document** icon on the Toolbar to open a new document window. (You can also press **Ctrl+N**, or choose **New** from the File menu.)

4. Type: **This is Document 3**.

Notice that the Title Bar for the new document says WordPerfect - [Document 3]. Until you save a document, it's identified by its document number.

In Figure 26.1, I have the third document on screen, and I've pulled down the Window menu.

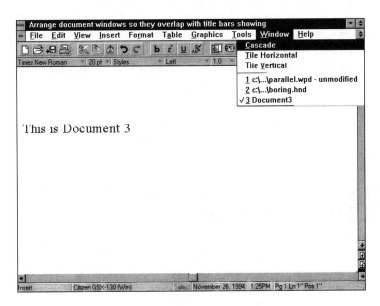

Figure 26.1 *The Window menu lists the three open documents.*

You're still only seeing one window at a time. As you open document windows, the other windows get hidden behind the current one, but they're still there. WordPerfect lists them at the bottom of the Window menu.

Switching Between Document Windows

There are three ways to move between document windows when you only have one window displayed:

❖ Choose the file you want from the Window menu by choosing **Window** and clicking on your choice. If you're using the keyboard, you can type the number next to your choice after you open the Window menu.

❖ Press **Ctrl+F6** to cycle forward through your open documents, or **Ctrl+Shift+F6** to cycle backward.

❖ Click on the **Control Menu Box** to the left of the word File on the menu bar to activate the document's Control menu. Select **Next** to switch to your previously opened document. When the document is not maximized (see the following section on "Using the Restore Button"), you will find the Control menu box at the left of the document title bar.

Try it. Notice that the document you choose from the Window menu instantly appears on your screen. When you press **Ctrl+F6**, the last document you opened is displayed. If you keep pressing **Ctrl+F6** or **Ctrl+Shift+F6**, you move through all of your open documents in sequence.

Now you can work with several documents at once and instantly switch to the one you want. But what if you want more than one document displayed on your screen? Coming right up.

DISPLAYING AND ARRANGING MULTIPLE DOCUMENT WINDOWS

Unless you specify otherwise, every new or opened document is displayed in a maximized window, which means that it covers any other open documents you might have. Well, let's specify otherwise.

Using the Restore Button

When a document window is maximized (this is the default state), there are two buttons in the upper-right corner of your computer screen. One is directly over the other, and each one has two little triangles, one pointing up and the other pointing down. The top button works with the WordPerfect program as a whole (more about that in the Warning that follows). The one we want, though, is below it, directly to the right of Help in the menu bar. This button is called the **Restore** button. When you click the **Restore** button on a maximized window, the window is restored to a smaller size within the WordPerfect window. Figure 26.2 shows a maximized WordPerfect document window, and Figure 26.3 shows the same document after clicking on the **Restore** button.

If you don't like choosing between buttons that look identical (I can emphathize with this), you can just restore all opened documents by choosing **Cascade** from the Window menu. More on this later, in the section "Arranging Windows Automatically."

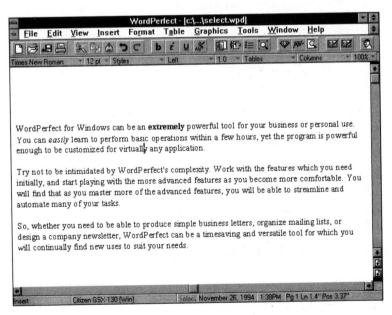

Figure 26.2 *A maximized WordPerfect document window.*

WARNING

Notice that there are two **Restore** buttons, one right above the other. The button on the very top is for WordPerfect itself, and so is the **Maximize** button just to its left. If you click WordPerfect's **Restore** button instead of the **Restore** button for the document window, the WordPerfect program window changes size and the **Restore** button turns into a **Maximize** button (an up arrow). If this happens, just click on the **Maximize** button to get WordPerfect back the way it was.

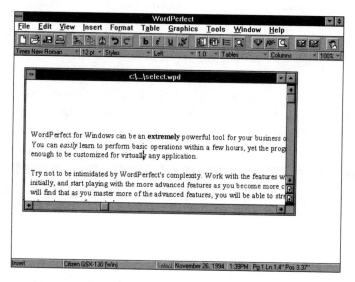

Figure 26.3 *A document restored to "normal" size.*

Notice that the **Restore** button for your document also changed to a **Maximize** button. You can click on this **Maximize** button to return the document window to full size (or double-click on the document's Title Bar).

Sizing Document Windows

Sizing a document window is very much like sizing a graphics box:

1. Make sure the window you want to size is active (the active window is the one with the highlighted Title Bar). If the window is already maximized, you can't resize it. You'll have to first use **Restore**, **Cascade**, or **Tile**.

NOTE

Here's a hint—If you can see any part of an inactive window, a quick way to switch to that window is to click anywhere in the part of that window that is visible.

2. Move your mouse pointer over one of the window borders until the pointer turns into a double-headed arrow.

3. Drag the mouse in the direction you want to size the window. As you drag, a shaded outline shows you what's happening to the size of the window.

4. Release the mouse button when the window is the size you want.

NOTE

Here's another helpful hint—If you want to change the height and width at the same time, position your mouse pointer over a corner border until the pointer turns into a diagonal double-headed arrow. Then click and drag as above.

If you don't have a mouse (or if you aren't fond of small furry rodents), try this—press **Alt+ -** to activate your document's Control menu, then choose **Size**. Use the **Up Arrow** and **Down Arrow** keys on your keyboard to make the window taller or shorter. Use the **Left Arrow** or **Right Arrow** to change the window's width. If you want to fine-tune your window's size, hold the **Ctrl** key down while using the **Arrow** keys. Press **Enter** when the window is the size you want.

Moving a Document Window

Moving a document window is exactly like moving a dialog box. Just position your mouse pointer over the Title Bar and drag the window wherever you want it.

Using the keyboard: With the window you want to move active, press **Alt—** to activate the window's Control menu. Choose **Move**, then use the **Arrow** keys on your keyboard to move the window in the direction you want. If you want to fine-tune your window's position, hold the **Ctrl** key down while using the **Arrow** keys. When you're done, press **Enter** to anchor the window in its new location.

Arranging Windows Automatically

WordPerfect's Window menu has three commands that automatically arrange all of your open document windows: Cascade, Tile Horizontal and Tile Vertical.

Cascade

When you choose **Cascade** from the Window menu, all of your open documents are displayed as shown in Figure 26.4. The documents are layered so that the Title Bar of each document is visible.

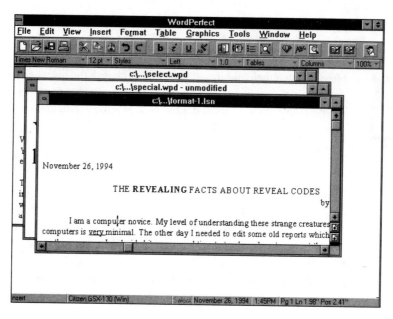

Figure 26.4 *Cascaded documents.*

As soon as you click on a Title Bar, the document you choose becomes active and jumps to the front. You can also switch between cascaded documents using the Window menu, the document's Control menu (click on the **Control Menu Box** at the upper left corner of the active document), or the keyboard techniques (**Ctrl+F6** or **Ctrl+Shift+F6**).

Tile Options

There are two tiling options in the Window menu: **Tile Horizontal** and **Tile Vertical**.

When you choose **Tile Horizontal** from the Window menu, your open documents are displayed one on top of the other as shown in Figure 26.5. **Tile Vertical** arranges the documents side by side, as shown in Figure 26.6. You can see a portion of each document, and they're arranged like floor tiles, with none of the windows overlapping.

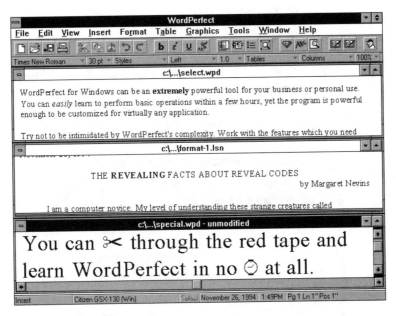

Figure 26.5 *Horizontally tiled documents.*

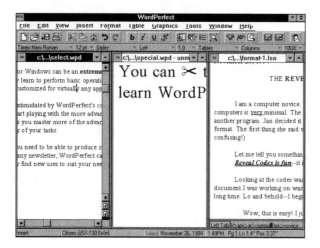

Figure 26.6 *Vertically tiled documents.*

WordPerfect tries to give each document window an equal amount of space. Figure 26.7 shows five documents tiled. In this case, WordPerfect splits the left side of the screen in half, and the other three documents are on the right. In other words, WordPerfect does its best to fit all of your documents on screen without overlapping any of the windows. When you have more than four open documents, **Tile Vertical** and **Tile Horizontal** can have the same effect.

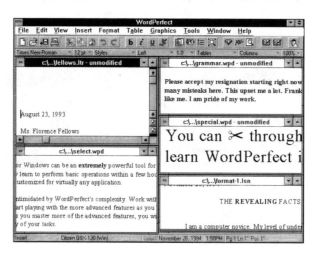

Figure 26.7 *In this example, it doesn't matter whether you choose.* ***Tile Horizontal*** *or* ***Tile Vertical.***

You can click anywhere in a document window to make that document active. And, of course, you can use the Window menu or the keyboard to switch between documents.

Cascading and tiling are quick ways to arrange your documents and see what you have. If you move and size several document windows, you can end up with a fairly confused (and confusing) arrangement, with some document windows hidden and others taking up too much space. Just choose **Cascade** or one of the **Tile** options to force some order into the situation.

Minimizing Document Windows

You can minimize any document window that's been sized, tiled, or cascaded. Just click on the **Minimize** arrow (the down arrow in the upper-right corner of the document window). Minimizing shrinks the document to an icon. In Figure 26.8, I show four minimized documents below an open document. Notice that the minimized documents still show up on the Window menu, so you can easily switch to any of them.

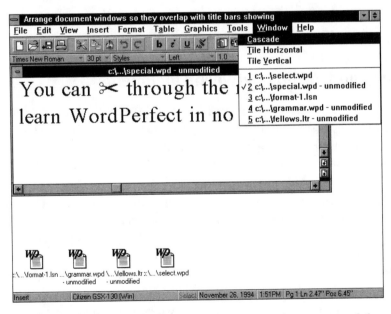

Figure 26.8 *Minimizing shrinks documents to icons. The minimized documents are still listed on the Window menu.*

Minimized documents aren't included when you choose a **Tile** option or **Cascade**—but when tiling or cascading, WordPerfect sees to it that the document windows don't cover up any minimized document icons.

NOTE

Restoring Minimized Documents

You can restore a minimized document to whatever size and position it had before it was minimized in myriad ways:

- ❖ Double-click on its icon.

- ❖ Select the icon and open its document Control menu by clicking on it, then choose **Restore.**

- ❖ Select the icon by pressing **Ctrl+F6** until the title of the icon is highlighted, press **Alt—** to activate its Control menu, then choose **Restore.**

- ❖ Choose the name of the document from the Window menu.

You can also maximize the document window by clicking once on the icon to open its Control menu and choosing **Maximize**.

Cutting and Pasting Between Documents

In Chapter 6, "Moving and Copying Text," you learned how to select blocks of text and move or copy them to the Clipboard. Once the text is in the Clipboard, you can paste it to a new location. Well, that new location isn't limited to your current document—text or objects in the Clipboard can just as easily be pasted into a different document.

Whatever you cut or copy to the Clipboard stays there until you cut or copy something else, so you can cut something from one document, open another document, and then use the **Paste** command to bring the information into the new document.

The easiest way to cut and paste between documents, however, is to have both documents on your screen at the same time. That way, you can zip back and forth between the documents by clicking anywhere in the document window. Cut or copy something from one document, then click in the other document, move your insertion point to the location you want, and choose **Paste**. It's as simple as that. Figure 26.9 shows one example of a screen arrangement that would make it easy to work with two documents at once. I opened both documents, then moved and sized the document windows. I can click in either document to activate it and use the scroll bars to move wherever I want.

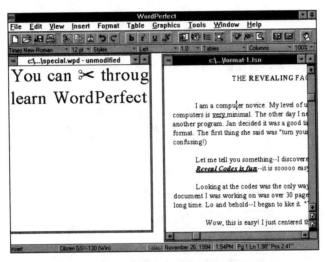

Figure 26.9 *Two document windows side by side.*

SWITCHING BETWEEN APPLICATIONS

In this chapter, we've been talking about displaying and working with multiple documents in WordPerfect. But Windows also allows you to work with more than one program at the same time. You can switch between programs as easily as you can between WordPerfect documents.

Alt+Tab

Alt+Tab is the magic key combination that takes you back and forth between programs. Right now, you probably just have WordPerfect running. When you press **Alt+Tab**, it takes you back to Program Manager. Go ahead, try it. From Program Manager, you could start another program without closing WordPerfect. (How many programs you can have open at one time depends on the size of your hard disk and how much memory you have.)

If you have more than two programs open, hold down the **Alt** key while you tap the **Tab** key. As you press the **Tab** key, the names of your open programs are displayed in sequence in the middle of your screen. When you see the name of the program you want to switch to, release the **Alt** key.

The Task List

The Windows Task List is a handy tool that you can use from any place in Windows. Just press **Ctrl+Esc**, and you'll see a dialog box like Figure 26.10.

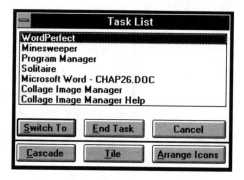

Figure 26.10 *The Windows Task List.*

The Task List contains a list of all of the programs you are currently running. You can switch to any one of them by double-clicking on the program's name (or by highlighting the name and choosing **Switch To**). You can also close a Windows program from the Task List by highlighting the program's name and choosing **End Task**.

Refer to your Windows manual for more detailed information about working with multiple applications.

FROM HERE ...

Well done! You're well on your way to becoming a WordPerfect wizard. As you keep working with the program, more and more of the features will start to become second nature, and you'll find yourself experimenting with new ways to approach your tasks.

The next and final chapter contains brief discussions of additional features that you can explore at your own pace. None of them is essential to working effectively with WordPerfect, but you might find a feature or two that fits your specific needs.

CHAPTER 27

Grab Bag

(Everything You Ever Wanted to Know about More Features, but Were Afraid to Ask)

Let's talk about:

- ❖ Abbreviations
- ❖ Binding Options
- ❖ Comments
- ❖ Converting files
- ❖ Document Compare
- ❖ Document info
- ❖ Document Summary

- ❖ Equation Editor
- ❖ Hidden text
- ❖ Hypertext
- ❖ Importing and linking spreadsheets and databases
- ❖ Kerning, word spacing, and letter spacing

- ❖ Line height and leading
- ❖ Line numbering
- ❖ Overstrike
- ❖ Passwords
- ❖ Repeat
- ❖ Tables of authorities
- ❖ WP Draw

This chapter is a laundry list of features that weren't covered in the other chapters. Some of them have very specialized applications (for example, a table of authorities is used only in the legal profession), and some are just extra added attractions. I'll describe each feature, give brief instructions for accessing it, and add any applicable notes or warnings. (For your perusing pleasure, the features in this chapter are covered in alphabetical order.)

By now, you have all of the tools you need to explore features in more depth. If you find something in this chapter that meets your needs (or kindles your curiosity), play around with it. And don't forget to use the online Help system to get more information. Have fun!

ABBREVIATIONS

The Abbreviations feature lets you use shortcuts to type words or phrases you use frequently and then expand the abbreviations when you're ready. For example, I created an abbreviation for WordPerfect for Windows so that I wouldn't have to type it out repeatedly. Whenever I used WordPerfect for Windows in a sentence, I just typed *wpw*. When I was done with each chapter, I ran the EXPNDALL macro to expand all of the abbreviations.

Do It

To create an abbreviation:

1. Type and select the text you want to abbreviate. Using the above example, you would type **WordPerfect for Windows**, then select the entire phrase.

2. Choose **Abbreviations** from the Insert menu.

3. Choose **Create**.

4. Type the shortcut letters in the **Abbreviation Name** text box, choose **OK**, and close the Abbreviations dialog box. (Using the example, you would type **wpw**.)

From this point on, wherever you would type the whole word or phrase, just type the abbreviation.

To expand an abbreviation:

1. Place your insertion point anywhere in the abbreviation.

2. Press **Ctrl+A**. That's the keyboard shortcut for expanding an abbreviation, and it's the fastest way. You can also choose **Abbreviations** from the Insert menu and choose **Expand**.

NOTE

WordPerfect comes with two macros that make it easier to work with abbreviations. ABBREV displays a dialog box that remains on screen so that you can create multiple abbreviations. EXPNDALL automatically expands any abbreviations you have included in your document—even if you have only used a couple of abbreviations, it's much easier to run this macro than to move to each abbreviation and expand it. Also note that abbreviations *are* case-sensitive. If you enter the abbreviation as **WPW**, WordPerfect won't recognize *wpw* as the same abbreviation.

BINDING OPTIONS

If you're going to bind a document that's printed on both sides of the page, you need to adjust the text so that's it's not all squished next to the binding. The binding options feature can make this adjustment for you automatically. You just tell WordPerfect which edge will be bound and how much space you need for the binding.

1. Choose **Page** from the Format menu, then choose **Binding/Duplex** from the cascading Page menu. The Binding Options dialog box is displayed, as shown in Figure 27.1.

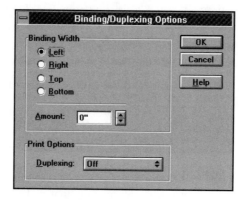

Figure 27.1 *The Binding Options dialog box.*

2.   Select the appropriate radio button and fill in the Amount text box.

3.   If your printer is capable of printing on both sides of the page (duplex printing), choose one of the **Duplexing** options.

It's a good idea to specify your binding options before you format the document. Changing binding options at the end could cause unwanted formatting changes.

NOTE

CHARTS

See the WP Draw section at the end of the chapter.

COMMENTS

You can add nonprinting comments to any part of a document (including footnotes, endnotes, and outlines). Comments are handy when you want to stick a note in a document to remind yourself (or someone else) to double-check information or flag an area that needs more work. You can turn existing text into a comment, or you can create a comment from scratch.

Do It

To add a comment:

1. Place the insertion point where you want the comment, or select the existing text that you want turned into a comment.

2. Choose **Comment** from the Insert menu, then choose **Create**.

3. If you're creating the comment from scratch, type the text for the comment and choose **Close** from the Feature Bar. In page view, a comment is displayed as an icon in the left margin. Click on the icon to display the comment, then click again to hide it. In Draft view, you see the comment as shaded text.

You can convert a comment to regular document text by placing your insertion point after the comment you want to convert, choosing **Comment** from the Insert menu, and choosing **Convert to Text** from the cascading Comment menu.

NOTE

See "Hidden Text," later in this chapter. Comments and Hidden Text are somewhat similar (and often confused).

CONVERTING FILES

WordPerfect can convert files created in most other word processing programs, and you can save a WordPerfect file in any of the supported formats.

When you try to open a file that was created in another program, WordPerfect displays the Convert File Format dialog box with its current format displayed in the **Convert File From** box. If the displayed format is correct, choose **OK**. If not, choose a format from the drop-down list. Figure 27.2 shows the Convert File Format dialog box with the drop-down list open. Notice that there's a scroll bar in the list box—if the format you want isn't visible, just scroll through the list.

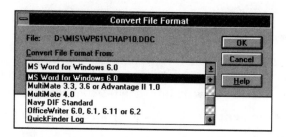

Figure 27.2 *The Convert File Format dialog box with the drop-down list opened.*

To save a WordPerfect file in another format, choose **Save As** from the File menu (or press **F3**), then choose the format you want from the Save File As Type drop-down list.

WARNING

Features don't always translate perfectly between programs. Even though WordPerfect can open files created in most word processing formats, some of the more complex formatting might not come through. Be sure to check converted documents carefully. If you're planning to save a WordPerfect document in another format, try to use fairly simple formatting features. That way, you won't lose formatting when you convert the document.

NOTE

WordPerfect automatically converts files created in WordPerfect 5.0, 5.1, 5.2 or 6.0 format. When you open a file created in one of these formats, you won't see the Convert File Format dialog box. If you want the file to retain its old format, make sure you use **Save As** and select the format you want from the Save File As Type drop-down list. Otherwise, the document is automatically saved in WordPerfect 6.1 format.

DOCUMENT COMPARE

You can use document compare to compare different versions of a document. With the latest version of the document on screen, do the following:

1. Choose **Compare Document** from the File menu.
2. Choose **Add Markings** from the cascading menu.

3. Make your selections in the Add Markings dialog box shown in Figure 27.3 and choose **OK**. By default, the document on screen is compared to the older version of the same document. Enter a file name in the Compare Current Document to text box if you want to compare the file on screen to a document with a different name.

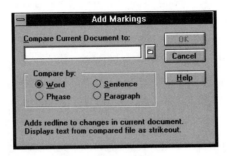

Figure 27.3 *The Add Markings dialog box.*

When you are ready to approve the changes, you can remove the markings by choosing **Compare Document** from the File menu and **Remove Markings** from the cascading Compare Document menu.

DOCUMENT INFO

You can get statistics about the document on which you are working by choosing **Document Info** from the File menu. Figure 27.4 shows the Document Information dialog box.

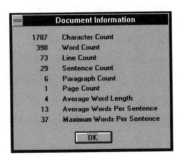

Figure 27.4 *The Document Information dialog box.*

DOCUMENT SUMMARY

You can use document summaries to help you identify documents by author, subject, and other descriptive information. Document summaries can be useful if you work in an environment where a lot of documents are shared. A document summary is attached to the document—it can be viewed or printed, and you can save the summary as a separate file. To create a document summary:

1. Choose **Document Summary** from the File menu.
2. Fill in the appropriate text boxes in the Document Summary dialog box, shown in Figure 27.5.

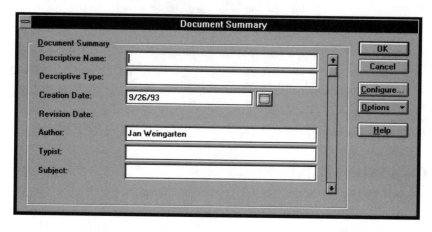

Figure 27.5 *The Document Summary dialog box.*

The Document Summary dialog box is set up with default text fields, but you can customize it to suit your needs. Just choose **Configure** to display the Document Summary Configuration dialog box shown in Figure 27.6. In the Available Fields list, check the fields you want to use and uncheck the ones you don't. You can also change the order of the fields by dragging items in the Selected Fields list.

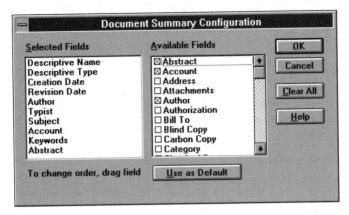

Figure 27.6 *The Document Summary Configuration dialog box.*

Once you've chosen **OK** or pressed **Cancel**, you'll be back in the Document Summary dialog box. Choose **Options** if you want to print the summary, delete it, or save it as a separate document. You can also use the Viewer in any file list dialog box to view a document summary.

DRAWING

See the section on WP Draw at the end of this chapter.

EQUATION EDITOR

WordPerfect includes a full-featured equation editor that's capable of creating complex mathematical and scientific formulas. The equation editor contains an awesome array of options—what you'll see in this chapter is just the briefest glimpse. The "Equations" section in your WordPerfect manual covers the feature in detail (including several examples), and the manual also has an "Equation Commands" appendix that lists all of the available commands, symbols, and mathematical functions.

Do It

To create an equation:

1. Place your insertion point where you want the equation.
2. Choose **Equation** from the Graphics menu to open the Equation Editor, shown in Figure 27.7.

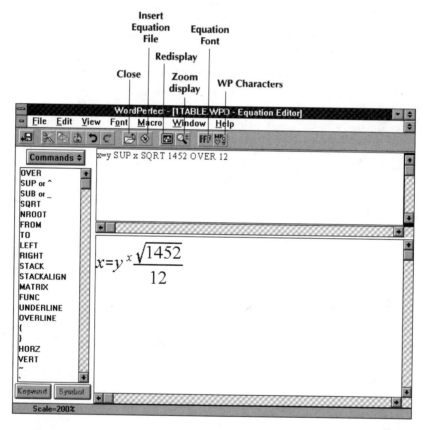

Figure 27.7 The Equation Editor with a sample equation entered.

3. Enter the equation in the editing window (the top window in Figure 27.7). Type the variable information and insert commands and symbols from the equation palette (the list at the left edge of the screen).

4. Click the **Redisplay** button to see how the equation will look in the display window. (Or choose **Redisplay** from the View menu.)

5. When you're done, choose **Close** from the File menu. The equation is displayed in your document.

When you create an equation, it's placed in a graphics box—it can be edited, moved, or sized using the same techniques you learned for working with graphics boxes. The equation is saved with the document, but you can also save it in a separate file by choosing **Save As** from the Equation Editor's File menu.

NOTE

The Equation Editor won't perform calculations for you—you have to figure that part out for yourself. But it does greatly simplify the chore of entering and formatting complex equations in a document. Also notice that the Equation Editor displays custom button and menu bars.

HIDDEN TEXT

Hidden text, like comments, is a feature that can be used to prevent text from printing.

Do It

To hide text:

1. Make sure **Hidden Text** is checked on the View menu.

2. Select the text you want to hide, or place the insertion point where you want the hidden text to begin.

3. Open the Font dialog box, choose **Hidden** from the Appearance area, and choose **OK**.

4. Unless you selected text before you chose the hidden attribute, type the text you want to hide.

5. Choose **Hidden** from the Font dialog box again to turn off the feature.

Notice that you can still see the text on screen. You display or hide the hidden text by checking or unchecking **Hidden Text** on the View menu.

If you're a teacher, take a look at this feature. You could write a test and enter the answers as hidden text. (Just make sure you actually hide the answers before you give the tests to your students!) Then, when you're ready to correct the tests, just uncheck **Hidden Text** on the View menu, and all of your answers will be there for you.

HYPERTEXT

You've already used hypertext. You may not realize it, but all of those green underlined words and phrases in the online Help system are actually hypertext links. When you click on one of them, it takes you somewhere else. In Help, the hypertext links jump you to a related Help topic.

You can create your own hypertext links so that readers can jump to different parts of a document or even to another document. For instance, you could create an on-screen presentation where a reader could click on a hypertext link to jump to a chart or table that's related to the subject you're discussing. A hypertext link can be tied to a bookmark, a macro, or another document. (The bookmark, macro, or document must exist before you can create the link.) Hypertext is a big word for something that WordPerfect has made very easy to create and use.

Do It

To create a hypertext link:

1. Select the text that you want to use as hypertext (that's the text that readers will click on to jump to a different location).

2. Choose **Hypertext** from the Tools menu to activate the Hypertext Feature Bar.

3. Choose **Create** to display the dialog box shown in Figure 27.8.

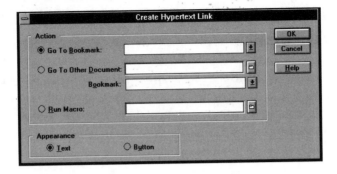

Figure 27.8 *The Create Hypertext Link dialog box.*

4. Enter the name of the bookmark, document, or macro you want to link to in the appropriate text box. (You can also use the drop-down lists or file icons to select the bookmark or filename from a list.)

5. Choose **Text** if you want the hypertext link to be displayed on screen as underlined green text (just like it does in Help). Choose **Button** if you want the hypertext link to look like a command button.

6. Choose **OK** when you've made all your selections.

Now, whenever you click on the hypertext link, you'll jump to the attached bookmark, document, or macro. When the Hypertext Feature Bar is active, you can move between links by choosing **Next** or **Previous**. You can return from a jump by choosing **Back** from the Hypertext Feature Bar. This returns the insertion point to the hypertext link.

To delete a Hypertext link, place your insertion point anywhere inside a link and choose **Delete** from the feature bar.

NOTE

If you click on a hypertext link and nothing happens, check to make sure the links haven't been deactivated. If you see an Activate button on the Hypertext Feature Bar, click on it to activate your links. If the button says *Deactivate*, you're okay.

IMPORTING AND LINKING SPREADSHEETS AND DATABASES

You can insert information from a spreadsheet or database file into a WordPerfect document. If you want, you can link the two files so that you can easily update your WordPerfect document to reflect changes in the original spreadsheet or database.

Do It

To bring spreadsheet or database information into a WordPerfect document:

1. Place your insertion point where you want the data to be inserted.

2. Choose **Spreadsheet/Database** from the Insert menu.

3. Choose **Import** if you want to retrieve the information into your document without creating a link. When you import a spreadsheet or database file, the actual data is inserted in your document, and there's no connection between the data and its original file. So if you make changes to the data in its original program, the data you imported into WordPerfect doesn't change.

    Choose **Create Link** if you want to connect the information between the two files. With this option, the data in your WordPerfect file can be automatically updated to reflect the current data in the original spreadsheet or database file.

    Depending on which option you choose, either the Import Data or the Create Data link dialog box is displayed. Both dialog boxes contain exactly the same options. Figure 27.9 shows the Create Data Link dialog box.

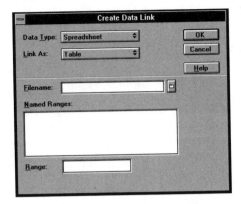

Figure 27.9 *The Create Data Link dialog box.*

4. Select a format from the Data Type pop-up list. Figure 27.10 shows the pop-up list with the available spreadsheet and database formats.

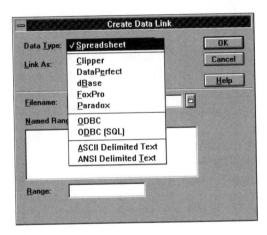

Figure 27.10 *The Data Type pop-up list.*

5. Choose an option from the Link As pop-up list. You can import a spreadsheet or database as a table, regular text, or a merge data file.

6. Enter the name of the file you want to import in the Filename text box (or click on the file icon and use the Select File dialog box to make your choice).

7. If you want to import only a portion of the file, fill in the Named Ranges or Range box.

8. Choose **OK** to import the file.

You can have WordPerfect automatically update any spreadsheet or database links whenever you open the document:

1. Choose **Spreadsheet/Database** from the Insert menu.

2. Choose **Options** from the cascading Spreadsheet/Database menu.

3. Choose **Update on Retrieve** in the Link Options dialog box.

If you haven't chosen **Update on Retrieve**, you can update your links at any time by choosing **Update** from the cascading Spreadsheet/Database menu.

KERNING, WORD SPACING, AND LETTER SPACING

You have several options for adjusting the amount of space between words and letters. *Kerning* is a typesetting term that refers to the process of adjusting the amount of space between specified pairs of characters. You can turn on automatic kerning if you want WordPerfect to automatically adjust the spacing between character pairs. For each font and point size, only certain pairs of letters are predefined for kerning.

Do It

To turn on automatic kerning:

1. Place your insertion point where you want to start kerning (or select the text you want to kern).

2. Choose **Typesetting** from the Format menu, then choose **Word/Letterspacing** from the cascading Typesetting menu.

3. In the Word Spacing and Letterspacing dialog box shown in Figure 27.11, check the **Automatic Kerning** check box and choose **OK**.

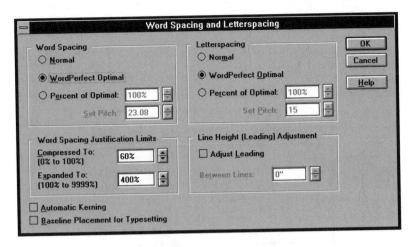

Figure 27.11 *The Word Spacing and Letterspacing dialog box.*

This dialog box also contains options for adjusting the space between words and letters. If you make a change in the Letterspacing area, it will affect all of your text, not just the kerned pairs.

You can use manual kerning to adjust the spacing between any two characters by an amount you specify:

1. Place the insertion point between the two characters you want to kern.

2. Choose **Typesetting** from the Format menu, then choose **Manual Kerning** from the cascading Typesetting menu.

3. In the Manual Kerning dialog box, specify the amount by which you want to decrease the space between the two characters.

4. Choose **OK**.

LINE HEIGHT AND LEADING

Line height is the distance from the top of one line of text to the top of the next line. When you choose a font and point size, WordPerfect automatically adjusts the line height, but you can specify a different setting.

1. Place your insertion point where you want to change the line height (or select a group of paragraphs to apply the line height change to).

2. Choose **Line** from the Format menu, then choose **Height** from the cascading Line menu. The Line Height dialog box, shown in Figure 27.12, is displayed.

Figure 27.12 *The Line Height dialog box.*

3. From the Line Height dialog box, select **Fixed**, enter a number in the text box, and choose **OK**.

You can further refine the space between lines by making a leading adjustment. In the early typesetting days, a strip of lead was actually inserted between each line of type. So the term *leading* literally referred to the amount of white space between lines. In WordPerfect, you adjust the leading by adding to or subtracting from the line height.

1. In the Word Spacing and Letterspacing dialog box (see Figure 27.11), choose **Adjust Leading**.

2. In the Between Lines text box, enter a positive number to increase the leading or a negative number to decrease the leading, and choose **OK**.

LINE NUMBERING

WordPerfect's line numbering feature can display and print the line numbers in your document. Many standard legal documents use line numbering to make it easy to refer to a particular section. You can number lines continuously throughout a document, or you can choose to begin with new numbers on each page.

Do It

1. Place the insertion point where you want the numbering to start.

2. Choose **Line** from the Format menu, then choose **Numbering** from the cascading Line menu. The Line Numbering dialog box, shown in Figure 27.13, is displayed.

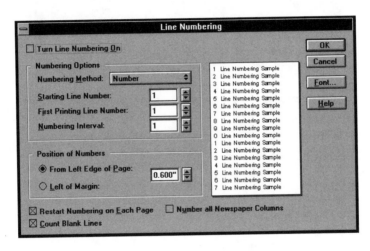

Figure 27.13 *The Line Numbering dialog box.*

3. Choose **Turn Line Numbering On**, change any options you want in the dialog box, and choose **OK**.

OVERSTRIKE

The WordPerfect Characters dialog box (**Ctrl+W**) gives you access to a wide range of special characters. But if you can't find what you want, you can create your own custom character combinations with the overstrike feature. For example, you could combine the number 7 with a hyphen to create a European-style number (with a line through the 7). To create an overstrike character:

1. Place your insertion point where you want to insert the character.

2. Choose **Typesetting** from the Format menu, then choose **Overstrike** from the cascading Typesetting menu. The Overstrike dialog box, shown in Figure 27.14, is displayed.

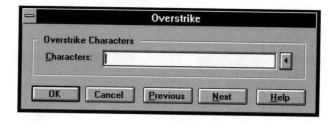

Figure 27.14 *The Overstrike dialog box.*

3. Type the characters you want to combine in the Characters text box (don't add spaces between the characters). You can enter the characters in any order. In the example I used above, I would type **7** and **-** (a hyphen).

4. You can add attributes to the overstrike character (like bold, italics, or superscript) by clicking on the left-pointing arrow next to the text box and choosing from the pop-up list.

5. Choose **OK** to insert the character in your document.

PASSWORDS

When you save a document, you can assign a password to protect confidential information. Once you've assigned a password to a document, no one can open or print the document without the password.

WARNING

A couple of cautions before you proceed. If you forget the password that you've assigned, you're out of luck. WordPerfect cannot help you recover the file. Also, be aware that assigning a password doesn't prevent a file from being deleted.

Do It

To assign a password:

1. Choose **Save As** from the File menu (or press **F3**).

2. Enter the name of the file you want to save in the Filename text box (or select a file from the file list to add a password to an existing file).

3. Check the **Password Protect** check box (in the lower right corner of the dialog box) and choose **OK**. The Password dialog box, shown in Figure 27.15, is displayed.

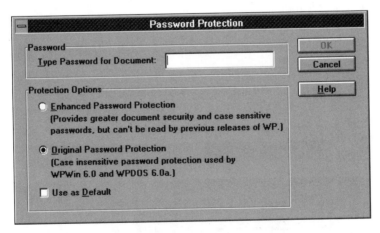

Figure 27.15 *The Password dialog box.*

4. Type the password you want and choose **OK**. (For security reasons, you won't see the password while you're typing—only a series of Xs will display.)

5. WordPerfect asks you to confirm the password by retyping it. Do so and choose **OK**.

From now on, when you try to open or print the document, you will be prompted to enter the password. If you can't supply the correct password, you'll be denied access to the document.

REPEAT

The Repeat feature can save you time if you need to type the same character or enter the same command several times in a row. For example, you could use repeat to insert a row of asterisks across the page without having to press the asterisk key 89,000 times (okay, that might be a bit of an exaggeration).

Do It

To use the repeat feature:

1. Place your insertion point where you want to insert the characters or begin the action.

2. Choose **Repeat** from the Edit menu. The Repeat dialog box, shown in Figure 27.16, is displayed.

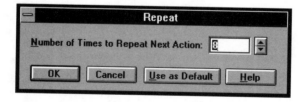

Figure 27.16 *The Repeat dialog box.*

3. Enter a number in the Number of Times to Repeat Next Action text box and choose **OK**.

4. Perform the action. Using the asterisk example, you would just type an asterisk as soon as you close the Repeat dialog box, and the asterisk is repeated however many times you specified.

TABLES OF AUTHORITIES

WordPerfect has a Table of Authorities feature that can automate the process of creating a list of citations for a legal document. The process of creating a table of authorities is very similar to that for creating a table of contents or an index: you design and define the table, mark your entries, and generate the table.

Do It

To define a Table of Authorities:

1. Decide which sections you want to include (for example, cases, statutes, legislative materials).

2. Choose **Table of Authorities** from the Tools menu, then choose **Define** from the Table of Authorities Feature Bar. The Define Table of Authorities dialog box is displayed, as shown in Figure 27.17.

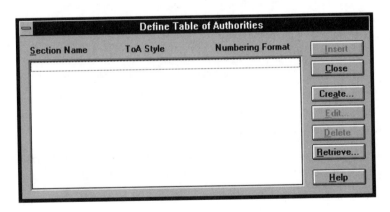

Figure 27.17 *The Define Table of Authorities dialog box.*

3. For each section you want to include, choose **Create**. Enter a name for the section and specify formatting options in the Create Table of Authorities dialog box, shown in Figure 27.18.

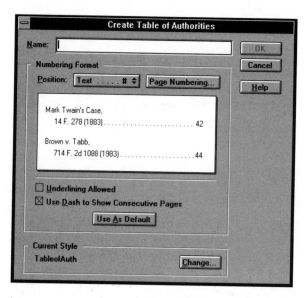

Figure 27.18 *The Create Table of Authorities dialog box.*

Once you have defined the table, mark the authorities in your document. The first time you cite an authority, you need to create the full form (the entire text of the citation as you want it to appear). Additional occurrences of the authority use short form marks. To mark an entry:

1. Select the text that you want to mark.
2. Choose **Table of Authorities** from the Tools menu.
3. For the first occurrence of a citation, choose **Create Full Form** from the Table of Authorities Feature Bar. To mark additional occurrences of the same citation, choose from the Short Form drop-down list.

4. If you are creating a full form citation, enter the appropriate information (specify the section and assign a unique short form name) in the Create Full Form dialog box and choose **OK**.

Before you generate the table, you have to tell WordPerfect where the table should be inserted in your document:

1. Place your insertion point where you want the table to appear.

2. Choose **Table of Authorities** from the Tools menu, then choose **Define** from the Table of Authorities Feature Bar.

3. Select a section and choose **Insert**. If you have not already defined the section, you can do it at this point by choosing **Create** from the Define Table of Authorities dialog box.

4. Repeat steps 2 and 3 for each section you want to include in the table of authorities.

When you are ready to generate the table of authorities, choose **Generate** from the Tools menu or from the Table of Authorities Feature Bar.

WP DRAW

Make sure you don't have any urgent deadlines before you start playing with this feature! Once you start experimenting with drawing and charting, it's hard to stop. WP Draw is a full-featured drawing and charting program that can be used to edit and add text to clip art images, create your own drawings using the freehand and shape tools, and create many different styles of charts (everything from eight different kinds of pie charts to three-dimensional stacked bar charts).

To use Draw, you can choose **Draw** from the Graphics menu, or double click on any graphic image in your document. Figure 27.19 shows one of WordPerfect's border images that can be enhanced using Draw's tools.

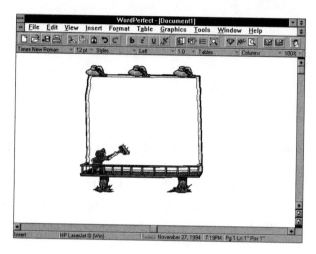

Figure 27.19 *Nice border, but it needs some work.*

By double-clicking on the border, Draw opens a drawing area around the image, as you can see in Figure 27.20. All the tools for sprucing up the image are at your disposal.

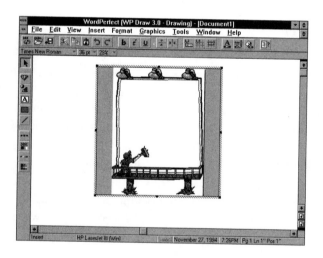

Figure 27.20 *The drawing area around the border and WP DRAW on the title bar tell you you're ready to draw.*

Figure 27.21 shows the image with text and an ellipse added.

Figure 27.21 *There! Now the border's more useful.*

You create and edit drawings by selecting tools from the tool palette on the left side of the drawing window or by making choices from the pull-down menus. WP Draw has its own Help system that can guide you through the process of working with drawings and charts. Figure 27.22 shows the How Do I window next to the Tool Palette Help window.

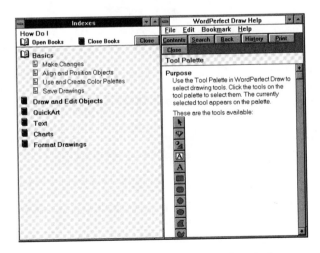

Figure 27.22 *Sample WP Draw Help windows.*

If you're the methodical type, explore WP Draw's capabilities by working your way through the Help system.

If you like to learn by the seat of your pants, just start choosing tools from the tool palette to see what they do. Notice that Help prompts display on WP Draw's title bar as you move your mouse pointer over the tool palette items, so you can get an idea of what a particular tool does before you choose it. After you choose a tool, keep an eye on the information at the bottom of the drawing window for instructions on using the tool.

Choosing **Chart** from the Graphics menu takes you to WP Draw, with the Chart Editor active. In Figure 27.23, I chose **Chart** from the Graphics menu, then **Gallery** from the Chart menu.

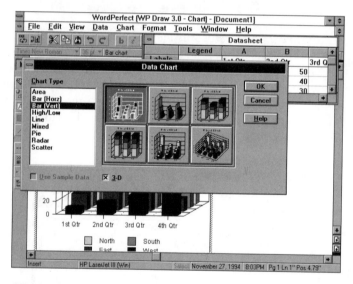

Figure 27.23 *WP Draw with charting tools and Gallery of data chart types displayed.*

Well, that was a whirlwind tour of WP Draw. Now that you know it's there, you can explore it at your leisure. The ability to customize your graphic images and create impressive charts to showcase your data can add the crowning touch to your arsenal of WordPerfect wizardry.

FROM HERE ...

We've reached the end of the road. But the end of this road is really a freeway on-ramp. WordPerfect is an incredibly rich program—there's much more depth and many more features than could possibly be covered in a book this size. It's time for you to make WordPerfect work for you. Use and master the features that fit your needs—as you gain experience with a particular feature, you'll continue to discover new shortcuts and possibilities. Enjoy!!

Installing WordPerfect for Windows

If WordPerfect 6.1 for Windows isn't installed on your computer, follow the instructions in this appendix to install it. The files on the WordPerfect disks are in a compressed format, so you can't just copy them to your hard disk. You have to use the Setup program.

1. Start Windows.

2. Insert the Setup disk in drive A (or drive B).

3. Choose **File** from Program Manager's main menu, then choose **Run** from the File menu.

4. Type **a:setup** to install the program from drive A (or **b:setup** if you're installing from drive B) and choose **OK** or press **Enter**. You'll see a dialog box that tells you WordPerfect is copying the work files it needs to begin the installation. When the files have been copied, the WordPerfect 6.1 for Windows Setup dialog box is displayed.

5. Choose **Install**. This takes you to the Registration Information dialog box.

   Note the **Uninstall** option. Use this if you ever want to remove WordPerfect from your system.

6. Enter your name and WordPerfect license number in the text boxes and choose **Continue**. The Installation Type dialog box is displayed.

7. Choose the type of installation you want to do. If you need help figuring out which type of installation to choose, click on the **Help** command button to get online Installation Help.

NOTE

You can cancel the installation process at any time by choosing **Cancel.**

❖ A **Standard installation** requires 32Mb of disk space. If you have the space available, this is the way to go. This option installs all of the files that come with WordPerfect, including all of the extra fonts, graphics images, etc. The only thing that isn't included in a standard installation is the Macro Help file, and you can always install it later using the Custom installation option.

❖ A **Custom installation** can take anywhere from 12Mb to 34Mb of disk space depending on the options you choose to install. With a custom installation, you can specify which file options you want to install and which directories you want to install the files to.

   If you choose **Custom**, follow the on screen instructions to specify the options you want to customize, then choose **Start Installation** from the Custom Installation dialog box. All of the dialog boxes have **Help** buttons—use them if you need additional information on any of the installation options.

❖ A **Minimum installation** requires approximately 12Mb of disk space. With a minimum installation, WordPerfect installs only the files that are necessary to run the WordPerfect program. You don't get any extras (like graphics images, macros, Help files, WPDraw, Spell Checker, or Thesaurus). Because a minimum installation really limits your ability to work effectively with WordPerfect's features, I recommend it only if you're extremely tight on disk space and don't need anything other than the basic word-processing features.

❖ If you choose **Network**, be sure to click on **Net Info** in the Network Installation dialog box before proceeding. This accesses online Help for network installations.

NOTE

The rest of these instructions take you through a standard installation.

If you have more than one hard drive, the Select Drive dialog box is displayed. Choose the drive that you want to install WordPerfect to and choose **OK** (or press **Enter**).

As soon as you press **OK**, WordPerfect begins installing the files. During the installation, watch the "commercials" that display. They point out some of WordPerfect's features and give you tips for making the best use of the program.

The first commercial reminds you to fill out your registration card and send it in (a great tip!).

As the installation proceeds, the Install Files dialog box tells you which files are being installed and displays the progress of the installation for the current disk and all disks, so you can tell how much farther you have to go.

Depending on how fast your computer is, the installation can take a while. You might want to have a good book handy (or go run around the block). A dialog box will display when it's time to insert the next disk. Just follow the on-screen instructions: Insert the requested disk and choose **OK** or press **Enter**.

NOTE

Don't worry if WordPerfect doesn't ask you for some of the disks—it only asks for the disks it needs to perform the installation you requested. Depending on your computer and the options you choose, WordPerfect may not need to use all of the installation disks.

At the end of the installation, WordPerfect asks if you want to view the README files. Choose **Yes** if you want to read them now. (You can choose **No** without causing a problem with the installation.)

As soon as you close the View README Files dialog box, you should see a dialog box that tells you the WordPerfect for Windows installation has been successfully completed. Choose **OK** to close this dialog box.

You're returned to the Program Manager window, with the new WPWin 6.1 program group active. To start WordPerfect, just double-click on the WPWIN 6.1 icon.

INSTALLING A WORDPERFECT PRINTER DRIVER

To install one of the WordPerfect printer drivers:

1. From Program Manager, double-click on the **WPWin6.1 Installation** icon in the WPWin program group.

2. Choose **Options** from the Installation Type dialog box.

3. Choose **Printers** from the Additional Installation Options dialog box.

4. Enter the appropriate information in the Select Printer Directory dialog box. By default, printer files are installed to C:\OFFICE\SHARED\WPC20.

5. Insert the requested installation disk and choose **OK**.

6. Choose the printer you want to install from the **Printers** list in the WordPerfect Printer Drivers dialog box. You can double-click on the printer name or highlight the name and choose **Select**.

7. Choose **OK** to begin the installation.

The next time you start WordPerfect, the printers you installed will be available in the Select Printer dialog box.

You can install more than one printer at a time. Just repeat step 6 until all of the printers you want to install are listed in the Printers to be Installed box.

Customizing WordPerfect for Windows

Throughout this book, we've used WordPerfect's default settings. If they work for you, that's great. You don't have to change anything. But almost every single setting can be customized to meet your individual needs. You change the default settings by choosing **Preferences** from the Edit menu, which displays the Preferences dialog box shown in Figure B.1. You can also access specific Preferences areas through QuickMenus—I'll point those out as we go along.

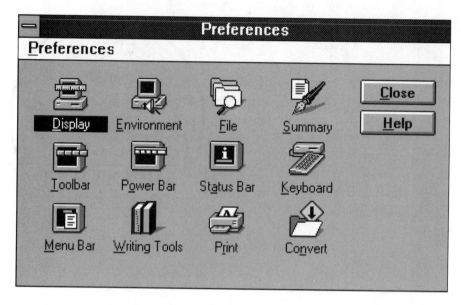

Figure B.1 *The Preferences dialog box.*

Double-click on one of the Preferences icons to open the dialog box associated with that icon (or press the **Tab** key until the icon you want is highlighted and then press **Enter**). You can also choose options from the Preferences pull-down menu. I'll go over each of the Preferences areas to let you know what you'll find and how you can make changes.

Any changes that you make through Preferences will remain in effect for all of your documents until you change them again.

DISPLAY PREFERENCES

From the Preferences dialog box, double-click on the **Display** icon to display the Display Preferences dialog box. You can also get to Display preferences by clicking the right mouse button on a scroll bar and choosing **Preferences** from the QuickMenu.

Document Display Preferences

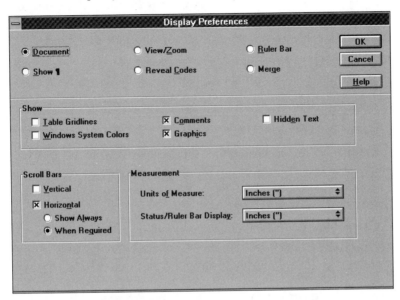

Figure B.2 *The Display Preferences dialog box.*

When you first open the Display Preferences dialog box, the Document radio button is selected. Document display preferences contains options that affect the document window. You can make the following changes to document display preferences:

❖ **Table Gridlines.** Check this box if you want the Tables feature to display dashed lines as guides when you've created a table without lines.

❖ **Comments.** By default, **Comments** is checked, which means that any document comments display as icons (or as shaded text in Draft view). Uncheck **Comments** to turn off the default display of comments.

❖ **Hidden Text.** Check **Hidden Text** to turn on the default display of any hidden text in your documents.

❖ **Windows System Colors**. By default (with this option unchecked), if you pick a different color for your text, the color you choose is displayed on your screen. If Windows System Colors is checked, all text displays in the colors you've chosen through the Windows Control Panel.

❖ **Graphics.** When **Graphics** is checked, all of your graphics boxes and lines display on screen. Turning off graphics display can speed up your screen redraws. When graphics display is turned off, your graphics display as empty boxes.

❖ **Scroll Bars.** Make changes in the **Scroll Bars** area if you want the vertical and/or horizontal scroll bars to be displayed all of the time. By default, scroll bars are only displayed when needed (when there's more document than you can see on your screen).

❖ **Measurement.** By default, all of your measurements are shown in inches on the Status Bar, the Ruler Bar and in any dialog boxes where you specify measurements or positions. You can change the display to show centimeters, millimeters, points, or 1,200ths of an inch. Choose **Units of Measure** to change the displayed unit of measurement for dialog boxes and reveal codes. Choose **Status/Ruler Bar** display to change the display for the Status Bar and Ruler Bar.

View/Zoom Display Preferences

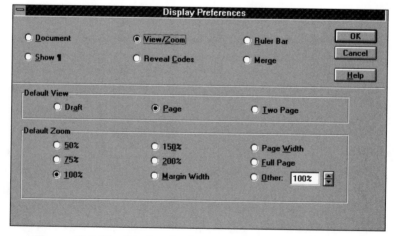

Figure B.3 *The Display Preferences View/Zoom dialog box.*

Select the **View/Zoom** radio button in the Display Preferences dialog box to customize the following options:

❖ By default, your documents are displayed in Page View. Choose **Draft** or **Two Page** to change the default view mode.

❖ Choose one of the radio buttons in the **Default Zoom** area to change the view percentage. By default, text is displayed at its actual size (100% View).

Ruler Bar Display Preferences

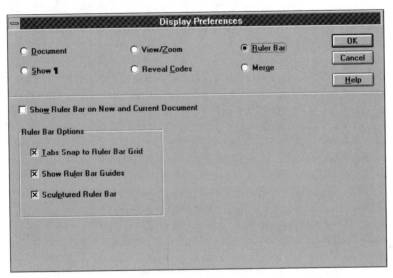

Figure B.4 *The Display Preferences Ruler Bar dialog box.*

Select the **Ruler Bar** radio button in the Display Preferences dialog box to choose from the options listed below. You can also access Ruler Bar preferences by clicking the right mouse button on the Ruler Bar and choosing Preferences from the QuickMenu.

❖ **Show Ruler Bar on New and Current Document.** Check this box if you always want the Ruler Bar displayed.

❖ **Tabs Snap to Ruler Bar Grid.** By default, your tab settings on the Ruler Bar are confined to invisible grid lines a millimeter apart. In most cases, this should work for you. To get rid of this restriction, uncheck this check box.

❖ **Show Ruler Bar Guides.** The Ruler Bar Guides are the dashed vertical lines that help you out when you use the Ruler Bar to move tab or margin markers. If you uncheck this box, the guides won't be displayed.

❖ **Sculptured Ruler Bar.** Uncheck this box if you don't want the default three-dimensional Ruler Bar display.

Show Display Preferences

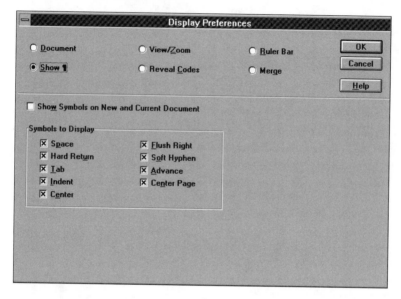

Figure B.5 *The Display Preferences Show dialog box.*

Double-click on the **Show ¶** radio button in the Display Preferences dialog box to specify how you want symbols displayed.

❖ By default, **Show Symbols on New and Current Document** is not checked. If you want to see a symbol on-screen whenever there's a hard return, a space, a tab, or any of the other symbols listed in the **Symbols to Display** area, check this box. Then check the boxes for the symbols you want to display, and uncheck the symbols you don't want to display.

Reveal Codes Display Preferences

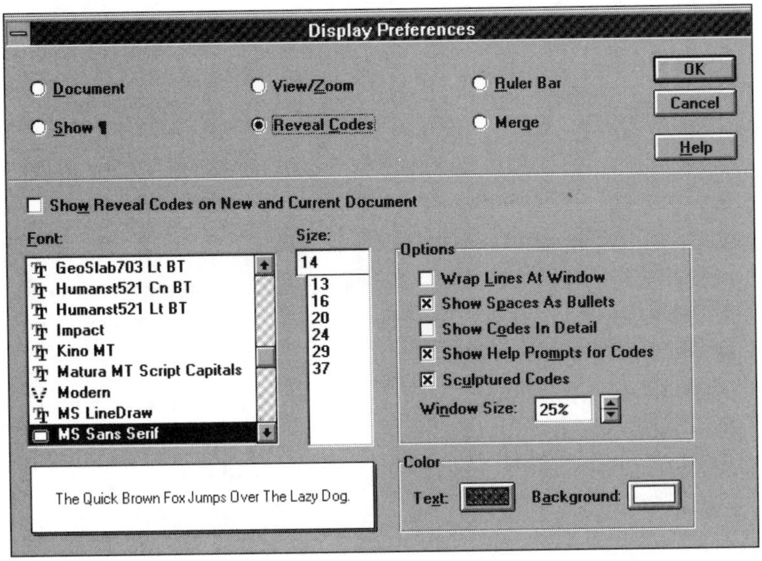

Figure B.6 *The Display Preferences Reveal Codes dialog box.*

Select the Reveal Codes radio button in the Display Preferences dialog box to choose from the options listed. You can also access Reveal Codes Preferences by clicking the right mouse button in the Reveal Codes window and choosing Preferences from the QuickMenu.

❖ **Show Reveal Codes on New and Current Document.** Check this box if you want the Reveal Codes window to be opened automatically whenever you start WordPerfect or open a document.

❖ You can change how your text appears in Reveal Codes by choosing a different font, size, or color. You can even change the background color for the Reveal Codes window.

❖ **Wrap Lines At Window.** Check this option if you want to see all of your codes without having to use the horizontal scroll bar. By default, codes can extend past the right edge of the screen, which can make them difficult to find.

- ❖ **Show Spaces As Bullets.** In the Reveal Codes window, spaces are displayed as diamond-shaped bullets. If you uncheck this option, there won't be any visible display of spaces in Reveal Codes.

- ❖ **Show Codes in Detail.** Check this option if you want all of the formatting information displayed for each code. By default (with this option unchecked), codes are displayed in a condensed fashion, and you can expand a code by placing your insertion point just to the left of the code.

- ❖ **Show Codes Help Prompt.** By default, Help prompts are displayed on the Title Bar when you place your mouse pointer on a code in the Reveal Codes window. To turn off the display of Reveal Codes Help prompts, uncheck this box.

- ❖ **Sculptured Codes.** By default, codes are displayed as buttons, with a three-dimensional appearance. If you want to display codes inside flat boxes without any shading, uncheck this option.

- ❖ **Window Size.** This is the percentage of your screen that the Reveal Codes window takes up. By default, it's set at 25%. This percentage is only relevant if you open Reveal Codes by pressing **Alt+F3** or choosing **Reveal Codes** from the View window. If you use the Scroll Bar to open Reveal Codes, you determine how much space Reveal Codes occupies based on how far you pull the sizing bar.

Merge Display Preferences

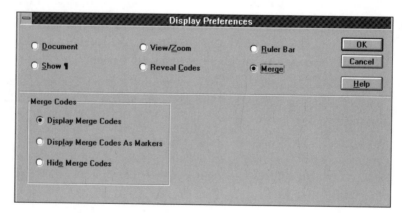

Figure B.7 *The Display Preferences Merge dialog box.*

Select the **Merge** radio button in the Display Preferences dialog box to specify how you want merge files displayed.

By default, all of your merge codes in form and data files are displayed on screen as codes (for example, at the end of each field in a data file, you see an ENDFIELD code). Choose **Display Merge Codes as Markers** or **Hide Merge Codes** to change the way merge codes are displayed in your documents.

ENVIRONMENT PREFERENCES

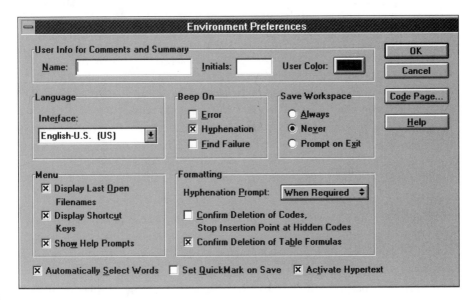

Figure B.8 *The Environment Preferences dialog box.*

From the Preferences dialog box, double-click on the **Environment** icon to display the Environment Preferences dialog box.

❖ **User Info for Comments and Summary.** If you enter your name and initials in the **User Info** area, you can use that information when you create comments and document summaries.

❖ **Interface.** English-US is the default. Any additional language module you have installed will be listed here. Selecting a different language will cause WordPerfect to use the document formatting conventions for that language. This option is also available in the Spell Checker, Thesaurus, Grammatik and Hyphenation. You will have to exit and then reenter WordPerfect for language changes to take effect. You may have to use **CodePage** to change the ASCII or ANSI character set for the selected language as well as specify default delimiters for ASCII delimited text files and import and conversion options for WordPerfect 4.2, DCA, DisplayWrite documents, and Windows metafiles. If the preceding sounded like a foreign language, you probably don't need this option. If the terms are meaningful to you, the dialog box is self-explanatory.

❖ **Beep On.** If you want to hear a beep when WordPerfect can't find a word or code you're searching for with the find and replace feature, or when there's an error condition, check the appropriate boxes in this area.

❖ Save **Workspace.** The workspace is the document or documents on which you are currently working. If you save the workspace, WordPerfect automatically opens the same document the next time you start the program. Choose **Always** if you want to save the workspace every time you exit WordPerfect. Choose **Prompt on Exit** if you want WordPerfect to give you an opportunity to save the workspace whenever you exit the program.

❖ **Menu.** This area controls the display of filenames on the File menu, Help prompts, and shortcut keys. Uncheck **Display Last Open Filenames** if you don't want the last four documents you opened to be listed at the bottom of the File menu. Uncheck **Display Shortcut Keys** if you don't want shortcut keystrokes to be listed next to items on the pull-down menus. Uncheck **Show Help Prompts** to turn off the display of all Help prompts on the Title Bar.

❖ **Formatting.** Use these options to control how WordPerfect deletes codes and how often it asks you questions. When you're using the hyphenation feature, you can choose to have WordPerfect prompt you when required (the default), always, or never. **Confirm Deletion of Codes** is unchecked by default. This means that WordPerfect can delete codes without asking you if it's okay. If **Confirm Deletion of Codes** is checked, WordPerfect stops at hidden codes and asks if you want to delete them (unless Reveal Codes is turned on, in which case, it assumes that you know what you're doing since you can see the codes). **Confirm Deletion of Table Formula** protects you from accidentally deleting a formula in a table. **Hyphenation**

Prompt lets you determine when you want to be prompted for hyphenation.

❖ **Automatically Select Words.** This is the default. When this option is checked, WordPerfect selects text word by word instead of character by character.

❖ **Set QuickMark on Save.** If you check this option, a QuickMark is inserted whenever you save a document. With the QuickMark, you can easily return to the same location next time you open the document by pressing **Ctrl+Q** (the shortcut key for Find QuickMark). Uncheck.

❖ **Activate Hypertext.** When selected, WordPerfect activates all hypertext links in the document you create.

FILE PREFERENCES

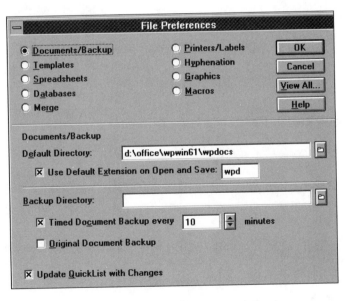

Figure B.9 *The File Preferences dialog box.*

From the Preferences dialog box, double-click on the File icon to display the File Preferences dialog box.

The File Preferences settings tell WordPerfect where to find different types of files on your computer. The initial location of files is determined when you install WordPerfect. If you chose a standard installation, WordPerfect created separate directories for macros, templates, and graphic images. If you did a custom installation, you had the opportunity to specify your own directories.

Each of the File Preferences radio buttons displays options related to that type of file. When you first choose File Preferences, the **Documents/Backup** radio button is selected. This is where you specify defaults for the documents you create. You also use Documents/Backup File Preferences to set automatic backup options.

Default Document Directory

If you enter a directory path name in the **Default Directory** text box (or click on the **File** icon and choose a directory from the Select Directory dialog box), that directory is automatically Selected whenever you choose **Open** from the File menu. And when you save a document, it is saved to that directory unless you specify a different one.

If you check **Use Default Extension on Open and Save**, all of your documents are automatically saved with the extension entered in the text box unless you specify a different extension when you save.

Automatic Backup

Even if you save your documents frequently, it's a good idea to use WordPerfect's automatic backup feature. That way you won't lose your work if the power goes out or something goes wrong with your computer. The backup files are stored in your Windows directory unless you specify another location.

❖ Enter a directory path in the **Backup Directory** text box (or click on the file icon and choose from the Select Directory dialog box) to specify a location for your backup files.

❖ By default, WordPerfect is set up to do a timed backup every 10 minutes. Uncheck **Timed Document Backup every** to turn off this feature. To change the amount of time between backups, enter a different number in the text box.

❖ Check **Original Document Backup** if you want WordPerfect to create a backup file every time you save a document. With this option checked, the new version of your document (the one on screen with your latest changes) is saved with the document's filename, and the original version (the one stored on disk the last time you saved) is kept and given a BK! extension.

Other File Preference Options

Click on one of the **File Preferences** radio buttons to specify file preferences for a particular type of file. For each file type shown, you can specify a default directory. In most cases, you can also specify a supplemental directory. A supplemental directory is often used in a network environment, where files and directories are shared by many users.

The **File Preferences** options for templates also allows you to specify a filename. WordPerfect uses STANDARD.WPT as the default template (which means it's used as the basis for all your new documents). To use a different template, just click on the **Templates** radio button and fill in the Default File text box.

Choose **View All** from the File Preferences dialog box to display a dialog box that lists the current settings for all of the File Preferences options.

TOOLBAR PREFERENCES

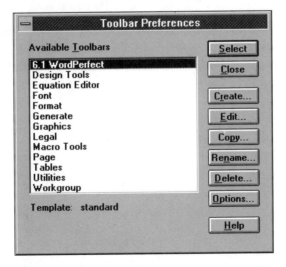

Figure B.10 *The Toolbar Preferences dialog box.*

From the Preferences dialog box, double-click on the Toolbar icon to display the Toolbar Preferences dialog box. You can also access Toolbar preferences by clicking the right mouse button anywhere on the Toolbar and choosing **Preferences** from the QuickMenu.

You can use Toolbar Preferences to change the location and appearance of Toolbars on your screen. You can also edit the predefined Toolbars or create your own custom Toolbars.

Changing the Location and Appearance of the Toolbar

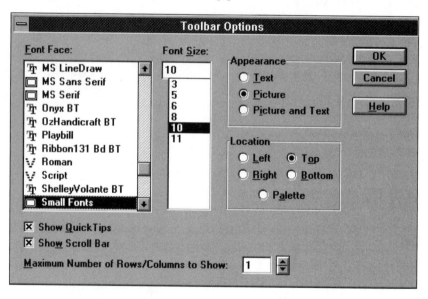

Figure B.11 *The Toolbar Options dialog box.*

From the Toolbar Preferences dialog box, choose **Options** to display the Toolbar Options dialog box.

By default, the buttons on the Toolbar display and graphics with no text; the text is in a 10 point font, and the Toolbar is at the top of the screen, just under the menu bar.

❖   Make selections from the Font Face and Font Size lists if you want the Toolbar text to appear in a different type style or size.

❖ Choose **Text** or **Picture and Text** if you want the buttons to display just text or pictures and text.

❖ Choose an option in the Location area to have the Toolbar display at the top, bottom, left or right of your screen. Choose **Palette** to display the Toolbar as a floating palette that you can move around.

You can also move the Toolbar by positioning your mouse pointer on a blank area of the Toolbar. When your mouse pointer turns into a little hand, you can drag the Toolbar wherever you want. As you drag, an outline of the Toolbar appears. If you let go of the mouse button when the outline is rectangular, the Toolbar becomes a floating palette. To position the Toolbar at the top or bottom of the screen, drag the Toolbar near the top or bottom and let go of the mouse button when the outline becomes a horizontal bar. To position the Toolbar at the left or right edge of the document window, drag the Toolbar to the left or right until the outline turns into a vertical column, and then let go of the mouse button.

❖ **Show Quick Tips**. Quick Tips provides information about the Toolbar button or icon your mouse pointer is currently resting on. This option is checked by default**.**

❖ **Show Scroll Bar**. Choose this option if you want the Toolbar scroll bar displayed. By default, it is not checked.

❖ If you want to be able to display more than one row or column of buttons, enter a number in the **Maximum Number of Rows/Columns to Show** text box.

Creating and Editing Toolbars

You can create your own Toolbars from scratch, and you can add buttons to or delete buttons from any of the predefined Toolbars.

To create a Toolbar, choose **Create** from the Toolbar Preferences dialog box, enter a name, and choose **OK**.

To edit a Toolbar, highlight the Toolbar you want to edit in the Toolbar Preferences dialog box and choose **Edit**. Or, to edit the currently displayed Toolbar, click the right mouse button anywhere on the Toolbar and choose Edit from the QuickMenu. The Toolbar Editor dialog box is displayed. The name of the Toolbar you're editing displays in the Title Bar.

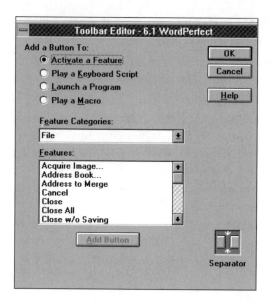

Figure B.12 *The Toolbar Editor dialog box.*

❖ You can add a button for any of the features in the Features list. Select **Activate a Feature**, highlight the feature you want to add, and choose **Add Button**.

❖ You can create a button that will enter text in your document. Select **Play a Keyboard Script**, type the text you want in the text box, and choose **Add Script**. Whenever you click on the button, the text you typed is inserted in your document.

❖ You can add a button that starts another program. Choose **Launch a Program**, choose **Select File**, and select the file that runs the program

❖ You can attach any of your macros to a button. That way you can run the macro just by clicking on the button. Choose **Play a Macro**, click on the **Add Macro** button, enter the name of the macro in the text box (or choose the macro from the Select File dialog box), and choose **Select**.

If you add more buttons than you can see on screen, scroll arrows are displayed to allow you to move between the rows of buttons.

When you're in the Toolbar Editor, you can make the following adjustments to the current Toolbar:

❖ You can add a space between buttons by dragging a separator bar onto the Toolbar. Move your mouse pointer over the Separator icon (in the lower-right corner of the Toolbar Editor dialog box) until the pointer turns into a hand, and drag the separator to the location you want.

❖ You can rearrange the order of the buttons just by dragging buttons wherever you want on the Toolbar.

❖ You can delete a button or separator by dragging it off the Toolbar.

❖ You can change the text and graphics for a particular button—you can even customize the text displayed in the Help Prompt. From the Toolbar Editor, double-click on the button you want to change. The Customize Button dialog box contains options for changing the appearance and text for the button. You might want to use this option when you create custom buttons to play scripts or macros. For example, you might edit the button text to display the name of the macro and create a Help Prompt that describes what the macro does.

When you've added your buttons and made all the changes you want, choose **OK** to return to your document. If you created a new Toolbar, its name is displayed on the Toolbar QuickMenu.

POWER BAR PREFERENCES

From the Preferences dialog box, double-click on the Power Bar icon to display the Power Bar Options dialog box. You can also access Power Bar Options by clicking the right mouse button on the Power Bar and choosing **Options** from the QuickMenu.

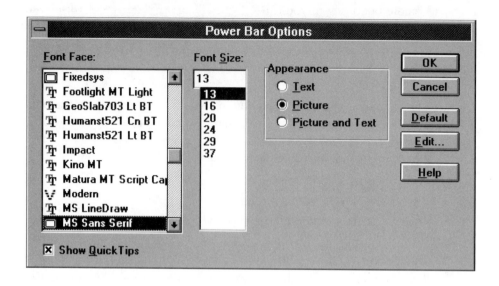

Figure B.13 *The Power Bar Options dialog box.*

❖ Make selections from the **Font Face** and **Font Size** lists if you want the Power Bar text to appear in a different type style or size.

❖ Choose **Text** or **Picture** if you want the buttons to display just text or pictures.

Choose **Edit** to add or delete items from the Power Bar or rearrange the order of the Power Bar buttons

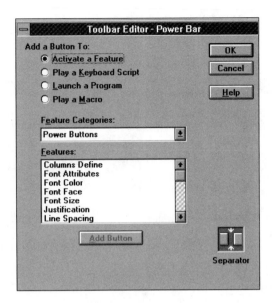

Figure B.14 *The Toolbar Editor - Power Bar dialog box.*

This works exactly like the Toolbar editor discussed in the previous section.

If you want to return the Power Bar to its default settings (the way it was when you installed WordPerfect), choose **Default** from the Power Bar Options dialog box.

STATUS BAR PREFERENCES

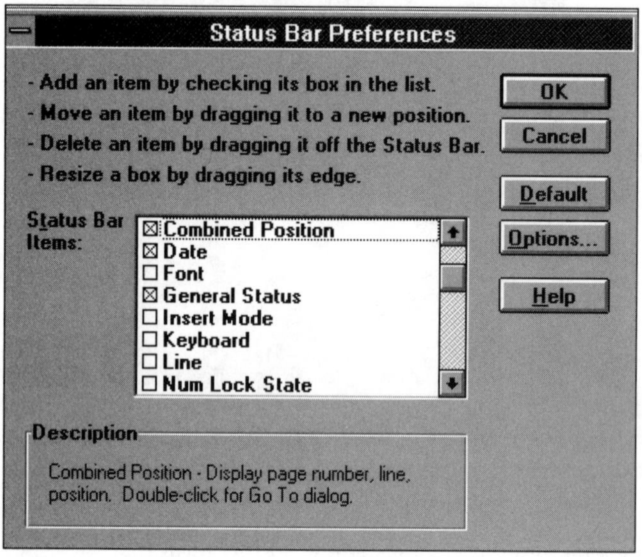

Figure B.15 *The Status Bar Preferences dialog box.*

From the Preferences dialog box, double-click on the Status Bar icon to display the Status Bar Preferences dialog box. You can also access Status Bar preferences by clicking the right mouse button on the Status Bar and choosing Preferences from the QuickMenu.

Use Status Bar Preferences to customize the information that's displayed on the Status Bar.

❖ The Status Bar Items list contains all of the items that can be added to the Status Bar. Check the boxes for items you want to add and uncheck the boxes for items you want to delete. You can also delete an item by dragging it off the Status Bar.

❖ You can change the size of the box for a Status Bar item by moving your mouse pointer over the right or left border of the box until the pointer turns into a double-headed arrow. Drag the arrow to the right or left to make the box larger or smaller.

❖ Rearrange Status Bar items by dragging the boxes to new locations.

❖ Choose **Options** to change the font, point size, and other display attributes for Status Bar items.

❖ To return the Status Bar to its default settings (the way it was when you installed WordPerfect), choose **Default**.

KEYBOARD PREFERENCES

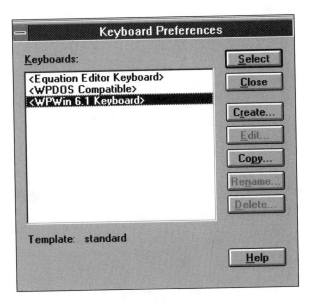

Figure B.16 *The Keyboard Preferences dialog box.*

From the Preferences dialog box, double-click on the Keyboard icon to display the Keyboard Preferences dialog box.

WordPerfect comes with three predefined keyboard layouts: Equation Editor, WPDOS Compatible, and WPWin 6.1. WPWin 6.1 is the default keyboard, and it includes the keyboard shortcut assignments that you've been using throughout this book. For example, you're able to press **Ctrl+D** to insert date text because WordPerfect assigned the date text feature to the **Ctrl+D** key combination.

You can select a different keyboard to use by highlighting it in the Keyboard Preferences dialog box and choosing **Select**. The Equation Editor keyboard contains keyboard shortcuts that help when you're creating equations. The WPDOS Compatible keyboard contains keyboard assignments that are familiar to people who've used the DOS versions of WordPerfect.

Creating or Editing a Keyboard Layout

You can't edit the predefined keyboards, but you can create a new keyboard layout that uses one of the predefined keyboards as a basis and later edit your new keyboard layout.

❖ Highlight the name of the keyboard you want to use as a basis for the new keyboard and choose **Create**. Enter a name for the keyboard in the **New Keyboard Name** text box and choose **OK**. Or, to edit an existing keyboard, highlight the keyboard and choose **Edit**.

The Keyboard Editor is displayed, with the name of your keyboard in the Title Bar.

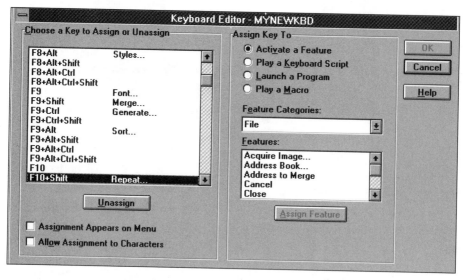

Figure B.17 *The Keyboard Editor dialog box.*

The list of keys on the left side of the Keyboard Editor shows which features or objects have been assigned to which keys. Use the scroll bar to see assignments for keys that aren't visible in the list box.

Highlight the key that you want to assign something to and do one of the following:

❖ To assign a feature to the key, select the **Activate Feature** radio button, choose a feature from the **Features** list, and choose **Assign Feature**. For example, if you highlight **F1** and choose **Cancel** from the Features List, **F1** becomes the **Cancel** key for that keyboard.

❖ If you want the keyboard combination to insert text in your document, select **Play a Keyboard Script**, type the text you want in the text box, and choose **Add Script**. Whenever you press the keyboard combination, the text you typed is inserted in your document.

❖ You can assign a keyboard combination to start another program. Choose **Launch a Program**, choose **Select File**, and select the file that runs the program.

❖ You can assign a macro to a keyboard combination. That way you can run the macro just by clicking on the button. Choose **Play a Macro**, click on the **Assign Macro** button, enter the name of the macro in the text box (or choose the macro from the Select File dialog box), and choose **Select**.

❖ Choose **Unassign** to remove the assignment from the highlighted key.

❖ Choose **Assignment Appears on Menu** if you want the keyboard shortcut to is displayed on the pull-down menu. This does not work for character assignments.

❖ Choose **Allow Assignment to characters** if you want to activate a feature with a number or letter without modifier keys. For example, if you map the Print command to the letter P, hitting P will put you in the Print Dialog Box. You will no longer be able to type the letter P in your documents

Copying a Keyboard Layout

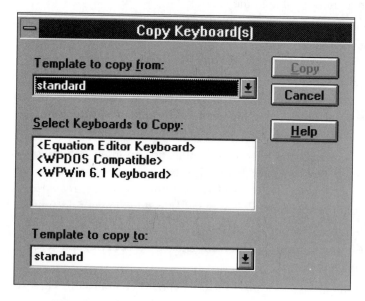

Figure B.18 *The Copy Keyboard(s) dialog box.*

You can copy a keyboard layout from one template to another.

- ❖ Choose **Copy** from the Keyboard Preferences dialog box.
- ❖ Select the template you want to copy the keyboard from.
- ❖ Highlight the keyboard you want to copy.
- ❖ Select the template you want to copy the keyboard to and choose **Copy**.
- ❖ If a keyboard with the same name already exists in the template you're copying to, you'll get an opportunity to rename the keyboard.

MENU BAR PREFERENCES

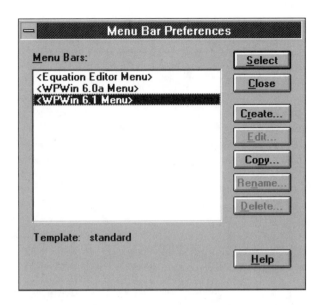

Figure B.19 *The Menu Bar Preferences dialog box.*

From the Preferences dialog box, double-click on the Menu Bar icon to display the Menu Bar Preferences dialog box. You can also access Menu Bar preferences by clicking the right mouse button on the Menu Bar and choosing **Preferences** from the QuickMenu.

WordPerfect comes with three predefined pull-down menus: The WPWin 6.0a menu, the WPWin 6.1 menu, which is the one you see most of the time, and the Equation Editor menu, which is activated when you create or edit an equation.

You can customize the pull-down menus to display only the items that you use, and you can move menu items to locations that make sense for your situation.

To create a new menu that's based on the WPWin 6.1 menu:

❖ Highlight WPWIN 6.1 in the Menu Bars list and choose **Create**.

❖ Enter a name for your menu in the New Menu Bar Name text box and choose **OK**. The Menu Bar Editor is displayed.

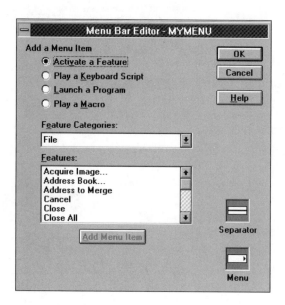

Figure B.20 *The Menu Bar Editor dialog box.*

❖ To add a menu item for a feature, select the **Activate a Feature** radio button, choose a feature category, and hold down the left mouse button on the feature you want to add. The mouse pointer turns into a hand holding a little bar. Drag the item to the Menu Bar. Release the mouse button when the item is positioned where you want it in the menu. Instead of dragging the item, you can select it and choose **Add Menu Item** to add the feature as a new menu item at the right end of the Menu Bar.

❖ If you a want a menu selection to insert text in your document, select Play a Keyboard Script, type the text you want in the text box, and choose **Add Script**. The script is added as a new menu item at the right end of the Menu Bar.

❖ You can add a menu item that starts another program. Choose **Launch a Program**, choose **Select File**, and select the file that runs the program. The menu item for the program is added at the right end of the Menu Bar.

❖ You can add a menu item that plays a macro. Choose **Play a Macro**, click on the Assign Macro button, enter the name of the macro in the text box (or choose the macro from the Select File dialog box), and choose **Select**.

❖ You can drag features to different locations on the menu.

❖ You can delete menu items by dragging them off the menu.

❖ You can add a dividing line to a menu by dragging a separator icon to the location where you want the line added.

❖ You can edit the text for any item you have added to the menu by double-clicking on the item in the menu bar and entering the information you want in the Edit Menu Text dialog box. If you want a character to be a mnemonic (an underlined character that can be used as a shortcut to access the menu item), type an ampersand (**&**) in front of the character.

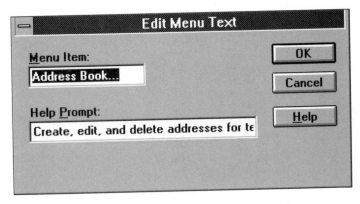

Figure B.21 *The Edit Menu Text dialog box.*

When you've made all of the changes you want, choose **OK**. To use your new menu layout, choose **Select**.

There's a special option for adding graphics box styles to the Graphics menu. Choose **Graphics Styles** from the Graphics menu, and choose **Menu** from the Graphics Styles dialog box. The Edit Graphics Menu dialog box contains a list of all of the available graphics style items. Check the items that you want displayed on the Graphics menu and uncheck the ones you don't want to display.

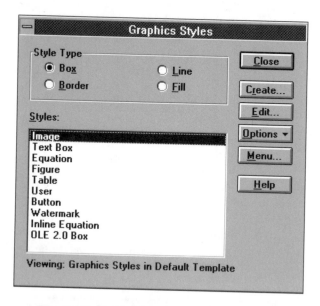

Figure B.22 *The Graphic Styles dialog box.*

PRINT PREFERENCES

Figure B.23 *The Print Preferences dialog box.*

From the Preferences dialog box, double-click on the Print icon to display the Print Preferences dialog box.

❖   The **Size Attribute Ratio** options are the relative sizes you get when you choose **Relative Size** from the Font dialog box. For example, if you choose **Large**, the text will be 120% of the size of your current font. You can change the relative sizes by editing the percentages in any of the **Size Attribute Ratio** text boxes.

❖   Enter a number in the **Copies** text box if you always want to print more than one copy of your documents.

❖   Choose **Printer** from the **Generated By** pop-up list if you want documents generated by the printer instead of by WordPerfect.

❖   In the Document Settings area, you can specify *high, medium,* or *draft* as your default print quality; choose **Full Color** to print your documents in color (sorry, this won't work unless you have a color printer); or **Black** to print in black and white. Check **Do Not Print Graphics** if you don't want graphics boxes, lines, and images to print.

APPENDIX C

Using the Templates Disk

The templates on the disk included with this book combine forms and macros. Once you have installed the files on your computer, you can use any of the templates by choosing **New** from the File menu (or pressing **Ctrl+T**) to open the New Document dialog box. Select the group that contains the disk templates (if you followed the disk installation instructions on the inside back cover, the templates are in a group called TYSWP61). Then double-click on the template you want to use (or highlight the template's name and choose **Select** or press **Enter**).

For most of the templates, you'll see one or more dialog boxes that need to be filled out. Enter the appropriate information and make the necessary choices. Click in the field you want or press the **Tab** key to move between fields in the dialog boxes. With most of the dialog boxes, pressing **Enter** is the same as choosing **OK**, so pressing **Enter** closes the dialog box even if you haven't completed your entries.

Since the templates perform varied tasks, I don't have any more general instructions for you. Just follow the on-screen prompts.

Once you've opened a template and filled in the requested information in the dialog boxes, what's left on your screen is a regular WordPerfect document. You can make any changes you want and save the document using any valid filename.

A few of the templates contain sample text. To create your own document, just delete the sample text and enter your own. In some cases, the sample text includes tips or instructions that will help you customize the document. Take a look at the sample text before you delete it.

WHAT DO THE TEMPLATES DO?

The rest of this appendix describes each template and gives you additional instructions. Figures showing each template (C.1 through C.16) are found at the end of this appendix.

Amortization Table (AMORTIZE.WPT)

Enter the amount of the loan, the interest rate, and number of payments, and the table calculates the amount of each payment that is applied toward interest and principal. The table expands to include the number of payments for your loan.

Audio Cassette Liner (CASSETTE.WPT)

This template creates an audio cassette liner that can be folded to insert into a plastic cassette case. A dialog box allows you to type the title of the cassette, headings for side A and B, and the text that prints on the back flap. Crop marks are printed to make it easy to cut the printed form to the proper size. This template uses the Tables feature.

Billing (BILLING.WPT)

This template allows you to track the amount of time you spend on various projects. You can create a permanent log to track the date, start and end time, client, and description. After you run the template once to create the log, a macro is provided that should be used rather than the template. The macro displays a dialog box asking for the time, date, and project information, and inserts information into your log file.

Brainstorm Session (BRNSTORM.WPT)

This template uses the Hypertext feature to set up a brainstorming document. The dialog box lets you enter several topic headings. The topics you enter are inserted into a header as hypertext—you can quickly move back and forth between topics by clicking on the green underlined topic heading. You can add more topics at any time.

Calendar (CALENDAR.WPT)

Pick the month from a dialog box and a calendar for that month is created. This template uses the Tables and Graphics features.

Checkbook Balance (CHECKING.WPT)

Calculate the balance for your checking account and reconcile it to your bank statement. A dialog box asks for your starting balance and inserts the starting balance into a table with columns for check number, date, amount, description, deposit. There's also a column to indicate whether the check has cleared. Click on the Perform Reconciliation button above the table when you're ready to calculate your balance. The button runs a macro that determines the balance on the bank statement by looking at only those checks that have cleared the bank. This template uses the Tables, Hypertext, and Macro features.

Diskette Label for 3.5″ disks (DISKLABL.WPT)

This template creates a label with nine diskette labels per page. A dialog box allows you to type a title and subtitle for the disk. If there is an install program on the disk, installation instructions can be inserted just by selecting a radio button. The form contains a button that allows you to fill the page with nine identical labels. The Labels and Hypertext features are used.

Exercise Chart (EXERCISE.WPT)

This template creates a table form that you can use to keep track of your exercise program. A dialog box asks you what columns you want in your chart. There are several predefined columns, which you can select by choosing the check boxes you want. The template also provides an edit box that lets you customize the chart with your own column headings. The exercise chart is in portrait orientation unless you specify seven or more columns. If you have more than seven columns, the chart will be in landscape format (sideways on the page) to allow enough space for the columns. This template uses the Tables feature.

Expense Report (EXPENSES.WPT)

You can use this template to create a form that tracks your expenses for a one-week period. The table (in landscape orientation) includes several expense categories and spaces for dollar amount, descriptions, and clients to bill. Totals are calculated for each expense category, and a grand total is calculated for all expenses during the one-week period. Expense category headings use graphics boxes to rotate text. Read the dialog boxes for hints to speed up the display of tables and graphics.

Font Sample (FONTSAMP.WPT)

You can use this template to take a close look at how a particular font will appear in several different sizes. It displays the entire alphabet in a large point size, along with a paragraph printed in various point sizes. When you select this template, choose the font you want to sample from a list box that includes all of the fonts on your system. This template can be very useful to examine the subtle differences between typefaces. Just run this template for as many different typefaces as you want, and print the resulting document.

Home Inventory (HOME_INV.WPT)

This template creates a table you can use to keep track of your household contents. There are no dialog boxes.

Invoice/Purchase Order (INV_PO.WPT)

This template automates the process of creating an invoice or purchase order. It automatically calculates totals. A dialog box asks whether you want an invoice or a purchase order, and you can select various column headings to include. After making your choices, another dialog box prompts you for the information that will be entered in the invoice. After you answer the questions, the invoice is created and filled in with the information you supplied. You can add more rows to the table, or edit it any way you want.

Keyboard Template (KEYTMPLT.WPT)

This template creates an actual keyboard template that can be placed above the function keys on your keyboard. Several predefined templates are included— select one of them by clicking on the appropriate radio button. There is also an option for creating a custom template, which gives you a blank form that you can fill in yourself. The template uses the Tables feature.

Legal Forms (LEGALDOC.WPT)

This template is actually a collection of several common legal documents, easily accessible through custom pull-down menus. The template changes WordPerfect's default menus so they are instead categories of documents, and each item in the menu represents a particular document. To retrieve the document you want, simply select it from the menu. The document can be edited, saved, or printed like any other WordPerfect document.

Letter to Senators (SENATORS.WPT)

This template asks you to select the state you want from a list box. It then inserts the names and addresses of both senators from that state and creates a blank letter for each senator. Just enter the text for one letter, copy the text to the other letter, use WordPerfect's Envelope feature to print the envelopes, and you have two letters ready to mail.

Net Worth Form (NETWORTH.WPT)

This template can calculate your assets, liabilities, income, expenditures, and total net worth. A dialog box asks for income and expense information. When this is filled out, another dialog box displays check boxes for various types of assets and liabilities. The next set of dialog boxes asks questions about the categories you selected. You can insert up to four entries for cash, stocks and bonds, and real estate. The dialog boxes for other assets and liabilities will change size based on the number of categories you checked. After you complete your entries in the dialog boxes, the information you entered is inserted into the table and the results are calculated.

Newsletter (NEWSLTR.WPT)

This template creates a two-column or three-column newsletter. A dialog box asks how many columns you want, the newsletter title, the volume and issue number for the newsletter, and the date. All of this information is automatically inserted into the newsletter. A table of contents is predefined, but can be eliminated by unchecking a check box in the dialog box. The date and volume/issue number print as white text inside a solid black text box, showing you how to create reverse text. The table of contents marking codes are included in the heading and subheading styles used with this template, and the table of contents is in a text box on the first page.

The sample text in the newsletter gives you instructions and tips for creating your own newsletter. To create your newsletter, delete the sample text and insert your own text and graphics.

Resumes (RESUMES.WPT)

This template allows you to choose from three different resume forms by clicking on a button underneath a thumbnail picture of each resume. Each resume is in a different format.

Three-Panel Brochure (BROCHURE.WPT)

This is a two-page template that is designed to be photocopied or printed to create a double-sided brochure. Fold it into thirds and you have a brochure. Two of the panels are predefined, but you can customize them to contain whatever you want. The cover panel contains a drop-shadow box with a title and whatever else you want. The mailer panel contains the return address, mailing address, and a place stamp here box. Since the text in this panel is rotated, a dialog box asks what you want included (include nothing if you don't want the brochure to be a self-mailer) so you don't have to rotate the text yourself.

WordPerfect Test (WP_TEST.WPT)

Test your WordPerfect skills by taking this test that covers many of WordPerfect 6.1 for Windows' features. Each dialog box asks you a question with four possible answers. After answering all 20 questions, the results are tabulated in a table. The table contains the question, the correct answer, and your answer.

Amortization Table

Amount borrowed	$1,000.00
Interest rate	8.00%
Loan period (months)	18
Monthly payment	$59.14

Period	Interest	Principal	Ending Balance
1	$6.67	$52.47	$947.53
2	$6.32	$52.82	$894.70
3	$5.96	$53.18	$841.53
4	$5.61	$53.53	$788.00
5	$5.25	$53.89	$734.11
6	$4.89	$54.25	$679.86
7	$4.53	$54.61	$625.26
8	$4.17	$54.97	$570.28
9	$3.80	$55.34	$514.95
10	$3.43	$55.71	$459.24
11	$3.06	$56.08	$403.16
12	$2.69	$56.45	$346.71
13	$2.31	$56.83	$289.88
14	$1.93	$57.21	$232.67
15	$1.55	$57.59	$175.08
16	$1.17	$57.97	$117.11
17	$0.78	$58.36	$58.75
18	$0.39	$58.75	$0.00

Figure C.1 *AMORTIZE.WPT.*

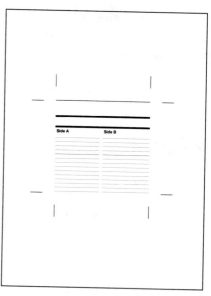

Figure C.2 *CASSETTE.WPT.*

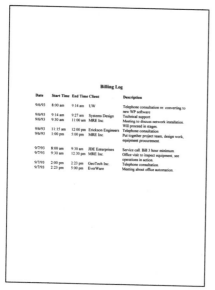

Figure C.3 *A sample billing log created with BILLING.WPT.*

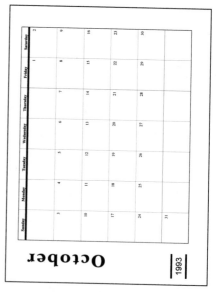

Figure C.4 *A sample calendar created with CALENDAR.WPT.*

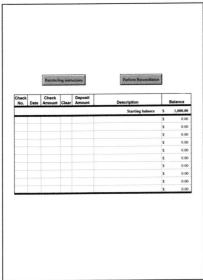

Figure C.5 *CHECKING.WPT produces this table.*

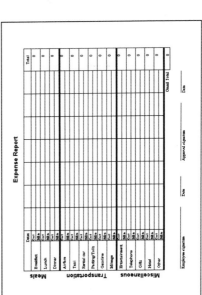

Figure C.6 *DISKLABL.WPT creates a form with nine labels to a page.*

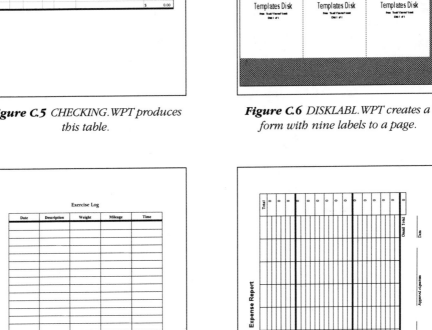

Figure C.7 *A sample exercise log created with EXERCIZE.WPT. You can create your own customized column headings.*

Figure C.8 *EXPENSES.WPT produces this table.*

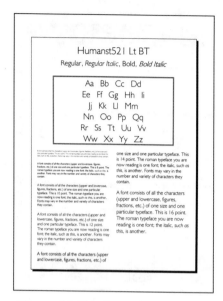

Figure C.9 *This figure shows the result of running FONTSAMP.WPT.*

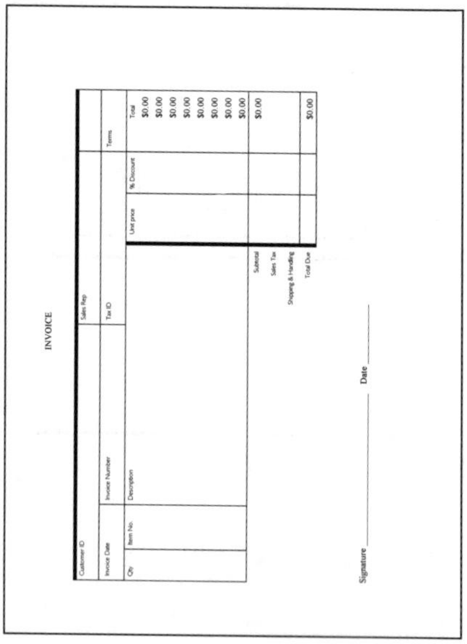

Figure C.10 *A sample invoice created with INV_PO.WPT.*

Figure C.11 *HOME_INV.WPT.*

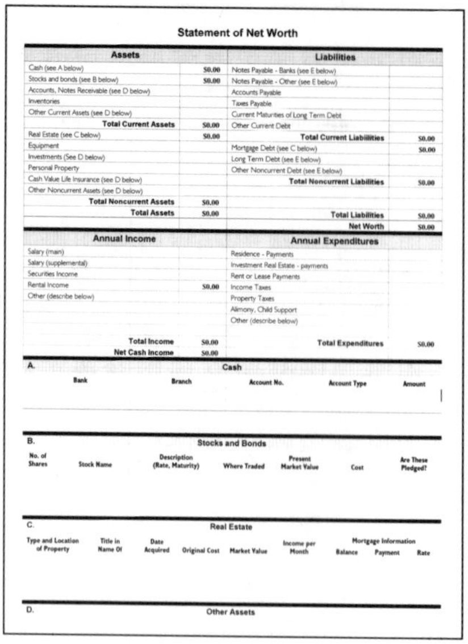

Figure C.12 *NETWORTH.WPT produces this table. It can be customized to contain information specific to your situation.*

Figure C.13 *A sample three-column newsletter created with NEWSLTR.WPT.*

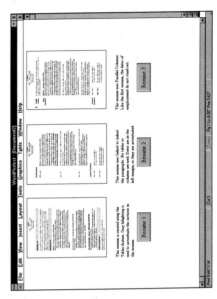

Figure C.14 *RESUMES.WPT allows you to choose from three different resume styles.*

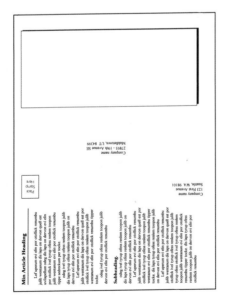

Figure C.15 *This brochure was created with BROCHURE.WPT. Your completed brochure can be folded into a three-panel mailer.*

Figure C.16 *Use WP_TEST.WPT to test your WordPerfect skills. After you answer all of the questions, this answer table is displayed.*

Test Question	Correct Answer	Test-Taker's Answer
What does Justification	All do?	Justifies every line in a paragraph, and can be used to force a heading to be the width of the margin.	Correct!
How do you select an entire paragraph using the mouse?	Either B or C	Correct!
What is the easiest way to indent an entire paragraph to the next tab position?	With the insertion point at the beginning of the paragraph, press F7.	Correct!
How do you center one line of text?	Position the insertion point at the beginning of the line, then press Shift+F7 (Layout | Line | Center).	Correct!
How do you add a WordPerfect document to the end of a document that is already on your screen?	Place the insertion point at the end of the document on screen, choose Insert	File, and specify a filename.	Correct!
What options are available in the Font dialog box?	Typeface, point size, appearance, color, relative size, superscript/subscript, and other special-purpose selections.	Correct!
What does Page View display that is not visible in Draft View?	Headers, footers, footnotes, watermarks, and the actual page margins.	Correct!
How would you spellcheck page 3 of a document on screen?	Position the insertion point on page 3 and choose Tools	Speller (or click the Speller icon on the Power Bar). From the Speller's Check menu, choose Page.	Quadruple-click on page 3 to select it, then choose Tools	Speller
How would you double-space a paragraph?	Double-click in the left margin beside the paragraph to select it. Choose Layout	Line	Spacing (or click on the Spacing button on the Power Bar). In the Spacing dialog box, type '2'.	Select the paragraph. Choose Layout	Paragraph	Spacing. In the Spacing dialog box, type '2'.
What is the fastest way to delete one word?	Position the insertion point anywhere in the word and press Ctrl+Backspace.	No answer selected.
How would you print 2 copies of the current page?	Choose File	Print or click on the Print button on the Power Bar), select the Current Page radio button. Type '2' in the Number of Copies text box, then click on the Print button.	Choose File	Print	Multiple Copies, then type '2' in the Number of Copies dialog box. Choosing File	Print, selecting the Current Page radio button and clicking on Print will now print 2 copies.
How many text blocks can WordPerfect store in its Undelete buffer?	Three.	Correct!
What is the easiest way to insert a hard page break?	Press Ctrl+Enter	Correct!
If you want your document to use Palatino as the default font, what is the best way to specify it?	Choose Layout	Document	Initial Font, then select Palatino from the list.	Select the entire document and click on the Font button on the Power Bar (or press F9 or Layout	Font) and select Palatino from the font list.

INDEX

Installing the Files from the Templates Disk

The files on the templates disk are in a compressed format, which means you can't run the templates directly from the disk. There are two files: TMPLT.EXE and MACRO.EXE. TMPLT.EXE contains template files that need to be copied to your default template directory. MACRO.EXE contains macros that are associated with the templates; it needs to be copied to your default macro directory. The following instructions tell you how to create a new group for the templates, copy the files from the floppy disk, and expand the files for use in WordPerfect.

1. In WordPerfect, choose **New** from the File menu (or press **Ctrl+T**).
    This opens the New Document dialog box.
2. Choose **New Group** from the Options drop-down list.
3. Type **TYSWP61** in the New Group Name text box. (If you want to give the group a different name, type that name instead.)
4. Exit WordPerfect and Windows (return to a DOS prompt).
    The rest of the steps tell you how to copy and expand the files using DOS. You can also use Windows File Manager to copy and expand the files. If you are familiar with File Manager, feel free to use it to install the files.
5. Insert the templates disk in drive A (if you are installing from drive B, substitute B for A in this step and the following instructions).
6. To copy the template files, type:
    ```
    COPY A:TMPLT.EXE C:\OFFICE\WPWIN\TEMPLATE\TYSWP61
    ```
7. To copy the macro files, type:
    ```
    COPY A:MACRO.EXE C:\OFFICE\WPWIN\MACROS
    ```
8. To expand the template files, type:
    ```
    C:\OFFICE\WPWIN\TYSWP61\TMPLT
    ```
9. To expand the macro files, type:
    ```
    C:\OFFICE\WPWIN\MACROS\MACRO
    ```

The templates are now installed and ready for you to use. For information about using the templates, refer to Appendix C.